Moscow
1905

Moscow, 1905

LAURA ENGELSTEIN

Moscow, 1905

WORKING-CLASS ORGANIZATION
AND POLITICAL CONFLICT

———————

STANFORD UNIVERSITY PRESS
Stanford, California   1982

Stanford University Press
Stanford, California
© 1982 by the Board of Trustees of the
Leland Stanford Junior University
Printed in the United States of America
ISBN 0-8047-1118-6
LC 81-50786

Published with the assistance of the
National Endowment for the Humanities

To my parents
and to the memory of
Morris and Riva Greenfield

Preface

My research on the social history of Moscow's 1905 revolution is based primarily on published sources, especially contemporary newspapers and official statistics compiled and published by the tsarist census bureau and by the Moscow city administration. I used these and other printed material at the following libraries: the Bibliothèque de Documentation Internationale Contemporaine, Nanterre, France; the Bibliothèque Nationale, Paris; the Helsinki University Library; the Hoover Institution, Stanford, California; and the New York Public Library. An early version of Chapter 11, based on these sources alone, appeared as "L'Insurrection de Moscou," in Jacques Baynac, ed., *Sur 1905* (Paris: Editions Champ Libre, 1974).

I spent the academic year 1973–74 in Moscow, under the sponsorship of the IREX Graduate Student Exchange with the Soviet Union. My experience in the archives, however, was not a happy one. I was given access to a very limited amount of material in the Central State Archive of the October Revolution (TsGAOR) in Moscow and in the Central State Historical Archive of the Soviet Union in Leningrad (TsGIAL). The documents I saw were useful in supplementing other sources, but represented only a minute sample of the riches in those archives.

In the early stages of this project I benefited immensely from the encouragement and intellectual stimulation of Lynn A. Hunt, whose work on the history of the 1789 French Revolution greatly influenced my thinking. Throughout my stay in France, Marion Bieber offered generous hospitality. I also profited from the exchange of ideas and sharing of work in progress with Diane Koenker and Gerald Surh. Leopold Haimson read an early version of the manuscript and offered helpful suggestions. Most of all, I would like to thank Reggie Zelnik for his encouragement, invaluable critical advice, and friendship. Without his persistence and support, this book would not have been written. J. G. Bell at Stanford University Press introduced me to the joys of revision with good-humored ruthlessness. The anonymous outside readers provided excellent criticism, which helped me improve the manuscript at various stages. Barbara Mnookin at Stanford University Press did a magnificent job of editing, and Itsie Hull helped me live through the whole process in relative sanity.

Dates are in the old style, that is, according to the Julian calendar, except when otherwise noted. In the twentieth century, the Julian was thirteen days behind the Gregorian calendar used in the West. The transliteration follows the Library of Congress system, except for well-known names. Foreign surnames and almost all firm titles, however, are left in transliteration, because many defy retranslation.

L. E.

Contents

Moscow, 1905

1

INTRODUCTION

In the 1905 revolution, widespread political dissatisfaction among the upper classes of Russian society joined with massive working-class and peasant unrest to produce, for the first time in Russian history, a nationwide movement for social and political change. The movement was not of a piece: its goals ranged from the moderate constitutional aspirations of progressive landowners, through the more democratic ambitions of liberal professionals, to the socialist program of the revolutionary intelligentsia, speaking in the name of the working class. What the educated contributed in rhetoric, ideology, and organizational skills, the peasants and workers contributed in the form of direct action: the strike and the jacquerie. As the crisis developed, the working class acquired a political education, and the privileged learned to use the instruments of collective action. The resulting combination, in conjunction with rebellious stirrings in the armed forces, frightened the tsarist regime into making the first constitutional concessions in its history.

What was the contribution of the working class to the nationwide opposition movement? It consisted first in massive work stoppages in the major cities, which virtually paralyzed the economy at crucial moments during the year. Communications, transportation, manufacturing, and vital public services ceased when white- and blue-collar workers went off the job. Without this popular movement, educated society might not have been able to convince the government that political change was desperately needed. The mobilization of the urban masses also helped move the liberal reform program in a more radical direction than it might have taken on its own. The voice of the revolutionary intelligentsia carried far greater weight in progressive circles when it appeared to speak for thousands, indeed hundreds of thousands, of agitated workers.

Not only did workers strike and demonstrate in greater numbers than ever before, but they also took part in the creation of representative institutions, through which they expressed their grievances and desires. The 1905 revolution witnessed an astonishing proliferation of grass-roots organizations, from factory and strike committees, labor unions, and community councils, to the St. Petersburg Soviet of Workers' Deputies, capstone of the October general strike. Many of these associations were the product of intelligentsia initiative, but party activists were themselves surprised at the enthusiasm with which the blue-collar ranks responded to their appeal. The revolutionaries were not always successful, however, or not always in the manner they had anticipated: many factory and shop workers were hostile to their approach and to their persons; others interpreted the political message in their own peculiar fashion; those who took part in worker organizations often departed from the original intentions of their intelligentsia sponsors and used the organizations in ways that suited their own needs and their own view of the world. The mobilization of the working class enabled the radical left to put pressure on its liberal allies, but it also pressured the socialist parties into altering their own expectations and strategies.

The working class was not a passive element in the revolutionary upheaval. It is clear that educated political leaders were not free to manipulate the masses in whatever direction they desired. It is difficult, however, to determine the degree to which socialist ideology corresponded to the workers' actual motives and desires. Few have left a record of their personal experiences. The memoirs that exist speak the language of ideological hindsight, the language of the victorious October Revolution. These insist that the Social Democrats rightly interpreted the workers' needs, political as well as material. Those who wish to discredit the popular movement contend that radical activists imposed their own political vision on the workers, who had no grander aspirations than the pressing desire to alleviate economic misery. But did the workers not have positive goals of their own? Were they insensitive to questions of social injustice and personal dignity? Lacking adequate literary evidence, the historian must approach this question by examining the pattern of working-class behavior in the course of the revolution. The changing structure of collective action, both from the sociological and from the organizational point of view, is the documentary legacy of 1905 that may allow us to understand the nature of the popular contribution to revolutionary politics.

Focus on this kind of evidence may not provide access to the "psychological dimension" of the revolutionary experience. But it does more than describe the external impact of popular actions, the role they played in the larger social equation. Patterns of behavior reveal attitudes, points of view, levels of political understanding. These express themselves in such particulars as the readiness to cooperate, the consistency of response, the emergence of rank-and-file leadership, and the nature of the goals adopted by the collectivity. These criteria provide a vocabulary that may enable us to avoid speculation about "consciousness"—that is, articulated self-awareness—without ignoring that crucial ingredient of revolutionary politics, the popular state of mind.

The working-class contribution to the revolution took two forms, as we have noted: massive strikes and demonstrations, and participation in grass-roots organizations. But the popular movement did not arise in isolation, as part of a closeted dialogue between revolutionary activists and their exclusive labor constituency. Much historical study has focused on the way outside groups provoked and channeled lower-class unrest. But the generation of political militancy was a many-sided process, involving interaction among different social strata. Workers not only responded to example and exhortation, but themselves provided inspiration. This, too, must be credited to their account. On the one hand, factory and shop workers struck on the suggestion of professional revolutionaries, rebellious students, and dissatisfied administrative and clerical employees. On the other hand, blue-collar strikes that began as modest bread-and-butter conflicts grew in proportion and political significance as they attracted outside support and sometimes prompted other groups to take similar collective action. Labor unrest achieved political results in 1905 because it was part of the general mobilization of urban society.

Soviet scholarship tends to reduce the question of outside influences on the working class to the question of party influence, specifically of Bolshevik party influence. Likewise, it views the development of worker organizations as the result of Bolshevik party leadership, or, in the case of developments that clashed with Bolshevik expectations or of tactics that failed, as the result of Socialist Revolutionary or Menshevik interference.[1] More than one historian has held a match to these straw men, and we shall do little to stir the ashes. Intelligentsia activism (let alone Bolshevik leadership) was but one of many forces shaping the worker's experience and his perception of that experience. Government and management policy and the educational activities of establishment liberals also contributed to worker self-awareness, promoted a sense of class solidarity, and prompted workers to fight their economic battles by collective means. The worker's response to such influences—his willingness to take action and his ability to take part in organization building or to assume leadership himself—depended on a variety of circumstances. Social background, education,

familiarity with city life, social contacts (not merely political contacts) outside the factory milieu, position within the plant hierarchy, wage level,
family and community involvement—all these facets helped form a
worker's political identity. The revolutionary events themselves changed
the way people saw their own position in society and opened up new pos-
sibilities of political action. This was true throughout the social hierarchy.

In Moscow, formal labor organizations were most successful when they
corresponded to the structures of everyday life: the neighborhood, the
plant, or the individual trade. The clever organizer, interested in attracting real grass-roots support, recognized these limitations and made the
most of them. In St. Petersburg the citywide soviet exercised considerable political authority, and workers from heavy industry played a dominant role in animating and in leading the strike movements. But in Moscow, centralized committees and unions never got off the ground; the
workers were not ready for them. Local, small-scale organizations had
much greater vitality. The situation there, in fact, tends to demolish two
chestnuts of Soviet historiography: the importance of the industrial "proletariat" as the keystone of the mass movement, and the emergence of a
serious political split between representatives of the working class and
those of the professional and "bourgeois" classes.

The Moscow working class, as we shall see, was in fact a congeries of
disparate social groups. Small-shop craft production still flourished alongside large-scale, mechanized industrial plants. Light industry, in particular clothing, textiles, and food products, dominated the city's economy.
The apparel trade was almost exclusively artisanal. The food and textile
industries, by contrast, relied in the main on a supply of unskilled labor
capable of relatively simple manual or mechanized operations.[2] A high
proportion of workers in both sectors worked in large plants and lived in
factory barracks; a large proportion were women, on the average less literate than men.

Such unqualified workers constituted the majority of factory laborers in
Moscow. They were "proletarians" by virtue of the circumstances and
quality of their work experience; they did not correspond, however, to
the Marxist type of urbanized industrial laborer with a developed sense of
class identification. In Soviet parlance, these were the "backward" element: unhappy and volatile, but culturally and politically unsophisticated. Their actions in 1905 were not uniform, however. Indeed, most
textile workers were slow to respond to the political crisis and were unprepared to form their own organizations. Workers in tobacco and tea factories, on the other hand, were notable for the coherence and deliberate-
ness of their strike actions. They were also highly responsive to political

leadership, proving only how dangerous it is to deduce politics directly from sociology.

The printing and metal industries to a much greater extent combined elements of artisanal and factory labor: like the garment trade, they employed vast numbers of skilled workers in small shops, though a significant number worked in larger enterprises. Metal and print factories, however, were organized on a different basis than food and textile plants, and they demanded a different kind of laborer. The paragon of the self-aware proletarian was in fact the skilled metalworker. Literate, well-trained, well-paid, and citified, the metalworker responded eagerly to socialist propaganda, urged his fellows to confront management, led them onto the streets, and got himself elected to shop and union committees. In the big metal works, such skilled workers formed a majority; textile mills and other factories employed them in smaller numbers in repair and maintenance shops. Some, with long seniority and good wages, were committed to stability. But others, by age or temperament more restless, were often in the front ranks of factory protests.

But probably only a minority of skilled metalworkers in Moscow were skilled factory workers. Moscow's metal industry was composed largely of small and medium shops, many of which engaged in finely crafted metalwork, a form of artisanal, not industrial, production. And yet there was a close affinity between the industrial "avant-garde" (the *peredovye rabochie* of Soviet literature) and the skilled craftsmen. They were similar in social background, in nature and degree of training, and even in the character of their work environment. The machine shop inside a large plant had much in common with the small, independent shop in terms of authority structure and of the work process itself. The skilled, literate blue-collar worker, whether in large- or small-scale production, retained the independence and pride of the artisanal craftsman.

The distinction between factory and nonfactory production was not the critical determinant of working-class behavior. High skill level and a sense of trade identity generally separated militant from passive workers in 1905. In the industrial setting, the labor elite supplied initiative and leadership. But traditional small-shop trades also proved extremely active, both in the strike movement and in trade-union organizing. Thus engravers, ribbonmakers, gold- and silversmiths, tailors, carpenters, and others far surpassed the unqualified factory masses in degree and sophistication of political involvement. Protest on the part of metalworkers in private industry and in railroad shops and of printers had a much wider impact on the mass movement as a whole than did strikes among food and textile workers, who collectively outnumbered them.

Another group that made a vital contribution to the labor movement in 1905 was the white-collar employees in the nonmanufacturing sector. They identified with the working-class cause, provided organizational guidance, and joined their blue-collar fellows in the meeting hall and on the street. Without them, no coherent movement would have emerged among either railroad workers or municipal employees, two groups indispensable to the success of the revolution in Moscow.

Thus the Moscow labor movement of 1905 was not, strictly speaking, a "proletarian" affair. It was a working-class movement in the most generous sense of the term, and it depended for its success on the support and participation of non-working-class groups. The leadership of the movement was equally heterogeneous. In St. Petersburg, the October general strike, highpoint of the revolution, was led by the Soviet of Workers' Deputies, dominated by representatives of metal and machine factories. In Moscow, it was led by a mixed committee of liberal professionals, white-collar employees, and representatives of industrial and craft trades. By the time a soviet came into being in Moscow, the mass movement was already on the decline, and the organization never commanded the authority of the St. Petersburg model. Independent working-class leadership in Moscow was not strong enough to threaten the oppositionist coalition, which indeed showed remarkable durability. A violent counterrevolutionary movement created a powerful bond between liberals and radicals. This bond survived the October Manifesto, despite a growing liberal nervousness with revolutionary tactics and an increasing tendency toward strident rhetoric on the part of intelligentsia radicals. "Bourgeois" Moscow did not abandon the working class, even when the workers took part in that most chilling of popular exercises, the armed insurrection.

Widespread sympathy for the workers' cause was not merely a function of negative circumstance: a common enemy and the relative weakness of labor leadership. Educated circles remained faithful for reasons of their own. True, many of the industrialists considered themselves progressive, but they resented the growing power of labor organization and resisted making economic concessions in the face of collective pressure; and many liberals were wary of association with political extremism. The socialist movement was surprisingly popular, however, among white-collar and professional groups, who often adopted Social Democratic or Socialist Revolutionary jargon to express their own political goals. Pharmacy clerks, for example, railed against their "economic exploitation" by their "class enemy," the pharmacy owners, and proclaimed their solidarity with the proletarian class struggle. Marxist class terminology may have accorded ill with social reality in imperial Russia, but it eloquently expressed the sense of social and political injustice bitterly felt by almost all members of

Russian society. This may account for its tremendous symbolic appeal outside the committed radical minority, especially in the heat of the revolutionary crisis.[3]

If the time was ripe for proletarian revolution, this meant that historical developments had already fatally weakened the old regime. Logically,
defenders of the status quo were eager to prove that social change was far
less advanced than partisans of revolution liked to believe. Throughout
the nineteenth century the tsarist government had attempted to prevent
the emergence of a proletariat, and down to the revolution itself its spokesmen insisted that Russia did not have one. "In Russia," wrote Count S.
Iu. Witte in 1895, "there is fortunately no working class in the Western
sense, and therefore there is no labor question." Likewise, the equally
high-ranking K. P. Pobedonostsev in 1897: "Conditions are different here
than in the West: we still uphold patriarchal relations between factory
owners and workers, who have not lost their ties with the land."[4] As late
as 1907, Factory Inspector I. I. Ianzhul denied that the Russian working
class had become a proletariat; unlike Europe, which had had the misfor-
tune to develop a permanent urban labor force, Russia had only a mass of
displaced, migrant peasants—the hyphenated worker still rooted in the
countryside, whose sense of identity and world view continued to be defined by the traditional, hierarchical categories of premodern society.[5]
Industrialization might prove necessary—indeed unavoidable—but its
social consequences were not therefore inevitable. The purpose of tsarist
social policy in the nineteenth century was to keep the peasant-worker
marginal to urban society. He remained a peasant by legal estate; his
movements were controlled by the village, and he had no right to take
part in public life within the city.[6] To ensure further that the displaced
peasants maintained their traditional subservience to authority, even in
the novel urban context, the government embarked on a policy of factory
legislation designed to protect the workers from destitution and to keep
them from becoming a chronically dissatisfied mass. The regime thus cast
itself as a benevolent force acting on the workers' behalf and expected
them to respond with gratitude and continuing political loyalty. Ingrati-
tude, in the form of strikes and collective disobedience, was in any case a
criminal offense. If the state interfered in the workings of the labor market, it did so not in the interests of social justice, but in those of social
harmony. To quote Count D. A. Tolstoi, Minister of Internal Affairs in the
1880's: "Factory hiring not only represents a civil contract, like any other
private contract, but directly affects the interests of social order and
peace."[7] Factory legislation was, above all, a police measure.
This policy, however, had the paradoxical effect of reinforcing the sense

of class identity that the government had all along been at pains to undermine. Each worker now had a wage booklet, and each knew he had certain specific rights, among them the right to legal redress of grievances. The law recognized the worker-management relationship as a formal, contractual arrangement to which both sides were legally beholden. It thus acknowledged the transformation of traditional, paternalistic customs into the kind of impersonal, businesslike relations characteristic of modern society, the society of rational contracts so deplored by nineteenth-century conservatives.[8]

With the establishment of uniform procedures and the singling out of factory workers as a distinct category, the workers themselves gained a new self-perception. There is evidence, for example, that skilled workers, who liked to see themselves as a breed apart, were forced to acknowledge what they had in common with other laborers. Under the law, they were all *rabochie*.[9] Although workers in the majority were still by origin peasants, it was clear that the authorities now recognized them as something else. Insofar as the regulations and procedures established by the new legislation did not adequately protect the workers' interests, they contributed not only to a sense of group identity, but also to a common sense of social injustice.[10] When the Russian worker first encountered Marxist propaganda, it was not the first time he had heard he was something other than a peasant and something more than a turner, fitter, or machine operative. The idea that he was a member of a special class was already explicit in official labor policy.

If the regime feared the political consequences of industrialization—heightened social tensions and increased lower-class unrest—it also recognized that the modern state could not rest on a traditional economy. Nineteenth-century Populists, by contrast, wished to transform the country's political system without altering its basic economic structure. In common with conservatives, Populists saw the preindustrial way of life as a positive feature of Russian society. In general, they condemned modernization as a source of increased economic and spiritual misery for the laboring classes: urban poverty was no improvement on rural poverty, and had the added disadvantage of lacking the communal satisfactions and communal values that the peasant derived from village life.[11] But the Populists also condemned autocracy as unjust, and wished to destroy the social and political hierarchies intrinsic to the old regime. They of course welcomed signs of popular insubordination as harbingers of social revolution. They did not view change in the mode of production as a precondition for political change.

Marxism, on the contrary, considered socialist revolution a consequence of the industrial revolution. Marxists therefore celebrated the ad-

vent of capitalist society and the emergence of a class of urbanized, prop-
ertyless laborers engaged in industrial mass production.[12] A proletariat in
the Marxist sense constituted only a small part of the Russian working
class in the 1890's. But by then Marxism had won the favor of the radical
intelligentsia, eager to believe that the logic of historical development ensured the success of their revolutionary project. Even the beginnings of a
proletariat represented a definitive and irreversible break with the old
order. Nicholas might wish to hold back the tide, but he himself had
weakened the dike by encouraging a policy of rapid industrialization.

Even if the actual proletariat was only in an embryonic stage of development, the idea of the proletariat had an independent political reality.
Marx's concept of the proletariat as the carrier of an egalitarian, democratic ideal, as the missionary of social transformation, had entered European political discourse before even the European working class had fully
assumed its modern guise. Marx's political vision helped change the way
the working class in transition thought about itself and also the way it was
perceived by other classes. Social development in Russia lagged behind
Europe, but ideas traveled faster than changes in the mode of production.
To some extent, the injustice felt by the working class was the injustice
experienced by every member of Russian society, only writ large: exclusion from public life and from political participation, inadequacy of legal
redress for social and political wrongs, limitations on cultural freedom,
subjection to the arbitrary and often cruel application of state power. The
fate of the working class was the fate of society itself, as Marx had warned.
Its hope was society's hope. It is possible that the proletariat achieved
such symbolic popularity in Russian educated circles not only because it
was the most impoverished and disadvantaged of urban classes, but also
because it represented the Future pounding at the bulwark of a rigid,
outmoded regime.

In the Marxist tradition, Soviet historians like to explain the activism of
Russian workers in 1905 as part of a process of social change already set in
motion. To the extent that capitalist development was under way, to that
extent had the working class begun to act like a proletariat, entering the
political arena to challenge the class structure of the old regime and the
economic domination of the bourgeoisie.[13] Conservative Western historians, by contrast, attribute working-class unrest to the opposite cause: to
Russia's social and economic underdevelopment.[14] In fact, they argue,
mature capitalism produces a tranquil labor force, integrated into society
at large, sharing in the general material well-being made possible by a
modern economy. Only the early stages of industrialization, the tumultu-
ous period of the industrial revolution, produce the kind of social unrest
that occurred in early-twentieth-century Russia. The recent migrant to

the city, the uprooted peasant, confused by social change and marginal to the urban environment, is the worker who rebels and the worker to whom the radical slogans of Marxism are most attractive.[15]

In fact, as we have noted, the Moscow working class was neither predominantly proletarian, in the Marxist sense, nor massively disoriented by the recent move to the big city. It contained a substantial number of urbanized, skilled workers, both inside and outside the factory. It was this group, along with white-collar and service workers, that provided the cutting edge of the political mass movement in 1905. Workers new to the city and to the factory often went on strike, but the skilled took the initiative and supplied the leadership. Weak ties to city life and a low standard of living did not promote, but rather retarded, collective action and, especially, political organization. This pattern appears to have characterized nineteenth-century working-class movements in Europe as well.

Despite the advanced development of large-scale mechanized production in Russia, the Moscow working class of 1905 did indeed still resemble the European working class in the early stages of industrialization, both in its structure and in its political behavior. By midcentury, Europe had already embarked on economic modernization, but traditional forms of production and traditional social groups were still strong. By then, however, it was also clear that Europe had a "labor question": the working class was changing, and the results presented a danger to social stability. In the crisis of 1848, the workers acted with a degree of cohesion and political aggressiveness they had never before shown. They acted in the name of the modern class they were in the process of becoming; but the leaders of the movement were, by and large, members of the established, traditional strata. E. J. Hobsbawm writes that the labor movement of 1830–48 involved a broad common front of urban workers, which derived its unity from "the programme and ideology of the proletariat, even though the industrial and factory working class as yet barely existed, and was on the whole politically very much less mature than other sections of the labouring poor."[16] The worker who responded positively to socialist propaganda in this period was the wage-earning craftsman, in both shop and factory— the skilled "labor aristocrat," not the impoverished manual laborer.[17] The European working class of midcentury was thus distinguished by its mixed social complexion and by the radicalism of its most stable and most socially privileged sector.

Such radicalism was not merely a rearguard action on the part of "declining artisans" anxious to defend privileges threatened by social progress.[18] Recent work challenging this interpretation argues that artisans did not, in fact, dissociate themselves from factory workers; rather, industrial and craft workers both identified themselves as part of a broader class movement. On the basis of a study of Berlin in the 1840's, Frederick D. Marquardt has shown that no sharp distinction existed between skilled workers inside the factory and artisans plying similar trades in traditional settings. The skilled and well-paid in both contexts distinguished themselves from the lower-status journeymen and semiskilled and unskilled laborers. Although the skilled elite felt superior to the rest, it nevertheless suffered under the same civic disadvantages with respect to middle- and upper-class society. "Workers of all types," writes Marquardt, "tended to develop a vague sense of common identity, as members of an outcast 'working class.'"[19] In March 1848, workers joined ranks in a single political movement, in which the skilled acted as spokesmen and leaders. The best-organized groups came from established crafts: tailors, gold- and silversmiths, printers, and bookbinders. Despite their craft identity, these journeymen acted independently of the guild associations and in a manner that challenged the principles of guild organization. They rejected the old corporatist categories and formed embryonic trade unions.[20] This occurred, according to Marquardt, because traditional corporate institutions were already losing strength. Although mechanized industry was still in its infancy, social categories within the working class were shifting their boundaries, and new coalitions were emerging, along with new forms of collective action.[21]

In a study of Marseille workers during the Second Republic, William H. Sewell, Jr. suggests an explanation for the relative activism of different working-class groups and for the important role played by certain traditional trades during moments of political crisis. He divides the Marseille working class into three categories: exclusive, open, and unskilled trades. The first consists of those in highly paid, membership-restricted occupations, such as dockworkers, shipbuilders, coopers, tanners, and masons. The members of the open trades, skilled craftsmen such as joiners and cabinetmakers, shoemakers, metalworkers, bakers, and tailors, were only slightly less well paid, but unlike the exclusive trades, these trades readily accepted recruits from outside. The unskilled, at the bottom of the scale, earned poor wages, changed jobs frequently, were often without work, and formed no lasting attachments to particular industries. Of the three groups, the second—the open trades—was the most militant, in terms of both organization and street demonstrations. They had many of the social advantages of the first group of closed crafts, but enjoyed much wider contact with other classes. The exclusive trades tended to take a conservative position in defense of their existing privileges; unskilled laborers, for their part, went out into the streets but remained largely unorganized. Sewell thus correlates political activism with two circumstances: economic well-being (high skill and wage level) and social integration.[22] A certain degree of stability and continuity are necessary for a group to act with any cohesion. Yet isolation from the general community inhibits a group from identifying with the common lot.

In a study of glassworkers in late-nineteenth-century France, Joan W. Scott offers similar findings. She notes that artisanal glassblowers began to form labor organizations when the modernization of the industry produced a fall in the demand for skilled labor. This in turn weakened the craftsmen's bargaining power and reduced their control over work conditions. It also cut back on their geographic mobility. As a result, they became more deeply involved in the urban community and came into greater contact with other working-class groups. They turned to the collective strategies favored by miners, for example, when they could no longer rely on craft control to protect them. The master glassblowers "used their position at the pinnacle of the hierarchy of skill to establish the union," at a time when they began to realize they shared the same economic and social disadvantages as less privileged, noncraft workers.[23]

The fact that such groups formed worker organizations did not mean that they all thereby acquired radical political goals. This is what bothered Lenin, when he looked at the example of late-nineteenth-century Britain.[24] There the working-class group most likely to unionize was the so-called labor aristocracy, distinguished from the ordinary laborers by superior social and economic standing and broader contacts among other social strata. Indeed, in some communities, even artisans and clerks were considered to form part of the laboring elite. But its core consisted of craftsmen whose skills were crucial to factory production, such as turners, fitters, and mechanics in the metal industry, and engravers and compositors in printing.[25] The emergence of this elite was a consequence of the incompleteness of modernization: "Factory production, or analogous systems," writes Hobsbawm, "only gave rise to a sizeable labour aristocracy in the nineteenth century where machinery was imperfect and dependent on some significant manual skill."[26]

The majority of unions formed by these trades were conservative. They did not take a combative attitude toward management or identify with the unskilled masses, but rather tried to defend their superior position against the threats posed by mechanization.[27] This was the kind of reformist trade unionism that Lenin saw as a threat to the revolutionary movement. The First World War caused an influx of semiskilled and unskilled workers into British industry, along with an increase in white-collar personnel. The labor aristocrats lost ground to the new industrial workers, and their trade organizations took on a more radical cast.[28] In this instance, they did not react to their decline in status by isolating themselves from the more unfortunate majority—another caution against facile generalizations.

These examples show that the upper-working-class strata were more apt to form labor organizations than their less-privileged fellows, but that the political consequences of their activity, and indeed their own professed goals, varied considerably. The behavior of the working class in mid-nineteenth-century continental Europe shows some striking resemblances to the behavior of workers in Moscow during 1905. In both cases artisanal and factory craftsmen supplied the labor movement with its most active members. In Russia, they responded eagerly to socialist leadership.

The key to the radicalism of skilled Moscow workers in 1905, it seems to me, is the fact that professional and white-collar groups were already seething with political dissatisfaction. It is clear that contact with the middle social strata had an important effect on the attitudes of the working-class elite in European societies, usually in a conservative direction. But in a period of general political discontent like the one that preceded and characterized the revolution of 1905, the direction was reversed. The radical intelligentsia alone was not enough to move the working class in times of general stability. The working class first mobilized and responded to political leadership in significant numbers at a moment of national crisis when the entire urban community, from top to bottom, was moved to action.

The political school of revolution, as Rosa Luxemburg called it,[29] is the subject of this study. In the following chapters, as we examine the reaction of Moscow society to the crisis of 1905, the particular focus will be on the behavior of the working class. Discussion of left-wing tactical and theoretical debates will arise only in connection with specific events or crucial decisions in which the interaction between workers and professional revolutionaries was a central factor. This is not to say that the parties failed to play a significant role in the mass movement, or that socialist theorists, preoccupied with class and political change, have examined the historical issues in an entirely misguided fashion. Quite the contrary: the terms of their debate have greatly enriched historical discourse. The present emphasis, however, serves to shift our focus from the point of view of the educated minority to the social environment in which it operated.

The second chapter describes the social and economic structure of Moscow on the eve of revolution. It locates the working class within the social hierarchy, and describes its internal stratification and its place in the civic community. The third presents the political background to the revolutionary crisis, beginning in the 1890's, and sketches the developments between January and August 1905. The remainder of the study consists of a narrative account of the events of the fall and winter of 1905, the political climax of the revolution and the apogee of labor unrest. In that context, it examines three aspects of working-class behavior: first, the various forms of collective action, including strikes, demonstrations, and mass meetings; second, conflict with other social groups and with the authorities, both violent and nonviolent; and third, organization building. The hallmark of popular activity in 1905 was the creative transformation of existing institutions, the structures of everyday life, into the structures of organized collective action. This did not result from the careful planning of intelligentsia militants. Indeed, intelligentsia initiative was successful only when it respected this basic popular impulse. As E. J. Hobsbawm has said: "Men [and women] live surrounded by a vast accumulation of past devices, and it is natural to pick the most suitable of these, and to adapt them for their own (and novel) purposes." [30]

2

THE URBAN COMMUNITY, I:

CLASS AND WORK

During the course of the 1905 revolution, the vast majority of Moscow's working population participated in some form of collective action. From the mill hand and the clerk to the lawyer and the physician, almost no occupational group remained uninvolved in the critical events of that year. Likewise, there was hardly a street or neighborhood, hardly a municipal or private institution in the city of Moscow that did not experience the impact of massive work stoppages or of violent conflict. The historian who seeks to record and catalogue the full extent of this mobilization is obliged to examine the city's social class structure in both occupational and geographic cross section.

This study focuses on the "working class" in relation to other groups or classes with which it cooperated or came into conflict. But what, or who, in 1905, was the working class? Can one define it, describe it, count it, and then track down and analyze its contribution to the revolutionary movement? One dreams, along with generations of labor historians, of linking socioeconomic circumstances to patterns of collective behavior. Finding the data to draw such connections is no easy task, complicated in the case of Russian history by the political and bureaucratic obstacles to research in Soviet archives. More basic and no less difficult, however, is the problem of definition. How does one classify the data one gathers? What categories are meaningful? Which distinctions in the socioeconomic realm will prove critical in determining the variety of response to the political crisis? Such difficulties plague labor historians in every cultural context. The peculiarities of Russian legal and social structure do not substantially affect the basic terms of the discussion, though they raise specific questions of their own.

It is hard to make such definitional decisions in advance. First of all, as the following chapters should make clear, the crucial distinctions that governed political choices were not always social or economic in the simple sense of the word. When pharmacy clerks insisted they were proletarians, they were not merely deluding themselves. They were defining their class position in relation to an ongoing social conflict. Second, reality itself is dreadfully unclear and contradictory. For example, it is notoriously dangerous, even in the European context, to draw a clear line between artisanal and industrial labor, though historians have used this distinction to explain differences in political behavior. One can find actual examples of the contrasted terms: the skilled master craftsman, at one extreme, who owns his tools, works in a small shop, completes his product, and identifies with his trade; at the other extreme, the factory operative, with no skill, no tools of his own, no sense of professional identity or pride, who merely serves the machine and the rationalized process of mass production. But gray more often drowns out black and white, as an examination of the Moscow working class will show. Within the small shop, as within the large plant, one finds a wide range of occupational types. Even at the time enterprises themselves so resisted classification that no two contemporary sources of data on manufacture and industry agree in their proportions. It is no easier, one must add, to distinguish between working class and lower-middle class, between lower-middle and middle.

In short, classic definitions do not always fit social reality. Even if one could pin down one's specimens with some degree of accuracy, moreover, one might still wonder if those particular categories were most useful to the task of explaining, or understanding, political behavior. This historian has chosen a compromise course. To describe the civic hierarchy that existed in Moscow in 1905 I have selected categories from three sources: (1) contemporary classification, both legal and conventional; (2) class categories employed by labor historians and sociologists (sometimes also part of the contemporary's arsenal); and (3) distinctions that emerge from the political record of 1905 itself as keys to group or class self-definition. Broadly speaking, the "economically self-supporting" (samodeiatel'noe) population of Moscow—to use the language of the census—falls into three general categories: (1) industrialists, merchants, and bankers; (2) professionals and white-collar personnel; and (3) the "working class."

The Upper Ranks of the Civic Hierarchy

None of the non-working-class groups falls neatly within the traditional legal categories of tsarist society. Among the economic elite that dominated the world of finance, trade, and manufacture, one finds members of the hereditary nobility, personally ennobled individuals, people designated as honored citizens, members of the merchant class, and an occasional person of peasant origin.* They form a group by virtue of their key position at the top of the city's administrative and economic institutions and also by virtue of their wealth and high social standing. Moscow was a commercial center: money and status often went hand in hand.

The economic elite took a major part in administering urban affairs and also influenced government policy at the national level. Its members sat on the City Council. They participated in a number of associations that provided them with an informal leadership structure and sharpened their sense of common interest, such as the Merchants' Society and the Artisan Board, the Stock Exchange Society (dominated by cotton textile manufacturers), the Russian Publishers' Society, and the Russian Pharmaceutical Society.[1]

Not all merchants and shopowners were wealthy, to be sure. The proprietor of a small tailoring establishment cannot be compared to the head of a giant textile mill. On the smallest scale, the artisan-shopowner was often close in status, manner of life, and economic position to his own employees. The wealthy few took an active part in urban affairs during the crisis of 1905, whereas the petty entrepreneurs did not distinguish themselves politically, though there is some evidence that they occasionally organized in defense of their economic interests. Retail merchants also belonged to several corporations, but these corporations did not take public positions during the revolution.[2] The Stock Exchange Committee, on the contrary, was politically outspoken in 1905. In general, the economically powerful played a more important, or at least a more obvious role in 1905 than the small-scale merchants and entrepreneurs, and their political clout was greater.

The economic elite controlled most of the large industrial firms in which the politically active working class was employed. The size of the industrial or commercial enterprise, its legal structure, and the degree of the owner's personal involvement determined the extent of direct contact between worker and boss. In larger firms, where this contact was often mediated by a managerial and shop structure, the individual owner or board member was a purely symbolic figure to the factory work force: from the worker's perspective, Mr. Guzhon, Mr. Gopper, Mr. List, were

---

* Honored citizens included government officials, non-nobles with higher education, rich merchants, and industrialists. The person so designated was exempt from certain taxes, from military conscription, and from corporal punishment. Merchants were also exempt from certain tax levies and from corporal punishment. Small tradesmen (*meshchane*), artisans (*tsekhovye*), and peasants did not enjoy these privileges. See George Vernadsky and Ralph T. Fisher, Jr., eds., *Dictionary of Russian Historical Terms from the Eleventh Century to 1917*, comp. S. G. Pushkarev (New Haven, Conn., 1970), pp. 50, 60.

abstract beings; the foreman was "the boss." But management policy however impersonally administered, nevertheless had an immediate impact on the lives of the wage-earning population, whereas the civic activities of the commercial and industrial leaders affected them hardly at all until the political breakdown of 1905 forced the city fathers to make decisions of vital concern to the entire community.

The professional classes come next in the civic hierarchy and may be divided roughly into two groups: those of high prestige, civic involvement, and often considerable wealth, the doctors, lawyers, judges, university professors, and top-level administrators, on the one hand; and on the other, their less exalted cousins, the schoolteachers, pharmacy clerks, engineers, petty bureaucrats, and across the generation gap, university and other higher-level students. Like the business class, members of the professional class belonged to a variety of legal estates. The more prestigious professionals mixed comfortably with the economic elite, sat on the City Council, ran the universities, had close ties with government officials in Moscow and St. Petersburg, and influenced public opinion through the editorial offices of newspapers and journals. These people constituted the nerve center of educated society, the civic conscience of Russia, referred to by contemporaries simply as *obshchestvo*, or "society," in contradistinction to the state, which was thought to be short on civic consciousness. They became a stronghold, such as it was, of "bourgeois liberalism," though they were not an economic bourgeoisie, but a technical and cultural one. They were the privileged upper crust of the professional intelligentsia.

No less privileged in terms of formal legal status and general education, schoolteachers, nurses, statisticians, and others, for all that they were professionals, nevertheless worked long hours, were often ill-paid, did not qualify to serve on or vote for the City Council, and read but did not edit the daily papers. This was the group that supplied the so-called radical or revolutionary intelligentsia with much of its political support and many of its active members. But as a whole, the professionals threw their weight behind the liberal or progressive movement, when it finally emerged at the turn of the century. University and Gymnasium students represent a special case. In higher institutions alone there were over 10,000 students, including some 7,000 at Moscow University.[3] Often from noble, wealthy, or professional backgrounds, students nevertheless identified in large numbers with the revolutionary cause and earned for themselves a place in the radical intelligentsia, though many were later to hold chairs in history and philosophy, become judges, and join the Kadet Party.[4]

White-collar workers, such as shop clerks, bank employees, office workers, and administrative personnel, both in private firms and in the municipal and government bureaucracies (including transport and communications), resembled the low-status professionals in social background and in the nature of their work. The ordinary white-collar worker, the so-called *sluzhashchii* ("one employed in a service"), stood somewhere between the intelligentsia professional and the manual or blue-collar worker (*rabochii*), though he might earn more than some professionals and less than some workers.[5] Wages for commercial employees, for example,

TABLE 1

Economically Self-Supporting Population (Work Force) of Moscow, 1902

Census category	Number (000)	Percent of work force
Entrepreneurs[a]		
Nonmanufacturing	44.9	
Manufacturing	40.6	
Subtotal	85.5	11.3%
Professionals		
Education	14.0	
Medicine	10.6	
Clergy	6.8	
Science, art, literature	6.7	
Law	2.3	
Sport, entertainment	1.2	
Subtotal	41.4	5.5%
Employees[b]		
Manufacturing	10.8	
Finance, commerce	31.7	
Transport	11.8	
Public institutions	10.7	
Hotels, restaurants	3.2	
Subtotal	68.2	9.0%
Other non–blue collar		
Police, military	25.7	
Independent, pensioners	30.7	
Hospitalized, unknown, etc.	75.0	
Subtotal	131.4	17.4%
Total non–blue collar	326.5	43.2%
Total working class	429.0	56.8%
Total work force	755.5	100.0%

SOURCE: *Statisticheskii atlas goroda Moskvy* (Moscow, 1911), Table 26, pp. 47–49, supplemented with data from *Perepis' Moskvy 1902 goda*, part 1, vyp. 2 (Moscow, 1906): Table 7, pp. 136–37, 158–59. Totals are inflated from rounding off.

[a] Includes employed family members.

[b] White-collar workers and service employees.

ranged from 180 rubles a month for bookkeepers, to 40–60 a month for top-ranking clerks, to as low as 25 for the majority.[6] The employees and professionals together, in their various capacities, formed the backbone of political leadership in 1905. White-collar workers also played an important role in the trade-union movement.

In 1902, Moscow's economically self-supporting population constituted almost 70 percent of the city's 1,100,000 residents (see Table 1). The entrepreneurial, professional, and white-collar groups together made up a quarter of that population (which I shall call the work force in this discussion for convenience). Owners of commercial and manufacturing enterprises in the first of those categories ranged from independent artisans and small retailers to large-scale industrialists. Of the 40,600 entrepreneurs in the manufacturing sector, only 1,400, or less than 3.5 percent, were factory owners.[7] Almost 70 percent of the white-collar employees in manufacturing, however, were attached to factories. Data collected several years later indicate that at least 3,500 civil servants in the "employee" category worked in the municipal administration and at least 1,500 in the postal and telephone service.[8] Altogether, non-blue-collar groups made up less than half the total work force. Of the total population of Moscow, in other words, approximately 40 percent were actively employed as manual workers of some sort and belonged to the category that we shall designate as the working class.

The Working Class

Not all blue-collar workers were engaged in production. Almost 40 percent of them did manual labor in the nonmanufacturing sector of the economy (see Table 2). The state and the city government employed only 5 percent of the working class, but this small group played a central role in the political events of 1905. The census does not have a separate listing for the 12,000 blue-collar workers on the payroll of the municipal administration, a sector that included a vast array of occupations, ranging from printers to garbagemen, from laundresses to hospital orderlies, from bakers to street cleaners, and so forth. Included in this number were 2,600 engineers, coach and tram drivers, repair and maintenance crews, and other transport workers.[9] The salaries and wages of these city employees varied as widely as the range of skill and status. Senior technical personnel in the slaughterhouse, for example, might earn as much as 165 rubles a month; assistant engineers slightly less. Junior technical staff were paid an average of 50 rubles a month, qualified machinists 30 to 50, other machine shop workers as little as 25. Fifteen rubles was the average monthly wage for unskilled laborers. Women workers in city laundries earned as little as 12 rubles a month.[10]

TABLE 2

Composition of the Moscow Working Class, 1902

Census category	Number (000)		Percent of working class
Nonmanufacturing			
Finance, commerce	20.8		4.8%
Hotels, restaurants	31.6		7.4
Transportation	37.6		8.8
Railroads		9.0	
Municipal		2.6	
Private[a]		26.0	
Domestic service, janitorial[b]	78.9		18.4
Subtotal	168.9		39.4
Manufacturing			
Factory production	107.8		25.1
Artisanal production[c]	107.1		25.0
Apprentices[d]	32.7		7.6
Unskilled daylaborers	9.0		2.1
Unknown	3.6		0.8
Subtotal	260.2		60.6
Total working class	429.1		100.0%

SOURCE: See Table 1.

[a]Coachmen, carters, cab drivers. See M. N. Petrov, "Gorodskoe khoziaistvo," in *Istoriia Moskvy*, vol. 5: 702–3.

[b]On female servants, see Rashin, p. 240. Factories and shops employed a total of 16,400 menials, also called servants, of whom 15,300, 93 percent, were women. See *Perepis' Moskvy*, part 1, vyp. 2: Table 7, pp. 137, 159.

[c]Of these, 2,202 worked in domestic production.

[d]*Perepis' Moskvy*, part 1, vyp. 2: Table 7, pp. 136–37, 158–59, gives the number of artisanal apprentices as 25,400. The remaining 7,300 apprentices counted in the census are not identified by trade in *Statisticheskii atlas*.

Despite such radical differences in training and earning ability, the city workers showed surprising solidarity in 1905. Municipal "employees" (of which there were at least 3,500) and municipal workers (of which there were at least three times as many) used the bureaucratic framework that united them as a basis for political organization. The professional and white-collar staff took the initiative in political organization and supported rank-and-file efforts to better the workers' economic position and bargaining power vis-à-vis the city bureaucracy. In league with each other, the two groups had a powerful impact on the local level, both economically and politically, and were vital to the success of the mass movement in Moscow.

Another bureaucratic entity that united a broad spectrum of social and occupational types was the railroad administration. Moscow was the largest single rail junction in the Empire: ten major lines converged there,[11] compared with six in St. Petersburg. Line headquarters employed a staff of 3,000; workshops, railyards, and freight and passenger stations at least 9,000 workers.[12] The railroad union formed in 1905 operated on a nationwide scale, but its organizational center was Moscow. Like the municipal work force, the railroad workers cooperated across class lines. In terms of political leadership and strategic impact, the railroad workers were central to the strike movements of the fall.

Statistics about the railroad work force usually cover the entire network; the data on Moscow alone are sketchy. The railway system had four service divisions: administrative and technical (7 percent of workers and employees); traffic and telegraph (27 percent); track maintenance and construction (36 percent); and locomotives and rolling stock (30 percent).[13] The first two divisions consisted largely of permanent staff drawn from the educated urban classes, who enjoyed vacation, pension, and travel privileges, and job security. At their top ranks they earned up to 1,500 rubles a month; bookkeepers, clerks, and telegraph operators, at the low end, earned between 30 and 60 rubles a month, well within the range of the blue-collar workers.[14] Stationmasters, cashiers, conductors, and various kinds of guards and supervisors also belonged to these two divisions. Those in subordinate positions were not on the permanent payroll; many came from working-class backgrounds.

The other two divisions in the railway system were overwhelmingly blue-collar, and more than half their work force was engaged on a temporary basis. Nonstaff workers might hold a single position for long periods of time, but without job security and other benefits. The construction and repair service included the greatest number of unskilled workers, many from rural backgrounds, who retained strong ties to the village economy. But this division was underrepresented in Moscow, where shop workers and administrative personnel predominated. The majority of workers in the machine shops and depots that maintained the rolling stock were highly skilled. The shops were no different from large machine-building factories. The four largest in Moscow, for example, had about 1,500 workers each, which put them in a category with the five biggest machine and metalworking plants in the city. Wages for railroad shop workers ranged from 10 to 40 rubles a month.[15] The nature of their trade and their work environment qualify these workers for inclusion in the metalworking category of industrial labor, but historians and statisticians have usually considered them separately. In 1905, Moscow's railway shop and depot workers were not insensitive to the factory workers' movement, but at the crucial moments they responded to leadership from within the railroad system and directed their economic protest against the railroad administration, the common employer that gave the entire railroad movement a single focus. The shop workers had an impact on the mass movement, not merely as metalworkers, but as part of the collective mobilization of the socially diverse transportation work force.

According to the 1902 census, slightly over half the city's blue-collar workers were employed by privately owned manufacturing enterprises, 108,000 in factories and plants (*fabriki* and *zavody*)—the industrial labor force proper—and 132,500, including 25,400 apprentices, in artisanal production (*remeslennoe proizvodstvo*). (See Table 2.) However, no other published source of statistical data on the Moscow working class agrees with these figures.[16] The problem is primarily one of definition. As a leading expert on the subject, A.V. Pogozhev, cautioned at the opening of his 1906 study of the Russian working class: "The chaotic condition and the inadequacies of our manufacturing statistics are well known to everybody. All available official data suffer from the extreme vagueness of the terms 'factory, plant, and artisanal enterprise,' as well as from the irregular and incomplete registration of small establishments, and even of comparatively large manufacturing enterprises."[17]

Recent Soviet scholarship, benefiting presumably from access to the archives of private firms and of the relevant tsarist bureaucracies, has not substantially improved on the work of early researchers in this regard.[18] Soviet historians focus on what they call the proletariat, that is, on workers employed by industrial establishments. By and large, they ignore the artisanal periphery (a broad periphery indeed). But even to define (let alone count) the industrial proletariat in the narrow sense, one must solve the problem of boundaries: where does one draw the line between small-scale factory production and artisanal manufacture?

Even if it were possible to distinguish neatly between different types of enterprises, the work force itself would still present a confusing variety. A worker might well shift from one category to another in changing jobs: out-of-work factory hands often found temporary employment in small unmechanized shops, for example.[19] And the so-called industrial labor force included workers who by skill, length of training, social background, and role in the production process were little different from those employed in so-called artisan shops. This could be said of various bakers and precious-metal workers, for example. These anomalies, of course, contributed to the confusion of data collectors. In theory, the Factory Inspectorate had jurisdiction over all enterprises with mechanized equipment or with more than 15 workers. In practice, this criterion was violated in both directions. In one curious and oft-cited decision, the Inspectorate excluded from its purview the 385-worker Filippov bakery in Moscow because bakers belonged officially to the Artisan Board.[20]

It is clear that the term artisan, as employed by the census and the Factory Inspectorate, covered more than the traditional skilled craftsman, or craftswoman,* who had passed through an apprenticeship, owned his or her own tools, and worked in a small shop where the production process involved a complex variety of operations. In 1896, the Moscow Artisan Board had a total of 37,400 registered members: 13,330 master artisans (*mastera*), plus 24,070 journeymen and apprentices (*podmaster'ia* and *ucheniki*). These belonged to 23 guilds, including 6 in clothing, 5 in metalworking, 3 in textiles, 3 in food, and 2 in woodworking. Thirty years earlier, in the 1860's, artisans in the apparel business had constituted almost half the registered total, and metalworkers a fifth.[21] This was not a closed guild system or an exclusive legal category. Less than 10 percent of the 37,400 in 1896 were artisans by social estate; the others had only a "temporary" artisan status that derived from their occupational training, but it is not clear how much quality control the guild organizations exercised over their membership. By legal estate the vast majority of temporaries were peasants.[22] Like most industrial workers, who also retained this official status, many artisans had abandoned all ties with the countryside. Still, a good proportion continued to own land and keep their families in the village.[23]

Let us say that by 1905 there were as many as 55,000 guild artisans in Moscow.[24] Of these, perhaps one-third or two-fifths were master artisans, some of whom owned their own shops and employed other workers. The guild figures thus do not account for the 132,000 artisanal workers listed by the 1902 census in its occupational breakdown of the Moscow working class.[25] Of this larger number, 39 percent were in the apparel trade, 16 percent in metalworking, 12 percent in woodworking, 9 percent in construction, 7 percent in food products, and a mere 5 percent in textiles (the other 12 percent were thinly distributed in various other trades). In each of the artisanal trades, however, the census considered a certain proportion of workers to be factory labor. Thus, 90 percent of ribbonmakers are listed under the industrial heading, as are 35 percent of the braidmakers, 32 percent of those who worked with precious metals, 17 percent of the bakers, and 15 percent of the woodworkers. Tailors, furriers, hatmakers, and shoemakers, by contrast, rarely worked in factories; only 3 percent of apparel workers fall under the industrial category as defined in the census. Although the guilds did not include skilled factory workers or the majority of small-shop artisans, a strong sense of group identity seems to have lingered among the practitioners of the artisanal trades, even in

---

*In 1896, at least a third of Moscow's registered master artisans were women (Pazhitnov, *Problema*, p. 185). In 1902, 40% of all artisan entrepreneurs and 32% of all wage-earning artisans were female. In the garment industry, the figures were still higher, 58% and 48%, respectively (*Perepis' Moskvy*, part 1, vyp. 2: Table 7).

arge-scale enterprises. Such workers manifested an unusual capacity for collective action and for organization building. The union movement in 1905, by and large, followed craft, not industrial, lines.

The Factory File

The composition of the industrial work force reveals the close relation between craft and factory production that still prevailed in early-twentieth-century Moscow. The inconsistency of statistical data that so frustrates the labor historian is, in fact, an indication of this intricate connection. The above discussion of the size of artisanal trades in Moscow relies on data from the 1902 city census. Yet a comparison of those figures with payroll statistics from individual firms shows that the census figures for "factory workers" fall consistently below the number of workers actually employed in the larger plants (those with 100 or more workers). Published guides to manufacturing enterprises, for their part, fail to include a large number of small shops, though their total figures agree in general proportions with those in the census. In some cases, as we have noted, the census classed whole factories in the artisan category because of the traditional nature of the craftsmen they employed or because of affiliation with the artisanal boards. And indeed, clothing and bakery factories did not involve a greater degree of mechanization or a more complicated division of labor than smaller shops in the trade.

This study relies on data compiled from manufacturing handbooks that list individual enterprises by street address and payroll size.[26] Instead of trying to distinguish between factory and artisanal labor, an attempt at which many have already failed, I have organized the data according to the size of the plant work force and the location of the firm. This makes it possible to analyze strike reports that refer to specific enterprises. It allows one to generalize about the impact of plant size on worker behavior, an impact that was indeed most significant. One must not, of course, assume that differences in plant size always coincided with differences in the mode and organization of the production process, or that such differences were necessarily the crucial ones for explaining varieties of working-class protest. One must also consider plant location, neighborhood character, and the histories (social and political) and economic circumstances of the individual trades. Another virtue of the composite data base (which I have called the Factory File) is to provide a detailed picture of the industrial geography of Moscow.

The File's greatest weakness is to underestimate the number of workers in small shops.[27] This bias is perhaps mitigated by a similar neglect shown in the police reports on strikes and working-class unrest. Just as the guidebooks overlooked numerous small shops as too insignificant to mention or not worth the trouble of describing with statistical accuracy, so the police seem to have concentrated on larger enterprises. They reported on the behavior of individual firms in detail, but usually mentioned the dispersed, small-shop trades in general terms: "most carpenters," "thousands of tailors."[28] The File, like police and newspaper accounts, is most accurate for those industries in which factory production played an important part. It covers a total of 154,000 workers in 7 industries, as compared with 150,000 listed in the census in the same categories (see Table 3). It does not include woodworking, apparel, and construction (a total of 83,800 in the census), for which specific data are inadequate, and strike information scant and impressionistic. Despite its shortcomings, the File

TABLE 3

The Moscow Working Class: Comparison of the 1902 Census and the 1905 Factory File

| Branch of industry | 1902 census[a] | | | Factory file | | | File as pct. of census |
	Factory workers	Artisans	Total	Plant size 100 or more workers	Plant size under 100 workers	Total	
Textiles	51,932	6,179	58,111	58,506	5,018	63,524	109%
Metal, machine[b]	16,877	21,042	37,919	21,073	9,490	30,563	81
Food, tobacco, alcohol, tea	14,627	9,294	23,921	21,521	4,274	25,795	108
Printing[c]	6,767	1,228	7,995	8,251	4,270	12,521	157
Chemicals, minerals	6,046	1,674	7,720	6,116	2,091	8,207	106
Leather	3,093	4,323	7,416	5,382	1,472	6,854	92
Paper	2,214	4,381	6,595	4,664	1,696	6,360	96
Subtotal	101,556	48,121	149,677	125,513	28,311	153,824	103
Wood[d]	2,754	15,746	18,500	3,041	3,314	6,355	34
Apparel	1,837	51,447	53,284	578	1,163	1,741	3
Construction	15	11,979	11,994				
Miscellaneous	1,651	5,162	6,813				
Subtotal	6,257	84,334	90,591	3,619	4,477	8,096	9
Census total	107,813	132,455	240,268				

SOURCE: Census, *Perepis' Moskvy 1902 goda*, part 1, vyp. 2 (Moscow, 1906): Table 7, pp. 116–59. Factory File, basic sources, I. F. Gornostaev, ed., *Fabriki i zavody g. Moskvy i ee prigorodov: Adresnaia i spravochnaia kniga o fabrichno-zavodskikh, glavnykh remeslennykh i torgovopromyshlennykh predpriiatiiakh i drugie spravochnye svedeniia* (Moscow, 1904), and A. V. Pogozhev, ed., *Adresnaia kniga fabrichno-zavodskoi i remeslennoi promyshlennosti vsei Rossii* (St. Petersburg, 1905).
[a]Figures include apprentices as well as the census categories of factory and nonfactory workers (rabochie).
[b]This category covers census groups III, IV, and XIII: metal, machines, gas, and electric.
[c]This category covers census group XV and subsections 144, 145, and 146.
[d]This category covers census group VIII and subsections 147, 152, and 154.

provides a base figure against which to plot the year's changing strike movements.

Because of the combined weight of the textile and metal industries in the industrial economy of Moscow, textile- and metalworkers dominated the 1905 factory strike movements, at least numerically. Whether they played a dominant role in terms of political organization and leadership is a question the following narrative will seek to answer. The discussion of 1905 will also attempt to link the political behavior of workers in different kinds of production to the structure of the industry in which they were engaged. Let us begin, therefore, with a comparison of the four major branches of factory-dominated manufacture in Moscow, in terms of four characteristics: the scale and organization of the workplace; the social profile of the labor force; the economic position of the work force; and the workers' experience of technological, social, and economic change.

Factory Labor in the Metal and Textile Industries

The only other city in the Empire of a size comparable to that of Moscow was St. Petersburg, but the industrial economy of the two cities differed in important respects. Moscow was a textile center, whereas St. Petersburg was dominated by heavy industry. The contrast is striking: in St. Petersburg there were over two and a half times as many metalworkers as textile workers; in Moscow there were twice as many textile as metalworkers.[29]

Compared with the capital, Moscow was not a city of colossal industrial giants. Even though 60 percent of Moscow city's textile labor force worked in plants with 500 or more workers, this compares with a full 75 percent in St. Petersburg, a figure closer to the one prevailing in the more rural areas of Moscow Province.[30] The contrast in the metal and machine industry is even more startling. Large plants employed only 35 percent of metalworkers in Moscow city, half the figure for St. Petersburg.[31] Only in the outlying districts of Moscow Province did the metal and machine plants show a similar pattern of worker concentration to that of St. Petersburg.

Moscow's metal industry was extremely varied. This rubric, indeed, is known to harbor a variety of trades and types of manufacture. Pressed to define it, Britain's Balfour Committee agreed in 1928 that the metal industry was really "an amalgamation of a considerable number of separate industries differentiated by product but united by the fact that the basic metal working operations underlying them are all substantially the same."[32] Moscow boasted 10 large machine-building plants; 50 or so medium-sized firms (100–500 workers), ranging from industrial machine shops to bicycle factories; and at least 400 small shops that turned out everything from umbrellas and icon frames to bedsprings and carriages. Moscow was the nation's main producer of gold and silverware.[33] According to the census, 16 percent of metalworkers specialized in the precious-metal crafts, including jewelry manufacture.[34] Absent were the giant machine- and ship-building plants of St. Peterburg, such as Putilov with its 10,000 workers and the Baltic shipyards with over 5,000.[35] The largest firm in Moscow was the 2,500-hand Guzhon steel mill. As might be expected, St. Petersburg employed a considerably smaller proportion of its metalworkers in small shops.[36] Government armaments contracts did not play a role in Moscow's economy, and even railroad-car production was confined to a single large plant in Mytishchi, on the outskirts of Moscow. The majority of Moscow metal firms were not specialized enterprises or volume producers, but worked almost exclusively on special order, sometimes even for private parties.[37]

Metalworkers displayed a range of skills, educational experience, and economic well-being that reflected the variety of manufacturing specialties and forms of production within the industry. The payroll of the larger firms often represented the entire spectrum, from unskilled menials to the highest level of sophisticated craftsmanship. The big metal and machine works, such as Gopper, Guzhon, and Bromlei, resembled complex beehives of interlocking shops. Although contemporaries and historians often use the terms zavod and fabrika interchangeably, zavod refers specifically to such large-scale, internally differentiated plants.[38]

Each shop (masterskaia) concentrated on one part of the production process: patternmaking (a woodworking trade); iron or steel smelting or rolling; tool-and-dye making; painting; and so forth. Thus not all workers in the metal industry in fact worked with metal. The workers in the shop formed a tsekh, the same term used to designate the various artisan guilds or trades. As an adjective, tsekhovoi might describe work organized on a team basis, a member of such a team, a person belonging to the legal category of craftsman, or an attitude of identification with a craft specialty. Thus, the terminology of artisanal production applied to the industrial workplace as well. Certain customs were also common to factory and artisan shops: for example, newly hired hands were expected to treat their fellow workers to a round of free drinks. The traditional alcoholic initiation ceremony, enjoyed at the expense of the newcomer, was as prevalent on the machine shop floor as it was in the tailor's workshop.[39]

Skill, status, and power hierarchies common to the independent small shop also appeared in the factory. In the artisan shop (also the master-skaia), the master craftsman (master) supervised the work and exercised authority over journeymen and apprentices.[40] In the factory, this role fell to the foreman (likewise called the master), a skilled workman chosen by management to control and oversee the shop's functioning. He determined work hours, fines, and job assignments; and his authority extended over both the skilled workers (*masterovye*) and the unskilled workers (*chernorabochie*) in his purview.[41]

The skilled far outnumbered the unskilled workers in metal plants. They were better paid (sometimes four times as much), better educated, and, of course, better trained, and they often looked down on the unqualified laborers.[42] Most were loath to do unskilled tasks, even temporarily (the low pay, low status, and hard labor involved explain their aversion), and objected to being identified with the common rabochii.[43] The unskilled tended to have closer ties to their villages of origin, mostly as a form of economic insurance. In terms of job security, the chernorabochie were the first to go. Many were dayworkers and never knew from one morning to the next whether the same factory would take them on again. Some were attached to specific shops, but most constituted a floating labor force within the plant. Few, in these circumstances, had a chance to develop a sense of loyalty to a specific firm or to their co-workers.[44]

The masterovoi, by contrast, was usually on the monthly payroll or worked by the job.[45] Because the Moscow metal industry was technologically backward, "almost everything was done in a semi-artisanal manner"; hand tools vastly outnumbered machines, and work was commonly finished "by eye."[46] The skilled metalworker chose the tools appropriate to the job and exercised considerable control over how the assigned task was to be accomplished. Such workers rarely came from artisan stock, but they represented an extension of the principle of handicraft labor. As a historian of the English metal industry puts it, "Inside every engineering craftsman lay the ideal type, derived from the old millwright, of the man who is hired to do a job, and to do it from start to finish without interference from his employer."[47] This class of worker demonstrated a marked spirit of independence.

Many skilled workers built up substantial seniority; but many others changed jobs frequently. This was especially true in the late 1890's, a period of expansion in the metal industry when the demand for skilled labor was particularly high. Then, the restless mechanic, turner, or patternmaker would pack his toolbox (he owned his own tools) and leave one plant for another. The masterovye often went from town to town, in a manner reminiscent of European artisans in their *Wanderjahre*. The patternmaker Semen Kanatchikov, in his wonderfully vivid memoirs, describes his own progress from apprenticeship at the Gustav List plant, where he was fired for a three days' absence to attend a country wedding; to a job at the Bromlei plant, which let him go during the annual post-Easter spring cleaning of "undesirable" elements; to a well-paid position in the new railroad-car works at Mytishchi; to another job at Vartse and McGill in the city; to ill-paid, unsuitable employment in a small metal-working shop; and finally to St. Petersburg, the Mecca of the "conscious," or self-aware, worker, as Kanatchikov is fond of describing himself.[48] Indeed, Kanatchikov's inquiring mind, critical attitude, and interest in "ideas" made him suspect to factory management. His intellectual restlessness fed on contact with other such peripatetic workers, who conveyed a wide range of experience with factory life, along with a hodgepodge of acquired information and attitudes.

The metal industry's work force was thus in a state of constant flux, at both ends of the social scale, for different reasons. Whereas the shops were relatively isolated from each other within the plant,[49] the workers themselves changed places, exchanged information, and developed a network of friends and acquaintances. It is easy to understand how the good-sized plant might serve as the backbone of an industrywide strike movement: its structure of tightly knit subunits integrated workers of all skill levels and degrees of urbanization, under the established authority of the highly qualified, whose personal contacts extended well beyond the factory gates and whose activity was indispensable to plant operation. In the 1890's, when Social Democratic organizers began to recruit followers among the Moscow working class, they concentrated on a number of large metal plants. At Gopper and Bromlei, for example, entire shops became centers of political activity.[50] Individual workers moved easily from job to job, taking the radical message with them.[51]

Large-scale, mechanized production, as we have seen, played a larger role in the textile industry than in metalworking and machine building. Cotton mills in Moscow employed a third of all textile workers, wool factories a fifth.[52] Cotton was technologically the most advanced branch of textile production,[53] and this is reflected in a high degree of worker concentration in large, modern enterprises. Plants with 500 or more workers employed three-quarters of the cotton labor force, compared with less than 40 percent of wool workers. The truly vast textile mills (from 3,000 to 10,000 workers apiece) were located in the outlying areas of Moscow Province.[54] Typically, the closer to the capital itself, the smaller the size of the textile plants. But even inside the city limits there were three firms with 3,000 or more workers: Prokhorov Trekhgornaia, Giubner, and Zhiro.

Large textile mills differed in their organization from metal and machine works, and the textile labor force as a whole reveals a dramatically different outline. Most significant from the point of view of cultural development, the ratio of skilled to unskilled workers was reversed: the vast majority of textile mill hands were machine operatives.[55] Spinning was the most highly mechanized division of the manufacturing process; it thus had the highest proportion of unskilled hands and also the highest proportion of women workers, categories that correlate directly.[56] In 1905, the textile work force as a whole was about 45 percent female, compared with only 6 percent in metalworking.[57] As plant size increased (with a corresponding increase in mechanization), so did the percentage of women: in the textile giants (with 1,000 or more hands) they accounted for 50 percent of the work force, against 33 percent in shops with under 100 hands.[58] The skilled occupational groups found in textile factory workshops included engravers, fabric printers, mechanics, and carpenters; these trades virtually excluded women.[59] Such craftsmen showed higher literacy and wage levels than the machine operatives (two factors that also correlate directly).[60] Three-quarters of all male textile workers were literate, compared with one-quarter of the women; the rate for engravers and printers in the industry, by contrast, was over 90 percent, a figure that compares favorably with the 92 percent rate for metalworkers.[61] These craftsmen also showed greater average seniority than the unskilled textile hands. Their wages might be as high as 60 rubles a month, compared with a low of 10–12 rubles a month for unskilled female operatives. Overall, women earned only half to three-quarters as much as male workers.[62] The average metalworker earned almost twice as much as the average textile worker in this period.[63] In both industries the average wage was highest in very large plants and lowest in very small ones.[64]

Textile production was much more labor intensive in Moscow and Moscow Province than in Europe or even in St. Petersburg. This is yet another indication of the slow rate of technological progress in the central industrial region as compared with the capital. In the 1890's England had an average of 3 operatives per 1,000 spindles in its cotton-spinning factories, Germany and Switzerland an average of 6, and St. Petersburg Province an average of 15. The average for Moscow Province at this point was 40.[65] The cotton-dyeing and fabric-printing factories of Moscow Province were only half as productive as those of St. Petersburg as measured by the ruble value of annual output per worker.[66] Technological backwardness in this case meant a lower standard of living for the workers: between 1901 and 1906, the average Moscow textile worker never earned more than two-thirds the wage of his St. Petersburg counterpart, with the result that throughout the period, the Moscow workers' average wages fell consistently below the national mean for the industry.[67]

Metal and textile workers also differed in terms of social origins and way of life. The overwhelming majority of textile hands (over 85 percent) were peasant by legal category, compared with something like two-thirds or three-quarters of metalworkers (this latter proportion holds for mechanics in textile plants as well).[68] Nominal peasant status did not necessarily mean, however, that a worker was fresh from the village. In fact, two-thirds of all Moscow residents in 1902 fell into this official category, but many had no more connection with the countryside than Moscovites in the urban civic ranks.[69] One such nominal peasant was Ivan Belousov, born in Moscow in 1863, the son of a furrier, whose family had resided in the city and plied its trade for several generations.[70] Still, in 1902, the factory worker was less likely to have been born in Moscow than a worker in the census's artisanal class (7 percent as opposed to 10 percent natives). White-collar employees (26 percent native) were over three times as likely as blue-collar workers to be Moscow-born.[71]

The trades also differed in their recruitment patterns. Better educated and trained workers more often came from families already rooted in the city, or else accustomed to urban employment. In Moscow Province as a whole, metalworkers showed a slightly higher tendency than textile workers to be second-generation factory hands.[72] Machine operatives were more likely to be the first in their families to enter the ranks of industrial labor; the skilled trades on the factory payroll tended to be those that had developed a hereditary work force.[73] Generational continuity was important in shaping a worker's self-definition; urban lore and perhaps even skill might be passed on from father to son. But at the same time that occupational traditions were established, it was not uncommon for Moscow workers to resist permanent transfer to the city. Many kept their families in the village, where children were born and raised until they were old enough to come to town.[74] Apprenticeship customs also united town and country. The artisan class was more firmly rooted in the city than the factory labor force, and many artisans followed the calling of their fathers, but small shops often drew apprentices directly from the countryside.[75] Likewise, factories attracted young peasants or village-born sons of workers, who then learned their trade on the job.[76] Artisan shops did not supply the factories with a class of worker long settled in the city and attached through generations-long tradition to a particular trade.

In the aggregate, textile workers and metalworkers contrasted markedly in social background and experience with city life. But one must beware of exaggerating these distinctions and forming neatly opposed stereotypes: the rude, illiterate textile hand, disoriented by his or her recent move to the metropolis, still tied emotionally and economically to the land; the more sophisticated town-bred mechanic, thoroughly accustomed to factory, tavern, and street. As Robert E. Johnson, a student of working-class formation, has shown, the contradictions are too various to sustain such a schema: veteran workers often maintained economic as well as familial ties with the village; workers of all kinds commonly left town on the holidays; and many workers returned to their own or to other villages when they retired from the factory, fell ill, or became unemployed.[77] Thus, Johnson concludes that town-country interaction was an ongoing, two-way process in Moscow Province at the end of the nineteenth century. In his view, the move to the city did not involve the sudden rupture of rural ties, but simply saw the transfer of many former associations into the urban context.[78] Migrants from certain provinces tended to settle together in selected sections of the city. Hiring patterns often followed regional groupings, both because recruiters sometimes concentrated their activities in particular areas and because individual workers relied on personal connections to gain entry into the factory labor force. Johnson sees the newcomer as profiting from a network of existing relationships, rather than suffering from the sudden dissolution of all accustomed social ties. Even the experienced worker appears to have retained such ties well beyond the initial period of residence in the city.

If few workers were fully separated from the land, it is clear enough that a permanent working class existed. What is less clear, and indeed doubtful, is whether more than a small number of workers represented the ideal type of the modern proletarian: bereft of all economic resources but his own labor and dependent on a social network fully integrated into urban life. It is also clear that the life of the recent migrant was more stable than the stereotype suggests. Whether or not continued contact with the village retards or promotes the tendency toward worker radicalism is a separate question. Johnson, for one, argues that the persistence of old village ties did not necessarily impede the process of mass mobilization; it may even have contributed to its effectiveness.[79] This view is based on the assumption that protest behavior, however disruptive its results, demonstrates clear patterns of group cohesion. A lack of data makes it hard to tell whether traditional ties were useful in maintaining such cohesion simply because they provided a convenient organizational network, or whether attitudes peculiar to the countryside caused workers to mobilize.

It is certainly true that politically sophisticated workers like Kanatchikov (along with intelligentsia Social Democrats) made a social distinction between types of workers, which they linked with corresponding political attitudes. Kanatchikov is a good example of a village-born worker who reached the top of the skill hierarchy and who fashioned for himself a way of life based on a distinctly urban model. In this, he was characteristic of a large group of skilled workers. He dressed well, aspired to culture, and rejected the "backward" ways of less-sophisticated workers, habits he associated with country life: religiosity, drunkenness, servility, living from hand to mouth. Almost all male workers drank, most to excess at least on occasion;[80] few were as fastidious as Kanatchikov. But his story makes clear that the workers themselves distinguished a cultural hierarchy in their own midst: at one end of the scale, the proud, self-reliant master-ovoi; at the other, the unskilled, "unenlightened" masses, still attached to what were seen as peasant ways. Even if the unskilled factory worker was instinctively belligerent, he remained politically uncritical; he might assault a policeman on the beat, but he revered the Tsar nonetheless.[81]

The evidence indicates that textile workers indeed fell into the culturally less-urbanized category.[82] The organization of the large textile mills worked to perpetuate the textile hand's relative isolation from city life and to retard the transformation of his habits and attitudes. Large metal and textile plants had much in common: a high degree of administrative control and surveillance (collection and registration of passports, distribution of numbered identification tags, and sometimes internal security forces); the punitive use of fines; the granting of arbitrary and extensive authority to foremen.[83] But the large textile mill had a broader impact on the workers' lives. In effect, it constituted a world apart. Whereas metalworkers usually found their own housing, often in communal apartments away from the plant, a large proportion of the textile workers lived in factory dormitories and ate in factory canteens or bought food at the company store. In controlling these basic necessities, the plant thus gained effective control of its workers' lives.[84] When, in addition, the firm was located on the outskirts of the city, the workers' contact with the town was severely limited. On the other hand, such close communal living may have endowed these workers with a sense of community or at least offered them the physical site for collective action. The giant Prokhorov cotton mill, for example, provided workers with a convenient base of operations during the climax of the December strike and uprising.[85] Here is an instance where persistent rural ties reinforced the strength of newly acquired urban association: family and village relations on the factory floor and in the dormitories made the worker feel more at home in the mill, which was otherwise an alien and impersonal environment.

The case of the textile workers demonstrates, however, that giant plants functioned as political catalysts only under certain circumstances. The textile work force was highly concentrated, as we have seen. Yet in 1905 it was the last segment of the industrial labor force to mobilize in support of the strike movement, it was the least responsive to the organizational efforts of intelligentsia activists, and it rarely engaged directly in political conflict. This may be explained in several ways. Textile workers in large plants located in isolated outlying districts were cut off from workers in other types of production and from city life in general. Even in mills closer to the center of town, textile workers retained more active ties with the countryside than those who worked in the metal and printing industries. Their social networks in the city were less well developed. They also had a place to run away to and an economic alternative—however poor—to factory employment. The high proportion of women in the textile labor force also discouraged political activity, because women were less educated, which tended to make them less interested in politics, and more easily replaced than men since they were not as skilled. Factory size alone was thus never enough to generate worker activism when other critical ingredients for political mobilization were absent.

Factory Labor in the Printing and Food Industries

Workers in the printing industry played a central role in the development and leadership of the working-class movement in Moscow. Fortunately, and certainly not by accident, they have been the subject of unusually intense sociological scrutiny. In particular, a statistical survey published by the Imperial Russian Technical Society in 1909 provides a wealth of detailed information, based on questionnaires distributed to workers throughout the industry.[86]

On a scale of cultural sophistication and economic well-being, printing workers most resembled the metal industry's labor force. Both groups were over 90 percent male and over 90 percent literate; and the average wage in printing was second only to that in the metal industry.[87] At the time of the survey, 22 percent of printing workers were Moscow-born and 38 percent had broken all ties with the countryside. The higher the worker's skill level, the less likely he was to be actively involved in the rural economy.[88] It is important to note, however, that fully 62 percent of the workers in this most urbanized of industrial trades* still retained economic or personal ties (or both) with the village.

Again like the Moscow metal industry, printing was a trade in which small shops predominated. At least 85 percent of the printing enterprises in Moscow had fewer than 100 workers (in metal the analogous figure is 80 percent), and 60 percent of them had fewer than 50.[89] There was, however, an increasing tendency for firms to consolidate and modernize. Thus, by 1905 two-thirds of Moscow printing workers (like the 70 percent in metal) were concentrated in factories employing 100 or more workers.[90] The largest private company, the Sytin Corporation, had 1,110 workers.

The degree of large-scale, mechanized production achieved in Moscow by 1905 meant that the printing trade, like the metal industry, was far from uniform.[91] Both included a wide variety of businesses representing a broad range of technological and organizational development and a vari-

---

*Not only were the printing workers themselves highly urban, but very few printing shops in Moscow Province were to be found outside the city (Pogozhev, *Adresnaia kniga*, pp. 108–9).

ety of working conditions. Only the large firms could afford to mechanize. The history of the Sytin company illustrates the way large establishments grew and diversified by incorporating smaller companies. Between 1885 and 1904, it acquired four smaller plants and two newspapers. Between 1900 and 1904 alone, it doubled the number of its presses and typesetting machines, doubled the size of its work force, and more than doubled its annual profits.[92] Lithography remained, by and large, a handicraft trade. Letterpress printing modernized more quickly, especially in newspaper publication, where the number of rotating presses and typesetting machines rose dramatically after the turn of the century. One typesetting machine did the work of four handworkers. Firms did not use skilled workers to operate the new machines, however, but trained men specifically for the new job. The machines made their first appearance in Moscow in 1903, after a large-scale printers' strike induced owners to grant a rise in typesetting wages. Only the Sytin, Levenson, and Kushnerev plants had them.[93]

Like the metal industry, the printing trade involved an assortment of occupations. The large firms often included under one roof all the stages and the various techniques of the printing process and therefore employed workers in all categories. Sytin, for example, was a combined machine-printing and hand-printing plant with its own bindery and presses for newspaper publication.[94] The "aristocrats" of printing were the skilled lithographers (engravers, draftsmen, and the like) and the hand-typesetters; at the bottom of the skill and wage scale were the bookbinders and unskilled machine operatives. The typesetters were by far the most mobile, changing jobs and cities more often than any other group.[95] They were also, however, extremely vulnerable to periods of unemployment. Each summer the printing industry traditionally cut back its payroll and rehired again in the fall. In 1904, it is important to note, the industry took back fewer workers than usual. In addition to this seasonal fluctuation, the trade was notably affected by political changes: when censorship eased, employment rose; when repression intensified, more printers found themselves jobless.[96]

The basis on which workers were paid reflected their standing in the labor force. The greatest proportion of the printing workers, 47 percent, were dayworkers (the least well paid and the least prestigious type of labor); 36 percent were paid by the month, and 17 percent by piecework. Piece rates predominated in trades that still demanded skilled handiwork: book composing, typemaking, engraving, color lithography, and so on. But it was the newspaper compositors, many of whom were now semi-skilled machine operatives and hired on a monthly basis, who commanded the highest wages in the business.[97] Although piecework was sometimes used in large factories as a method of increasing worker productivity,[98] it was a hallmark of artisanal labor. Most tailors, for example, were paid in this manner, though the ones who worked at sewing machines in the factories earned a monthly wage and were paid at a rate that compared favorably with the pay of skilled handworkers.[99] In contrast to the textile industry, where machine operatives were the least-favored class, the garment industry, like the printing industry, seems to have rewarded machine operatives with good pay and relative job security. Modernized enterprises (usually larger in scale) offered better pay, shorter hours, and better conditions to all categories of workers.[100] To the seamstress in a subcontracting sweatshop or the printer in a small basement shop, the factory was indeed a positive alternative. Within the printing plant or clothing factory, mechanization may have threatened the jobs of some, but it provided new and better opportunities for others.

The workers in the food industry (which by the Factory Inspectorate's definition included alcoholic beverages and tobacco) were a large and, in 1905, an active group. In Moscow, this sector employed over 6,000 workers in 300 bakeries, 7,000 in 30 candy factories, 4,500 in 20 or so tea-packing firms, and 4,000 in 5 cigarette and cigar plants. There were, in addition, some 9,000 workers sprinkled about in such diverse enterprises as vodka factories, breweries, sugar refineries, macaroni factories, and sausage-making shops.*

The bakery industry was officially an artisanal trade. Bakery owners belonged to the Moscow Artisan Board, which regulated rates and working conditions. In the face of worker unrest, the board represented the owners' collective interests.[101] Only one establishment employed over 100 workers: this was the main Filippov bakery on Tver Street, with 385 workers, the largest branch of a chain of bakeries scattered throughout the city. Among the identifiable firms, however, the average employed fewer than 40 workers. Almost all employers required their bakers and salesclerks to live and take their meals on shop premises.[102] Cash wages were therefore low. They ranged from 15–18 rubles a month for master bakers to 6–8 for journeymen and as little as 1.5–3 for young apprentices. Bakery-shop clerks earned an average of 6–8 rubles monthly, another example of the economically thin line that sometimes divided white-collar and manual labor. When it came to taking collective action, however, the

---

*This total exceeds the 26,000 in the Factory File. The extra 4,500–5,000 worked in bakeries and tea factories that cannot be identified individually or cannot be located by address. For the overall figures cited here, see *PDMP*, p. 24, and *Istoriia odnogo soiuza* (Moscow, 1907), Appendix. *Perepis' Moskvy*, part 2, vyp. 1: Table 7, lists only 24,000 food workers.

clerks stood apart from the bakers. They preferred petitions to strikes as a means of improving their position, since they viewed the strike as a pre-eminently "working-class" instrument.[103]

The practice of obligatory room and board was typical of the artisanal trades. Workers commonly described themselves as "living at Filippov's," for example, rather than as "working in the Filippov factory." The system was not only a form of economic exploitation, but a hallmark of traditional employer-worker relations.[104] It was more widespread in shops with no pretensions to modernity (Filippov's was clearly an exception to the modernizing trend in this regard). The pattern stands out clearly in the garment industry, organized along the same lines as the bakery industry: a higher proportion of tailors in the better establishments than in the subcontracting sweatshops lived and ate off the premises. Like the large-scale factory dormitory, in-shop living arrangements increased the owner's control over his employees. The practice differed from the industrial analogue in being more restrictive: the artisanal workers' direct contact with the employer in the smaller shops made them feel the weight of their dependence more acutely; and such workers did not have the option open to factory workers of choosing to live on their own. The freedom to do so became an issue in 1905, when workers sought to enlarge the scope of their civic rights. The bakers, for example, made the abolition of room and board one of their recurrent strike demands.

The largest firm in the candy industry was the giant Einem Corporation, which employed 1,900 workers in the manufacture of chocolates, cocoa, preserves, candy, and biscuits. About two-thirds of the Einem workers were women, a proportion common among firms in the trade. Einem was known as a model factory: it provided dormitories, libraries, and pensions, and paid better-than-average wages.[105] Three other factories employed about 800 workers each. Altogether, 60 percent of all candy workers were concentrated in large enterprises with 500 or more workers; only 12 percent were in small shops, averaging 50 workers apiece.[106]

Few of the workers in the tea, alcoholic beverages, sugar, and tobacco industries were employed in small establishments. Nine tea firms monopolized the trade's labor force, and the five tobacco factories had an average of 775 workers. Neither tea-packing nor tobacco-handling demanded skilled labor. The work consisted largely of simple, repetitive manual operations: the weighing, packing, labeling of tea; the rolling of cigarettes and wrapping of cigars. Both industries employed a high proportion of female and adolescent workers. Half of the 900 workers at the Vysotskii tea company, for example, were in their teens, and it was these child-workers who lived in the plant dormitories, under management supervision and control.[107] It is one of the curiosities of Moscow's industrial development that alongside the large, compact tobacco factories, vestiges of cottage production managed to survive. It is another curious fact that tobacco workers across the board, from unskilled factory hands to the home-based cigarette rollers, participated actively in the 1905 strike movements.[108]

As a rule, artisanal craftsmen made common cause with factory workers in the political movements of 1905, and many white-collar workers in office jobs supported blue-collar strikes. Other white-collar groups, such as the bakery clerks, who took action on their own, were careful to preserve their social distance, while remaining sympathetic to the strike movement. Sausage makers in small shops stood out for their ability to act together in 1905. These workers and some of the slaughterhouse workers saw themselves as working class. Butchershop employees, however, were notorious for their militant right-wing sympathies. Like other retail food shop employees, they viewed the working class and its form of political behavior as a threat to the social order, of which they considered themselves the loyal defenders. For their part, the factory workers, who were the emblem of urban social oppression, were not uniformly interested in politics. Some were indifferent to collective action, others openly hostile. Those who became active did so for a variety of motives, in the service of various goals. Such contrasts reveal the many social and economic distinctions concealed behind the broad class categories. They also demonstrate that political self-definition often transcended simple sociology.

3

THE URBAN COMMUNITY, II:

SOCIAL GEOGRAPHY AND PUBLIC LIFE

Industrialization began in earnest in the Russian Empire during the last decade of the nineteenth century. In demographic terms alone, the changes it entailed were dramatic. Between 1890 and 1900, Moscow's population increased about 30 percent, St. Petersburg's almost 40 percent.[1] In 1902, nearly three-quarters of Moscow's inhabitants had been born outside the city, and less than a third of this group had lived in Moscow for longer than ten years.[2] As we have noted, a disproportionately large number of these newcomers were in the industrial working class. By 1900, Moscow had half again as many workers as it had in 1890. Meanwhile, St. Petersburg's working class had grown at an even faster rate, 88 percent, an eloquent sign of the intensity of industrialization in the capital city. There, employment in the metal industry showed the greatest gain: up 150 percent over the decade. In Moscow, the number of men employed in machine-building increased 85 percent, but the metalworking labor force as a whole grew only 69 percent. Textile employment rose more gradually: up 23 percent in Moscow, 41 percent in St. Petersburg. In Moscow, food production expanded most rapidly of all: its work force grew 89 percent over the decade. In St. Petersburg, where light industry was less important, the number of food workers rose only 9 percent.[3]

The explosion in the size of the urban work force was the product of an intense entrepreneurial fever. A full 40 percent of all Russian firms in business at the turn of the century had been founded after 1891. Almost 90 percent of these were small establishments with fewer than 100 workers.[4] Meanwhile, many of the existing firms had expanded as the new ones were being formed. Thus, despite the increasing number of small businesses, an ever-growing proportion of factory workers came to be employed in large and giant plants. The work force of the average textile factory in the city of Moscow grew 69 percent between 1890 and 1900, that of the average metal factory 37 percent.[5]

At the turn of the century Russia was hit by an economic crisis that put a stop to such rapid industrial expansion. In the five years preceding the revolution, Moscow's working class continued to grow, but at a much slower rate than in the previous decade. In Moscow Province as a whole, the number of employed industrial laborers rose only 6 percent between 1901 and 1905; the metal labor force increased 4.5 percent, that in textiles, 6.5 percent. The food industry even contracted, with a 7.6 percent drop in employment by 1905.[6]

During this slowdown, however, large firms took on new hands at more than double the average growth rate. The number of textile workers in large plants (500 or more workers) increased 16 percent in this period, while the number in small factories fell 16 percent. The data do not indicate whether this shift involved a rearrangement of the existing work force or a laying off and replacement of workers by new recruits. Between 1901 and 1905, the work force dropped 11 percent in small metal shops and rose 13 percent in large metal plants (500 or more workers).[7]

The trend toward worker concentration was evident in the food and printing industries as well.[8] The printing industry as a whole expanded considerably between 1901 and 1905. Factory Inspectorate data (incomplete but consistent over the years) show that the existing large firms grew still larger, increasing their payrolls 35 percent, while a number of middle-sized firms went out of business, along with an even greater number of very small establishments. The work force in the smallest shops under the inspectorate's jurisdiction decreased 18 percent.[9]

This depression, which was part of a general European crisis, hit heavy industry most severely. Metal production in the Russian Empire fell off 12 percent between 1900 and 1902, and the number of metalworkers declined 6 percent between 1901 and 1903.[10] In Moscow Province, however, where metal production was tied more closely to the local market, layoffs were few. Employment of male workers fell only 2.2 percent in 1902 and had recovered by the next year. The pattern of female employment shows, however, that Moscow metal firms were not unaffected by the national slump. Although skilled workmen in the large plants lost their jobs, the industry hired cheap, unskilled labor: the only metalworkers hired in Moscow Province in 1902 were women; in 1903, they constituted 58 percent of newly engaged workers.[11] In both years, moreover, wages were lower than they had been in 1901.[12] Not all firms recovered quickly from the crisis. Guzhon, the largest metal factory in the city of Moscow, cut back its labor force 12 percent in 1902 and did not return to its 1901 complement until 1905.[13]

Light industry throughout the Empire, and in Moscow Province in particular, continued to prosper during the economic downturn.[14] Textile employment and wages generally rose between 1901 and 1903, except in silk production, and the food industry was hardly affected at all.[15] Those printing companies that produced for the industrial market (preparing food labels, for example) did well during the crisis, but book publishing cut back, and a number of firms folded.[16] Because light industry predominated in Moscow, the city experienced a relatively mild setback at the turn of the century.

Nationally, the Russo-Japanese War, which began in January 1904, seems to have given an added boost to the economic recovery under way by 1903.[17] But the war's effects on industry in Moscow Province were uneven.[18] For example, although the value of metal production in the Empire rose, metalworkers in the province tended to be laid off, not hired, in 1904. The workers who were kept on in the larger factories enjoyed wage increases, but small metal shops clearly suffered during the war: their workers lost both jobs and money in 1904.[19] In the textile industry, production was up in both wool and cotton as a result of military orders. In the cotton mills, workers were in demand and wages rose, probably in connection with the rise in prices for finished cotton goods on the Moscow market.[20] But the growth in wool production had an opposite effect: prices for wool yarn fell slightly in 1904, employment and wages also fell, and the proportion of female workers increased slightly.[21] Silk production suffered most, because of the interruption of supplies from the Orient. One-quarter of the province's silkworkers lost their jobs in 1904, and the rest got lower wages.[22] Food workers likewise experienced a rise in unemployment and a drop in wages.[23]

As a result of these developments, when the prices of basic consumer goods in Moscow rose in 1904, after being depressed in 1902–3,[24] the real wages of textile workers and food workers fell off sharply. As a group, the metal and printing workers had made large enough wage gains to offset the price rise.[25] Overall, workers in small establishments tended to be less well paid than those in medium and large firms.[26] Although craftsmen in the city's artisan shops had also made some wage gains between 1902 and 1903, the pay rates fell abruptly in 1904, and they too were hurt by the rise in consumer prices.[27] Unemployment was rampant among artisanal workers, especially in the countryside around Moscow,[28] but also in smaller shops within the city limits.[29] It is thus clear that workers in small-scale manufacture, whether industrial or artisanal, found themselves in a particularly weak position on the eve of 1905.

Factories and Neighborhoods

The tsarist regime deprived the nonprivileged classes of access to social and political institutions. Intelligentsia radicals and liberal democrats alike tried to involve the working class in formal organizations, in order to raise its cultural level and to control its political behavior. But labor organizers were unable to fill the gap in the institutional structure of Russian society. In general, the urban masses did not respond to centralized leadership. In 1905, the workplace and the neighborhood, not large-scale unions or political parties, formed the backbone of collective organization for the majority of Moscow's working-class population.

The giant firm, as we have seen, was an environment in which groups of different social, cultural, and occupational background interacted. It therefore constituted fertile ground for the development of politically sensitive workers. It also served as an effective instrument of mass mobilization in periods of crisis. As a rule, large factories were the first firms to go on strike in a given industry or a given area of the city. Their workers also tended to stay on strike longer than employees of small enterprises. The skilled workers within big plants were often the most politically active in the trade and served as leaders in moments of conflict. The big industrial plant constituted its own "small world" (tsel'yi mirok),[30] but this enclosed world formed part of another, larger one, the neighborhood. It was the relation of the large factory to its neighbors that often proved decisive in turning local disputes into movements of general protest. To understand the role of community in shaping popular response to the crisis of 1905, one must examine the social geography of Moscow at the turn of the century.

Moscow is shaped like a great wheel, with the Kremlin at its hub. Wide streets radiate out from the center like spokes, connecting two concentric rings of broad boulevards. In 1905, these circular thoroughfares contained parklike islands of grass and trees. Beyond the outer rim of the wheel, vast, irregular neighborhoods stretched outward until they merged imperceptibly with the surrounding suburbs. Contemporaries divided Moscow into six broad geographic areas, each composed of several police districts (chasti).[31] The population was distributed fairly evenly among them, but the six sections differed considerably in social and economic complexion (see Table 4).

Inside the circular parkways lay the heart of commercial and institutional Moscow. The City (Gorodskaia) district at the very center harbored a dense array of small shops and markets, the so-called trading rows

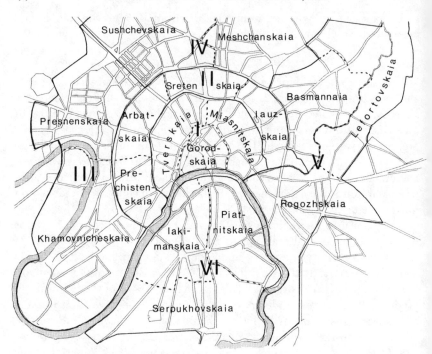

MAP 1. The neighborhoods and districts of Moscow in 1905. The boundaries of the six neighborhoods are based on I. Verner, *Zhilishcha bedneishego naseleniia Moskvy* (Moscow, 1902), p. 4. The map is from *Glavneishie predvaritel'nye dannye perepisi g. Moskvy 31 ianvaria 1902 g.* (Moscow, 1902).

(*torgovye riady*), which faced the northern edge of Red Square. Just behind the rows was the Stock Exchange building. Surrounding the Gorodskaia lay the Tverskaia and Miasnitskaia districts, full of fashionable shops, theaters, and elegant restaurants, and such official buildings as the Governor-General's mansion on Tver Street and the City Council building at the northern entrance to Red Square. Along the west side of the Kremlin, the Alexander Gardens stretched down to the river. At the upper edge of the gardens, across the street from the buildings of Moscow University, the Manège housed a thousand cavalrymen. In the eastern section of the Miasnitskaia district were the main post and telephone offices, the Polytechnical Museum, and the fashionable residences of the Maroseika, home to more than one city councilman.

Along the edge of Theater Square, near the Club of the Nobility, was another cluster of shops, the Okhotnyi Riad, or Hunter's Row, center of the retail butcher trade. In 1905, the butchers from Hunter's Row gave the place a reputation for right-wing violence. Most of the other trading rows were less faithful to their names: the Furrier's Row and the Cutlery Line, for example, housed a variety of shops. Some of the rows contained the retail outlets of fashionable and wealthy firms dealing in fur garments and jewelry. Others sold dry goods, candles, old books, household items, and clothing and food of all kinds.

Along the Moscow River, to the south and east of Red Square, lay the Zariad'e (literally, "beyond the rows"), an area dense in artisan shops: "tailors, shoemakers, capmakers, turners, bootmakers, hatmakers, furriers, pursemakers, buttonmakers, and glovemakers."[32] This was also the old Jewish quarter, and many of the artisans were Jewish. Farther to the east, behind the foundling hospital, at the periphery of the swank Miasnitskaia district, nestled the Khitrov Market, notorious as a refuge for impoverished transients, down-and-out artisans, and alcoholic factory workers who had pawned the clothes off their backs and drunk themselves out of a job.[33] The Khitrov flophouses supplied factory owners with strikebreakers, small shops with cheap labor, and right-wing mobs with belligerent volunteers.

Wrapped around the inner three districts (together area I), and falling between the two concentric rings of boulevards like a blanket of insula-

TABLE 4
Social Geography of Moscow, 1905
(Percent)

Area and districts	Share of total population	Share of working-class population	Share of population classed as peasant	Literacy rate	
				Male	Female
I: Gorodskaia, Tverskaia, Miasnitskaia	12%	7%	62%	83%	57%
II: Prechistenskaia, Arbatskaia, Sretenskaia, Iauzskaia	15	5	57	82	58
III: (Presnia-Khamovniki): Presnenskaia, Khamovnicheskaia	14	16	70	72	46
IV: Sushchevskaia, Meshchanskaia	22	14	66	74	48
V: Lefortovskaia, Basmannaia, Rogozhskaia	22	30	72	72	44
VI: (Zamoskvorech'e): Iakimanskaia, Piatnitskaia, Serpukhovskaia	15	28	69	72	46
Citywide average	—	—	66%	76%	50%

SOURCE: Total population, *Statisticheskii atlas goroda Moskvy* (Moscow, 1911), pp. 5, 9. Working-class population, Factory File (see Table 3 for sources). Peasant population, *Perepis' Moskvy 1902 goda*, part 1, vyp. 1 (Moscow, 1906): Table 8, p. 139. Literacy rate, *ibid.*, Table 4, pp. 115, 117, 119.

tion between the bustle of craft and commerce within and the sprawling squalor of the factory districts beyond, lay Moscow's fanciest residential section, area II. Together, the two densely populated central areas contained the core of socially and culturally prestigious urban society. These areas showed the highest proportion of residents belonging to the privileged legal categories.[34] Prechistenskaia and the Arbat, in particular, sheltered an unusually large number of administrative civil servants and professionals.[35] Because of the central location of Moscow University and the overwhelmingly upper-class background of students in higher educational institutions, over half, if not two-thirds, of such students living in Moscow resided in the two central zones.[36] Mortality rates were below average in the center, and its literacy rates were the highest in the city.[37]

The proportion of downtown residents belonging to the working class and the peasant estate was also below average. Among peasant women, a higher proportion were employed as domestic servants here than elsewhere in Moscow.[38] Manufacture in the central districts was largely artisanal. In addition to the majority of garment workers, two-thirds of bakery workers and one-half the city's printers worked in areas I and II. One machine factory (Lipgart, with 500 workers), one textile mill (Butikov, with 1,600 hands, down in the southern tip of Prechistenskaia, near the river), two tea factories, and a sugar refinery constituted the extent of large-scale industry in the center of Moscow.

Despite the poor housing conditions in the Zariad'e and around the Khitrov Market, slum-dwellers were less common in the downtown area than beyond the boulevards.[39] Almost a quarter of the artisanal and factory workers in Moscow lived in dirty, run-down buildings where they were crowded into apartments in which each person had only a bed or part of one to himself. In the late nineteenth century, at least half the city's population lived in communal quarters or in the households of others, as lodgers or employees. Very few workers could afford to live in units centered around their own families, even when their dependents also lived in the city. Thus, whereas females constituted at least half the upper-class residents of Moscow, the proportion was only 39 percent in the peasant category, a clear sign of the fragmentation of working-class family life in this period.[40]

Beyond the boulevards and south of the Moscow River stretched the four manufacturing districts. These extensive, outlying areas were only a half to a third as densely populated as the center. But they were home to three-quarters of the city's residents and to almost 90 percent of its industrial working class.

The three districts tucked under the northward curve of the Moscow River were known collectively as the Zamoskvorech'e (literally, "beyond

the river"). This area (VI) had the greatest concentration of factory workers anywhere in Moscow. Its literacy rate was below average for the city,
and was especially low in the Serpukhovskaia district, farthest from the
center. Area VI also had the most large-scale industrial plants of any single neighborhood: of the city's 27 textile mills with 500 or more workers,
10 were located here, as were 5 of Moscow's 10 largest metal plants (see
Map 2). Almost three-quarters of the textile workers and half the metalworkers in the area were concentrated in giant enterprises, significantly
more than average for the two industries. The largest firms in the food
and printing industries were also in the area: Einem candy, with 1,900
employees, and Sytin, with 1,110 printers. The Zamoskvorech'e contained, in addition, a large proportion of the city's leatherworking shops,
including the immense Til' tannery, with 3,100 workers. More than 30
percent of the work force in area VI was in textiles, 25 percent in metal,
13 percent in food, and a mere 4 percent in printing. Large-scale machine
production was more important here than anywhere else in Moscow.

Four of the 10 big textile mills in the Zamoskvorech'e and four big
metal factories (Bromlei, Gopper, Zhako, Tereshchenko) were sunk in the
southernmost Serpukhovskaia district. Sytin was situated almost in dead
center of the entire area, a few blocks from two large wool-weaving factories, Shrader and Mikhailov (1,400 and 1,265 workers, respectively), and
not far from the Tsindel' cotton mill (2,400 workers). This conjunction of
massive enterprises proved to be a fertile breeding ground for worker
militancy in 1905. Another dangerous grouping, from the point of view of
strike contagion, was a string of factories perched on the southern embankment of the Moscow River. Directly across from the Kremlin was the
Gustav List metal works (440 workers), neighbor to the Einem candy factory and around the corner from the Golutvinskaia cotton mill (950 workers). Farther east, one encountered the Ding candy factory (470 workers)
and the Smirnov vodka plant (725), and not far away, the Dobrov and
Nabgol'ts machine factory (1,020). The river thus drew industry up to the
very doorstep of fashionable Moscow, but at the same time served as a
barrier between two very different worlds.

Second to the Zamoskvorech'e in density of working-class residents
were the three vast districts along the city's eastern periphery. This area
(V) had the highest proportion of inhabitants in the peasant category and
the lowest rate of literacy in the city.[41] Almost half the area work force was
in the textile industry, less than a fifth in metal, a bit fewer in food, and
around 5 percent in printing. Here giant plants dominated to a lesser extent than in the Zamoskvorech'e, employing only a third of the textile
workers and 44 percent of metalworkers (including 2,500 in the Guzhon
plant in Lefortovo, at the city's eastern limit). Metal and machine produc-

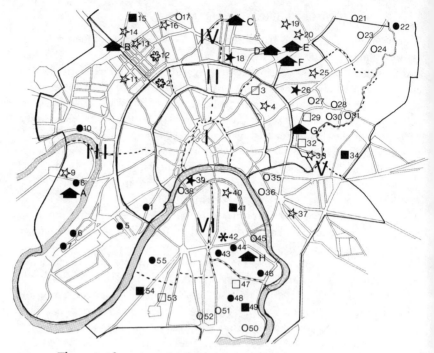

MAP 2. The major factories in Moscow in 1905. White symbols show a work force of 500–1,000 people, black symbols a work force of 1,000 and over.

KEY TO THE FACTORIES

■ *Metal Factories*
Belgian Electric 15
Bromlei 54
Dobrov & Nabgol'ts 41
Gakental' 32
Gopper 47
Guzhon 34
Lipgart 3
Tereshchenko 53
Veikhel't 29
Zhako 49

● *Textile Factories*
Alekseev, Vishniakov
    ribbon 36
Anonymous silk 17
Bundshukh dyeing 21
Butikov mixed weaving 1
Demin knitting 30
Diufurmantev wool 28
Dobrzhialovskaia canvas 8
Fletcher canvas 51
Gandshin & Virts
    ribbon 45
Giubner cotton 6

Golutvinskaia cotton 38
Kariakin wool 23
Konstantinov wool 31
Korochkin cotton 24
Meshcherin cotton 48
Mikhailov wool 43
Moscow Lace 7
Mussi silk 22
Nyrkov silk 35
Prokhorov cotton 10
Riabovskaia cotton 52
Shchapovy cotton 27
Shlikhterman cotton 50
Shrader wool 44
Simono silk 55
Tsindel' cotton 46
Zhiro silk 5

★ *Food Factories*
Abrikosov candy 19
Bostandzhoglo tobacco 26
Dukat tobacco 11
Einem candy 39
Gabai tobacco 14
Genner sugar 9

Gubkin-Kuznetsov
    tea 33
Moscow sugar 4
Perlov tea 18
Popov tea 20
Popov tobacco 37
Renomé candy 16
Smirnov vodka 40
Sui candy 13
Vysotskii tea 25

* *Printing Plants*
Kushnerev 12
Levenson 2
Sytin 42

◆ *Railroad Stations*
Brest B
Briansk A
Iaroslavl E
Kazan F
Kursk and Nizhnyi
    Novgorod G
Nikolaevskii D
Saratov H
Windau C

tion was not on the same scale as in the Zamoskvorech'e, but was still larger than average for the industry as a whole. These three districts were the center of the precious-metal trade: almost half Moscow's jewelry makers and gold- and silversmiths worked in the area. Rogozhskaia, for its part, was the heart of the city's wholesale meat industry. It contained the municipal slaughterhouse and a host of small sausage-making shops.

Industrial plants were scattered throughout area V, but the Moscow-Kursk railroad station, on the border of Basmannaia and Iauzskaia (part of area II), formed the center of an industrial concentration that served as a focus of working-class activity in 1905. The railroad shops alone employed 1,650 workmen. Within a narrow radius one came across two large metal plants (Veikhel't and Gakental', with 800 and 540 workers, respectively), the giant Bostandzhoglo tobacco firm (1,550 workers), and farther east, three large textile mills (employing almost 2,000 workers between them), all on a single street.

Presnia-Khamovniki, the two districts to the south and west (together, area III), were the textile capital of Moscow. Somewhat fewer textile workers lived and worked here than in area V, but nowhere did textile production so monopolize an area's labor force: two-thirds of all factory laborers in Presnia-Khamovniki worked in textiles (half of them in cotton). This explains the relatively high proportion of women among the residents in the peasant category.[42] Metalworkers, by contrast, were few (under 8 percent of all factory workers in the neighborhood) and employed exclusively in small and medium shops. In textiles, five giant firms employed over 80 percent of all mill hands in the area, including Zhiro silk (3,400), Giubner cotton (3,000), Dobrzhialovskaia canvas (1,600), and Moscow Lace (1,000)—all in Khamovniki. Three of these plants were situated near the riverbank, behind the Briansk railroad station. The fifth giant in area III was the largest single factory in the city of Moscow: the 6,000-hand Prokhorov Trekhgornaia Manufaktura. The Prokhorov cotton mill, established in 1842, overlooked the river from Presnia's southern edge, just east of the Trekhgornaia Gates. The mill housed half its labor force in vast factory barracks. The rest lived in squalid slums crowded around the factory. This quarter presented the classic picture of working-class misery: ramshackle wooden houses crammed along mud streets, in which workers rented cots or corners in rooms that were unsanitary, vermin-ridden, and overcrowded.[43] Presnia's western periphery was "a center of hooliganism, petty thievery, cheap prostitution," an area so dangerous even to its lower-class inhabitants that police permitted workers at the Mamontov varnish factory, near the Presnia Gates, to carry guns for self-protection.[44]

But the area south of the river was neither squalid nor heavily industrial. Indeed, Khamovniki included some fancy residential districts, near the Medical Institute and in the vicinity of Smolensk Boulevard. Still, even here industry had begun to infringe on the province of luxury. Tolstoi's residence, for example, was located on Khamovniki Way, adjacent to the Khamovniki brewery, whose smokestack towered over the writer's garden.

Between Presnia on the west and Basmannaia-Lefortovo on the east lay the two northern districts of Sushchevskaia and Meshchanskaia (area IV). Among the four industrial neighborhoods, this area had the lowest concentration of factory workers, the lowest proportion of residents in the peasant category, and the highest literacy rate. Here small-scale production predominated. Of the 18,500 carpenters and cabinetmakers throughout the city, at least a third were to be found in this area. Metalworkers made up one-quarter the local work force, but half of them worked in small shops. There was only one large metal plant nearby (Belgian Electric, with 1,300 workers). There were comparatively very few textile workers here (6 percent of the city's total), and only two textile firms of any size (in the 500–1,000 category).

The food industry was strong in the north and was concentrated in large firms: two big tea plants (Perlov and Popov, 1,500 and 500 workers, respectively), Gabai tobacco (600), and three candy factories, Siu (920), Abrikosov (800), and Renomé (600). This area also boasted the second-largest printing establishment in the city: the 900-worker Kushnerev Corporation. A good number of these big plants were grouped at the outer limits of the area, around the Brest railroad station at the Tver Gates, on the west, and behind the Nikolaevskii, Iaroslavl, and Kazan stations circling Kalanchevskaia Square, on the east. The Brest and Kazan stations had large shops, with 1,200 and 2,500 workers, respectively. These became a focus of working-class activity in the vicinity. Their position at the edge of Presnia, to the west, and of Basmannaia, to the east, made them natural rallying points for workers in these two heavily industrial areas, as well as for those to the north.

An overview of Moscow's social geography thus shows that commerce, civic administration, and artisanal production were concentrated within the circular boulevards, and that industry occupied the outlying areas, with the western districts specializing in textiles, and the southern in machine building. Factory workers lived in relative isolation from other social classes. Their daily life revolved around the workplace, the dormitory or communal apartment, and the tavern. They maintained an active commerce with the countryside. Many had spent long years in the city and had developed a distinctive sense of identity and of local community. Yet, in the cultural sense as well as the geographical sense, the factory labor force remained on the fringe of urban life.

City Government and City Politics

The opportunity to participate in public life was severely limited for all social classes in tsarist Russia. There was nevertheless a hierarchy of access to civic and political activity that reflected the social hierarchy. All but a small handful of Moscovites were completely excluded from such activity. Less than 2 percent of the city's economically self-supporting population was employed in the management of public institutions and in civic administration. An even smaller proportion was eligible to participate in elections for the City Council, the only organ of municipal government that was not part of the imperial bureaucracy. Men over twenty-five could vote if they met the property qualifications set forth in the Urban Statute of 1892.[45] (Women, of course, were excluded.) But even then, fewer than a fifth of the 8,817 eligible voters (1,665 men, or 0.15 percent of Moscow residents) participated in the City Council elections of 1904.[46]

Family connections dominated the world of industry and commerce in Moscow, and business dominated public life.[47] Over a third of the 159 city councilmen elected in 1904 were in trade and manufacture; and over a third were professionals, the bulk of them lawyers (20 percent of the council).* Certain families predominated within the narrow elite of council members. One-fifth of the 1904 councilmen were related to at least one other council member. Three families alone—the Vishniakovs, the Bakhrushins, and the Guchkovs—accounted for eleven councilmen, and ten other names could be counted twice each. Eight additional councilmen belonged to families that had been represented on the council since 1897. Indeed, if one takes into account all the 232 men elected to the council between 1897 and 1904, the concentration of family influence is even more striking: more than a quarter of these men (61 individuals from 24 families) had relatives who had also served during this period, the Guchkov and Bakhrushin families again figuring most prominently, with five members each.

The civic activity of many councilmen extended to other organizations.

---

* Among the prominent factory owners on the City Council were V. A. Abrikosov (candy), the Bakhrushins (textiles and leather), P. D. Botkin (tea), M. N. Bostandzhoglo (tobacco), S. V. Gopper (machines), S. A. Popov (tobacco, tea), I. D. Sytin (printing), and I. M. Zhemochkin (leather). The occupations of a quarter of the 1904 councilmen are unknown. Statistical breakdown of the professional and economic ties of the city councilmen based on *Moskovskaia gorodskaia duma, 1897–1900* (Moscow, 1897), which includes brief portraits of all councilmen elected between 1897 and 1900; and on *Spravochnaia kniga po moskovskomu gorodskomu obshchestvennomu upravleniiu, 1904 g.* (Moscow, 1904), pp. 40–46.

Thirty of the 57 men who were active in commercial life were members of the business community's most influential institutions: the Stock Exchange Society, the Division of Trade and Commerce, the trading row directorates. Many also served as officers of the merchants' and small tradesmen's corporations and on the governing boards of various financial institutions.[48] The council members' residential patterns were as cliquish as their business associations. Not only were their homes clustered in the same neighborhoods; often several lived on the same street. Thus, of the 113 councilmen elected in 1900 for whom we have street addresses (90 percent of the total), almost a fifth lived in the Prechistenskaia district and another fifth in the adjoining Arbatskaia and Tverskaia districts. Fifty-four of these men lived on the same 19 streets; and eight resided on a single avenue, the Maroseika.[49]

City government itself constituted an extensive economic enterprise. The municipal administration was responsible for the provision of public services like sanitation, water, gas, and electricity; for the operation of workhouses, orphanages, and other charitable institutions; and for the physical upkeep of roads, bridges, and public buildings. The city owned and operated several enterprises, including a gas works, laundry, slaughterhouse, publishing house, bakery, and tram network. These, along with municipally owned properties, produced 40 percent of the city's income; another 35 percent came from property and business taxes, the remainder deriving from various fees and forms of direct taxation.[50]

Although municipal funds helped sustain the city's peacekeeping forces,[51] the City Council did not control the police or the prison system, and it had no influence in determining the use of troops quartered in the city. The chief of police (*gradonachal'nik*) was appointed by the Ministry of Internal Affairs in St. Petersburg, and his jurisdiction extended beyond simple matters of law enforcement. His office supervised the activities of the Factory Inspectorate and exercised ultimate authority over the functioning of the city government itself.[52]

In 1902, 21,000 troops were stationed in Moscow. The largest barracks were in lower Khamovnicheskaia (5,300 men); in Serpukhovskaia (3,600); at the southern edge of Meshchanskaia, not far from the Nikolaevskii Station (2,000); in lower Iauzskaia along the inner boulevard (1,800); at the city's northeastern boundary (1,500); and in lower Rogozhskaia near the embankment (1,200). The Manège across from the university housed 1,000 cavalrymen. Another 2,200 men were stationed in the military suburb of Khodinskoe Pole, outside the city limits north of Presnia.[53] The police force consisted of 3,500 patrolmen, whose duties were facilitated by the cooperation of some 2,000 night watchmen and the almost 17,000 concierges (*dvorniki*) employed by houseowners.[54] There were 3 uniformed policemen to every 1,000 Moscow residents, compared with 19 soldiers per 1,000. This ratio reflected the government's reliance on military force for peacekeeping purposes.

The tsarist regime was designed to restrict decision making to the highest echelons of national government. It not only limited the right to participate in local affairs; it also deprived local institutions of any real power or independence of action. The Moscow City Council and municipal administration were not autonomous organs of self-government, but essentially only managers of the city economy. Supreme authority was in the hands of a direct representative of the central government: the Governor-General, who was responsible to the Ministry of Internal Affairs. Many of the administrative bodies of the national bureaucracy (especially those under the jurisdiction of the provincial governor's office) provided for the participation of leading public figures,[55] but there was no exclusively municipal institution that had ultimate authority over its own functions. So unaccustomed were Russian subjects to the determination of their own affairs, that even in the crisis of 1905 Moscow's City Council refused to assume political responsibility. Nothing like the French municipal revolution of 1789 occurred in Russia's cities. For all its liberal sympathies, Moscow's urban elite showed itself fearful of changes in the authority structure of the regime that might unleash social forces beyond its control.

Although the members of Moscow's City Council did not enjoy the exercise of political power in any meaningful sense, they represented an oligarchy of wealth and civic status. Despite the intrusion of modern industry and the influx of foreign capital, local families still dominated commerce, manufacture, and public life. Moscow industrialists were more timid than their St. Petersburg counterparts in changing from traditional to technologically advanced forms of production; the average Moscow factory was run on a more personal, patriarchal basis than the modern St. Petersburg plant.[56] The industrial labor force expanded, but not as rapidly as in the capital, and when peasants moved in from the countryside, they did not so much break with tradition as perpetuate well-established habits of intercourse between town and village.

Moscow's heterogeneous working class included a wide range of occupational categories, from the skilled artisan to the untrained manual laborer. Workers also differed vastly in education, social background, and familiarity with city life. The industrial labor force itself displayed a variety of social types. The large manufacturing plant brought together different kinds of workers in a common, if stratified, framework. But the plant also isolated the industrial worker from other social classes. Large-scale manufacture was concentrated in the western, southern, and eastern areas of the city. Long work hours, segregated residential districts, and a profound cultural divide kept factory workers apart from the rest of the population.

The central neighborhoods grew more slowly than the outskirts,[57] composed as they were of upper-class residents, merchants, white-collar workers, and traditional craftsmen. Here were the offices, retail shops, and public institutions of Moscow. Blue-collar workers employed in the downtown area were less cut off from city life in general. Printers, in particular, occupied a strategic position in the social hierarchy; skilled, literate, living and working in the heart of Moscow, yet still working class by economic level and the nature and conditions of their labor, they were extremely sensitive to changes in the regime's cultural policies. What the intelligentsia experienced as spiritual deprivation, the printers experienced in unemployment and wage cuts. The printers, not surprisingly, showed a remarkable degree of group solidarity, political militancy, and organizational capacity in 1905.

The only other groups to rival the printers in the coherence and impact of their protest were the railroad workers and the municipal employees. These were bureaucratic, not social or economic categories. It was, in fact, the social diversity—the forced interaction of different classes—that generated political activism among them. The bureaucratic structure provided the means to guide and sustain the collective impulse. In terms of trade-union organization, the artisanal trades, whether inside or outside the factory, the white-collar groups, and the service professions were extremely active. The broad mass of blue-collar factory workers, however, did not become involved in union activity.

Despite the sharp class divisions in Moscow society, the revolutionary movement of 1905 was in fact a movement of class cooperation. The nationwide political crisis broke down social barriers, at least temporarily, and the crossing of boundaries is what gave the movement its power. The general mobilization of society at large drew the working class out of its isolation. The privileged recognized the social and economic problems of the working class as part of the political dilemma of society as a whole. And the working class, to some extent, was able to associate its own particular conflicts and needs with the larger issues at stake in the opposition movement. Though vastly outnumbering the mobilized professional and white-collar sector, Moscow workers did not impose themselves politically. Their great triumph in 1905 was merely to have joined the rest of the urban community.

4

POLITICAL BACKGROUND AND THE

OUTBREAK OF REVOLUTION

The movement for political change that sparked the crisis of 1905 began, not in the working class, but among the educated, privileged social strata. By the 1890's, progressive members of the landowning class were already agitating for political reform. In the cities, the process of gradual political mobilization began at the turn of the century, with the formation of unofficial corporate organizations. Members of the liberal professions and of the technical intelligentsia joined societies for the promotion of professional interests. University students formed clubs and associations designed to press for changes within the academic system. Despite a prohibition against public association, these organizations developed into forums for open political discussion and eventually, under the pressure of events, into instruments of political mobilization.

No mass workers' movement existed in Moscow in 1900. Although Social Democrats and other radical activists had been at work for almost a decade educating workers in socialist ideas, spreading news of worker unrest, and trying to lay the groundwork for labor organization, the results had been negligible. Intelligentsia socialists established study groups or served as teachers in factory- and government-sponsored Sunday schools and evening classes. The radicals used the classroom to discuss Marxism and to explain the principles of labor organization.[1] This approach produced a group of politically informed workers, but it did not convert them into revolutionaries. Influenced by the so-called agitation strategy developed in the Polish and Jewish labor movements, Moscow Social Democrats began to shift their attention from theoretical to practical issues, to the specific economic causes of worker discontent. Proponents of agitation did not by any means abandon the revolutionary goals of the Social

Democratic movement. The approach was based on the idea that workers would continue to find the intelligentsia's notions abstract and meaningless until they had participated in down-to-earth labor conflicts. Only on the basis of this collective experience could they achieve a political understanding of their own class interests.[2] As a first step toward the development of a mass-based labor movement that would concentrate on trade-union matters, Moscow Social Democrats gathered representatives from seven large metal factories, three railroad shops, and two wool-weaving mills. These formed the nucleus of an organization known as the Workers' Union (Rabochii soiuz).[3] Evidence suggests that the politically responsive workers were, by and large, skilled shop hands.[4] The union held two large public demonstrations in 1895, and by 1896 it claimed to have a membership of 2,000 workers and contacts at over 40 plants.[5]

Despite the propaganda efforts of intelligentsia activists, workers in Moscow Province remained calmer throughout the 1890's than those in other parts of the Empire.[6] St. Petersburg, for example, experienced a wave of strikes among cotton textile workers in 1896.[7] That was also a peak strike year in Moscow Province,[8] but considerably fewer workers were involved there than in the capital. Most of the strikes that occurred in Moscow during 1895–96 were independent of the Workers' Union, and Moscow workers did not respond when the Social Democrats launched a leaflet campaign calling for solidarity with workers in St. Petersburg.[9] Only in those few plants, mostly in the metal industry, where the union had established strong contacts did the Social Democrats successfully lead strikes in the late 1890's. In 1895–96, the union helped promote related actions in the neighboring Kursk railroad shop, Veikhel't machine plant, and Perepud metal factory, clustered together at the inside corner of the Basmannaia district.[10] Workmen in the Kazan railroad shop, also under union influence, struck more than once during 1896–97. At the same time, there were strikes at three other metal plants with ties to the union: Guzhon, Bromlei, and Dobrov and Nabgol'ts. In early 1897, management at List and Dobrov and Nabgol'ts voluntarily shortened the workday, thereby putting a stop to further unrest among the metalworkers and setting a new standard for the industry, as smaller firms followed their example.[11]

Textile workers, by and large, had little contact with the union, and those that struck seem to have done so on their own initiative. Weavers at the Prokhorov mill, for example, led three strikes, one in 1895, another in 1898, and still another in 1901. In all cases, the strikers articulated specific grievances relating to work conditions, pay scale, and wage inequalities among workers in the plant. Police reports do not suggest that intelligentsia activists were behind these outbreaks, though Workers'

Union leaflets were found in the Prokhorov mill in July 1896, that is, after the first strike. In 1898, the giant Giubner cotton mill in Khamovniki also struck, led by workmen from the printing department.[12] By this time, Social Democrats had begun to organize the engravers (skilled metalworkers employed in calico printing) at the Prokhorov and Tsindel' mills. It is possible that the Giubner strikers, many of whom had trained at Prokhorov and attended organizational meetings, acted under this influence.[13]

Despite such examples of intelligentsia involvement, the level of strike activity in various plants and industries in Moscow Province during the 1890's did not by and large correlate with the presence of radical organizers. In general, large enterprises in a given sector took the lead. Among provincial textile workers, those in cotton mills were the most active. The metal industry, however, was relatively stable.[14] The same was true of St. Petersburg, where metalworkers lagged behind textile hands in strike propensity. The reasons for this are unclear. Gerald D. Surh suggests that metalworkers were relatively well off in the 1890's as a result of industry expansion and a shortage of skilled labor. Textile workers were presumably at a greater disadvantage, since machine operatives were easy to recruit and easy to replace.[15] But being at a disadvantage can inhibit rather than promote strike activity. The question remains open.

Even in St. Petersburg, where worker unrest was substantial in mid-decade, Social Democratic leadership was weak.[16] It was all the weaker in Moscow. Workers' Union leaders deplored their isolation from the majority of workers. They saw the strike wave as a vindication of the new agitation approach: the need to abandon "abstract politics" and to concentrate instead on the concrete grievances that troubled the rank and file and had led them to mobilize on their own.[17] Despite this sensible resolve, the Workers' Union never got very far. By the spring of 1897, police had arrested the majority of intelligentsia leaders and many of the union's adherents. Workers became fearful of joining socialist-sponsored groups.[18] Activists still at large now worked in isolation from each other and remained largely independent of the Moscow Committee of the Russian Social Democratic Workers' Party (RSDWP), which came into being the next year.[19] Intelligentsia members of that committee were promptly arrested, in March 1898; others were arrested in 1900, along with a circle of worker sympathizers, including several typesetters, a patternmaker, and a skilled mechanic.[20]

Despite these setbacks, the early organizational activities of the Social Democrats ultimately did bear fruit. Numerous propaganda circles (kruzhki) had brought skilled and literate workers into contact with members of the radical intelligentsia. These so-called conscious (soznatel'nye) workers often resented the authority of their intelligentsia mentors, but they themselves exercised a similar authority over their less enlightened fellows. They bridged the social chasm that separated professional revolutionaries from the culturally inaccessible multitude. In the words of one such product of *kruzhok* education: "The mass of workers at that time [the 1890's] did not understand the intelligentsia's language. Thanks only to a cadre of translators, so to speak, from the ranks of semi-intelligentsia workers was [organizational] activity at all successful."[21]

Although the politicized minority lost contact with party militants in the late 1890's and early 1900's, many of its members reemerged to lead strikes, meetings, and committees in 1905.[22] The small but influential worker-intelligentsia nurtured by the Social Democratic movement contributed to the spread of worker militancy in a more indirect fashion. After the turn of the century, the government attempted to counteract socialist influence by forming official labor associations. This project depended for its success on the cooperation of educated workers. The police managed to recruit a good number from among those who had been schooled in Social Democratic circles.[23] In this way, the worker-intelligentsia helped extend a type of trade-union experience to a much broader section of the Moscow working class than the socialists could possibly have reached on their own.

These long-term consequences of intelligentsia activity were not immediately apparent, to be sure. In this period, radical organizations were weak and had little direct influence on popular behavior. Labor unrest all but disappeared in the last year of the nineteenth century. Meanwhile, however, political discontent had begun to surface in the Empire's universities and technical schools in response to a law of July 1899 threatening politically active students with expulsion from school and forced service in the army. In February 1901, students demonstrated in St. Petersburg, in Kharkov, and in Moscow. A number of the Prokhorov workers, then in their third strike, wandered downtown from the industrial Presnia district and joined the student protestors. Police attacked the demonstrators and arrested many of the participating students. Some 500 of them were expelled from Moscow University. Like the law itself, repression served only to radicalize, not to intimidate, its victims. The severity of the official response succeeded in broadening the focus of student discontent from issues of academic concern to matters of more serious political consequence.[24]

The conjunction of student and worker unrest had been accidental.[25] Nevertheless, the authorities decided that energetic measures had to be taken to safeguard the lower classes from political contagion.[26] In the same paternalistic spirit that lay behind nineteenth-century factory legislation, the Moscow Secret Police, with the blessings of their superiors in the Ministry of Internal Affairs, set up a network of officially sponsored labor organizations. These were designed to counteract the effects of revolutionary propaganda by providing a legitimate outlet for worker grievances and helping to remove the economic causes of worker discontent. The project's master mind was S. V. Zubatov, head of the Moscow Secret Police. He had explained the notion of preventive unionization in an 1898 memorandum prepared for D. F. Trepov, then Moscow chief of police:

If the petty needs and demands of the workers are being exploited by the revolutionaries for such basically antigovernment ends, should not the government act as quickly as possible to remove this useful tool from the hands of revolutionaries and appropriate it for its own purposes? . . . As long as the revolutionaries merely preach socialism, one may apply simple repressive measures, but when they begin to exploit the petty inadequacies of the existing legal order for their own ends, repression alone is not effective; one must remove the very ground from under their feet.[27]

The project attracted the support of liberal professors from Moscow University like A. A. Manuilov, I. Kh. Ozerov, and V. E. Den, who lent an air of respectability to the undertaking. They helped draft corporate charters and held lectures on general problems of worker organization.[28] Ozerov justified their cooperation with the police on the grounds that the unions provided legitimate grievance procedures and thereby served the workers' interests.[29]

As one might expect, Zubatov's strategy ran into stiff opposition from factory owners, who did not wish to see social harmony achieved at the expense of their own economic interests, and who did not want to relinquish full autonomy in dealing with their own employees. Industrialist opponents of the Zubatov venture argued that unions as such, regardless of their ideological coloration, would contribute to the worsening of social conflicts. Any organization that developed a sense of class identity among industrial workers would encourage them to unite in defense of their group interests. It was better to leave them with the illusion that they still belonged to the amorphous peasant masses and thus had no special position to defend as laborers in the urban economy.[30]

This argument sounds surprisingly like one Lenin advanced in 1902:

In the long run the legalization of the labor movement will benefit us [the Social Democrats] and not the Zubatovs. . . . Inasmuch as you are taking a real step forward—even if in the form of a "timid zigzag," but a step forward—we shall say: Much obliged, pray go on! Only a real, even if tiny, increase of scope for the workers is a real step forward. And any such increase will be useful to us and speed the emergence of the kind of legal societies in which provocateurs will not be catching socialists but socialists will be catching converts.[31]

In the short run, however, the police unions proved disastrous to radical fortunes.

The first officially approved meetings of metalworkers, held in the Historical Museum, were chaired by the academic experts. Soon the workers themselves began meeting in neighborhood taverns. Representatives of these district gatherings (raionnye sobraniia) then obtained police permission to form a council of workers in metal production, which soon enlarged its membership to include workers in other industries. Workers brought their specific grievances to the council, which passed them on to the Factory Inspectorate. Council delegates sometimes intervened directly in factory disputes and even cooperated in the organization of strikes.[32]

The metalworkers' union attracted about 250 workers from at least four factories. A similar effort in the textile industry succeeded in organizing 1,200 workers, including engravers at Prokhorov, Tsindel', and Giubner, earlier the object of Social Democratic attentions. Weavers also joined in significant numbers. Zubatov's agents managed, in addition, to organize printers, buttonmakers, carpenters, and workers in candy, perfume, and tobacco factories.[33]

It soon became clear that the council's attempts to promote the workers' economic interests had not lessened working-class discontent. Indeed, convinced that the government had taken their side, workers became more aggressive in their struggle with factory management. The popularity and militancy of the Zubatov unions caused industrialists to go to the authorities in protest against the activities of the worker deputies.[34] Their objections were supported by the Ministry of Finance, which resented police interference in factory affairs.[35]

The Ministry of Internal Affairs soon had cause to regret the success of its own undertaking. The largest strikes in this period stemmed directly from the influence of police-backed organizers. When the workers at the Mussi silk mill in Lefortovo struck in 1902, the Zubatov workers' council intervened to represent the strikers' interests. The police pressured plant management not only to recognize the council's authority, but to accede to the workers' demands. The Secret Police, moreover, gave the strikers financial assistance, which enabled them to hold out for two months.[36] This affair was decisive in causing Zubatov's downfall in Moscow. Industrialists succeeded in convincing the ministries in St. Petersburg of the danger inherent in the pro-worker attitude of the Moscow police. It was thanks only to the intervention of the Moscow Governor-General, Grand Duke Sergei Aleksandrovich, that the Zubatov system was not immediately abolished.

On April 2, 1902, a Socialist Revolutionary terrorist assassinated D. S.

Sipiagin, the Minister of Internal Affairs. Sipiagin was replaced by V. K. Plehve, who preferred repression to more indirect forms of social control. Zubatov was transferred out of Moscow to head the Secret Police administration in the capital, and the character of the Zubatov unions changed decisively. The Moscow Secret Police terminated the lectures in the Historical Museum and restricted the activities of the workers' council, which was no longer permitted to hear worker grievances. The teaching of conservative religious principles replaced instruction in labor history. When workers at the Bromlei metal plant struck in July 1903 to protest fines and other hardships, the police failed to support their action, threatening the strikers with dismissal and banishment from the city if they refused to return to work.[37]

In June 1903, as part of the retreat from police unionism, the government established a system of factory elders (*starosty*), designed to preserve the illusion of worker self-representation and to channel discontent through official hands, while destroying the workers' freedom of action. Under this system, management supervised the election of worker-representatives, who were to serve as intermediaries in cases of conflict or dissatisfaction in the factory. But the workers understandably had no confidence in the elders, since the employers controlled the elections and prevented the workers from meeting publicly to discuss their grievances. Because the factory owners also distrusted the plan, the *starosta* system was not successful.[38]

In short, after Zubatov's departure from Moscow, the government reverted to traditional strategies for controlling the workers' movement. It ensured that the fiction of worker self-representation remain just that—a fiction. All the same, government labor policy was not entirely consistent; vestiges of Zubatovism remained. In September 1903, the Moscow police tried to ban a meeting of printing workers and arrested several of their leaders. In response to the ban, over 6,000 printers, led by the typesetters, went on strike to obtain specific improvements in wages, hours, and conditions. Plant owners willingly negotiated with the strikers and ended by granting many of the demands. This happy conclusion was crowned by the formation of a printers' union, which was sponsored by the old Zubatov workers' council. Patently in conflict with official policy, the union was nevertheless approved by the Moscow police at the end of the year.[39]

Another printers' union also emerged from the strike, an illegal association formed by Social Democratic organizers, known as the Union of Moscow Printing and Lithography Workers for the Struggle to Improve Conditions of Labor (Soiuz moskovskikh tipo-litografskikh rabochikh dlia bor'by za uluchenie uslovii truda).[40] The existence of this alternative did not prevent the majority of printing workers from supporting the police-sponsored organization. The Zubatov union did not merely attract the unskilled "backward" elements. Among the printers, the most enthusiastic participants in the union meetings were those who had learned the value of labor organization from the experience of the 1903 strike. The average worker did not view the Secret Police with the same hostility as the intelligentsia. He recognized that the Zubatov program, in fact, promoted his most immediate interests. The vast majority, even of printing workers, were suspicious of "politics" in the abstract. They valued the officially sanctioned meetings for allowing them to discuss questions that concerned them directly, such as conditions in the factories and the principles of cooperative association. The Social Democratic printers' union, by contrast, involved but a handful of sophisticated workers and their intelligentsia advisers. Its members did little more than write and distribute leaflets explaining the principles of socialism. They could not match the resources and freedom of action enjoyed by the government-supported union.[41] It was only the switch toward a conservative, pro-management attitude, forced on the Moscow police by St. Petersburg authorities, that finally alienated mass support for the official unions.[42]

Having undermined the Social Democrats, the Zubatovites were themselves languishing by 1904. The revolution of 1905, however, was to reap the rewards of the government's novel approach to social control. By 1904, a significant portion of the Moscow working class had taken part in basic trade-union procedures, such as the election of representatives and the process of formulating collective demands. In a sense, then, even as the Zubatov movement was destroying the organizational base of the radical intelligentsia and interrupting their contacts with the masses, it was doing their educational work for them.

The political climate in society as a whole had to move sharply to the left before Lenin's hopes for the paradoxical outcome of Zubatov's experiment were realized. While the Social Democrats were losing out to police unionists on the economic front, the movement of political opposition to the regime was gaining strength in educated circles. In the wake of the 1901 student protests, two new political groups were consolidated: the Socialist Revolutionary Party and the movement for liberal reform.

Like the Social Democrats, the Socialist Revolutionaries aimed at the socialist transformation of society, but they rejected the Marxist belief that the urban working class must lead the revolution. In the Populist tradition the Socialist Revolutionaries called for peasants and workers to fight side by side; and in the spirit of class cooperation they welcomed the support of liberal progressives. The liberal movement, as it emerged in 1902–3, represented the fusion of two trends: the tradition of zemstvo reformism and a more radical tendency that included among its prominent spokesmen such former Marxists as Peter Struve.* Most liberals rejected the use of violence, and few desired changes more extensive than political reform. The liberal movement was nevertheless willing to ally itself with socialist groups openly espousing revolution.[43]

As Minister of Internal Affairs, Plehve tried to stop the spirit of discontent from spreading throughout the ranks of Russian society by intensifying police repression. But repression could not restore the regime to popularity. The outbreak of war with Japan in January 1904 at first aroused a wave of patriotism in educated circles, but criticism of the government reached a new pitch as defeat followed defeat in the Far East. In July 1904, like his predecessor, Plehve was assassinated by a Socialist Revolutionary terrorist. A month later, the Tsar appointed Prince P. D. Sviatopolk-Mirskii to replace him. Mirskii hoped to regain the goodwill of "society" by renouncing Plehve's repressive methods. Such abrupt shifts were typical of government policy in this period. As Count Witte remarked, "It is in the Emperor's nature to act like a pendulum, swinging between two extremes."[44]

Taking advantage of the new mood, a national congress of zemstvo representatives met in St. Petersburg in November 1904 and called for the institution of some form of popular representation. To everyone's surprise, the group suffered no legal reprisals. Their example inspired a wave of similar resolutions by local civic institutions and citizens' groups unaccustomed to commenting on public issues. The Moscow City Council, for example, issued a resolution on November 30, 1904, calling for "the protection of the individual from extralegal surveillance; the abolition of extraordinary legislation; the protection of freedom of conscience and of religion, of speech and of the press, of assembly and organization— these rights to be guaranteed by the establishment of permanent and fundamental statutes, enacted with the participation of freely elected representatives of the population. Society must have the legal power to control administrative activity, thereby guaranteeing official respect for these constitutional rights."[45]

During the last two months of 1904, the liberals sponsored a series of banquets in 26 cities for the discussion of political questions. Although a moderate position in favor of constitutional reform predominated at most of these gatherings, the demand for a constituent assembly based on universal suffrage gained wide acceptance in the nonsocialist opposition.[46]

---

*The zemstvos, institutions of local administration established by Alexander II in 1864, became the center of a reform movement in the 1880's and 1890's. Progressive zemstvo members hoped to achieve civil freedoms and greater participation in government without altering the basic structure of the autocratic regime.

Before the government had time to curtail the growing outspokenness of respectable society, it faced a renewed upsurge of popular unrest. Students in both Moscow and St. Petersburg launched demonstrations in late November and early December; those in Moscow ended in violent conflict with the police. Members of the professional intelligentsia supported the student protests, but few workers were involved.[47] Working-class discontent expressed itself independently. On December 13, workers in Baku launched a general strike that lasted for 22 days. The beginning of 1905 witnessed growing unrest among the metalworkers of St. Petersburg.

The St. Petersburg police had sponsored a workers' organization similar to the Zubatov unions. Under the leadership of the Orthodox priest Father Gapon, the association attracted a substantial following, especially after Plehve's assassination, when membership swelled to include as many as 8,000 workers.[48] The rising enthusiasm for worker meetings paralleled the increasing fervor of discussion in other classes of the population. Although some workers who considered themselves socialists were active in Gapon's organization, the Social Democrats officially stood aside from the Gapon movement. The new vitality in working-class circles caught them unawares. Like the Moscow strikes of 1902–3, which had been organized by Zubatov's unionists, the strike of Putilov metalworkers in St. Petersburg was led by Gapon's followers.[49]

On January 9, 1905, Father Gapon led a peaceful procession of workers toward the Winter Palace, where they hoped to present the Tsar with a list of grievances. But as they reached the Narva Triumphal Arch, troops blocked their way and fired into the crowd, leaving about 1,000 demonstrators and onlookers dead or wounded. The Tsar's violent response set off a massive series of strikes throughout the Empire and accomplished the transition from the period of prerevolutionary ferment to the revolutionary crisis itself. In St. Petersburg, the Putilov strike, which had already mushroomed to involve over 100,000 workers, was sustained for another week.[50] In Moscow, strike activity began immediately, on January 10, and lasted for at least eight days. When labor unrest had reached a peak in 1903, the Factory Inspectorate recorded a total of 13,000 strikers for the whole of Moscow Province, or less than 5 percent of the entire provincial labor force.[51] Now, in January 1905, the inspectorate reported a total of 45,000 striking workers in Moscow Province; the police counted 42,700 inside the Moscow city limits alone.[52]

In some cities, the strike movement included non-working-class groups and took on the character of a political protest. In Moscow, however, the workers acted alone. The movement began in the Zamoskvorech'e (VI), led by the area's giant plants—Sytin printing; Bromlei, Dobrov and Nabgol'ts, and Veikhel't metal—all factories with previous Social Democratic or Zubatov contacts. As a group, the metalworkers were the most active in the January strikes, followed in order by workers in the food industry, textile workers, and printers. Almost all the large textile mills in the Zamoskvorech'e were affected, but only Prokhorov in Presnia shut down, and the majority of the city's smaller textile factories kept working. Over half the metal strikers came from the industry's bigger firms. As a result, the movement remained strongest in the Zamoskvorech'e, an area dominated by large-scale enterprise. The strike spread from factory to neighboring factory, by force of example or in the wake of enthusiastic crowds. Most strike demands involved economic grievances. There was little sense of professional solidarity among the strikers.[53] Most returned to work after two or three days, in the same uncoordinated manner in which they had first left their benches. The sudden mobilization had taken the Moscow Social Democrats by surprise, and they did little once the movement had erupted to increase its effectiveness.

The same caretaker strategy (*popechitel'naia politika*) that lay behind the Zubatov and Gapon experiments continued to inspire official labor policy in the wake of the January outburst.[54] The strike movement had begun in St. Petersburg, and it was there that the government focused its pacification efforts. At the end of the month, the authorities in the capital announced the formation of a special committee composed of elected worker-delegates and factory owners, who were jointly to work out a program of economic improvements. The so-called Shidlovskii Commission (after Senator N. V. Shidlovskii), like the Zubatov council, was designed to provide a legitimate forum for the expression of workers' grievances. It was also a means of pressuring industrialists into making economic concessions that would pacify their employees. The commission had the support of the new Governor-General of St. Petersburg, D. F. Trepov, who in his former capacity as Moscow chief of police had defended Zubatov's ideas against criticism from the Ministry of Finance.[55]

The St. Petersburg working class was eager to participate in the proposed elections. Some factories began choosing representatives to send to the commission's electoral assembly even before the official election date of February 13. But many workers were dissatisfied with the announced electoral procedure, and they presented Senator Shidlovskii with a number of demands for changes in the rules and for political guarantees. They insisted on the reopening of the Gapon locals closed by the police after the January strikes and on obtaining permission to use them for free discussion. They wanted full protection for commission delegates, freedom of expression in its sessions, and the release of workers arrested since the first of January. Two liberationist lawyers helped the workers draft their demands.[56] The Social Democrats, for their part, profited from the electoral campaign, which provided them with an invaluable opportunity to expand their audience. Thanks to socialist propaganda, as many as a fifth of the representatives elected in the factories declared themselves Social Democrats. Almost half, however, were Gaponites.[57]

When these representatives met on February 16 and 17 to conduct the second stage of the election process—the selection of deputies to the commission itself—they reiterated the demands presented earlier by individual factories. They also insisted that all the delegates be permitted to meet together in common session, and that all the commission proceedings be published in full in the press. When Shidlovskii failed to satisfy all these demands, the representatives announced a general strike in St. Petersburg. The strike was supported by the Menshevik faction of the Social Democratic Party and aroused widespread enthusiasm in the factories. Three days later, on February 20, the authorities disbanded the commission.[58]

Despite its premature demise, the Shidlovskii Commission had a profound effect on the workers' movement in the capital, and by extension in other cities as well. Instead of undermining the movement at its center, the commission helped it strengthen its organizational base. The commission provided St. Petersburg workers with their first experience in free elections and their first access to a public forum. The idea of collective worker representation thus gained wide publicity, and many of the former delegates continued to exercise leadership within their factories.[59] True, the experience was confined to the capital, but workers in other cities looked to St. Petersburg for an example, and the Social Democrats applied the lessons they had learned in connection with the Shidlovskii elections when it came time to establish worker organizations in other places.

After the failure of the commission, the government made one more effort to improve factory labor conditions. It invited representatives of the industrial community, along with experts on the labor question, to form another commission, this time under the chairmanship of the Minister of Finance, V. N. Kokovtsov.[60] This attempt at solving the worker problem was no more successful than the first, though for different reasons. The government's effort to improve the workers' lot was motivated by politically conservative calculations. Factory owners resisted the pressure for economic reform and called instead for changes in the political domain. Discontent, they claimed, was a response to oppression, not to hardship. A representative of the Moscow Stock Exchange Committee suggested that the workers be guaranteed the freedom to organize and the right to engage in peaceful strikes: "The present commission has not been called into being by conditions inherent in industial life, but rather in response to the massive wave of strikes that has overwhelmed all of Russia in recent months. These strikes have been motivated not so much by discontent with economic conditions as by factors external to the industrial context."[61]

While the Kokovtsov Commission languished, some manufacturers began meeting on their own. The Moscow Stock Exchange Committee called a congress of factory owners for mid-March in Moscow. The participants agreed to limit the extent of acceptable concessions to labor demands. Later, in May, the industrial community called for implementation of the Bulygin rescript and the accompanying decree of February 18, 1905.[62]

The Bulygin rescript, issued two weeks after the assassination of the Moscow Governor-General, Grand Duke Sergei, and at a time when the Japanese were routing Russian troops at Mukden, promised to allow popular representatives to play a limited role in the legislative process. The concession was designed to salvage the government's position in the face of domestic unrest and military disaster.[63] The decree that came with it granted Russians the right of petition.

The publication of the February 18 decree had given rise to a fever of meetings and organizational activity, despite the continuing restrictions on public assembly and on freedom of speech and association. Zemstvo liberals organized a number of congresses, and associations proliferated among the professional intelligentsia.[64] The professions displayed a broad range of political attitudes, from moderate reformism to pronounced radicalism.[65] The revolutionary movement found numerous sympathizers among teachers, doctors, lawyers, clerks, and zemstvo administrative staff (the so-called zemstvo third element). Most supported the popular cause without concern for the niceties of partisan rivalry, but some groups and many individuals associated themselves with the Social Democratic or Socialist Revolutionary position. In March, a congress of politically concerned physicians assembled in Moscow and declared itself ready to fight "hand in hand with the laboring masses against the autocratic-bureaucratic-system." Teachers held a national congress in May, at which they declared their preference for the Socialist Revolutionary point of view.[66] In the same month, 14 professional organizations joined together under the leadership of P. N. Miliukov to form a loose confederation. This group, known as the Union of Unions, adopted the political position shared by left-leaning liberationists and the socialist parties: it called for a constituent assembly elected by universal, direct, and equal suffrage and by secret ballot (the so-called four-point formula).[67]

Other groups critical of the existing regime and of the Tsar's vague plans for reform were not ready to support this demand. Representatives of the zemstvos and the cities called for guaranteed civil rights and for the creation of a representative assembly with an active role in legislative affairs. They approved of universal suffrage but wanted no part of the rest of the Union of Unions' four-point formula, refusing to endorse the principles of the secret ballot, direct elections, and equal representation.[68]

In July, industrialists from a number of major cities met in Moscow to discuss the government's plans for an advisory national assembly (Duma) without law-making powers—the so-called Bulygin project, the details of which had just recently been made public. The conservatives present, including representatives of the Moscow Stock Exchange Committee, endorsed the official proposal, while the more progressive among them called for a Duma with legislative powers. But they too held back from adopting the four-point formula as the basis for popular representation.[69]

By early summer, the government's reformist intentions had lost whatever credence they might initially have enjoyed. A wave of pogroms hit numerous Russian cities, and the Ministry of Internal Affairs pursued an increasingly intolerant policy.[70] In May, Trepov became Assistant Minister of Internal Affairs in charge of the police.[71] His appointment dashed progressive society's remaining hopes of political liberalization. The authorities responded to signs of labor unrest with the wide use of courts-martial, the frequent invocation of the death penalty, and the use of troops to suppress civil disorders. They showed a similar intransigence toward members of educated society. In April, the government attempted to repress student agitation by closing dormitories and dining halls, and threatening a mass dismissal of students and faculty. In May, it prohibited parents and students from meeting in common. In June, teachers were enjoined from issuing political resolutions. The courts began prosecuting lawyers and engineers for belonging to professional associations affiliated with the Union of Unions.[72] In July, Trepov attempted—though without success—to prevent the fourth zemstvo congress from holding its sessions. In early August, police arrested members of the Union of Unions' central bureau, meeting in Miliukov's apartment. Even moderate liberals had begun to lose hope that the Tsar would be responsive to their petitions. The Union of Unions declared that government policy justified the use of all possible means in the fight against autocracy.[73]

In this period, while educated society was feeling the brunt of repression and agitating for political reform, the revolutionary parties were able to profit from the expanded opportunities for propaganda. After the January strikes, Moscow Social Democrats had successfully infiltrated a number of the Zubatov-sponsored workers' assemblies. In St. Petersburg, elections to the Shidlovskii Commission allowed the socialists to address large sections of the working class. During February and March, illegal literature proliferated, and activists were able to hold outdoor rallies that attracted a wide worker audience. Police could not check the increased tempo of left-wing activity. In his memoirs, the Moscow Bolshevik S. I. Mitskevich attributes their failure to two circumstances. The sudden rise in worker unrest broadened the scope of Social Democratic contacts and made it harder for police agents to penetrate the movement, as they had done so successfully in the 1890's. More important, interest in the popular cause was so widespread among the population at large that police repression no longer sufficed to contain the symptoms of discontent. In Mitskevich's words:

The [Moscow] resident had formerly been indifferent or even hostile to the revolution. Now, sympathy for the revolution began to infect the broad mass of the intelligentsia, white-collar employees, residents. It became easier to find apartments for assemblies, secret meetings, storage places, printing presses. Sympathy for the revolution even began to penetrate the milieu of concierges, doormen, and the police themselves. Their enthusiasm for espionage and denunciation diminished, and occasionally they even cooperated [in illegal activity].[74]

The impact of stepped-up socialist propaganda did not immediately show itself in a surge of working-class recruits to party organizations or in greater party control over the labor movement. Despite increased Social Democratic contacts in the factories, the number of workers with distinct political loyalties was extremely small.[75] Nor were intelligentsia leaders able to guide the course of worker unrest. In Moscow, for example, when the Social Democrats tried to launch a general strike in May, the workers were indifferent to their appeal.[76] As the party paper *Iskra* noted, "The masses were learning how to think under party tutelage, but they would not listen to the party's instructions on how to act."[77] In other parts of the Empire, the mass movement spread during the months of April, May, and June, largely independent of Social Democratic initiative.[78] Not the least disturbing event, from the government's point of view, was the June mutiny of sailors in the Black Sea Fleet.[79]

But the weakness of organized socialist leadership at this point does not mean that the active proselytizing of the summer months had had no effect on the revolutionary movement. In a manner that is hard, if not impossible, to document precisely, the workers surely absorbed the socialist message on some level of awareness. At the least, they had been exposed to a set of ideas that, however meaningless or threatening they seemed at the time, would later offer them a framework for interpreting the political developments of the fall. One can safely say that the Moscow working class increased its familiarity with socialist ideology during the summer months, without falling into the error of concluding either that the workers necessarily understood what they had heard (that they had suddenly become "conscious"), or that they therefore owed an organizational allegiance or a personal loyalty to intelligentsia leaders.

The month of August constituted a turning point in the development of the revolution. On August 6, the Tsar finally issued a decree confirming the exact nature of the national assembly first proposed on February 18 and further elaborated in June, along with the procedure for electing representatives. The Duma did not have the power to legislate, but could only advise the Tsar and his ministers. It was to be elected by means of indirect suffrage. The distribution of the franchise depended on a combination of status and property qualifications that excluded almost the entire urban intelligentsia as well as the urban lower classes. Most of the inhabitants of non-European Russia were also excluded, as were all women throughout the Empire.[80]

The provisions of this act proved disappointing to almost all partisans of constitutional reform.[81] The Moscow City Council greeted the law as a step in the right direction, an indication that the Tsar was willing to consider changes in the bureaucratic regime, but the majority of the councilmen found the act itself inadequate. They insisted on the need for legally guaranteed civil rights and liberties, and supported the goal of universal suffrage.[82] Progressives debated whether to boycott the elections or to participate in the hope of achieving further constitutional change.[83]

Along with the August 6 announcement, the Tsar rescinded the decree of February granting limited rights of political discussion.[84] This renewed restriction on freedom of speech and assembly prompted local authorities to crack down on public activity. Thus, the Moscow Governor-General P. P. Durnovo announced: "I *will no longer tolerate* any private gatherings whatsoever in the city of Moscow or any zemstvo congresses; nor will I allow any type of collective discussion of state affairs at private meetings or in zemstvo assemblies. The question of state reform must be considered at an end."* Thus unleashed, the Moscow police showed themselves no respecters of social class in their display of antilibertarian zeal. On August 20, they interrupted a meeting of city councilmen, professors, and representatives of the nobility taking place in a private apartment, and dispersed a meeting of the organizational bureau of the congress of city and zemstvo representatives.[85]

The authorities soon modified this policy of crude police harassment

---

*Quoted in *Pravo*, no. 32 (Aug. 14, 1905): 2616. Gen. P. P. Durnovo was the second Governor-General of Moscow to have been appointed since the assassination of Grand Duke Sergei in February. The post had been filled first by Gen. A. A. Kozlov; he held it from April 14 to July 15, when he was replaced by Durnovo. Adm. F. V. Dubasov in turn replaced Durnovo on Nov. 24, 1905.

when the Treaty of Portsmouth on August 23 (N.S.) ended the war with Japan but failed to alleviate the general mood of resentment and dissatisfaction.[86] Once again, repression was mitigated by a calculated thaw, this time in the form of a decree granting administrative autonomy to the universities. The measure was designed to pacify the politically restless professoriate, as well as the volatile student body.[87] The students had been on strike since February. The university was in a strategic position to unite the disparate opposition forces. It naturally brought together liberals from the educated professional classes and radicals from the nonacademic intelligentsia (in many cases ex-students themselves). The university could even attract members of the urban lower classes as well, as it had in 1901 when workers joined students in street demonstrations.

The declaration of university autonomy did not calm the agitated student body. On the contrary, it proved to be "the first breach in the Government's fortifications."[88] Adopting a Menshevik suggestion, the students decided to end the academic strike by turning the university into a forum for political education and revolutionary agitation. Thousands of students from all over the city gathered daily in the university lecture halls during the first weeks of September to attend marathon meetings that often lasted for hours.[89] It was the first time the Social Democrats had enjoyed such broad public exposure. The few voices of dissenting conservative opinion were drowned out in the general enthusiasm.[90]

On September 11, the majority of students present supported a resolution pledging to fight hand in hand with the laboring masses for the overthrow of the tsarist regime and the establishment of a democratic republic. The students followed the Social Democratic line in condemning all compromise with the government; in particular they refused to accept the conditions of university autonomy or to participate in elections to the State Duma. Revolution, the students declared, was the only form of political struggle they found acceptable.[91] On the following day, the students voted to establish formal leadership organizations. They formed two committees. One was to operate publicly to represent the student body in dealings with the university administration. The other was conceived as an illegal organ of political propaganda.[92]

When classes resumed on September 15, some 3,000 students showed up at the university, but fewer than half sat in the classrooms. The rest marched through the halls, interrupting lectures and singing revolutionary songs. Although classes continued to be held in the days that followed, attendance was minimal. Meetings still attracted large audiences.[93] The political tenor of the discussions and the presence of outsiders disturbed the university authorities. But though they believed the university as an institution should remain outside politics, the administrators were reluctant to resort to repressive measures. Their restraint reflected the liberal principles of the newly elected rector, Prince S. N. Trubetskoi, and his assistant, A. A. Manuilov.[94]

Despite the revolutionary rhetoric that dominated student discussion in early September, the lot of the working class remained a largely theoretical concern, since few workers participated in the meetings held inside the university. Before student agitation had entirely died out, however, new signs of labor unrest appeared in Moscow. Students—through no effort of their own—soon found themselves in the company of proletarian comrades. On the evening of September 21, a crowd of over 3,000 persons forced its way into the Law Auditorium. Almost a third of those present were striking workers. It was the first occasion on which more than an insignificant proportion of the audience consisted of nonstudents,[95] and their participation produced a state of euphoria among the student radicals. The meeting lasted from eight o'clock in the evening until midnight, and a holiday atmosphere reigned. As one professor noted: "Yesterday's meeting was attended by experienced leaders, whose speeches aroused the wild enthusiasm of their young listeners, even of the 'academics' [i.e., moderates] in their midst. Many said they considered the time spent at that meeting to be the happiest moment of their lives."[96]

The mixture of striking workers, radical organizers, and rebellious students, reminiscent of the situation in 1901, worried the police. While the meeting was in progress, the chief of police told the rector that a large number of troops had been stationed in the Manège across from the university, ready to use armed force against student demonstrations. Fearing that some radical groups might want to provoke just such a confrontation, the rector ordered the closing of the university.[97] For the time being, student unrest faded into the background, as the working class began to mobilize in larger numbers than at any time since the beginning of the year.

5

THE SEPTEMBER STRIKE MOVEMENT

After the January and February strikes, labor unrest in Moscow diminished sharply.[1] It was not until the fall that workers once again left their benches in large numbers. The September strike movement began in the printing industry as a dispute over hours and wages. Workers in other trades soon followed the printers' example. In little more than a month's time, the initial conflict had mushroomed into a massive labor walkout that crippled the nation's economy and forced the Tsar into political compromise.

Five groups formed the backbone of the September strike movement: printers, bakers, carpenters, tobacco workers, and metalworkers. The strike was not planned by intelligentsia radicals, and it was not inspired by political motives. The strikers wanted better pay, better conditions, and better treatment. But the factories that initiated the September strikes had two things in common: all had previous contact with socialist organizers (some also with Zubatov unionists), and all had struck earlier in the year or before 1905. Once the key plants had gone on strike, other workers in the same industries followed suit. Printers, bakers, carpenters, and tobacco workers all showed a high degree of group solidarity. Printers and carpenters even formed special councils to coordinate their strike efforts. But no overarching leadership organization developed until the strike had already subsided.

In September, striking workers crowded the downtown streets and mingled with students and middle-class residents. Anxious to restore order and to prevent a politically volatile situation from developing, the authorities attempted to clear the streets by force. Their crude, indiscriminate methods created a sense of solidarity among disparate social groups and taught them that no public action could remain unpolitical in a regime so terrified of conflict.

The printers were not new to collective action. July 1903 had witnessed a series of printers' strikes in Kiev and the southern cities of Baku, Tiflis, and Batum; and inspired by this example, Moscow typesetters had begun agitating for higher wages and shorter hours. The printers were convinced that the law of 1897 had instituted a ten-hour day. They refused to believe they were mistaken (the law set an eleven-and-a-half-hour maximum) and decided to strike for their "legal rights." In planning their 1903 strike, the printers acted on their own initiative. The leaders had wanted to meet at a central location in the Tver district: on Nikitskaia Street, across from the music conservatory and not far from the university. The police denied them permission. So the printers congregated instead in a working-class tavern, in the southern, industrial fringe of elegant Prechistenskaia (area II). The tavern was near the river and a block away from the giant Butikov textile mill, yet still within range of the majority of print shops in the downtown area. When Police Chief D. F. Trepov realized what was afoot, he declared the place off limits, and the printers retreated to the suburbs. Thus did the police try to banish labor unrest by forcing the instigators into ever greater isolation from their fellows and from the rest of the city. The tactic did not succeed, but it showed a true understanding of the dynamics of popular mobilization.[2]

The tactic did not succeed because dissatisfaction had already come to a head in the key large plants. On September 9, 1903, workers struck at Levenson, Sytin, Iakovlev, Mamontov, the Russian Printing and Publishing Corporation, Kushnerev, and Mashistov; and from there the movement spread.[3] The printers presented a list of 23 demands to the Society of Printing Entrepreneurs, an owners' association. These concerned improvements in work conditions, such as better health care and plant hygiene; the regulation of apprenticeship; the abolition of punitive fines; the use of polite address by foremen and management; the institution of a nine-hour day and limits on overtime; wage and piece-rate increases; and the application of the starosta system. The owners finally granted many of these points. Among other things, they agreed to a ten-hour day and a 38 percent pay raise for typesetters. The printers had no formal organization, but their discipline and solidarity impressed an official of the Factory Inspectorate, who commented on the seriousness and orderliness of their behavior. For this reason, he noted, the strikers were all the more surprised to find themselves arrested and in prison when the strike was over.[4]

The authorities responded to the strike in two ways, the familiar carrot and stick of tsarist labor policy: they arrested the ringleaders, and they authorized Zubatov to set up the last of his unions. It was at this moment, as noted earlier, that the Social Democrats first got their foot in the door. The way this happened deserves attention, because it illustrates a pattern that reappears throughout 1905: the importance of nonparty white-collar and intelligentsia contacts in promoting working-class organization. The hero in this case was a certain Sofia Germanovich Khrenkova, who worked as a proofreader. She was a Social Democratic sympathizer, but not a party member; later she joined the Socialist Revolutionaries. She helped the families of arrested workers by collecting money from her intelligentsia friends. It was under her influence that some of the strike leaders still at large formed the Union of Moscow Printing and Lithography Workers for the Struggle to Improve Conditions of Labor as an alternative to the officially sponsored typographers' association. The illegal union adopted the Social Democratic program but did not join the party. It also adopted its own slogan: "The right to fight is a human right." This simple, nonideological formula accurately reflected the average worker's indifference, if not hostility, to "politics." The union confined its activities to issuing a newsletter filled with articles on general political themes written by intelligentsia activists. It soon lost contact with the factories and left the field open to Zubatov. By the end of 1904, the union's original working-class roots had dried up; it had become, in the words of the Menshevik labor organizer V. V. Sher, "a typical Social Democratic committee," that is, an intelligentsia core cut off from the rank and file.[5]

The strike movement of 1905 revived the union. In January, about 3,000 Moscow printers struck after hearing of the massacre in St. Petersburg. This was a spur-of-the-moment reaction, but it reawakened interest in organization. By midsummer, the printers' union had acquired 300 members, and most big plants had formed factory committees. These sent representatives to three district assemblies: Gorodskoi in the center, Butyrskii at the northern end of Sushchevskaia, and the Zamoskvorech'e in the south. These assemblies in turn sent delegates to a central committee. Thus reestablished on an elective basis, the union began concentrating on bread-and-butter issues. In August, it joined the Social Democratic Party, choosing to associate with the Menshevik faction. It was a sign of how far the workers had come, notes Sher, not without a touch of irony, that joining the party did not cause them to desert the union.[6] Indeed, as late as July 1905, printers were still attending mass meetings led by Zubatovite organizers.[7] It is clear that their interest in the "political" aspect of the printers' union was minimal. Well into the September strike, workers continued to voice suspicions about the union's ultimate goals. In St. Petersburg, where the Social Democrats also established a printers' union after January 9, the group declared itself to be a legal organization.[8] The Moscow union, however, remained "underground" until after the September strike.[9] Only then did it shed its conspiratorial posture for open trade-unionist activity.

Despite the organizational progress made during the summer, the union did not initiate the September movement. The printers' strike actually began in August, for reasons undoubtedly connected with seasonal fluctuations in hiring. It was customary for printing factories to lay off workers in the summer. But unemployment was particularly high for compositors in the spring and summer of 1905 because the political crisis had caused book publishers to curtail production.[10] Perhaps in anticipation of the fall rehiring, workers at Kushnerev (900 workers, in Sushchevskaia, area IV) petitioned for shorter hours. At this point, the union stepped in and urged the printers not to appeal to management on an individual factory basis, but to prepare instead for an industrywide action in support of a common set of demands. Before launching the strike, the union hoped to allow time for workers to discuss the proposed demands at the shop level. Workers at Sytin (1,110 workers, in the Zamoskvorech'e, area VI) disrupted these plans by presenting management with their own demands on August 11.[11] These included a nine-hour day, half-pay during illness, and a series of graduated pay raises designed to introduce greater economic equality in the factory.[12] On September 13, the firm's directors agreed to the first two demands, but not the last. Shorter hours at the same rate of pay meant a loss of earnings for pieceworkers. Monday, September 19, was payday. After receiving their wages, the typesetters and bookbinders, both of whom worked by the job, declared themselves on strike. The rest of the Sytin workers joined them.[13]

The next day, September 20, the union called for a general strike in support of the Sytin men.[14] By September 21, a quarter of the city's printing workers were out; and by September 24, almost half.[15] Workers in the larger factories took the lead. As a result, the strike began in the outlying districts and only then spread to the central, downtown areas where most small printing enterprises were concentrated.* It remained most intense in areas III, IV, and VI. The walkout closed over two-thirds of the city's

* Between September 21 and September 24 the number of striking printers in area I doubled and the number in area II tripled. In areas III, IV, and VI, however, the strike had reached its maximum extent by September 21. In these three areas, the first plants to close were Mashistov in Presnia (325 workers), Kushnerev in the Sushchevskaia district (600 out of 900 workers), and Sytin in the Piatnitskaia district (1,110 workers). Area V had one fairly large plant (Khudiakov, with 300 workers, in the Rogozhskaia district), but it did not join the strike until September 22. In areas where the industry was dominated by smaller shops, the same pattern prevailed, with the largest plants taking the lead. The Russian Printing and Publishing Corporation in Iauzskaia, with 430 workers, was the first to strike in area II. It was joined the next day by the Levenson plant in Arbat, with 500. The first plant to strike in the Tver district was the largest in that area (the Iakovlev factory, with 470 workers).

larger firms (those with 100 or more workers), including all three private firms with 500 or more workers. Altogether, more than half the work force employed in larger plants joined the strike, compared with only a third of the workers in smaller shops. Throughout the year, larger plants repeated this pattern of speedy mobilization and greater intensity of strike participation (high strike propensity) in most industries.[16]

Few plants striking after September 19 announced economic grievances specific to their own factories. Most struck without any demands at all, from a sense of solidarity or for fear of reprisals from strikers.[17] Once the strike had caught on, the printers' union attempted to create a unified leadership structure. The union issued a set of general demands applicable to all factories involved in the strike. The most important of these demands, both in practical and in symbolic terms, called for management recognition of worker-deputies. This amounted to an acknowledgment of the right to trade-union representation and collective bargaining.

In each factory [read the union's statement] all sections must have permanently elected workers' deputies. The deputies will handle all business concerning their factories and represent them in dealings with the owners. Each worker will communicate with the owner through the deputies. The owner does not have the right to negotiate with individual workers over the heads of the deputies.[18]

The union demanded that deputies have the power to sanction hiring and firing, to review cases of violations of factory rules, to suggest the dismissal of individual members of the factory administration, to supervise sanitary conditions in the shops, and to set pensions for widows and disability pay. Without waiting for management's response to their demands, many workers proceeded to elect representatives. These deputies, even when they had no power to negotiate with the owners, exercised great authority among the workers themselves. They formed factory strike committees and cooperated with intelligentsia organizers in formulating demands and coordinating strike activity. Worker-deputies also played a central role in organizing trade unions later in the year.

Other union demands included the institution of an eight-hour day; the abolition of the system of subcontracting, which increased the power of foremen; equal pay for women; paid maternity leave; annual paid vacations; and sick pay. In addition, the printers demanded that they be addressed in the polite form, and that they no longer be subjected to body searches on leaving the factory. Strikers commonly adopted these human-dignity demands throughout 1905. The printers also wanted the right to live and eat outside the shop or factory. This, as we have noted, was part of a move away from the traditional worker-employer relations characteristic of artisanal production. The printers demanded cash payments instead of room and board (a form of wages in kind) as a way of increasing their independence and of raising the actual value of their income.

One of the most important economic demands concerned the piecework system. Piecework was a critical issue for the skilled craftsmen, among whom it was a common mode of payment. Workers paid by the job tended to work longer hours than others, restrictions on overtime did not apply to them, and they were more vulnerable to the whims of shop foremen than were workers with guaranteed monthly wages. They were also the first to feel the effects of unexpected supply shortages or production cutbacks.[19] The printers' union wanted to have bookbinders, engravers, draftsmen, and newspaper compositors taken off piecework and put on the monthly payroll.[20] The last of these groups, the newspaper compositors, of whom there were about 200 in the city, had the most success in redefining and improving its status in 1905. As we saw in Chapter 2, in the preceding years newspaper typesetting had undergone a technological revolution in Moscow. In 1905, work conditions were revised to fit modern standards: these typesetters changed from piecework to monthly wages, at higher rates, and on the basis of an eight-hour workday. In the less-mechanized book industry, typesetters and bookbinders continued to work under the old artisanal conditions.[21]

In an effort to increase the union's contacts among the mass of striking printers, the union's Menshevik leaders formed a new organization, the Council (Soviet) of Deputies from Printing and Lithography Plants,* composed of worker-delegates elected in the shops. The Moscow City Board, the city's nonelected governing body, allowed the delegates to as-

*The Russian word soviet is usually used to refer to this printers' organization. I have chosen to use the English translation instead, to avoid the inaccurate implication that this early group had more in common with the later soviets than it had. This semantic problem has historical and political significance. The term soviet in itself means simply council. Professional strike committees formed in the course of 1905 were referred to as soviets: for example, the Ivanovo-Voznesensk textile workers' soviet of May, the ribbonmakers' soviet of August, and the printers' soviet of September. Only later in the year were citywide soviets formed, first in St. Petersburg and then in Moscow. These organizations were intended to unify and amplify the functions of the earlier committees; in the process, a new type of institution emerged, significantly different in structure and political consequences from the antecedent models. Some historians prefer to retain the designation "soviet" so as to underline the genealogy of the later institution. But the word itself acquired its special significance only after the final stage of that development; to project backward is to endow Social Democratic organizers with more foresight than they actually possessed. The word soviet becomes important in the later period of the revolution as a challenge to other forms of organization. The liberal-dominated Moscow Strike Committee created in October played much the same role as the earlier professional "soviets." When the Social Democrats, in their struggle to counteract the committee's influence, established an independent organ of strike leadership, they called it simply the Soviet. This name had the virtue of association with prior Social Democratic committees. It had the additional polemical advantage of representing in linguistic terms the break with liberal principles. The word soviet has retained this political connotation down to the present.

semble in a school building not far from the university, in the Tver district, where they met for the first time on September 25. The council held nine additional sessions before October 4. Its membership grew from an initial 87 deputies representing 34 printing plants, to 264 deputies from 110 plants. Among the first firms to send delegates were the three biggest plants and at least half the shops with 100 or more workers. Seven newspapers and two railroad print shops also sent delegates.[22] The council thus represented a much broader constituency than the union alone. The council delegates elected 15 of their own number to form an executive committee. Its primary job was to conduct negotiations with the united factory owners and to make certain that the final settlement in each firm satisfied the basic demands adopted by the council. The executive committee was also responsible for announcing future meetings of the plenum, making arrangements with the city administration for suitable meeting places, establishing the agendas, and handling the collection of strike funds.[23]

The union's Social Democratic organizers hoped the council would extend and deepen their control over the strike movement. It did so in a practical but not an ideological sense. The council's meetings attracted a wide variety of workers, few of whom were interested in political theory. Some had been members of the police-sponsored union; they retained a respect for legality and a distrust of subversive organizations. Political ideas unconnected with immediate strike issues met with suspicion even among the council delegates, and workers frequently interrupted socialist speakers who addressed their meetings. Disrespectful mention of the Tsar provoked indignation at some of the early sessions.

The willingness to join the trade union, the demonstration of professional solidarity in September 1903 and again in September 1905, the readiness to elect factory and committee delegates, all show that the printers as a group had a fairly advanced sense of collective identity, compared with other sections of the Moscow working class. There were some, certainly, who belonged to the select class of educated workers with close contacts among the intelligentsia. But the average printer did not embrace the socialist ideology with which the intelligentsia justified its organizational efforts. The fact that the workers were eager to participate in running their own affairs testifies to a certain independence of spirit among the rank and file, but it says nothing about their appreciation of the larger political context within which their own actions played a part.

The idea of workers' deputies, for example, won immediate popularity.[24] And the council itself found ready acceptance because it represented a transformation of earlier experiences; it was not an entirely new invention. The Zubatov unions, the starosta system, and the January strike movement had all involved the election of factory delegates. The workers now wanted to control the choice of their own representatives and to keep them independent of management or government influence.[25] This concern reflected a desire to change power relations in the workplace; in that sense, it held the germ of political awareness. But the workers' demand for greater autonomy did not, at this stage of the movement, entail an interest in more explicitly political issues.

This may explain why the city authorities did not at first view the council with alarm. The first session was small and innocuous. It was so small in fact that the council's leaders feared they might not have the support of the majority of strikers. They therefore called a general open meeting for September 26. The announcement had already reached the plants when the police chief decided to ban the assembly. That evening, the workers appeared at the meeting hall to find it surrounded by Cossacks. The delegates from the printers' council wished to avoid conflict and urged the crowd of almost 3,000 to go home quietly. While backing down from immediate confrontation, council and union leaders took the September 26 incident as proof that the fight for economic gains must inevitably lead to conflict of a political nature. Consequently, the union urged the workers to begin agitating for a general strike in support of their civic rights. More important, they must continue to meet and discuss—if not publicly, then in their plants, where discussion was still officially permitted. The union's organizers wished to avoid violence, but they hoped to perpetuate the spirit of solidarity generated by mass meetings even after the public forum had been closed to them.[26]

While the printers were busy organizing, the strike spread to other trades. Between September 25 and September 28, a good number of bakers and carpenters stopped work. Several big tobacco-processing plants, a large candy factory, and a group of metal factories, including the machine shops of the Moscow-Brest railroad, also struck. Mechanics in the city tram park and some workers in the city slaughterhouse and waterworks joined the strike as well. As a rule, workers in those factories or trades in which socialist or police organizers had been active before 1905 were more likely to strike than workers with no previous organizational experience.

Like the printers, the bakers had been the object of Social Democratic agitation for some years. As early as 1902, party organizers had been active in the city's largest bakery, the main Filippov plant on Tver Street (area I). At the same time, the Socialist Revolutionaries had set up study circles in some of the smaller bake shops.[27] Like the printers' strike, the bakers' strike stemmed from dissatisfaction with wages and with the behavior of factory management. In both trades, a single large plant played a crucial role in focusing and sustaining the movement.

The bakers' walkout in September was the continuation of an earlier conflict. In March 1905, the bakers had planned a strike to coincide with the busy pre-Easter season. They did not act entirely on their own in this; they were assisted both by Social Democratic organizers and by certain progressively inclined labor experts interested in building a stable trade-union movement in Russia. Nonsocialist professionals of this sort, in fact, played an important role during 1905 in laying the foundations for permanent labor organizations. Not only did they control considerable institutional resources, but their moderate credentials stood them in good stead both from the government's point of view and from the workers' standpoint, wary as they were of the overtly "political" appeal of socialist radicals. In St. Petersburg, for example, two liberal lawyers helped draft the demands the workers had presented to the Shidlovskii Commission in February. One of them, G. S. Nosar', won a position of lasting popularity among the capital's working class and eventually became president of the city soviet. In 1901, the Moscow branch of the Imperial Russian Technical Society founded an organization called the Museum for Assistance to Labor, with headquarters in a building on Rozhdestvenskaia Street (between the Tverskaia and Miasnitskaia districts of area I). Initially, museum members such as I. Kh. Ozerov participated in the Zubatov experiment, but they withdrew their support when the government no longer allowed the police-sponsored unions to act in the workers' own interests. The museum then concentrated on such educational services as the organization of popular lectures, the creation of workers' libraries, and the collection of labor statistics.[28] The museum once again became involved in labor organizing after March 1905, with the election of a new board of directors of predominantly left-liberal tendency.[29] It was this revived institution that came to the aid of the bakers.

Under the museum's auspices, the bakers held a number of mass meetings and drafted a list of common grievances. Up to 4,000 bakers attended these gatherings and endorsed a program of economic and work-related demands. These included pay raises, semimonthly paydays (irregular payment was common in small artisan shops), eight-hour shifts, the regulation of overtime and of holiday breaks, respectful personal treatment, and freedom to live off the premises. When the Moscow Artisan Board rejected these demands, the majority of bakers went on strike.[30]

The Filippov bakery on Tver Street provided a central meeting place. Its 385 employees included some of the trade's most politically experienced workers. This was the movement's center of gravity. On the management side, Filippov also "set the tone." In 1897, it will be recalled, the owners of the smaller metal factories waited for List or Dobrov and Nabgol'ts to adopt the ten-hour day before doing likewise. "When Dobrov cuts back, then so shall I," said the petty entrepreneur. In April 1905, D. I. Filippov was the first to break ranks with his colleagues and agree to various concessions. The others followed suit, to prevent Filippov from monopolizing the lucrative Easter business.[31]

The strike netted the workers substantial gains. It also generated a rudimentary labor organization. The workers' list of demands bore the signature of the Moscow Bakers' Union and the imprint of the Moscow Committee (Bolshevik) of the Russian Social Democratic Workers' Party. The union that emerged in April was in fact little more than a strike committee,[32] but it provided a framework for future organization and leadership. The union acted as a counterpart to the Artisan Board, which represented the owners' collective interests. Its very existence, as well as some of the specific demands in the workers' program, indicates that the bakers were on their way to breaking with the artisanal context. At the same time, the traditional structure of the trade helped them define their new identity, if only in a negative fashion, as the mirror image of the employers' united front.

It is perhaps not surprising that the largest, most modernized firm in the business should supply the impetus for such a movement. It is also perhaps for this reason that the Social Democrats were able to win a loyal following among the decidedly nonproletarian bakers. The evidence does not permit us to judge whether the Social Democratic union was of purely practical importance to the bakers (a means of achieving immediate, concrete goals), or whether it also satisfied symbolic needs (serving as a sign that the baker was acquiring a new social identity), or whether the union actually evoked a conscious, ideological response. Certainly, the evolution of working-class activism was never an even process. Traditional thinking not uncommonly went along with innovative behavior. The workers in the Ivanov candy factory, for example, struck in July 1905 to achieve a number of improvements, among which they listed the right to time off on a series of saints' days and other religious holidays. The Soviet labor historian who chronicles this event sees it as a sign of the workers' "low level of class consciousness."[33] In general, the strikes in early 1905 were marked by an absence of explicitly political rhetoric. Beginning in the fall, however, they began to show patterns of group cohesion, which might be considered a form of implicit or embryonic collective self-definition, independent of political ideology. The bakers, like the printers, displayed a remarkable degree of craft solidarity, which was not a product of

Social Democratic indoctrination, but rather the ground on which the Social Democrats were able to build subsequent organizations.

Just as the printers' strike of September 1905 repeated the pattern of September 1903, so the bakers' strike in September echoed the one in April and picked up the same themes. When bakery production returned to normal after the seasonal summer lull, the bakers saw their recent gains eliminated. The wages posted in most bakeries on September 10 were significantly lower than the ones agreed on in April. Workers who objected to the new conditions found themselves jobless, their places taken by others willing to settle for less.[34] When Filippov lowered wages in the Tver Street bakery, workers there announced a strike for September 25. On September 24, the police chief summoned the owners of the largest bakeries and persuaded them to honor the April agreement in order to avoid trouble. Nevertheless, the Filippov workers were out on the street at ten o'clock the next morning. At least 40 other bakeries also went on strike.[35] The bakers returned to work three days later, apparently satisfied with their symbolic gesture.[36] The owners had of course resolved the original economic issue by reinstating the April settlement, and therefore the strikers had already "won" before the walkout began.

Tobacco workers also went on strike over economic grievances, but they had more difficulty obtaining results. Only two of Moscow's five tobacco factories shut down in September: Dukat in Presnia (III), with 900 workers, and neighboring Gabai in the Sushchevskaia district (IV), with 600 workers. Zubatov labor organizers had been active in both factories since 1901. By 1904, Social Democratic and Socialist Revolutionary organizers were competing with the Zubatovites in the formation of study groups.[37] Gabai workers had struck in 1897, and both plants had closed down in January 1905.[38] The Gabai factory went on strike on September 22; Dukat followed two days later. The workers demanded institution of an eight-hour day (an SD-signature issue); the abolition of overtime and night shifts; the regulation of child labor; sick pay; and several other specific improvements.[39] During the strike, Social Democratic and Socialist Revolutionary organizers worked hand in hand, and the two plants were in close contact.

On September 26, police arrested two Gabai workers who belonged to the strike leadership and were associated with the Social Democrats. The Gabai strikers demanded their release as a condition for settling the conflict. Three days later, a delegation of workers accompanied the factory owner on a visit to the police chief, who personally ordered the men set free. The strikers considered this a great victory, and it strengthened their sense of solidarity. Sustained by financial contributions from workers in other tobacco firms, the Gabai strike continued for three weeks, until management finally agreed to new conditions.[40] At Dukat, the strike lasted 42 days. The administration refused to negotiate with the workers. The strikers were able to hold out because management at Gabai and at the still-larger firm of Bostandzhoglo (in Basmannaia, area V) hired a number of Dukat hands on a temporary basis and contributed to a strike fund. After being forced to make concessions themselves, Gabai officials clearly hoped to weaken the competition and make sure that Dukat did not profit from cheaper labor. In the end, Dukat agreed to a ten-hour day (down from eleven and a half) and various pay raises. None of the striking workers lost their jobs or received a dock in pay for the time lost.[41] Throughout, the tobacco workers showed remarkable discipline and responded readily to instructions from their leaders, who themselves followed guidelines set by radical labor organizers.

In contrast to the tobacco industry, the woodworking trade was organized in small or medium-sized establishments.[42] Because the work force was so dispersed, strike activity was coordinated by an assembly of workers from different enterprises. A large open-air meeting of 350 carpenters took place just outside the city on September 25. The participants drew up a list of demands, which included an eight-hour day, wage increases, the abolition of piecework, overtime, and fines, and the establishment of a worker emergency fund. The workers also demanded full pay for strike periods and the creation of a permanent commission of workers' representatives with power to prevent arbitrary firing practices.[43]

When police interfered with a second mass meeting on September 26, a group of workers under Bolshevik direction responded by forming a council (soviet) of deputies from the carpentry trade.[44] The self-appointed deputies urged their fellows to launch an industrywide strike in support of their demands. The council emphasized the importance of sticking together until the workers in all enterprises had obtained similar concessions. Like the printers' and bakers' strikes, the September woodworkers' strike began in the industry's largest firm, the Shmidt furniture factory in Presnia (III). The Shmidt factory had already been struck in January. Its 260 workers were the best paid in the trade. The purpose of the September strike was to bring other shops up to that level and then force them all to improve conditions. Shmidt workers spread the message by making the rounds of nearby shops and persuading other carpenters to join them. The strike reached its peak on September 28,[45] when it involved over 1,000 workers from 22 enterprises, plus some 400 cabinetmakers from small shops in the outlying Mar'inaia Roshcha area, just north of the Sushchevskaia district (IV).[46]

Moscow metalworkers struck in two waves during September: the first represents the typical craft, or artisanal, pattern of labor protest; the second is characteristic of industrial, or factory-worker, strikes during 1905. Early in the month, approximately 1,500 precious-metal craftsmen went on strike, following a meeting at which a small group of leaders established a strike committee and drafted a set of demands. This same group had met in July and August and decided to form a trade union. No union yet existed in September, but the handful of active workers had made themselves known in the trade and were able to coordinate a craftwide movement similar to the carpenters', bakers', and printers' strikes.[47]

During the last week of September, in the wake of the printers' strike, an additional 8,500 or 9,000 metalworkers left their jobs. The majority came from the large machine-building enterprises. No central committee existed, and demands varied from plant to plant. Workers in the largest factories struck first and then made the rounds of smaller firms in the neighborhood. The strike remained local and was largely restricted to a handful of big plants. Of the total number of metal strikers in late September, 75 percent worked in the Zamoskvorech'e and 60 percent were employed in factories with 500 or more workers, most of which had a history of labor unrest and of socialist contacts.

In the Zamoskvorech'e there were five key striking metal factories: List (440 workers), on the embankment across from the Kremlin; Dobrov and Nabgol'ts (1,020), to the east, in upper Piatnitskaia; and Bromlei (1,500), Zhako (1,400), and Gopper (600), all located farther south, in the Serpukhovskaia district. Of these, all but Zhako had been the focus of Social Democratic agitation during the 1890's, and all but Zhako and Gopper had participated in the January strike movement.[48] The first plant to stop work was List on September 25; the other four followed suit the next day, ahead of the rest of the industry. At the Dobrov and Nabgol'ts factory, workers met on September 25 to discuss their grievances, then left the premises on their own initiative. The Mensheviks distributed a leaflet condemning the dismissal of several workers and urging the others to protest on their behalf. The leaflet also exhorted the workers to continue meeting at the plant, despite a ban against assembly on the premises. The next day, September 26, the workers declared themselves on strike, following the appearance of a crowd from the List factory.[49] Workers in each of these large plants formulated a set of demands that they presented to the owners. Workers in all five plants wanted better pay and improved conditions; most insisted on the right to assemble peacefully, to strike, and to elect their own deputies. Workers at List, Zhako, and Dobrov and Nabgol'ts began choosing such deputies before they received a reply to their petition. The List workers were the only ones to mention overtly political issues, such as civil liberties, amnesty for political prisoners, and the creation of a constituent assembly.

Most of the smaller plants that struck on September 27 were either clustered in the immediate vicinity of one of the large plants or located on a major street directly connected to them. Dobrov and Nabgol'ts, for example, lay in the center of a heavily industrial area, not far from the militant Sytin plant, which was still striking at this time. Several smaller machine shops in the area stopped work after the appearance of large crowds. Similarly, the strike at Bromlei spread to two adjacent machine shops immediately after a meeting at which Social Democratic speakers addressed workers from all three firms. Only Gopper and Zhako, in eastern Serpukhovskaia, did not seem to spread contagion in their area. The workers from List were particularly active proselytizers. They laid siege to the neighboring Einem candy plant (1,900 workers) and forced it to close. Only police guards kept work going in the Golutvinskaia cotton mill (950 workers) on a nearby embankment. In addition, workers from the List plant on the river made contact with workers in the other branch of the List firm, located clear across the city in Butyrki, northwest of Sushchevskaia (IV). When the 800 workers there also struck, they in turn set out to stop work in other factories near them.

Despite the enthusiasm of workers in certain large plants, the work force in the heavy metal industry did not show the same unity and group consciousness as the precious-metal craftsmen. In the months that followed, the skilled artisans established the groundwork for a permanent labor union with a distinct craft identity. This identity was so strictly defined, in fact, that jewelers and gold- and silversmiths at first formed separate organizations and only after considerable negotiation agreed to combine into a single union.[50] The factory workers did elect shop delegates and form plant committees; and several factories sent representatives to trade-union congresses and to the Moscow Soviet in November. But the heavy metal industry never organized as a whole and never showed the professional solidarity of the narrow, more homogeneous trade.

The same distinction between craft and industrial protest holds for the textile industry. In August, there had been a ribbonmakers' strike, involving four factories. Workers from the two largest (Gandshin and Virts with 525 hands, and Sigalov, with 85) formed a strike committee, which drafted a set of general demands. The strike concluded before the end of the month with concessions from the owners. The committee later dubbed itself the Council (Soviet) of Ribbonmaker Deputies.[51] This council was in fact the first "soviet" in the city of Moscow. By adopting the title, the strike committee announced its intention of becoming a permanent body, the core of a labor organization with continuing functions that went beyond immediate strike issues. In September, the ribbonmaker delegates (including at least one associated with the Mensheviks) established a trade union for the specific purpose of protecting their constituents against an influx of unskilled labor.[52] In this case, it seems, the ribbonmakers, an artisanal trade within the textile industry, organized to defend a position of relative privilege. They made contact with Social Democratic organizers and demonstrated a sense of craft solidarity. There is no sign, however, that they identified their own conflicts with issues of concern to the working class as a whole. The August strike was a self-contained event. In September, only seven textile mills, none in ribbon production, staged strikes of their own. The total number of strikers (about 2,000) was negligible and far below the total for January.[53] The majority of textile- and metalworkers did not form industrywide associations or even central strike committees in 1905. The first three soviets in Moscow were composed of ribbonmakers, printers, and carpenters—all primarily artisanal trades, in which, however, large-scale production units had begun to make serious inroads.

The September strike movement began as a peaceful affair, centered on factory- or trade-related issues. In the first three days, there were few incidents of disorder, and police reported no violence.[54] But from the start it was clear that labor conflict was not going to remain peripheral, either in the geographic or in the political sense. There were two specific reasons for this: first, the concentration of printing workers in the downtown areas; and second, the state of political agitation that had seized the Moscow University student body in the wake of the August 27 autonomy decree. As a result of this geographic coincidence, politics moved into the open, under the very nose of the anxious and watchful authorities. It was not long before persons of all social classes found themselves shoulder to shoulder in public places, before the hostile eye of the police, who attempted, unsuccessfully, to send them home. This was the incendiary mix that the government perceived as most threatening to its own political safety.

As early as September 20, crowds were already filling the streets throughout the day and into the night. Workers, students, and other residents mingled along the first ring of boulevards. Large groups assembled to listen to speeches at various well-known points in the center of town, such as the Pushkin monument on Strastnaia Square, between the Tver and Arbat districts. There was no preconceived plan to the movement, and at first no sign of violent intentions.[55] As the authorities took a more active role in trying to clear the streets, attacks on property and police increased. Police, soldiers, and Cossacks began to chase the crowds from place to place, trying to break up meetings and keep strikers away from the print shops still in operation.

The first violent confrontation between workers and troops took place late in the afternoon on September 22. A group of about 100 striking printers, joined by some idle young boys, had set about stoning the windows of a print shop on Strastnyi Boulevard in the Tver district, publisher of the Monarchist newspaper *Moskovskie vedomosti*.[56] After being stopped and dispersed by the police, the crowd regrouped around the Pushkin monument. A witness described the scene that ensued:

[There were] Cossacks with unsheathed swords, infantry with guns cocked. The Cossacks closed in [around the crowd], forming a tight circle with only a narrow passage left for the public, through which I managed to squeeze myself. Suddenly shots rang out, one of the gendarmes tottered on his horse and fell. The crowd was frightened by the shots and turned to run. The Cossacks set upon those who tried to flee, and what followed defies description.[57]

The authorities, now thoroughly alarmed, decided stronger measures were needed to restore order. The Governor-General ordered all printing plants put under armed guard, and Cossacks were posted around Strastnaia Square. By 10:00 P.M. the streets were quiet.[58]

The next day not a single Moscow newspaper appeared. The tumult of street agitation remained largely confined within the inner ring of boulevards. Bands of striking typesetters, joined by some bystanders, continued to roam the area in groups of 200 or 300, breaking windows in plants still operating. Some owners closed down merely to avoid damage. Troops began firing rounds of blanks and later on real bullets.[59]

A certain amount of random vandalism occurred in the evenings. At dusk on September 26, for example, a large number of workers gathered on the northeastern end of the inner ring of boulevards. As they moved along the streets (down Miasnitskaia Street toward the Red Gates), they broke streetlamps, overturned benches, and knocked down trees. They threw stones into the windows of stores along the way and hurled bricks at policemen. One part of the crowd even tried to overturn a passing horse-drawn tram, but was thwarted by a company of grenadiers.[60]

During the afternoon of September 23, crowds made several attempts to stop work at newspaper print shops. Eleven men were arrested, for example, when a stone-throwing crowd in the Tver district attacked the offices of the right-wing newspaper *Moskovskii listok*. The police later released the men after deciding that they had not been ringleaders, but were merely peaceable bystanders. The records of this and of other such arrests allow one to discover who made up the crowds and how they came together.

All the arrested men worked at three printing plants in the immediate vicinity of the besieged press, two of which—employing eight of the eleven—were located on a single street. The men were not all residents of the area. Only four lived in the Tver and Arbat districts; four lived in Presnia, and the others in different areas. In this case, at least, the workers appear to have left their shops together and wandered out into the streets, rather than leaving from home and joining up with their neighbors. Shopmates furthermore appear to have stuck together once on the scene. The group was young but not adolescent. Five of the men were between twenty-one and thirty; four were under twenty-one, and two were in their thirties.[61]

Evidence from another group arrest, this one on September 26, supports the idea that the crowds trying to close down plants still in operation consisted of workers from similar enterprises, not of randomly assembled individuals. The arrestees, 15 workers who were part of a crowd of some 100 trying to stop work at a sausage factory, were all sausage makers themselves, employed by three other firms. Eight worked together in one firm, and four of these came from the same hometown as well. Six of the 15 (including those four) were natives of a single *uezd* (provincial district). Only one of this group was over thirty years old; eight were between twenty and thirty years old, and six were younger than twenty.[62]

The pattern repeats itself in yet another case, this one involving 20 upholsterers arrested in a crowd in the second Sretenskaia district (II) on September 27. Thirteen of these men came from one or another of four furniture shops in the adjacent Tver-Arbat area. Three were from a larger factory (Zibrekht) located outside the center, and these men all lived in the vicinity of the factory. The other 17, however, came from eight different parts of town. This group was slightly older than the others; only two men were under twenty-two, and nine were over thirty.[63] Other reports indicate that workers such as these were joined by students and street children, perhaps runaway apprentices or urchins from the Khitrov Market. Evidence does not permit us to tell, however, which members of the crowd resorted most readily to violent action.

The crowd did not always initiate the violence. Reports indicate that the Cossacks or gendarmes were at times guilty of attacking first, usually with swords and whips. Witnesses or people caught in the clashes were horrified by the use of these weapons, even when the troops were responding to provocation. A typical incident occurred at noon on September 26. A regiment of Cossacks returned a volley of stones with two rounds of bullets directed into an oncoming crowd on Nikitskii Boulevard. Ten bodies lay on the ground after the shooting. More injuries followed when the terrified Cossack horses bolted and ran wildly along the boulevard, trampling people who stood in their way.[64]

The indignation of the liberal press focused on a particularly violent clash in front of the Filippov bakery on Tver Street. Late on September 24, the bakery workers announced that they would go on strike the following morning. On emerging from the factory after the last night shift, the bakers found themselves confronted with police and Cossacks, who surrounded the building. The workers threw bricks and stones; the troops responded with fire. In the end, police arrested 197 workers, of whom 144 were under eighteen years of age; 34 workers were wounded.[65] That afternoon, several of the arrested men returned. Some were bandaged and bloody. They said they had been led to the courtyard of the police chief's residence and attacked by police, Cossacks, and gendarmes, using whips, rifle butts, and bayonets.[66]

The Filippov incident was the only major confrontation during the first week of the strike. By September 26, activity in the center of town had calmed down.[67] After September 27, fights began to occur between strikers and workers in the outlying areas who had not yet adhered to the movement. On one such occasion, over 200 strikers harried the workers at two adjacent furniture factories. The crowd threw stones and fired an occasional revolver shot at the buildings. One of the plants had struck earlier, and work had already partially resumed. Its employees resisted the crowd's appeal. When police arrived and tried to clear the grounds of outsiders, the workers inside came to their aid. Gunfire from the crowd wounded several officers. The police returned the fire. Eventually the plant closed, and its recently rehired workers left the premises.[68]

On the evening of September 27, deputies from two striking metal plants appealed to the workers in a nearby bicycle factory to leave their benches. The younger men at the plant wished to join the strike, but the older workers opposed the idea. The conflict resulted in a melee that was broken up by the police. The next morning a crowd of 400 to 700 strikers appeared and tried to prevent work from continuing. Cossacks and police summoned by the management shot 21 workers, four of whom died. The shooting went on for an hour, after which work at the factory was suspended. A twenty-year-old Moscow University student was arrested along with six workers. The student, whom the police suspected of being the ringleader of the incident, was armed with a revolver. Social Democratic leaflets were found on the others.[69]

The presence of agitators in the crowds led some commentators to blame the rise in violence on the machinations of revolutionary leaders. Right-wing newspapers accused left-wing extremists of encouraging the mob's criminal impulses.[70] Conservative citizens objected that the police were not using strong enough measures. "Everyone is cursing [Governor-General] Durnovo, [Police Chief G.P.] Medem, and, above all, Petersburg," wrote L. Tikhomirov, one of the editors of *Moskovskie vedomosti*, in his private journal. "If the police are blamed, it is because they have been deprived of all authority: they must submit to attack without being able to defend themselves."[71] The liberal press, on the other hand, argued that repressive legislation encouraged the authorities' use of violence. Since public assembly was unlawful, even peaceful meetings became a pretext for police intervention. Liberal journalists claimed that official reports exaggerated the number of wounded among the armed forces and ignored the number of civilian casualties.[72] The police reports even dismayed the most ardent partisans of law and order. "In the first place," wrote the same Tikhomirov, "everyone thinks [that the disproportionate number of uniformed victims] is a lie. In the second place, that if the reports are true, they're disgraceful. [The troops] are not only incapable of harming the Japanese; they cannot even cope with a crowd!"[73]

Moscow's liberal city councilmen objected especially to the use of Cossacks to control civil disorders. They proposed that the Cossack regiments quartered in Moscow be removed from the city. This suggestion was vigorously opposed by one of their fellow councilmen, A. S. Shmakov, who made no bones about his distaste for Jewish "intelligentsia-hooligans" and all liberals in the "Jewish camp."[74] Liberals, he claimed

[do] not want to know about facts that are already common knowledge: about Jewish propaganda, even among the troops; about the evil deeds perpetrated by Jews, using Finnish knives, revolvers, and explosive bombs. [These include] a number of political murders, whose victims have been Cossacks, dragoons, and infantry officers, as well as various officials and private individuals. One must keep in mind the horrors that the Jews and their sympathizers have perpetrated in Warsaw, Gomel, Odessa, and other centers favored by agitators, who can be stopped only by force.[75]

This speech offended the majority of the councilmen. But the language was not too outrageous to find favor in respectable conservative circles. Later in the year, extreme right-wing groups used similar anti-Semitic rhetoric to justify a massive antirevolutionary campaign, encouraged by public authorities and geared to win mass support.

By the end of the month, disorder in the streets had died down. But the strike movement did not abate completely. Some strikers returned to work, especially in plants such as Einem, which had closed in response to pressure from workers outside the factory. The printing strike dragged on, though workers in smaller shops were eager to return to the job.[76] During the first week in October, the strike spread to some previously uninvolved plants, but the overall number of strikers continued to decline.

By the end of the first week in October, half the printers who had struck in September were back on the job. Newcomers continued to join the strike as late as October 8, momentarily retarding the strike's dissolution, but most were as quick to withdraw as they were slow to join: almost three-quarters of the printers who struck for the first time after October 1 were back at work seven days later.

Strikers in the largest plants showed the greatest perseverance, a pattern that reemerged throughout the course of the year. The Sytin plant resumed operations only on October 4, after concessions from the owners. Workers at the second-largest striking firm (Kushnerev in the Sushchevskaia district, area IV) did not capitulate until October 19. Workers employed by medium-sized enterprises (100–500 workers) continued to account for the largest number of strikers in early October. But the vast majority of printers who struck for the first time after October 1 came from shops with fewer than 50 employees. These workers were not only the last to close down their shops, but the first to return to the job. Their short-lived enthusiasm hastened the final collapse of the printers' movement.

Individual enterprises began to defy or to ignore directives from the center. As early as September 28, the printers' council was obliged to appeal for continued discipline and solidarity:

In the event any factory wishes to return to work, it must present reasons for wanting to do so. If it is a question of insufficient funds, the council will try to help out the factory. If the reasons given are important enough, the council will give permission to resume work. If the council should not give its approval, however, the factory must without question submit to the council's decision.[77]

On October 4, the council laid down conditions for ending the strike. It urged the workers still on strike to pare down their demands to the conditions already granted by the Sytin administration (the nine-hour day, half-pay for the strike period, and various pay raises) and those who had gone back to work to support the others with financial contributions. Once back at the job, the council insisted, workers must defend their right to elected deputies. More than any other specific issue involved in the strike, the principle of collective representation was the key to building strong working-class organizations.[78]

The metal strike ran out of steam even faster than the printers' strike. Almost half the September strikers in the metal industry had returned to work before October 1. As in the case of the printers, the first to leave the strike were workers in the smaller plants. During the first week in October, the remaining strikers were joined by 2,000 new recruits, but the total number of striking metalworkers nevertheless declined. Also as in the case of the printers, strikers from small shops were more heavily represented among the October newcomers than they had been in the September strike. Altogether half the metalworkers on strike in the first week of October had either been dismissed or returned to work by October 8. Two large plants, List, and Dobrov and Nabgol'ts, closed their doors by management decision. Dobrov and Nabgol'ts fired its entire work force on October 5 and then weeded out certain undesirables when it rehired the workers two days later.[79]

Among workers who were not affected by management lockouts, the quickest to return to the job on their own accord were those who had only joined the strike in October. An exception to this pattern and to the general tendency of small shops to strike late and return to work early were the strikers from the precious-metal trade. They constituted at least two-thirds of the striking metalworkers from shops with under 100 workers. In early September, they had struck as a group, and they did so again in early October. Between the two strikes they held their first general trade-union meeting in a tavern on Pustaia Street, near Taganskaia Square in Rogozhskaia (area V), a center of the precious-metal trade. At the conclusion of the second strike, the union still existed only in outline, but with each strike episode, the determination to organize had grown stronger.[80]

Despite the influx of newcomers in the metal and printing strikes, the strike movement was clearly on the wane by early October. Of the other three major participants in the September movement, only the striking tobacco workers sustained their effort into the new month. The bakers, as we have seen, had already withdrawn from the strike. The woodworkers held out somewhat longer, but their ranks did not expand: the Shmidt workers returned to the furniture factory on October 4, after concessions from the owner; at least a third of the original number of strikers had resumed work by October 8; and the strike came to an end two days later.[81]

The September movement was confined to workers in the manufacturing sector. (For a breakdown of the strikers, see Table A.1, p. 229.) It did not involve educated professional groups, white-collar employees, service workers, or—with some minor exceptions—municipal and government employees. Apart from the tobacco workers, skilled groups formed the backbone of the movement: bakers, carpenters, typesetters, gold- and silversmiths, and machinists. In each trade, the largest plants took the initiative and exercised leadership over the movement.

The Social Democrats set up councils that helped the strike to spread along occupational lines. In early October, Menshevik organizers made an attempt to consolidate the councils into a permanent leadership body. They began the work of organizing what was to be the Council of the Five

Professions at two meetings, on October 2 and October 4, held in the Museum for Assistance to Labor. The founding meeting drew together 32 representatives from the five major striking trades. At the second meeting, the ribbonmakers were also represented. The participants were politically active workers; all either belonged to a Social Democratic group or were sympathetic to the Social Democratic position.[82] The printers, tobacco workers, Moscow-Brest shop workers, and ribbonmakers all sent Mensheviks, the carpenters a Bolshevik and a Menshevik. N. I. Chistov, president of the printers' council, chaired the sessions.[83]

The organizers wanted each trade to preserve its independence on the projected citywide council. Delegates elected by factories in each branch of industry were instructed to choose deputies to speak for the industry as a whole. Individual factories and districts did not have separate representation.[84] In addition to setting out future ground rules, the delegates at these meetings served as a provisional strike committee. Their major task, however, was to preside over the wind-down of the strike movement. On October 4, they issued guidelines similar to the ones suggested earlier by the printers' council. The instructions aimed to produce an orderly retreat. Where there was no hope of concession from factory owners, all workers in a given trade should resume work simultaneously, as an expression of continuing solidarity. In trades where some owners had conceded and others still held out, striking workers were to continue the struggle, with the moral and financial support of their successful comrades. The workers were also instructed to set up strike funds to support future actions. Above all, they were to regard the right to freely elected deputies and to free assembly in the factories as a central issue, to be defended at all costs.[85]

It is clear that centralized leadership played a minimal role in September and certainly did not account for the movement's wider impact on the city as a whole. This impact was due to other circumstances. Although the strike was concentrated in the manufacturing sector of the urban economy, it was not confined to the predominantly industrial areas of the city. Most printing plants were located in the central downtown area, which included the commercial and financial district, police and administrative offices, the university, and the major shopping area. As soon as the printers stepped out of their shops into the streets, their strike became a public issue. Freed from the narrow confines of their trade, the printers provided a mass audience for student and intelligentsia agitators. Conflict over economic issues involved the workers in illegal forms of public behavior and brought about a confrontation with authority. The printers' council concluded from the experience of September that political struggle had become inevitable. In the current crisis no strike could remain "unpolitical," however modest its original goals.

We began with a peaceful struggle for the improvement of working conditions [read a union leaflet in early October]. We began the fight against one enemy— the owners—but we were met along the way by troops, police, and Cossacks. We realized that the bakers were not beaten by accident, nor was it accidental that peaceful meetings of the Sytin printers were prohibited inside the factory. We understood that the Cossacks, policemen, and gendarmes were carrying out the will of the authorities, who in turn depend on higher authority—on the auto- cratic government. We saw that another enemy confronted us—a fierce and terri- ble enemy—our government. Our peaceful economic struggle has led us straight to the very thing that some had previously wanted to avoid—it has led us to politi- cal struggle, to struggle with the autocracy. Even those who were decisively against politics have been forced by experience to change their minds.[86]

Violent clashes between government forces and civilians in the central streets and boulevards also made an impression on city residents, who would not have been affected had the strike remained confined to trade- union issues in predominantly working-class districts. The funeral of Prince S. N. Trubetskoi in early October gave the public an opportunity to show its growing support for the opposition movement. The Prince, rector of Moscow University and a prominent liberal, had died on Sep- tember 29, while on a visit to St. Petersburg. In Moscow, a large crowd of students, and professors, along with the representatives of various profes- sional unions, gathered at the Nikolaevskii Station on October 3 to meet the train bringing his body back home.[87] The crowd accompanied the body as it was carried across town to the university. A service was held in the university chapel, which overflowed with wreaths and mourners. The procession then set out again toward the Donskoi Monastery in the lower Zamoskvorech'e. The cortege represented a cross section of educated so- ciety. Students carried the coffin. Red flowers and red ribbons speckled the crowd, which included priests as well as many solid citizens. The So- cial Democratic parties did not send representatives, but the singing of revolutionary songs alternated with the chanting of the liturgy.[88] Great crowds gathered to watch the procession, but no police were present. At five-thirty, as it was already growing dark, the coffin arrived at the cemetery.[89]

While the professors were eulogizing their deceased colleague, a crowd of almost 2,000 students had gathered at the cemetery gates to listen to revolutionary speeches. When the burial was over, the students set out in the direction of the university. This time, the swell of revolutionary lyrics was not interrupted by the counterpoint of priestly chants. The "Mar- seillaise" alone echoed through the darkened streets. The students had crossed less than half the Zamoskvorech'e when they were met by a squadron of Cossacks. In the two skirmishes that followed, several students were beaten with whips and 23 were arrested. The police chief later insisted that the students had begun firing random shots at the troops, but as in most such cases, who fired first is unclear.[90]

The incident so outraged public opinion that the police were obliged to issue an official justification, which appeared in all the daily newspapers. Those in the liberal camp were incensed. It was not that they shared the students' political goals or approved of their rhetoric. Trubetskoi himself had been a paragon of moderation. But the funeral symbolized the right to public assembly and to open expression of political opinion. The attack on students who had honored Trubetskoi's memory struck at the heart of the liberation movement. Instead of repudiating the young radicals, establishment liberals saw the students' fate as symbolic of their own situation. They also identified with the students as members of their own class. Some were perhaps their very own children. The autocracy was no respecter of class differences when it came to politics. Public demonstrations, open discussion, collective action, autonomous labor struggles—all were equally vulnerable to repression, no matter what the social standing of their participants or the temper of their ideological spokesmen. Physical brutality threatened anyone who dared take a public stand; good breeding was no protection.

For educated society, government policy thus underlined the basic issues that bound liberals and radicals together in common opposition to the established order. For the working class, government violence transformed local factory conflicts into confrontations of obvious political significance. The policeman who locked you up after a drunken brawl was only doing his duty; he was an accepted hazard of everyday life. The gendarme or Cossack who beat you or shot your mate for assembling on street corners, or for joining hundreds of others in a fight for better conditions, or for the right to a living wage—that was a different matter. It served the owners' interests. It offended your sense of justice, and it betrayed the promise of benevolent impartiality represented by the factory inspector and Zubatov's men. The disturbing iconoclasm of the radicals sounded suddenly less extreme. During the autumn phase of the revolution, observed the Menshevik P. A. Garvi, "the miracle of the workers' psychological transformation took place literally before our very eyes."[91] As part of this process, the strikes and violence of September helped forge the liberal-radical, professional-proletarian alliance that succeeded, in October, in bringing the autocracy to a standstill.

6

THE OCTOBER GENERAL STRIKE, I:

RAILROADS AND FACTORIES

Representatives of the factory work force were conspicuously absent from the Trubetskoi funeral demonstration. The September strike movement, which dragged on into early October, was already on the decline. It looked as though the working class was ready to settle down. Labor organizers used the moment of calm to consolidate the newly formed organs of strike leadership, which threatened to dissolve once the conflict was over. They had barely taken the first steps in this direction when a renewed surge of labor unrest interrupted their efforts and set off the massive social movement known as the October general strike. This attracted the support and active participation of the entire urban community. In Moscow, it represented the high-water mark of liberal-socialist alliance and of interclass cooperation during 1905.

The September strike consisted of a series of simultaneous but unrelated and basically uncoordinated actions involving several trades. By contrast, the October strike began as a calculated move on the part of an organized sector of the labor force—the railroad workers—a move designed from the start to attract wide-ranging support. The railroad workers were uniquely situated to spearhead a nationwide movement and to ensure its effectiveness. The railroads penetrated to all corners of the Empire. Their operation was indispensable to a functioning economy. The railroad administration was an arm of the imperial government. A railroad work stoppage reflected directly on the wisdom of government policies and underlined the intimate connection between the economic and the political causes of labor unrest. Furthermore, since the railroad work force represented almost the full spectrum of Russian society, the mobilization of transport workers across the board meant that general dissatisfaction with the existing state of affairs had reached serious proportions indeed. Even without the support of other sectors, railroad militancy promised to affect the entire economy and the entire social hierarchy.

But railroad leaders had every intention of attracting the widest possible support for their efforts. They announced the project for a nationwide shutdown at the October 4 meeting of the Council of the Five Professions.[1] This signaled their desire to cooperate with existing working-class organizations to build a powerful, all-encompassing movement. In this they eventually succeeded. As the center of the railroad leadership, Moscow was destined to play a crucial role in the development of the mass movement that crowned the revolutionary year.

The Railroads Mobilize

The railroad workers themselves had only recently established the kind of centralized organization that enabled them to launch such a movement. This organization, the All-Russian Union of Railroad Workers and Employees (Vserossiiskii zheleznodorozhnyi soiuz sluzhashchikh i rabochikh; shortened to All-Russian Union in the following text), had its roots in the labor conflicts of January and February. It held its founding congress in April, thanks to the combined efforts of Social Democratic, Socialist Revolutionary, and liberal organizers. The union's hybrid political leadership and mix of social groups did not prove a disadvantage, but were in fact the organization's source of strength. The early phases of railroad militancy showed that no group could act alone and lead a successful movement. What was true for the railroad workers in particular was true for the general strike as a whole: without substantial white-collar and professional participation, blue-collar protest remained a marginal affair. The railroad union represented in microcosm the dynamic political formula of the 1905 revolution: white-collar leadership of a united front of working-class and professional groups, using the strike and the trade union—characteristically "proletarian" instruments—to achieve democratic or basically liberal aims, such as greater economic equality and the right to self-representation.[2]

The gradual mobilization of the railroad work force followed the same pattern as the mobilization of the wider community. Agitation began among skilled blue-collar workers, but remained isolated and confined to shop-related issues until organized protest from the outside provided political focus. Only in the end did the broad, unskilled masses enter the picture. In Moscow, railroad unrest began as an incidental part of the factory strike movement. Shop workers on the Kazan, Kursk, and Brest lines struck in January; the shop workers at several other lines went out with them,[3] but station personnel, telegraphists, linemen, and administrative staff remained uninvolved.[4] Social Democrats had been active in the three main striking shops, which may account for the uniformity of certain of the workers' demands, such as the eight-hour day, the right to strike without reprisals, and the recognition of elected deputies as a permanent feature of worker-management relations. Other demands included an end to punitive fines, body searches, and overtime; improved health care and sanitary conditions; the institution of pension plans; and civility on the part of supervisors.[5]

Despite Social Democratic influence, the petitions contained no political language or references to the general crisis and state of labor unrest that followed the events of January 9. Railroad discontent was a reaction to powerlessness on the job and to economic hardship. Workers in the Moscow-Kazan shops and depot were the most restless of the lot, perhaps because of the intransigence of the director, who was quoted as saying he would rather lay golden rails from Moscow to Kazan than give in to worker demands.[6] Yet even the Kazan shop workers had not lost faith in government authority. As late as August, they petitioned the Governor-General of Moscow to intercede on their behalf, to convince management of the fairness of their economic grievances. "We have the honor," they wrote, "most humbly to beg Your Excellency to accept our petition from our elected representatives and humbly to beg you to examine all our demands and needs."[7] However naïve and unsophisticated the workers' expectations, however passive the majority of the rank and file,[8] the January strikes represented an important step forward. The worker-delegates elected in the shops continued to exercise authority among their fellows and to provide leadership throughout the rest of the year.

The other railroad workers and employees did not begin to mobilize until February. The link between the blue- and white-collar movements is difficult to establish. V. V. Romanov, vice-chairman of the All-Russian Union, remembers that the office and line employees felt betrayed by the shop machinists, who returned to work just as the staff decided to go on strike. It was only later, in March, after the government attempted to destroy railroad labor activity across the board, that the two groups drew closer together.[9] The Soviet historian I. M. Pushkareva emphasizes the importance of the "proletarian element" to railroad organization. She asserts that the administrative staff and linemen were inspired by the example of the shop workers' militancy and were radicalized by contact with Social Democratic workers.[10] But she also presents evidence suggesting that the unrest among blue- and white-collar workers had different and independent origins. She cites the memoirs of a former clerk in the financial office of the Vladikavkaz railroad, who claimed that the clerical staff showed no signs of dissatisfaction with their lot or interest in social issues until the Russo-Japanese War "awakened public opinion" (*obshchestvennaia mysl'*). Only when educated society began to grumble did the office staff first consider the possibility of banding together to improve their own situation.[11]

The example of the shop strikes may well have inspired the clerks to stop work when the time came, but it is important to note that working-class unrest by itself was not enough to move them to action. The railroad union grew out of white-collar, not blue-collar, mobilization, and it retained its connection with the professionally based liberation movement. Like left-liberals in general, the railroad leaders shared the broad democratic assumptions at the heart of Social Democratic ideology. Like other professionals, the railroad staff adopted the classic strategies of the labor movement: the strike and the trade-union form of organization. But as the Social Democrats never tired of complaining, the railroad union was resolutely radical-democratic (petty bourgeois, in the Marxist lexicon) in outlook. This is precisely what enabled it to appeal both to working-class and to professional groups.

The administrative clerical staff were from the first better organized than the shop workers had been in January. The various lines elected leadership committees, which communicated with each other by telegraph and drew up demands for each service. Line employees followed their initiative, and some shop workers also struck in February. Like the shop workers, the employees wanted a say in their own affairs: the right to elected deputies, the right to peaceful assembly, and the right to petition for the redress of grievances figured prominently alongside a host of specific economic demands.[12] Socialist language is absent from their programs. "We are united," said the office workers' committee of the Moscow-Kazan administration, "in the attempt to win our human rights" (*chelovecheskie prava*).[13] During the February strikes, which lasted almost three weeks, employees used the Museum for Assistance to Labor as a central meeting place. In early March, representatives of the various line committees decided to combine into a central bureau of employee representatives. They also appealed to the police chief for permission to set up a mutual-aid society of railroad employees. Permission was never received.[14]

Indeed, the Ministry of Communications took pains to prevent the further growth of autonomous railroad organization. On February 8, the government issued the so-called Temporary Rules on Worker Deputies in Shops and Engine Depots on State Railroads. These had two parts: the first, an attempt to stem labor unrest with judicious economic concessions (e.g., the nine-hour day, revised piece rates and overtime pay), and the second, a measure designed to replace worker-controlled deputies with management-approved spokesmen (an extension of the starosta law of June 10, 1903, to railroad shops). The promise of a nine-hour day was especially effective, as it turned out; news of the concession prompted many shop workers to call off their strike.[15] Three days later, on February 11, the government declared the railroads temporarily under martial law: striking workers were now subject to arrest and imprisonment of up to eight months.[16] In late March, the ministry issued two circulars affirming the imposition of martial law, restricting the right of petition, and rejecting employee demands for the recognition of permanent "elected organizations to participate in questions of firing, hiring, and transfer of employees." The ministry also rejected proposals to establish a special employees' bureau. Beyond this, it declared null and void all economic and organizational concessions granted by local rail administrations in January and February.[17] Thus, in one blow the government wiped out all the movement's concrete achievements and destroyed its chances of future legal development.

Far from stifling unrest, the government succeeded only in politicizing the railroad movement and in strengthening the bond between shop workers and line and administrative employees.[18] The railroad intelligentsia responded to the ministry's challenge by forming a national union. The founding congress met in Moscow on April 20–21. Sixty persons attended, representing ten lines, seven of them in Moscow. Only one delegate was a blue-collar worker.[19] The congress elected seven members to a central bureau, which co-opted additional members in July. Five of the initial seven had technical and white-collar jobs. Of the final dozen or so, only two were shop workers. At least three (and probably four) members of the enlarged bureau were Socialist Revolutionaries, two were Social Democrats (one Bolshevik and one Menshevik), and the rest were nonparty, including one anarchist and one unknown.[20] The nonparty members were in fact close to the Socialist Revolutionaries or to the liberal left, and almost all of them joined the bureau in July, perhaps to strengthen union popularity among the politically uncommitted rank and file.

The Socialist Revolutionaries continued to dominate the railroad union leadership throughout 1905. Their position was eminently suitable as an ideological standard for the railroad movement. They aimed to change society through the united efforts of all working people—proletarian, white-collar, and peasant alike. The Socialist Revolutionaries were popular among educated urban groups who considered the liberals too moderate in their strategy and insufficiently democratic in their aims, but who shied away from the Social Democrats. The Social Democrats' sociological approach to "proletarian" politics put them at a disadvantage with respect to white-collar and professional groups. Strictly speaking, the office clerk was no proletarian; he represented the petty-bourgeois enemy. The Social Democrats actually undermined railroad solidarity by emphasizing class differences. Romanov recalls that the Social Democrats tried to "sort out the railroad work force into 'purely proletarian elements,' on the one hand, and 'bourgeois-liberal and radical [elements],' on the other. They explained the essence of the class struggle, using the antagonism between these two social forces as their example."[21] Such an attitude did not prevent the Social Democrats from trying to win the clerks' support with appeals to their sense of social justice. The Social Democrats' strained and inconsistent relations with the All-Russian Union demonstrates that they never resolved this essential conflict in their own position.[22] The Socialist Revolutionaries, on the other hand, did not see a contradiction between the economic and the political interests of salaried and wage labor. The secretary and the clerk could fight for their own material needs and at the same time feel themselves part of a larger movement for social change.

The first railroad congress adopted a program based on principles acceptable to all members of the progressive coalition. The union defined itself as a professional corporate organization for "the defense of the economic, legal, and cultural interests of railroad employees and workers of all categories." Since any autonomous civic activity, however modest its goals, was impossible under the existing "political-bureaucratic order," the first and basic priority was the destruction of the autocratic regime and the establishment of a society based on truly democratic principles. The union considered itself part of "that liberation movement [osvobo-ditel'noe dvizhenie] that has already involved the enlightened members [soznatel'naia chast'] of all civic and professional groups." It supported the principle of a constituent assembly of popular representatives elected on the basis of the four-point formula. For the achievement of such a goal, the statement went on, legal means were not appropriate, since the goal itself was incompatible with the existing order. The union therefore pledged itself to a campaign of strikes, not merely for professional economic purposes, but for political ones as well. This did not mean, however, that the union could afford to join any one political party. In order to unite the full spectrum of railroad workers and employees, without alienating either the unsophisticated or the revolutionary activists, the union must refrain from partisanship.[23] In the words of the union's vice-chairman, the union decided to take a political position because autocracy gave it no choice, but it refused to make a virtue of necessity. The union merely "formulated those simple, logical propositions suggested to the wide railroad strata by the very course of events, with the gracious assistance of the railroad administration and other authorities. In the given circumstances, these authorities did the union's agitational work for it."[24]

Such "tailism" (allowing events to set the political agenda and speaking to the lowest common social denominator) was anathema to the Bolsheviks, who feared the flow of events might strand them on the quiet shores of bourgeois compromise. They were headed for the rapids of social revolution, with proletarians at the engines and Marxists at the helm.[25] Their most consistent strategy was therefore to organize the railroad shop workers on a separate basis. In February, the Bolsheviks issued a leaflet in the name of the Union of Railroad Workers, Attached to the Moscow Committee (Bolshevik) of the RSDWP. By April, they had changed the name of this organization to the Union of Railroad Employees of the Moscow Network, Attached to the Moscow Committee of the RSDWP, presumably to attract a wider following. This was already a compromise with principle.[26] Bolshevik influence remained strong (though not exclusive) among shop workers and in some local line committees.[27]

But Social Democratic organizers cooperated with the All-Russian Union; indeed, they helped form its program and sat on its central committee. Mensheviks welcomed broad-based labor organizations as a means of widening the mass movement. Bolsheviks were in principle hostile to politically independent organizations, but in the summer of 1905 they agreed to work within the framework of nonparty unions. Their independent, party-based union had little success on its own. The All-Russian Union was in fact a loose federation of autonomous committees, and the Social Democrats were free to operate on a local basis.[28] The central union continued to draw the bulk of its supporters from the employee category,[29] whereas the shop workers tended to be guided by the local line committees. By the time the union's second congress met in July, Social Democrats controlled six of the 19 lines that sent delegates, and they attracted considerable support for their stand on specific issues.[30]

Despite the Social Democratic influence within the union, the organization retained its close association with the liberation movement. In May, the All-Russian Union sent delegates to the founding congress of the professionals' and white-collar workers' Union of Unions. That organization was an even looser one than the railroad union and did not impinge on the latter's independence. The decision to join merely reflected the importance of the railroad intelligentsia in determining union policy.

Although the railroad leadership remained essentially liberal, the liberals themselves were moving to the left under the force of government repression and the realization that the constitutional reforms promised in February were likely to prove disappointing. In late May, the Union of Unions announced its support for "any and all means of struggle" against the existing government.[31] During June and July, the All-Russian Union, along with other organizations, such as the newly formed unions of municipal employees, retail shop clerks, and printers, held large open meetings in and around Moscow. Police reported, for example, that crowds of workers and employees from different Moscow railroads met regularly in the woods around Perovo, a suburb of Moscow and the site of machine shops attached to the Moscow-Kazan line. Here the crowds listened to revolutionary speeches, free from official interference. The police complained they did not have the manpower to disband or even to keep track of these gatherings.[32]

The subject of discussion at the summer meetings was the possibility of launching a general political strike to protest the forthcoming announcement of voting regulations for the so-called Bulygin Duma. Bolsheviks hoped the strike would soon lead to armed insurrection, but the majority of the union leaders wanted only to pressure the government into broadening its concessions. In May, the Bolsheviks tried to lead a general strike on their own. Their failure taught them to cooperate more closely with the nonparty unions, which they learned to value for their broad contacts among the rank and file.[33] At its second congress in July, the railroad union declared itself in favor of a nationwide general strike to begin at an appropriate moment in the near future.[34] By the time the union issued its cautious pronouncement, Moscow workers had already been discussing such a possibility for two months.

Indignation rose to a climax in educated circles after the publication of the Duma electoral rules on August 6, but the working class remained quiescent. As we have seen, it was only in September that labor unrest picked up again in Moscow, for reasons unconnected with the general political situation. The railroad workers, for their part, were preoccupied with their own affairs in September and did not respond at once to the Moscow labor walkout. In May, the government attempted to undercut the railroad movement by the familiar strategy of economic appeasement. It announced the formation of a special commission in which representatives of the workers themselves would consider the revision of their pension system. The central bureau of the railroad union, with the support of many Social Democrats, wanted to boycott the commission, for fear that the partial satisfaction of economic grievances would dampen worker militancy. The majority of railroad workers nevertheless took part in the government-called election of delegates.

When the commission finally met in St. Petersburg on September 20, the delegates immediately manifested a surprising degree of independence. They rejected the officially designated chairman and met separately to elect a chairman from their own ranks. They decided to exclude all nonelected delegates from future meetings, and they refused to limit their discussions to the narrow question of pensions.[35] The 35 delegates were almost all middle-level employees. Only one was a blue-collar worker. Their activities nonetheless aroused great interest among the railroad rank and file. Reports on the congress appeared in the daily papers and in the union newsletter, and the delegates received up to 30 telegrams a day.[36] The commission achieved no concrete results, but its significance lay outside its actual accomplishments. The experience proved to be an important step in the development of group solidarity among railroad employees. "It turned out that the importance of the commission lay not in the activities of the delegates meeting in St. Petersburg," says the Soviet historian M. N. Pokrovskii, "but in how the commission was conceived all over the country. For the railroad workers this was a kind of constituent assembly. It seemed to them that the commission was about to proclaim a democratic republic. And when the rumor arose that the conference had been dispersed and the delegates arrested, everyone believed it."[37]

The rumor circulated in early October, and though unfounded, it contributed to a state of growing agitation among the railroad workers. This unrest began with a local conflict in the Moscow-Brest shops (in Presnia, area III). Some 1,000 Brest workers struck on September 27, under Menshevik leadership. These machine shops were "a Menshevik citadel," "the brain of the [Presnia] district." They employed "many old, politically conscious metalworkers," that is, a worker-intelligentsia with a history of socialist activism. Even so, the majority of Brest workers were not ready for political explanations and found it hard to stand up to management pressure.[38] The Ministry of Communications refused to consider the strikers' demands or to recognize their elected deputies. Administrative employees and line workmen stayed on the job. On October 3, the strike ended abruptly when the administration dismissed the entire shop and rehired only those workers who signed a pledge not to strike in the future.[39]

On that day there was some sporadic strike activity on other lines: in the Kazan and Iaroslavl shops and among the Kursk conductors. The All-Russian Union decided to call for a general strike in support of a national railroad walkout. It announced this decision at the October 4 meeting of the Council of the Five Professions.[40] The Moscow Bolshevik Committee, along with a minority on the All-Russian Union's central bureau,[41] did not think the factory workers were ready for a general strike, since many were returning to their benches after the September walkouts. The Bolsheviks urged their followers in the railroad shops to begin local strikes, but they did not link this action to a broader movement. By October 6, no shop workers had responded to their summons.[42] The All-Russian Union's central bureau then issued a general strike call for October 7, addressed to the entire railroad work force. The Moscow Bolshevik Committee supported this decision, since its own independent effort had failed.[43]

Once the strike was under way, the Social Democrats cooperated actively with the All-Russian Union. But this cannot disguise the fact that the great general strike of October 1905 was not the product of Social Democratic (let alone Bolshevik) leadership. The October strike was not primarily proletarian, either in ideological inspiration or in its social complexion. Far from rushing to the support of the railroad initiative, the Bolsheviks did not announce their official endorsement of the general strike as such until October 10 in Moscow and October 12 or 13 in St. Petersburg.[44] The Bolsheviks distrusted amorphous strike movements as a diversion of popular energy toward vaguely defined reformist, or "merely democratic," goals. To achieve the victory of socialism, they held, revolutionaries had to focus on the destruction of state power. This was the necessary precondition for true democracy and social equality. To act otherwise was naïve or petty-bourgeois. The Bolsheviks therefore introduced the slogan of armed insurrection into many of their leaflets supporting the strike. "Lay down your tools and take up arms," the leaflets read. "Long live the armed uprising of the exhausted people!"[45] But the Bolsheviks were not in fact ready to launch such an undertaking. The slogan was merely a rhetorical device that allowed them to distance themselves (in principle, at least) from their allies: they were not syndicalists or fuzzy-minded democrats, but partisans of the proletarian class struggle, which meant a struggle led by the Social Democratic Party. Since they were in no position to direct the movement that had broken out around them, they were correct, from their own (tautological) point of view, to distrust it. They did not, however, stand aside once the strike had caught on. The October movement netted the liberals and moderates a constitutional compromise; it netted the left-wing parties increased popular support and expanded opportunities for labor organization among wide segments of the working class.

The General Strike Begins

The October strike began on the Moscow-Kazan railroad, where the local committee included both Socialist Revolutionaries and Social Democrats.[46] This was not an accident. In fact, neither group could do without the other. On the evening of October 6, several Moscow-Kazan machinists, including a member of the All-Russian Union's central bureau, got hold of an engine and drove to the Perovo Station, where the administrative head was a fellow union member. Perovo telegraphists sent a message to stations throughout the Empire, announcing the strike call. They then walked off the job. That same evening, Moscow-Kazan freight engineers stopped work. At dawn the next day, October 7, police arrested several engineers and a telegraph operator at the Moscow-Kazan station. In response, workers, administrative personnel, and passenger engine drivers joined the strike. Strikers from the Kazan station then crossed Kalanchevskaia Square to the Iaroslavl station, where they had no trouble getting the staff and workers to walk out.[47]

On October 8, contingents of railroad employees belonging to local line committees made the rounds of the city's other stations. V. N. Pereverzev, chairman of the All-Russian Union's central bureau, later described their activity:

Work stopped immediately in all the railroad administrations. The administrative personnel, mainly young men and women, set out in crowds to visit all the stations in the Moscow network and persuade the remaining workers and employees to leave their work. By this time the stations were already under armed guard, but the soldiers did not show the slightest desire to interfere with the strikers in their criminal activity. It was common to see soldiers as well as officers manifesting a definite sympathy for the strikers. Some officers flirted with the girls and offered cigarettes to strikers. On that day, the young men and women of the administrative staff were responsible for spreading the strike among those very workers in the machine shops who, according to the original [i.e., Social Democratic] plan, ought to have begun the strike themselves.[48]

Newspaper reports of the beginning of the railroad strike in Moscow confirm Pereverzev's impressionistic account. At three stations, the administrative personnel first struck alone; at two others the engineers and traffic supervisors joined them in initiating the walkout; and at another station the administrative personnel led the strike along with shop workers: thus, white-collar employees took part in the first day of the strike at six of Moscow's ten stations. Engineers and traffic supervisors struck alone at two others and shop workers at the remaining two.[49]

The amount of violence involved in the spread of the railroad strike seems to have been minimal. The conservative daily *Moskovskie vedomosti*, which eagerly detailed the criminal acts of strike participants, cites only three incidents in which the workers used force against a person. On the evening of October 6, striking workers beat up a locomotive engineer who was reluctant to leave his post, and fired shots at a supervisor who tried to interfere. The shots missed. On two other occasions strikers threatened a signalist and a telegraph operator with revolvers, but did not hurt them. Groups of 300 to 500 strikers entered freight and passenger stations, to mount the locomotives, release the steam pressure, and shut off the engines. Occasionally they got into fights with other workers who tried to protect the trains. Strikers also destroyed some signal apparatus, broke windows, and tore down telegraph wires.

By October 9, all Moscow stations were under armed guard, and the soldiers tried to keep the strikers out. After October 10, outgoing railroad traffic ceased on all lines but the Nikolaevskii, connecting Moscow with St. Petersburg, and incoming trains went no farther than suburban stations. The Kazan and Kursk passenger stations were crowded with travelers caught between connections. The railroad administration lodged them in stationary railroad cars and gave them a small daily allowance. The wealthier passengers hired cabs at exorbitant.rates to take them on into the city. Military battalions manned the few trains that still maintained communication between the two capitals.[50]

On October 7, the All-Russian Union formulated the following demands in connection with the growing strike:

1. Pay raise for all railroad workers
2. Institution of an eight-hour workday
3. Formation of a bureau of deputies composed of railroad workers and employees, which would meet with the administration to resolve questions of hiring and firing
4. Abolition of existing pension funds
5. Radical reorganization of medical aid
6. Opening of a sufficient number of schools, libraries, and reading rooms for railroad staff
7. Freedom of speech, press, and assembly; the right to trade-union organization and strike activity; inviolability of person and domicile
8. Calling of an all-Russian congress of delegates, elected by railroad personnel and workers, to formulate a new statute for railroad employees and workers
9. Calling of popular representatives with legislative power, elected by the entire population of the nation
10. Legal immunity for all participants in the strike
11. Full amnesty for all political and religious prisoners[51]

On October 10, the Minister of Communications, Prince M. I. Khilkov, met with a delegation of 40 railroad workers in Moscow. The delegates insisted that all arrested strikers be released as a condition for negotiations. There was nothing he could do about this, the Prince regretted. He entreated them to speak openly with him about their grievances anyway, and to trust him as a former worker himself. On the subject of overtime, he recalled how he had once been eager to work 16 hours a day to increase his earnings. He contrasted his own former zeal and the high productivity of foreign labor with the inefficiency of contemporary Russian workers. In fact, said the Minister, he still worked harder than they did, rising at seven in the morning and ruining his eyesight over heavy paperwork. The delegates objected that their own 16-hour workday left no time for reading or study. If they really wanted to, the Prince replied, they could still fit in an hour of reading, which over a year amounted to ample time.[52] Nothing better illustrates the paternalism of tsarist officials than the Minister's sermon to the railway workers.

On his return to St. Petersburg, the Minister commented on the meeting:

The deputies insisted on demands that are not within my power to grant: that is, political rights and the liberation of individuals arrested by the police. Material questions are of secondary importance. I am doing everything possible to calm the striking railroad workers, but it is uncertain how long the strike will continue. Measures are being taken to restore the normal state of affairs, but until the general agitation has diminished, it will be hard to count on the resumption of normal service.[53]

Politics appealed primarily to the technical and skilled members of the railroad work force. They mingled freely with other professional groups and had already acquired the habit of political discourse. Their presence was common, for example, at mass meetings in the university. The less-skilled workers, by contrast, could not comprehend the heady political questions that interested their leaders:

When, on the third day of the strike, the halls of the university and the Technical Institute suddenly filled with the genuine gray masses from the workers' districts, then the picture changed significantly. Economic demands now came to the fore, and agitators could no longer introduce political slogans without difficulty. "We thought that real business would be discussed here, and once again they're trying to stuff us with politics!" Such outbursts were heard frequently from those workers who were completely new to the mass movement. This suspiciousness was especially strong among unqualified railroad workers—signalmen, line workmen, and the like.[54]

The Strike Spreads to the Factories

No more sophisticated than these "unqualified railroad workers," the industrial workers nevertheless began to respond to the railroad union's example. Over 25,000 of them struck in the ten days following October 7. This does not count the 8,000 workers remaining on strike from September. The total number of strikers, 33,300, or about one-fifth of Moscow's industrial labor force, was higher than in September, but less than in January. Even in St. Petersburg, factory strikes were less extensive now than they had been in January and February.[55] The October factory strikes in

Moscow were not as well organized as the September strikes, and they spread along neighborhood rather than occupational lines. As in January, the textile workers constituted the largest group of strikers in Moscow, followed by the metalworkers and the food workers. (See Table A.1 for a breakdown of the numbers.) The movement was largely concentrated in the city's eastern and southern districts: one-third of October's factory strikers worked in area VI, the Zamoskvorech'e, and close to a third worked in area V, Basmannaia-Rogozhskaia-Lefortovo.

The occupational groups that had struck in September did not display the same degree of solidarity they had shown earlier. The carpenters' strike petered out by October 10.[56] The striking tobacco workers hung on but did not increase in number. The bakers did not strike as a group, nor did the printers, though several individual printing factories were still on strike. The new strike affected perfume, candy, and paper factories, tea-packing firms, flour mills, and wineries. The 2,700 workers in chemical, leather, and paper manufacture who joined the strike after October 7 did not constitute coherent professional groupings (with the exception of the perfume factories), but were drawn into the movement primarily by geographical accident.[57] Most of these diverse enterprises were located in the Sushchevskaia-Meshchanskaia (IV) and Lefortovo (V) districts (the outer north and northeast sections of the city), and many were situated near striking metal or textile firms.

Approximately 9,200 metalworkers, or almost a third of the industry's work force, went out on strike between October 7 and October 17. Of these, 3,000 were survivors of the September movement. Among the new adherents were 800 craftsmen from precious-metal workshops, including a group of enterprises clustered together in Rogozhskaia (V). The core of the strike movement in the metal industry consisted of workers in a handful of large firms: six of Moscow's ten machine factories with 500 or more workers struck in October. Five of these had struck at least once before in 1905. Four plants in the Serpukhovskaia district in lower Zamoskvorech'e (VI) together supplied over a third of October's striking metalists. These were Bromlei (1,500 workers), Zhako (1,400), Gopper (600), and Tereshchenko (500). Firms in area V employed another quarter of the metal strikers. But the enormous Guzhon steel mill in that area did not strike; its 2,500 workers stayed on the job, despite attempts by strikers from a nearby tea factory to get them to stop work.[58] Altogether, fewer metalworkers struck in October than in September or January.

In the textile industry, the number of strikers almost reached the January level and far exceeded the figure for September. Altogether 12,000 textile hands struck between October 7 and October 17, or about one-fifth the industry's work force. The textile strikes were concentrated in the same districts as the metal strikes and were likewise focused on a limited number of key firms. Six of Moscow's 27 large textile mills (500 or more workers) struck in October. The strike affected a greater proportion of textile workers in the Zamoskvorech'e (VI) than elsewhere in the city: the area employed only a quarter of the industry's workers, but supplied over half its October strike participants. Almost all the area's 6,000 textile strikers, moreover, had already been on strike at some time since January 1905.

The textile workers in the Zamoskvorech'e who were the most active and the best organized were concentrated in four large firms, which together accounted for half the total textile strikers in October: the Tsindel' cotton mill (2,400 workers); two wool mills, Mikhailov (1,265) and Shrader (1,400); and the Ganshin and Virts ribbon factory (525). All four were located in the same section of the Piatnitskaia district of the Zamoskvorech'e, and all had previously struck in January. Tsindel' and Ganshin and Virts, moreover, were among the first textile mills to close after October 7. Socialist organizers had been most active among the Tsindel' workers, who presented their management with a list of 24 demands, ending with a call for worker solidarity, civil liberties, and a constituent assembly elected on the four-point formula.[59] At the Shrader plant, workers and management agreed between them to close up shop. The workers nevertheless considered themselves on strike and not merely shut out. Two days after the plant closed, Shrader workers appeared at the Mikhailov plant to persuade those workers to join them. The Mikhailov workers had already formulated their own demands and did not need much persuasion.[60] The disproportionate share of strikers from large plants, however, did not necessarily reflect a uniformly high degree of political awareness, or even of trade-union militancy, among the mass of workers. Even at Tsindel', for example, only 500 workers initially wanted to strike; the others stopped work only after a day of noisy agitation and threats by the strikers.[61]

Force of example, often reinforced by crowd pressure, drew textile workers in smaller plants out onto the streets. Many of the striking firms in Lefortovo (V), for example, were located in two small areas, each of a three- or four-block radius. Among them were eight firms (with a total of 1,540 workers) that struck for the first time on October 12. These were clustered on four adjacent streets, and the workers in all eight were subjected to crowd pressure. In each of the three major branches of textile production—cotton, silk, and wool—considered separately, the largest firms were the most militant, with the very smallest next in order.

In the ten days following October 7, the number of industrial workers affected by the strike continued to mount, but the attrition rate was also high. As new recruits left their benches, other workers just as steadily went back to their jobs. A minimum of 2,000 striking metalworkers resumed work between October 8 and October 17, leaving no more than 7,000 on strike at the end of the period. This is but one indication of the relatively low level of organization among October strikers in the factory work force.

The sudden upsurge of enthusiasm among industrial workers had taken the Social Democrats by surprise. Menshevik and Bolshevik militants at work in the industrial neighborhoods had judged the strike movement to be on the wane in early October. Those party organizers who had been busy in the meeting halls of the university and other educational institutions had not expected the railroad strike to have immediate repercussions in the working-class districts.[62] The Social Democrats, as we have seen, did not issue their own strike call until October 10.

There was no organized connection between the railroad strike and the renewed activity in the industrial districts. Crowds of striking railway workers carried their message to the factories in person. They played the same role as the printers had in September. Both printers and railroad workers were scattered throughout the city. Each group had a unified and politically conscious leadership. The first to leave their jobs, these workers provided a free-floating mass to which other strikers could then attach themselves. As each new factory struck, the body of proselytizers increased, and subsequent attempts at persuasion became even more forceful. Socialist Revolutionary and Social Democratic organizers wove their way into the crowds, repeating the same slogans at different factories and in different districts, until they became the catchwords of the movement.[63]

The strikers' use of physical intimidation increased after October 13. Between October 13 and October 17, few factories appear to have closed simply on the initiative of their own workers, and the presentation of demands rarely accompanied the decision to strike. Management began shutting down to avoid property damage inflicted by proselytizing strikers. Violence did not always originate with the strikers, to be sure. During the second week of the strike, the police became more aggressive and occasionally took shots at peaceful crowds. Such incidents too moved a number of factory owners to close up shop in the desire to avoid bloodshed.[64] Four giant textile firms closed their doors in this period: two cotton mills, Giubner (3,000 workers) and Prokhorov (6,000), both in the Presnia-Khamovniki area (III); and two silk mills, Zhiro (3,400), also in Khamovniki, and Simono (1,000) in the Zamoskvorech'e (VI). The workers took advantage of the lockout to formulate demands and declare themselves on strike.[65]

The majority of October strikers in the industrial sector were motivated by the desire to obtain specific improvements in their economic situation. Socialist organizers tried to demonstrate the political implications of the strike, but they were not always successful in making their ideas understood. The example of the strike itself was more effective than political propaganda in winning recruits in the factory districts. Railroad and factory workers had been on strike for almost a week before they were joined by workers in the nonmanufacturing sector. It was only after this that the strike acquired a central leadership committee, which acted as spokesman for the movement as a whole.

7

THE OCTOBER GENERAL STRIKE, II:
PROFESSIONALS AND POLITICS

The railroad strike had begun in Moscow, because of the city's central position at the hub of the Empire's transportation network. By October 12, the movement had spread throughout European Russia and Poland. A general work stoppage, accompanied by a fever of political meetings, affected major provincial cities, as well as the capitals.[1] For a week after the railroad union's announcement, the St. Petersburg Bolshevik Committee refused to come out in support of the strike. It did so only after the movement had spread from the industrial suburbs to the factory districts and had white-collar and professional support. By then it was October 13.[2]

The Mensheviks were quicker to take advantage of the strike. On October 10, Menshevik leaders in St. Petersburg decided to create a citywide committee of worker-deputies, and their idea won the support of left-leaning liberals.[3] Just as the workers had earlier chosen delegates to the Shidlovskii Commission, they now elected deputies to the central workers' council. Some of the deputies who met for the first time on October 13 were in fact former delegates to the commission. It was not until the strike committee's third session, on October 17, that it adopted the title Soviet.[4] The delegates at this time also selected an executive committee and announced the publication of a newsletter. By the end of November, the soviet consisted of 562 deputies representing 147 factories and 34 shops, as well as 54 representatives of various trade unions. Two-thirds of the factory delegates came from metal factories and machine shops. Since metalworkers constituted about a third of the city's industrial labor force, they were thus overrepresented on the soviet, a sign of their political activism. Among the unions represented were several involving white-collar or artisanal groups: office workers, retail and pharmacy clerks, tailors, shoemakers, watchmakers, and jewelers. Industrial categories predominated, however.[5]

Like the All-Russian Railroad Union, the St. Petersburg Soviet remained officially nonpartisan. Its president was the left-liberal lawyer (later turned Menshevik) G. S. Nosar', now using the name Khrustalev-Nosar'. The Social Democrats could outvote their Socialist Revolutionary rivals, but they could not impose their views on the membership. The Bolsheviks initially insisted that the soviet adopt a Social Democratic platform, but the delegates refused.[6] The St. Petersburg Soviet exercised strike leadership for 50 uninterrupted days, during the remaining weeks of October and throughout November. Besides acting as a strike committee, the soviet formed a militia and negotiated with the city council, the mayor, and the post office and railroad administrations. It also served as a coordinating center for independent workers' organizations, such as the railroad and postal unions.[7]

In Moscow, the working class played a much smaller role in the direction of the strike movement. Professional and white-collar groups predominated on the Strike Committee formed on October 12; the committee included factory delegates, but they were far in the minority. Among the organizations represented were, first of all, the All-Russian Railroad Union's central bureau, as well as the strike committees of individual city and suburban lines. Municipal employees sent delegates from three associations: technicians, engineers, and administrative personnel. Other professional and white-collar groups participating were the telephone workers; the bank and retail clerks; the Union of Unions member unions of lawyers and engineers; and the engineering students' association. Only three blue-collar groups took part: delegates from joinery shops and factories; from various machine factories; and from the Iakovlev printing plant. In addition, six political organizations participated independently: the three socialist parties; the Union of Unions; and two Union of Unions member unions—the Union for Women's Equality and the Peasant Union.[8] This social mixture led the Menshevik delegate P. A. Garvi to describe the committee as a kind of political Noah's ark.[9]

The committee's financial support reflected its composition. Individual contributors donated one-third of the funds collected (three alone gave half that amount); 40 percent of the money came from professional and white-collar groups, including medical personnel, lawyers, journalists, teachers, and bank and administrative employees (icon painters and actors also sent some money); another quarter of the total sum came from political or civic groups. Students and railroad workers contributed only a negligible amount.[10]

The Social Democrats tried to counteract the dominant influence of the professionals in two ways. They tried—unsuccessfully—to increase worker representation on the Strike Committee itself. In addition, the Mensheviks tried to create a soviet on the St. Petersburg model. They held three meetings in October, but nothing came of their plans.[11] The Social Democratic challenge was not serious enough to undermine the Strike Committee's leadership during October. It was not until late November that something resembling a central workers' council finally took form in Moscow.

The White-Collar/Blue-Collar Alliance

With the formation of the Strike Committee, professional and white-collar groups other than the employees of the railroad administration began to join the strike. The first to do so were the employees of the Moscow city administration.[12] The strike of the municipal civil servants had two important consequences. All the essential public services immediately ceased: the city's waterworks, gas and electric plants, and slaughterhouse closed, and the city administration was paralyzed by the strike of its technical and clerical personnel. In addition to crippling daily life, the walkout of the municipal employees brought about a direct confrontation between the strike movement and the City Council, which was affected both in its role as employer and in its role as guardian of the peace.

As we have seen, the city administration, like the railroads, employed a variety of skilled and unskilled workers and professionals. The first to form their own organization were the white-collar personnel. Manual and factory workers generally followed their leadership.[13] As in the case of the railroad shop workers and administrative personnel, the municipal workers and employees drew closer together under the impact of political events and formed a united front against their common employer. In both cases, the salaried staff was the most politically articulate and independent group, and in both cases, the white-collar and professional intelligentsia embraced the workers' cause as their own. They used socialist rhetoric to underline the seriousness of their political commitment, but did not accept the formal leadership of any one revolutionary party.

In late January 1905, some 200 municipal employees, meeting in the Museum for Assistance to Labor, had formed an association known as the Corporation of Employees in the Moscow City Administration (Korporatsiia sluzhashchikh po moskovskomu gorodskomu upravleniiu). Its goal was to achieve "recognition of the need for corporate organization of all salaried employees of the city administration, [in the form of] a permanent committee of elected representatives, to handle all questions concerning the corporate interests and needs of city employees."[14] In late

April, another organization appeared: the Corporation of Workers and Low-Ranking Employees in the Moscow City Administration (Korporatsiia rabochikh i nizshikh sluzhashchikh v moskovskoi gorodskoi uprave). Both groups emphasized the need to increase wages and to equalize pay levels.[15]

Like the railroad administration, the city authorities at first viewed organization in itself as a threat. The City Council only reluctantly recognized the corporation of city employees on August 6.[16] It was more resolutely hostile to the joint association of workers and low-ranking employees. At their second meeting, on July 30, the workers' corporation drew up a list of specific demands, which included a minimum wage of 25 rubles a month, the abolition of overtime, two days in a row off per week, improved housing and work conditions, the right of worker-representatives to conduct organizational business in city enterprises, and the institution of an eight-hour workday.[17] On August 19, the City Council and city administration created a special commission to consider these demands. Its members met for the first time on September 2, with the participation of five representatives from the workers' corporation. The commission recognized the justice of many of the grievances, including the need for higher pay and shorter work hours.

While the councilmen debated the commission's report, the two corporations held a joint meeting on September 18 in the City Council building, at which they affirmed their solidarity. A crowd of several thousand attended.[18] The city government, however, refused to make concessions and finally rejected the workers' program on September 23.[19] In early October, the managers of city enterprises endorsed the workers'.demands as reasonable—and in fact beneficial from the point of view of efficient operation. Municipal engineers and middle-ranking technicians also indicated their support.[20] The favorable opinion of the commission and of the managerial staff made the council's stubbornness all the more intolerable to the workers. An early settlement might have averted a crisis. Procrastination forced the workers' hand and transformed a labor conflict into a political confrontation.

When the municipal work force finally joined the general strike, it did so in support of its own particular demands. The timing of its decision had less to do with the general situation or the railroad union initiative than with the response of its own employer, the city government. Like the railroad administration, the City Council was a political as well as an economic agent: its decisions reflected political as well as material considerations. The general strike generated a mood of confrontation and raised general issues that certainly affected the workers' stance. They also affected the way in which the city councilmen responded to the workers' appeals.

From the workers' point of view, however, the real issues at stake concerned work conditions, material well-being, and the right to organize in defense of these interests. The demand for self-representation, of course, was a de facto challenge to legal restrictions on collective activity and reflected the prevalent spirit of political defiance. Perhaps because of the overheated political atmosphere, the city councilmen declined to meet the workers on these specific issues. The council's right wing was hostile to worker organization in principle. But even the liberals refused to consider the workers' actual demands. The liberals' close and uneasy alliance with the political left may have caused them to jump at the specter of social revolution symbolized by the militant "proletariat" (in this case, their own blue-collar work force). They may have smelled the rat of Social Democratic propaganda. The moderates among them were more than a little wary of the radicals, who presented a threat to the success of their own, more modest undertaking: the campaign for democratic political reform. Perhaps they feared that the "social issue" might jeopardize their political goals. In a curious parody of Social Democratic logic, the liberal councilmen rejected the workers' economic demands in the name of political change. In so doing, they did not win the workers to the cause of moderate reform. Instead, they gave the workers reason to accept the radical claim that "bourgeois ideology" merely concealed the selfish interests of the class enemy.

Seven representatives of the corporation of workers and low-ranking employees attended the October 11 session of the City Council.[21] They demanded official recognition of their organization. They also insisted on immediate satisfaction of the July demands. If not, municipal workers were ready to strike at a moment's notice. The city administration had already forfeited the workers' goodwill by failing to take action earlier. The delegation spokesman reproached the liberal councilmen in particular. They professed concern for working-class interests, yet they refused to endorse the municipal workers' specific demands. The large public audience gathered in the council chambers greeted this remark with prolonged applause. Councilman S. A. Muromtsev, the renowned legal scholar and zemstvo constitutionalist, assured the delegates of the liberation movement's sympathy.* But, he warned, the workers must under-

---

*Galai, *Liberation Movement*, pp. 19, 228, 258. The zemstvo constitutionalists were committed to working for the establishment of a constitutional regime (with or without monarchy), but did not fully support the more democratic program of the liberation movement. They began to campaign for a constitutionalist platform in November 1903. (See *ibid.*, pp. 178–79, 187–88.)

stand that economic concessions would not solve their problems unless the general political context was altered. He proposed a resolution demanding political reform as the only means of restoring social tranquility. The council adopted the motion with only four negative votes.

Muromtsev had confirmed the workers' fears that their best allies might hide behind their very liberalism to avoid practical concessions. In fact, he used the same argument often advanced by progressive industrialists: that political issues must take precedence over economic demands as the only way to calm social unrest and to improve the workers' position in society. It took a very sophisticated worker indeed, or a very credulous one, to interpret this reasoning as a token of political goodwill and not to see it merely as a self-serving pose that conveniently placed abstract ideas above the well-being of the lower classes. The council itself seemed to prefer general statements to concrete measures. The councilmen reaffirmed their sympathy with the workers' position as a matter of principle. They promised to provide them with hygienic apartments, but refused to act on other specific demands before November 15. The council warned that in case of a strike, it would take energetic steps to ensure the continuation of vital services. If necessary it would fire striking employees.

In their closing remarks, the worker-delegates promised that medical personnel would remain on the job out of concern for public welfare, but they warned that even hospital staff would quit their posts if the city administration used force or fired striking workers. The medical profession itself presented a united front that transcended class differences. That same day, October 11, head doctors in the municipal hospitals informed the mayor, Prince V. M. Golitsyn (also a zemstvo constitutionalist), that they fully supported the demands of their staff. They urged the city administration to recognize the hospital workers' recently formed corporation.[22]

The council's reluctance to act only strengthened the bond between professionals and blue-collar workers on the municipal payroll. The clerical and administrative employees of the City Council and of the city administration, most of whom were women, met on October 13 to affirm their sympathy with the workers' cause. Their statement, issued in the name of the Central Group of Municipal Personnel, was endorsed by the city's top-ranking technical personnel (engineers and architects). The statement read:

The workers have initiated a strike, which we consider to be one of the most powerful means of defending labor from the exploitation of employers and of influencing government forces and the bourgeois classes to improve the socioeconomic position of workers and other representatives of salaried labor. The commission of delegates representing all the corporations of employees in the Moscow city administration considers it indispensable above all to declare its full solidarity with the striking workers in city enterprises. [It] proposes that city employees declare themselves on strike until their [the workers'] demands are completely satisfied.

The Central Group designated a strike committee to work in close conjunction with the Social Democratic Party.[23] Thus the technical and white-collar elite drew the battle line above its own head, siding with the working class against the bureaucratic regime and the propertied classes. In this it echoed an old tradition in intelligentsia protest, which viewed the people and the enlightened few as allies in the struggle against the oppressive state and its economically powerful allies.

Not all civil servants, to be sure, rallied to the so-called proletarian cause. On October 11, a crowd of over 2,000 striking railroad workers entered the central post and telegraph office and tried to close it down. The postal and telegraph clerks refused to strike. Cossacks and dragoons broke up the crowd, with a liberal application of the whip, and the mayor had troops posted around the building.[24] But the striking railroad and factory workers continued to win the backing of salaried professionals. One of the first groups to support them was the Moscow pharmacy clerks.[25] They themselves had already struck on February 5, 1905, demanding minimum wage scales, shorter work hours, polite address, the right to chose their own lodgings (abolition of bed and board tied to the job), and the right to take collective action. This had been the first strike in the history of the pharmaceutical trade.

The profession had boasted a legal, nonpolitical association since 1895 —the Russian Pharmaceutical Society—whose members included pharmacy owners as well as employees. By 1905, the society showed a definite sympathy for the liberation movement. In May of that year, the pharmacy clerks crossed the line into illegality and formed a professional union, which profited from the existence of the Pharmaceutical Society in much the same way that other illegal unions flourished under the umbrella of the Museum for Assistance to Labor. The union's primary goal was to bring about "the thorough transformation of the structure of the pharmaceutical profession, in the interests of its own labor force [trud], as well as in the interests of public health [narodnoe zdravie]." It also aimed to improve the economic position of salaried employees. It recognized strike activity as "the only means of struggle against the existing pharmaceutical order and regime." As this language might suggest, representatives of the socialist parties took part in the union's meetings. One gets the impression that Socialist Revolutionaries and Social Democrats were both present. This might explain the union's officially nonpartisan position (political independence for trade unions was favored by Mensheviks and Socialist Revolutionaries) and also the fact that references to the proletarian class struggle appear in union resolutions from the very beginning. The influence of the Socialist Revolutionaries may be inferred from the union's decision in July to join the liberal-dominated Union of Unions. The vote was a close one, however, suggesting that the Social Democratic representatives argued against the move.

Pharmacy clerks in St. Petersburg went on strike on September 6. The Moscow union endorsed their action, but did not itself decide to strike until September 28.[26] The formal announcement had no effect, however, until the union felt its own existence threatened. At one o'clock in the morning of October 10, police interrupted a meeting of union representatives at the Pharmaceutical Society and forced them to disperse. The union responded by announcing the start of a strike "in defense of our interests, which coincide with the interests of the entire proletariat."[27] The executive committee formulated a general program that included demands for a two-week annual vacation, sick leave and pay, the right of employees to approve hiring decisions, shorter shifts, a minimum wage scale, and pay for strike time. In addition, the union's statement called for an end to the police regime, the establishment of civil liberties, amnesty for political and religious prisoners, and the calling of a constituent assembly based on the four-point formula.[28] By the end of the day, the majority of pharmacies in the city, both private and municipal, had closed.[29]

The pharmacy owners, many of whom were sympathetic to the platform of the liberation movement, promptly called a meeting and voted to close their establishments on October 12 to honor the strike.[30] The striking employees insisted, however, that their loyalties rested with the working class. They rejected the tradition of paternalistic fellowship that still characterized the profession. "We are glad you have reached political maturity," the strikers told their liberal employers, "but you are our enemies in the economic domain, and we do not trust you."[31]

Like the white-collar city employees, the pharmacy clerks used the language of class struggle to emphasize their desire for independence of action and self-expression. In July, the assistant mayor, I. A. Lebedev, had tried to convince city workers and staff that they did not need a special organization to promote their interests, because the City Council and city administration already had their best interests in mind.[32] The municipal workers and administrative employees insisted, however, on their right to represent themselves. They persisted in viewing their relationship to their employers as an antagonistic one. The municipal staff and pharmacy clerks alike were determined to organize on their own, to win economic improvements by means of strikes, rather than wait for the reaction to respectful petitions. They loudly proclaimed the fundamental contradiction between the interests of employees and employers. In so doing, they were asserting their right to political action. They called this acting in solidarity with the proletariat. For the proletarian cause represented a rejection of traditional hierarchical relations and an admission of the actual conflicts inherent in society. When, in defiance of sociological realism, the pharmacy clerks dubbed themselves "a part of the great proletarian army,"[33] they were not trying to ignore political issues by cloaking them in the rhetoric of economic struggle (the charge leveled by Muromtsev at the municipal clerks), but quite the reverse. They were insisting that politics could not be confined merely to the constitutional sphere, but must involve open conflict among social groups at the grass-roots level.

The government, of course, was not eager to see conflict openly expressed. But a policy of intolerance did nothing to calm the troubled waters. The regime contributed to the intelligentsia's view of itself as a pariah group by trying to stifle autonomous activity even in respectable circles (among lawyers, teachers, and engineers, for example). Repression, however, drove large sections of educated society, not merely the self-styled revolutionary intelligentsia, toward a symbolic alliance with the working class. A flesh-and-blood alliance was not always possible, since the ordinary worker was more often than not hostile to all intellectuals and professionals.* The regime's fear of conflict, coupled with its fear of change, made it in fact the most destabilizing force at work in society.

The authorities waged physical and ideological war against the militant pharmacy clerks. Cossacks and gendarmes set upon clerks who made the rounds of working pharmacies to spread the strike. Many of those assaulted were women.[34] The strikers also fell victim to racist denunciation in the right-wing press, a favorite tactic of reactionary rabble-rousers: "One must not forget," editorialized *Moskovskie vedomosti*, "that many pharmacists are Jewish, and the Jews are at present the Russian people's worst enemies."[35] Certain police officials seemed to make the same connection. The police captain of the second Tver precinct, for example, was convinced that most pharmacy clerks were Jewish and were conspiring to

---

*One eloquent example of blue-collar antagonism to educated people may be found in Mamontov, "Dvizhenie rabochikh," p. 193. The author was at the time a leader of the precious-metal workers' union. On Nov. 13, 1905, he was to address a meeting of 300 such workmen in a tavern on the northern edge of the city. Before he could open his mouth, however, he was attacked by a group from the audience. They calmed down only after their own local leaders explained that Mamontov was neither an intellectual nor a student. It must be remembered, in this connection, that the precious-metal workers were the most advanced in the metal industry in terms of trade-union organization and collective action.

terrorize their well-meaning colleagues. The Jews, he thought, wished to exert a stranglehold over the dispensing of medicine, in order to inflict the greatest possible harm on those in need.[36] A campaign of anti-Semitism served the useful function of increasing the distance between the educated minority and the popular masses, since the latter were no more friendly toward Jews than they were toward students and gentlemen in glasses. But in one sense, at least, the tactic backfired; instead of frustrating the disaffected clerk's desire to unite with the working class, official anti-Semitism only reinforced his sense of personal injustice and of social marginality. For these reasons, he clung the more ferociously to the values represented by those more downtrodden than himself.

The Problem of Violence

As the strike spread to all sectors of the city economy, the work stoppage began to affect every aspect of daily life. The anticipated disruption of public services had already created a mood of anxiety. On October 9, a temporary malfunction in the water supply produced panic in the city. When a muddy color appeared in the water, rumor spread that the strikers intended to contaminate the city's supply. Although the water soon returned to normal, the mayor asked that armed guards be posted around the two waterworks.[37]

The railroad strike soon stopped the flow of supplies into Moscow. By October 12, the price of meat had doubled, and milk was no longer available. The Grain Exchange Committee informed the Finance Minister that the city had only a limited store of grain left. The telephone was no longer in operation between Moscow and St. Petersburg. The rumor spread that strikers intended to attack banks and commercial establishments, but it proved unfounded. When the Electric Company informed its clients that service could no longer be assured, panicked residents immediately bought up the available supply of candles and kerosene. Electric trams stopped running. Shops closed their doors and boarded their windows for fear of nighttime rock throwing.[38]

Leaders of the industrial and financial community were divided in their response to the strike situation. The Moscow Stock Exchange Committee, chaired by N. A. Naidenov and representing the older generation of commercial entrepreneurs and the well-established Moscow banks, asked the Governor-General to declare a state of emergency. Another group of industrialists, chaired by S. I. Chetverikov and representing the city's more progressive industrialists of a younger generation, opposed that move; they urged that the population be granted broader political rights to help calm the situation.[39] A group of factory owners in the metal industry added their voices to the progressive camp; they resolved to reject the aid of Cossacks in settling disturbances connected with the strike.[40]

The Governor-General, P. P. Durnovo, tried to allay the public's fears and forestall the possibility of civic disorder. On October 14, he had notices posted all over the city denying that there were any serious shortages as a result of the railroad strike. In the same notice, acting on direct instructions from the Ministry of Internal Affairs,[41] he warned people of the penalties for any untoward activity:

> Since unscrupulous, evil-minded persons are continuing to provoke disorderly behavior among peaceful residents, I have ordered a sufficient number of troops to be posted throughout the city for the protection of the population. At the least gathering of persons and manifestation of criminal intentions, the troops will use their arms and open fire.
>
> Therefore, I urge all well-intentioned and honest residents to go about their business peacefully and, in the interests of their own personal safety, to avoid places where for any reason crowds are gathering.[42]

These admonitions notwithstanding, the authorities' anxiety over the effects of the strike and over the possibility of increased violence deepened as the shutdown spread to an ever greater number of services. Personnel in the remaining branches of administration—the Moscow Provincial and District Zemstvo boards—struck on October 14, as did workers in the Mytishchi waterworks. Telegraph operators stopped work, and most courts closed because of the militancy of lawyers and legal personnel; the reluctance of many judges to join the movement was not enough to keep the courts in session. Bank employees expressed their indignation at the Stock Exchange Committee's petition in support of martial law and declared their solidarity with the strike. Workers in the electric plant walked out. Gas was shut off. Middle and lower schools canceled classes, leaving the students free to roam the streets. By October 15, Moscow was "plunged in darkness."[43]

Despite the hardships wrought by the strike, the movement found widespread sympathy in educated circles. Even the City Council became more sensitive to the needs of its employees. On the afternoon of October 14, the council held an emergency closed meeting and decided to continue meeting daily as long as the situation remained critical. Aside from journalists, the only outsiders admitted were 17 delegates from the executive committee of the Corporation of Employees in the Moscow City Administration. The council officially recognized the corporation and gave it permission to meet on administration premises. In addition, the council agreed to periodic pay raises and an eight-hour workday for workers in all factory-type city enterprises.[44]

Not all the councilmen shared the sentiments of the majority. The delegates from the employees' corporation emphasized that they were acting in solidarity with their blue-collar comrades. The notion of a united front between municipal workers of different rank and economic status incensed the council's more conservative members. P. M. Kalashnikov told the delegates that they were victims of revolutionary propaganda. A. I. Guchkov, who himself sympathized with the moderate wing of the liberation movement, called the employees' radical statements a "shameful and black mark" on the movement, a manifestation of collective psychosis. His brother, N. I. Guchkov, argued that if the workers were exploited, then the office personnel themselves were responsible, since they were part of the administrative structure. A strike by salaried staff, moreover, would only aggravate the lot of the poor, who would be the first to suffer from the economic consequences. As a parting shot, Kalashnikov blamed the very existence of the employees' association for the chaotic functioning of the city administration. At this, the delegates left the meeting in indignation.[45]

Many liberals who supported the current tactics of the movement were uneasy about their possible consequences. Their fear of the disruptive potential of the mass movement was balanced, however, by an equal or greater fear of the government's capacity for violent reprisal. The Kadet Party, which held its founding congress in Moscow on October 12, rejected the possibility of negotiation with the politically bankrupt government and declared its full support for the strike movement.* The party's statement read:

The question is no longer whether or not political freedom will exist in Russia or whether it will be granted from above. The question is only whether freedom will be realized by violent or peaceful means, whether by the spontaneous outburst of popular forces or by their organized action. From this point of view, the Constitutional Democratic Party warmly welcomes the enormous step taken by the people in the same direction it has chosen itself: [it welcomes] the organized mobilization of the Russian working class. Though deprived of political rights, the working class is socially powerful. It is therefore menacing even when it remains peaceful.

It is up to the government to open the way for this great popular march to freedom—or else to turn it into bloody carnage. Having learned from the experience

*The Constitutional Democratic (KD, or Kadet) Party consisted of liberationists and zemstvo constitutionalists who decided to participate in the Duma elections in order to realize the liberation movement's program by peaceful means. These groups had first decided to form such a party in late August 1905, but it was not formally organized until October. P. N. Miliukov, who served as Foreign Minister in the Provisional Government of 1917, was one of the party's most prominent leaders. (See Galai, *Liberation Movement*, p. 260.)

of January 9, the government may hesitate to bring about a repetition of that event and earn for itself a second time the name of murderer. If that nevertheless happens, the government should know that all conscious and enlightened Russian citizens stand behind the people. The Constitutional Democratic Party proposes to take all measures within its power, as events may dictate, to prevent possible clashes. But whether or not it succeeds, the Party henceforth subscribes entirely to the popular demands. All its sympathy and moral force weigh in favor of popular liberation.[46]

Heedless of such warnings, the authorities refused to moderate the violence of their repressive measures. Two serious incidents occurred on the City Council's very doorstep.[47] At noon on October 15, a group of workers and their intelligentsia supporters arrived at the council building bent on attending a meeting of the various corporations of municipal employees taking place inside. I. A. Lebedev, the assistant mayor, did not allow them to enter, so they were left standing in the street. Some 200 onlookers had gathered by the time a detachment of dragoons arrived. The horsemen formed a semicircle, pinning the crowd against the council building. The dragoons ordered everyone to disperse, but before there was time to comply, they drew their swords and waved them menacingly. People began fleeing in terror, but not all managed to escape. The soldiers caught up with the stragglers, beat them with open swords, and trampled them under their horses' hooves. Policemen standing nearby joined in by beating up the victims as they lay. There were 40 wounded, some of whom were taken to the nearby university for treatment.

At this point, the conflict between different social groups was also becoming more brutal. The second violent incident of October 15 took place between one o'clock and three o'clock in the afternoon in Okhotnyi Riad (Hunter's Row), the street of butcher shops located behind Theater Square, between the City Council building and the university. It began when a crowd of some 2,000 persons, including many students of both sexes, entered the street and demanded that the shops close in accordance with the strike. When the owners refused, the crowd threw stones. According to the version that became current, various shopkeepers and their clerks, especially butchers, responded by beating up everyone in reach, using sticks, knives, and boards. When Cossacks arrived to restore order, they instead joined the attack, falling on the students with swords and whips, until several were beaten unconscious. The wounded were carried into the university for first aid.

In the days following this incident, Moscow newspapers printed letters signed by hundreds of persons who had resolved to boycott the merchants of Okhotnyi Riad. Some shop owners, however, were themselves supporters of the liberation movement. They replied to the threat of boycott by defending their own behavior and ascribing the violence to members of the Black Hundreds.* Shortly before the students appeared in the market, so they claimed, several men, including neighborhood policemen, had made the rounds of the shops, urging merchants to beat up any students, strikers, or pedestrians of intellectual appearance who might come their way. They themselves and their employees, of course, had not responded to the provocation. Those who had were the transient or marginal frequenters of the market: draymen, vendors, merchants from outside the city, and unemployed drifters, who as everyone knew were beggars or petty thieves. Despite the protests of the honorable minority, the shopkeepers of Okhotnyi Riad kept their right-wing reputation. Police complicity in acts of wanton violence had never been in doubt and was only confirmed in the wake of this incident.[48]

While these events were occurring barely a block away, some 300 citizens gathered in the City Council building to discuss the problem of restoring public order. Councilman Muromtsev had proposed the idea of consulting with civic leaders and groups, and he chaired the meeting. The assembled delegates reflected the entire range of urban society. They represented government institutions, the commercial and propertied classes, and skilled professional groups, as well as students, workers, and left-wing parties.[49] Individual strike committees also sent delegates, but they had no separate voice in the proceedings.

The meeting opened in an atmosphere of crisis, as reports of Cossack brutality on nearby streets reached the assembled delegates. A majority of the groups present favored the creation of a committee of public safety, charged with the task of forming a city militia. The militia should be open to all citizens of Moscow and be financed by the City Council. They also suggested that residents in each section of the city form local committees to discuss questions of defense and security. Only the Social Democrats objected seriously to this proposal. At this date, the Bolsheviks were already calling for armed demonstrations by the workers, though their calls went unheeded in the factories. The Mensheviks considered the Bolsheviks' position premature and irresponsible, and they condemned them for their "adventurism." But they stood with the Bolsheviks in wanting a mi-

---

*The traditional urban merchant estate was divided into corporations called *sotni*, or hundreds. The lower categories, such as petty traders and some artisans, were called the black hundreds (*chernye sotni*). This term became pejorative in 1905. Its use to describe antirevolutionary mobs reflects the general perception that the small tradesmen and their employees responded most eagerly to right-wing propaganda. On these terms, see *Entsikopedicheskii slovar'*, 41 vols. (St. Petersburg: Brokgauz-Efron, 1890–1904), vol. 30a: 942. See also George Vernadsky and Ralph T. Fisher Jr., eds., *Dictionary of Russian Historical Terms from the Eleventh Century to 1917*, comp. S. G. Pushkarev (New Haven, Conn., 1970), p. 139.

litia that would be free of the City Council's control. The Social Democrats suggested in all seriousness that the council resign and transfer its resources, along with its authority, to them. They would then create a truly popular national guard and hold elections to a popular committee, which would serve as the provisional administration of Moscow.[50]

Supporters of the majority proposal disagreed among themselves on how much influence to allow unofficial citizens within the proposed public safety committee. Members of the Moscow District Zemstvo voiced the most unorthodox proposal by suggesting that the committee reflect the composition of the present meeting, with the exception of councilmen and government officials. Other groups suggested that one-third of the committee members be city councilmen, one-third representatives of intelligentsia circles (kruzhki), and one-third representatives of workers and students. The lawyers offered an even less democratic proposal: they wanted fully half the committee to be city councilmen and only half chosen from other social groups.

The delegates waited until 2:00 A.M. to hear the council's decision. But the announcement, when it came, settled none of the issues. The councilmen had found it impossible to agree on any of the proposals offered that afternoon. The council's two most outspoken defenders of the liberation movement, Muromtsev and N. N. Shchepkin, felt that decisive action should be taken, but they could not rally more than a dozen of their colleagues to support them, and even they disagreed on the extent to which the council should share its authority with groups outside the government.[51]

In the debate over the composition of a public safety committee, the committee itself was lost sight of. The City Council had convened representatives of all segments of society, but it had not taken action on their suggestions, let alone allowed them to participate in the proposed solution. The council had no desire to challenge the basis of constituted authority by overstepping the limits of its own institutional competence. It issued critical statements and drafted petitions asking for expanded participation in national government, for changes in ministerial policy, and for guaranteed civil rights. But it did not question the legitimacy of the existing system. It certainly had no desire to assume power of any kind even on the local level. It refused to take action on its own, and it resisted public efforts to transform it into an instrument for political change. Even in a moment of crisis such as late 1905, when the imperial government had lost credit with much of moderate and progressive society, the City Council refused to step into the political breach.

The assembled delegates deplored the council's failure to rise to the occasion. They greeted its irresolution with cries of "Down with the City

Council!" and "Woe to the councilmen!"[52] Confidence in the civic authorities sank to a dramatic low, but the disappointed participants realized that even this defeat was meaningless. Prince D. I. Shakhovskoi, the most moderate of liberals, was heard to say, in discouragement:

Power in any case does not lie with the City Council, but with the Governor-General. Suppose the council did decide to organize a militia and actually designated funds for arms. We would never see that money, since money is in banks, and the banks are being guarded by soldiers. Suppose even that the money materialized—where would we buy arms? We must find other means. In the country, for example, I know of a certain revolver factory—why not try to get arms there?[53]

But if the council had disappointed the supporters of the liberation movement, it had not thereby improved its already compromised reputation in the eyes of the conservatives. For those defenders of Monarchy and Orthodoxy who saw the October 15 meeting as a concession to the revolutionary Jewish conspiracy, the City Council had forfeited its remaining claim to authority. The Monarchist Party demanded that the council be dismissed for engaging in revolutionary activity.[54]

The voice of reaction was indeed a minority in the City Council, and the number of enthusiasts for the status quo seemed for the moment insignificant in the flood of liberation opinion. But the enemies of the liberation movement were busy mobilizing their own forces. A small number of the monarchy's uncompromising defenders had previously formed an organization called the Union of the Russian People. Its purpose was to defend the principles of autocratic government and Great Russian supremacy, in an epoch when politically subversive attitudes seemed to have gained a hold at all levels of society.[55] When even the government appeared powerless to check the strike movement, the Union of the Russian People decided to counter the revolutionary threat with its own brand of mass mobilization. The union hoped to rally those segments of the urban population that had already been overtly hostile to the strike movement, to harness and thereby render more effective their spontaneous efforts to strike back at the revolutionary enemy. It therefore published a resolution calling for the formation of "peacekeeping detachments," to be organized in the parish churches with the cooperation of the local clergy. These neighborhood brigades were to "reestablish civic peace," without, however, resorting to "any kind of violent or extreme measures."[56]

This announcement appeared on Friday, October 14, spread in large type across the front page of *Moskovskie vedomosti*, mouthpiece of the Russian Monarchist Party.[57] It immediately aroused a stormy reaction. The liberal press thought the manifesto had government approval, especially since the Moscow chief of police, Baron G. P. Medem, was a member of the Monarchist Party. *Russkie vedomosti*, for example, called the union's appeal a blatant invitation to civil war. The paper distinguished between incidents of violence connected with the strike movement, the unavoidable by-product of a legitimate form of social action, and such deliberately provocative acts as the arming of private citizens at private expense. The editors endorsed the establishment of a militia composed of tax-paying citizens, financed by the city and dedicated to the maintenance of order and the protection of property.[58]

Popular antistrike sentiment focused with particular vehemence on the university. Thanks to the autonomy decree, Moscow's institutions of higher education continued to provide a meeting place where discussion and organization could take place without fear of police interference. So indifferent did the authorities seem to this state of affairs that the policeman stationed at the university entrance served willingly as unofficial doorman. He would open the door to arriving students and ask, "Where are you going? If you are looking for the Socialist Revolutionaries, turn to the right; the Social Democrats are this way, to the left."[59]

The university had been the scene of continual gatherings since early October. The socialist parties, along with various strike committees, had made it their headquarters.[60] On October 12, the University Council called for unrestricted freedom of assembly, arguing that existing prohibitions placed an unfair burden on the university. The following day, the government issued new regulations authorizing indoor public meetings on approved topics, subject to prior written permission and police supervision.[61] From the university's point of view, this did nothing to alleviate the situation. The Bolshevik organizer A. Sokolov remembered the varied and changing crowds that filled the city's academic establishments:

In early October, the meetings were concentrated mainly in the university and the Technical Institute. The two institutions attracted different audiences: students and intelligentsia/petty-bourgeois circles dominated in the university, whereas in the Technical Institute student blazers drowned in a sea of workers' jackets. Political sympathies, moreover, corresponded to the type of listener: SRs had the upper hand in the university, SD-Bolsheviks in the technical school. When the strike was declared, both of these "temples of science" turned into passageways through which the noisy, variegated crowd poured in a veritable torrent from early morning to late at night.

Who was not there! Workers, students, all kinds of professional people, tradition-minded merchants uneasily glancing around, earnestly trying to understand what was going on, suspicious types such as repentant police spies, fashionably dressed young girls, . . . and finally, peddlers selling candles (for which the demand had sharply risen since electricity was cut off), and apple vendors.

The mood of this fluid crowd was excited, joyfully enthusiastic, but completely undefined in terms of party sympathy. Individuals from different social strata here lost their natural coloration and unconsciously took on foreign hues. . . . Merchants from the Zamoskvorech'e shot glances of fellowship at workers, who responded in kind, while the wildly rapturous students were ready to embrace anyone who cried "Down with the autocracy!"[62]

To the monarchy's defenders, the university seemed like the head of the revolutionary dragon. Students began to take the matter of self-defense into their own hands. Meanwhile, the worried administration urged the City Council to protect the university with the forces of the proposed citizens' militia. The militia was still under debate, however, when the situation at the university reached a crisis.

On the evening of October 14, a crowd of over 1,000 persons of diverse occupations gathered in the university. They held a nightlong meeting in the light of flickering candles. The next day, the University Council suspended classes and prohibited further public meetings. The courtyards and auditoriums had not yet emptied when the victims of the attack in Okhotnyi Riad poured in from the street. The three students and five others suffering from sword wounds received emergency first aid. The refugees expected a Cossack attack on the university itself. They helped the other students collect material for barricades: flagstones, cobblestones, desks, metal rods, anything that came to hand went into the homemade fortifications. On top, they hoisted a Red Cross flag. The students made bonfires of classroom furniture and gathered in the courtyard to await the expected assault.[63]

They waited through the night in the barricaded buildings, but there was no attack. Troops surrounded the university, while members of the faculty begged the authorities to exercise restraint. Some of the leading agitators managed to slip out under cover of darkness.[64] Early the next morning, Sunday, October 16, the rector, Professor A. A. Manuilov, announced that the danger of attack had passed. The students were free to leave. Some 200 of them obtained permission from the central student committee to cross the barricades. They made their way past the soldiers, escorted by Manuilov and several other professors.

A general meeting of the remaining 1,500 students, speaking in the name of the "revolutionary proletariat and intelligentsia," demanded that the soldiers first be withdrawn. The police promised they could leave as a group, without danger of arrest, if they did not stage a demonstration on their way out. The students left the university in an orderly procession, led by the rector, some faculty members, and an assistant to the chief of police, an army general named Rudnev. When the group had dispersed peacefully, police locked the university and placed it under armed guard.[65]

The crisis in the university was handled without incident, thanks to the intervention of the rector and other liberal professors. But Sunday promised to be a day of even greater agitation. This was the day the Union of the Russian People had chosen to organize its antirevolutionary vigilance committees in the churches. The Governor-General condemned the criminal activity of revolutionary instigators who intimidated the "working people" and provoked them to disruptive behavior. He nevertheless warned publicly against the use of force by private citizens. He urged the population to cooperate instead with the legitimate forces of order.[66] But official peacekeeping efforts, as we have seen, were not notable for their restraint. Troops often behaved all too much like the right-wing enthusiasts themselves. Cossack officers, for example, showed little concern that troops billeted in the Manège across from the university regularly beat up students and other passersby.[67]

The episcopal authorities, it is true, warned the clergy that they would look unfavorably on the use of churches for any but religious functions. The Metropolitan specifically prohibited the selection of committees and asked the clergy to say special prayers for the restoration of public order. But he also instructed them to deliver a sermon written for the occasion by the right-wing editor V. A. Gringmut.[68] The contents of the sermon led the City Council to accuse the clergy of inciting the people to acts of violence. Some priests simply refused to read the text, publicly dissociating themselves from its "disgraceful tone and content."[69] High-ranking authorities thus tolerated or encouraged violence in practice, though they publicly condemned it in principle.

The Strike Wanes

Right-wing organizers won a popular following by playing up the inconvenience and hardship suffered by city residents as a result of the strike. On October 15, employees of the city waterworks decided to resume work to avoid aggravating the Black Hundred reaction. The railroad strike committee and the revolutionary parties supported their decision. Military engineers sent by the Governor of Moscow Province were already working to restore service. The City Council ordered the troops withdrawn and in a charitable spirit allotted 3,000 rubles to aid the families of striking city employees. Early in the morning of October 16, the workers returned to the waterworks, and the military engineers retired.[70]

Although the factory strike movement was still in full swing in St. Petersburg,[71] enthusiasm for the strike was weakening in Moscow, especially among unskilled workers. Even the railwaymen were discouraged:

On October 15 and 16, [the unskilled railroad workers, such as signalmen and line maintenance workers] had already begun to oppose the railroad strike committee, led mainly by higher technical personnel. . . . The [strike] situation was so unclear that the railroad union, formerly nerve center of the entire strike movement, had already begun to contemplate the liquidation of the strike. The strike had clearly come to a dead end.[72]

As the workers began to break ranks, the leaders' authority and self-confidence wavered. Plans for resuming operations at the city slaughterhouse aroused such conflict among workers that their own strike leaders were afraid to appear in person unaccompanied by a member of the City Board.[73] The machinists still supported the strike, but the butchers were eager to resume work. Only after the municipal official M. I. Priklonskii had promised to guarantee the machinists' personal safety did they agree to sit down with the butchers and discuss the situation. The strike leaders urged the assembled workers to hold out for the satisfaction of their political demands. But Priklonskii persuaded them to accept the economic concessions offered by the city. The majority agreed to resume work within two days' time, despite the unresolved political issues.

While these negotiations were in progress, a crowd of local meat merchants had gathered outside the slaughterhouse. The shopkeepers insisted that work resume immediately. They threatened to break down the gates and start butchering the livestock themselves. While some were busy arguing with Priklonskii, others had happened on a lone student near the slaughterhouse fence. They had just begun to beat him up when his cries attracted attention. The slaughterhouse butchers, Priklonskii, and a nearby policeman came to his rescue. Frustrated in their attack, the shopkeepers became even more belligerent. Priklonskii advised the workers for their own safety to reopen the slaughterhouse on the spot.

Toward the end of the strike, such conflicts became more common. Skilled workers tended to be more sensitive to political issues and less willing to concede defeat than other striking workers. Certain petty-bourgeois groups, notably shopkeeper-butchers and other small tradesmen, often expressed their hostility toward the strike by assaulting scapegoat figures such as students and members of the intelligentsia.

The ragged ending, however, only highlighted the extent to which the October strike itself had been a triumph of suspended conflict. Among the working class, skilled and unskilled had rallied together. Blue- and white-collar workers had supported each other's cause (as in the case of the municipal workers and the railroad workers). Even employer and clerk had found themselves caught in political sympathy (thus, pharmacist and pharmacy clerk, city councilman and city engineer).

With few exceptions, Moscow's administrators themselves desired change. The City Council never endorsed the strike, but many councilmen sympathized with the movement's political goals. In the words of M. Ia. Gertsenshtein: "We [the City Council] did not go on strike, but at the same time we announced in the council that we were not satisfied with the existing order and demanded that it be changed. The strikers have been demanding the same thing, only they have chosen different means."[74] The council nevertheless refused to break with the hallowed tradition of administrative inertia. The city's politically concerned groups were unwilling to seize the initiative themselves. They ended by passively witnessing the clash of forces raging around them. They thus abandoned the stage to the archenemies of change, who were less reluctant to take action.

The mass movement had meanwhile fashioned a new language that dispensed with institutionalized forms of expression. The general strike carried the demand for political reform to the attention of the imperial government by paralyzing the nation's economy. The government responded to organized coercion with organized repression, but in the end it was the first to concede defeat, thus enabling its challengers to claim victory. News of that concession, in the form of the Imperial Manifesto of October 17, did not reach Moscow until the evening. "The top [revolutionary] party leaders, sharply aware that the strike campaign was hanging by a thread, were prepared to awake the next morning to a regime of martial law; instead they awoke to find themselves in a 'constitutional state.'"[75]

Government repression and the violence of the right-wing reaction to the general strike had contributed largely to cementing bonds within the progressive movement. The bonds did not dissolve with the appearance of the manifesto, however. The reforms only increased the venom and frustration of the right. Many policemen and soldiers vented their rage on the joyful conquerors of imperial compromise. A period of unprecedented civil liberty followed the publication of the manifesto. It encouraged the growth of political differences within the ranks of the October alliance, but the strength of the counterrevolution prevented these differences from destroying the liberal-socialist partnership.

The October Manifesto was a victory for liberal aspirations: the desire to build a political system truly responsive to the country's social needs. The majority of moderate and left-of-center leaders welcomed the opportunity to engage in open political activity. Most strongly doubted the government's sincerity, but only a tiny minority pinned its hopes on the failure of compromise. Had the regime made good its promises, it would have strengthened its position immeasurably. The educated classes were eager to take part in representative government; the working class was eager to play a role in its own affairs, whether in shop committees or in trade unions. Social unrest, at least in Moscow, might have settled into stable institutional channels.

Government policy made this impossible, however. Just as the regime, by its uncompromising short-sightedness, had pushed the railroad union into the political fray, so the government eventually forced the Bolsheviks to make good their rhetorical bravado. In the wake of the manifesto, their call for insurrection seemed inappropriate and doctrinaire. But two months later, their thirst for conflict was satisfied, thanks to the regime's provocative strategy. The Bolsheviks' fixation on armed uprising reflected their conviction that Russian society could not change without the destruction of the state in its existing form, a state dedicated to the frustration of social progress and political life. In fact, Nicholas used violence and repression to undermine the compromise solution to the 1905 crisis and to force a confrontation between absolutes. In so doing, he validated the Bolshevik conception of revolutionary politics as a war between two enemy powers, the state and the party, for mastery over the political arena.

8

THE DAYS OF FREEDOM

Aftermath of the October Manifesto

The October Manifesto provided the conditions for legal political activity: freedom of conscience, speech, assembly, and union, and inviolability of person. Like the majority of workers, the mainstream members of the liberation movement were ready to take advantage of these concessions. But distrust of the government ran deep. The vague provisions for a national Duma satisfied only the most conservative liberationists. Those who found the manifesto acceptable called themselves the party of the October Manifesto, or the Octobrist Party, dedicated to full cooperation with the government.

The Kadets were no less eager to assume political responsibility within an institutional framework. But they shared the skepticism of the socialist left,[1] which viewed the manifesto as a tactical ploy to divide the opposition without altering the power structure of the existing regime. The Kadet leader P. N. Miliukov criticized the decree's ambiguity. It promised that legislation would be subject to the "approval of the Duma," which would participate in the "supervision" of state power. Part of the population was still excluded from the franchise, but the manifesto promised "further development of the principle of general suffrage [to be implemented] by the newly established legislative system." Miliukov wondered if the decree was only a "cunning ruse": "Why these three words 'development,' 'principle,' and 'general' instead of a direct proclamation of 'universal' suffrage? . . . Why did the manifesto speak only of 'approval'? . . . Why the word 'supervision' [over state power] instead of 'control'?"[2]

The Kadets nevertheless agreed to work within the proposed Duma to obtain further reforms.[3] The Union of Unions, by contrast, adopted a

position indistinguishable from that of the Social Democrats. In a resolution passed the very day the manifesto was published, it refused to credit
the government with a serious desire to institute reforms and emphasized
the continued need for revolutionary struggle. The same uncompromising attitude was reflected in the statement of the Moscow Strike Committee, where the influence of the minority Social Democratic and Socialist
Revolutionary members had increased, thanks to a leftward shift in the
dominant Union of Unions.[4]

The manifesto thus did not win the hearts of the political leaders of the
opposition. All groups nevertheless devoted their energies to the practical tasks of political organizing. Mensheviks, Socialist Revolutionaries,
and even Bolsheviks helped lay the foundations for a labor movement
focused on trade-union issues, rather than revolutionary confrontation.
The liberals, for their part, were eager to interpret the regime's intentions in the best possible light. But government policy soon robbed them
of their optimism. The credibility of the extreme left grew in proportion
to the rise in violent conflict and the increase in government repression.
The moderates were caught in the middle. The year's bloody climax was
not the product of left-wing conspiracy. It resulted from the regime's deliberate attempt to frustrate a compromise solution to the political crisis of
1905. This is all the more ironic in view of the popular enthusiasm for the
manifesto itself and for the work of trade-union organization.

The average Moscovite did not at first share the skepticism of opposition leaders. On the morning of October 18, an outburst of general euphoria greeted news of the decree. Crowds filled the streets, people embraced, and flags bedecked the town. Shops were closed. Police were
scarce and did not interfere with the joyful celebration. One journalist, at
least, could not disguise his own exultation: "On the streets and in the
squares, in taverns, restaurants, and bars—wherever one rode or walked
on that day—people were gathered everywhere, in groups of all sizes;
and the assembled throngs were tirelessly harangued by orators [mostly
Social Democrats] perched on makeshift platforms, on chairs, tables, and
upside-down barrels. These were the first free meetings."[5]

In legitimizing the aspirations of the liberation movement, the October
Manifesto seemed to exonerate the participants in the October strike.
Amnesty for political and religious prisoners became the central issue of
the post-manifesto days, in St. Petersburg as well as in Moscow.[6] In
Moscow, the demand for amnesty was endorsed by a chorus of progressive groups, including the City Council, the Moscow University Council,
the Lawyers' Association, and the Kadet Party. They were joined by the
more radical Union of Unions, Union of Workers in the Printing Trade,
and Union of Commercial Employees, as well as the Moscow Strike Com-

mittee, and the revolutionary parties. Along with amnesty, these groups also demanded the abolition of martial law and other emergency legislation as incompatible with guaranteed civil rights.[7]

Neither the Strike Committee nor any of the revolutionary parties, however, had mobilized the enormous crowds that gathered in the central squares and on the boulevards. The crowds were determined to obtain the immediate release of prisoners by exerting direct pressure on the authorities.[8] They were encouraged in this tactic by the fact that public assembly was no longer illegal. On October 18, the assistant police chief pledged not to interfere with street meetings. Rector Manuilov gave his blessings to a crowd of university students gathered in front of the City Council building. Emboldened by these reassurances, a group of 1,500 students and workers resolved to appeal for amnesty directly to the Governor-General in person. As they proceeded up Tver Street, red bunting was visible on every hatband and sleeve. The sounds of the workers' hymn and the revolutionary funeral march were greeted by raised hats and loud hurrahs from crowded windows and sidewalks. In keeping with the new spirit of toleration, the popular mood was genial: as the procession passed by the editorial offices of the Monarchist *Moskovskie vedomosti*, the marchers interrupted their singing for a concert of catcalls, whistling, and laughter, but made no violent threats.[9]

As if to confirm the miraculous transformation of government attitudes, Governor-General Durnovo appeared on his balcony and agreed to release the prisoners arrested in connection with recent events. Despite this assurance, however, the crowd seemed bent on direct action and continued up Tver Street to Strastnaia Square, headed for the Butyrskaia prison. Along the way, the marchers were distracted by the sight of a prisoners' transport van. In a sudden burst of indignation, they tried to seize the van, but were unsuccessful. The incident occurred across the street from Secret Police headquarters. The crowd gave vent to its frustration by throwing rocks at the building and trying to force its way into the court. It was but a moment before the police began shooting. The crowd replied in kind. In the end, two persons lay wounded and two dead.[10]

Undaunted by the first taste of violence in the era of freedom, the marchers proceeded toward the second ring of boulevards. By now, their numbers had grown to tremendous proportions. As many as 10,000 set off down Malaia Dmitrovka toward the prison.[11] The group consisted of students, both male and female, from high schools as well as higher educational institutions, the usual contingent of intelligentsia activists, and a large mass of workers.[12] In the course of the afternoon, authorities released 141 prisoners, who emerged in groups of ten, to the triumphant cries of their liberators. Another crowd, led by three barristers, obtained the release of 80 prisoners at the Taganka prison; they were escorted past the Cossack guard by the Assistant Governor-General, V. F. Dzhunkov-skii.[13]

Meanwhile, the throngs of demonstrators at the Butyrskaia prison, their mission accomplished, turned back toward the center of town. Along the way, another group joined the procession, which by six in the evening had swelled to over 30,000. As they approached the Triumphal Gates at the intersection of Sadovyi Boulevard, the marchers met up with a large group of demonstrators approaching from the direction of Strast-naia Square. The people in this group carried national flags and a portrait of the Tsar. When they demanded that the red-flag bearers step aside, the response was a round of shots. Two of their number fell wounded, and the rest fled in panic. Another crowd at the doors of the Taganka prison, bent on obtaining the release of the remaining prisoners, were less fortunate in their encounter with their antagonists: gunmen hidden in the shadows fired into the crowd, which dispersed in panic.[14]

The apparent immunity that the authorities had granted to the partisans of amnesty had barely lasted the day. The enemies of reform stepped up their attacks against anyone they thought of as responsible for the strike and its unwanted consequences, and the days following the manifesto's publication proved to be even more turbulent than the period of the strike itself. On October 19, there were further clashes between so-called patriotic, or Black Hundred, crowds and groups of students and workers carrying red flags. The most serious incident took place late in the evening in front of the Filippov bakery on Tver Street, where a group of more than 200 persons began beating up workers who refused to doff their hats at the sound of the national hymn. The workers sent to the university for help, and a squad of 20 armed students rushed to their defense. As usual, the question of who fired first was a matter of debate. The police reported that the students had begun shooting as soon as they arrived; the liberal papers contended that the first shots came from the other side. What is certain is that four persons were killed in the exchange, and as many as 15 were wounded.[15]

Official compliance with the new law did not long survive the first confused moments following its announcement. Many Cossack troops and some members of the police force shared the belligerent spirit of the anti-revolutionary throngs. Cossacks especially were known for their indiscriminate use of violence: one squadron, for example, was reported to have attacked a peaceful crowd of women and children gathered on the city's outskirts, leaving one victim dead.[16] Police not only encouraged lo-

cal toughs to beat up students and workers,[17] but eagerly joined in themselves. One witness reported the following incident on the morning of
October 18:

I saw a band of at least 20 city policemen hold and beat a young eighteen-year-old
worker in the presence of the captain of the second Iakimanskii precinct. The
worker's face ran with blood as he tried to ward off the rain of blows with raised
hands. [My woman companion] ran toward the assailants crying "How dare you
hit him, how dare you!" In a flash, we were surrounded by a dozen policemen
with frenzied, brutal faces, who turned on us with raised fists. We fled into the
courtyard of a nearby house to escape them, but there we were caught by other
police and taken to the captain who had presided over the beating of the young
worker; that poor victim had meanwhile been dragged into the police station. "So
you want to be witnesses!" the captain screamed at us. We asked him to arrest us,
but he signaled instead to some officers, who chased us to the street corner with
kicks and shoves, until we at last found refuge in a courtyard.[18]

The police authorities did not trouble to conceal their sympathies or
apologize for the actions of their subordinates. On October 18, Police
Chief Medem had asked his captains not to obstruct right-wing demonstrations. Indeed, he had instructed them to do more than that: "If patriotic sentiments should be expressed in public," they were told, "do not
merely refrain from interfering, but actively intervene to protect the patriots from attack by hooligans."[19] The captain of the second Tver precinct
complained that public opinion was interfering with the fulfillment of
these instructions. He regretted the narrow escape of a student who had
apparently fired into a nationalist crowd during one of the numerous confrontations of October 19. The captain explained that "troops had not
been summoned [to aid the policemen in hot pursuit of the fleeing stu-
dent], because the soldiers would without doubt have joined with the police in defending the nationalist group, a bloody clash would inevitably
have resulted, and the papers would then have been able to report the
next day that Black Hundreds led by police were responsible for shooting
at a crowd of demonstrators."[20]

The police defended the so-called patriots, and the liberal press denounced government complicity in right-wing violence. For supporters of
political reform, as well as for the advocates of revolution, the murder of
Nikolai Bauman came to symbolize the consequences of the unholy alliance between crown and mob. Bauman, a Bolshevik activist and veterinarian by training, had only just been freed from prison as part of the
post-manifesto amnesty. On the evening of October 18, he was among the
crowd at the Taganka prison demanding the release of those still being
detained there when he was shot and then beaten to death by a worker of

Black Hundred sympathies.[21] A group of lawyers, including Prince D. I. Shakhovskoi, complained to the Governor-General of police and Cossack brutality. They convinced Durnovo to keep troops and policemen away from the funeral ceremonies. A delegation of seven councilmen, headed by Prince V. M. Golitsyn, the mayor, endorsed their request.[22]

Bauman's funeral took on a demonstrational character reminiscent of the October 3 services for Prince Trubetskoi. Students and workers gathered around the Technical Institute at noon on October 20. The Social Democrats had not honored the late rector with their presence at his funeral. Now their organizations dominated the occasion, and their slogans were carried aloft on banners that read "Down with autocracy!," "Long live the provisional revolutionary government and the democratic republic!," and "Long live socialism!" The Bolshevik message was embroidered in "ornate" golden script on a "heavy velvet" background. The Menshevik standard had been hastily stitched together the night before by the wife of a party militant. (A group of anarchists, in even more haste, had simply chalked their slogans on swatches of black calico.) Radicals were not the only ones for whom Bauman's death had political significance. Representatives of various professional unions, including those of the engineers, lawyers, railroad employees, pharmacy clerks, and printers, took part in the ceremonies. The Kadet Party also sent delegates. The liberals displayed a poster that said: "To the victim of a freedom without guarantees."[23]

The marchers set out from the Technical Institute toward the center of the city, heading for the Vagankovskoe Cemetery, located directly across town beyond the Presnia Gates. Students formed defense squads to protect the procession against a possible Black Hundred attack. One of these bands preceded the coffin. Another, wearing Red Cross insignia, brought up the rear. There were as many as 100,000 marchers, of whom at least 10,000 were railroad workers and employees. They walked ten abreast, carrying wreaths and singing the funeral march and the "Marseillaise." The procession was enclosed by a chain of monitors linked arm in arm, mostly students and nurses, but also some soldiers. Red flags decked the houses along the route. A group of 30 army officers and soldiers joined the throng as it crossed Theater Square. As it passed the Conservatory on Bol'shaia Nikitskaia Street, the crowd acquired an orchestra. No unpleasant incident marred the occasion, and the procession reached the cemetery at eight in the evening.[24]

In contrast to Trubetskoi's staid burial service, the tone at Bauman's graveside was strident. There was no priest in attendance, and the widow's impassioned cry for revenge served as the funeral oration. As on the earlier occasion, most of the mourners quickly dispersed. A group of students, numbering up to 3,000, left together and walked silently back toward the university, which they reached at about eleven o'clock. Meanwhile, a mob of some 1,000 drunken men carrying national flags had gathered around the Manège, across from the university. When they saw the first students approaching, they began shooting. The student defense squad shot back. Their companions, caught in the crossfire, tried desperately to force their way into the locked university gates. As they struggled for safety, they heard rifle fire. The Cossacks quartered in the Manège were shooting in their direction. Students screamed in terror and fell to the ground while trying to flee. Six finally lay dead, and over 30 were seriously wounded.[25] Once again, ceremony had ended in bloodshed.

In the days that followed, the bloodshed increased. On October 22, the toll of innocent victims reached a new high: at least 14 persons were killed and 20 wounded.[26] Drunken crowds roamed the streets, shoving pedestrians off the sidewalks. Lone students were the favorite target of the "patriots"; conspicuous in their uniforms, they were often mobbed and beaten, to the enthusiastic cheers of bystanders.[27] A particularly bloodthirsty bunch actually bludgeoned a student to death and threw him into the river. The case was vividly recounted in *Russkie vedomosti*:

After hearing a speech delivered by [the] Governor-General . . . from the balcony of his house, the crowd carrying national flags and a portrait of the Tsar was given special permission to continue on its way. As it neared *Kamennyi most* [Stone Bridge], the crowd came across a lone student riding in a carriage, whom it proceeded to drag to the pavement. The student shot at his attackers three times in self-defense, killing one and wounding two. . . . The crowd thereupon grabbed him and kicked him from all sides. Cursing the already bloody victim, one of his assailants shot the student three times, at which the rest of the group turned to run and were restrained only by the threats of their ringleaders. The student had survived the shots and lay moaning on the ground. Whipped to a frenzy of brutality, the crowd continued to beat the body and then, shouting excitedly, dragged it by the arms along the street, head downward, until they reached the middle of the bridge, when they threw the body into the river. . . . The student, who was still alive when he hit the water, raised his head several times; but by the time he had reached the foot of the bridge, only his clothing was visible. The crowd meanwhile descended along the inclined bank and began pelting the body with stones, until it sank out of view.[28]

Such futile attempts at self-defense as the student's impulsive revolver shots only increased the fury of the hostile mob. Sometimes provocateurs deliberately stirred up animosity by mimicking this desperate tactic. The papers reported that witnesses had seen men dressed up as workers who had approached patriotic groups and fired into their midst with blank cartridges.[29] Contemporaries were not sure who made up the Black Hundred gangs. People assumed they were mainly shopkeepers, such as the butchers of Okhotnyi Riad.[30] Watchmen and concierges also counted for a good number. But the social stereotype did not always hold: in at least one case, a student was assailed by a crowd of striking waiters.[31]

Violence and vandalism were not confined to the right-wing fringe or to the downtown area. Gangs of striking workers did their share of intimidation and property damage in working-class districts. When strike activity picked up again after October 17, it often led to conflict among the workers themselves. One such volatile situation developed in Presnia (III), in the vicinity of several large plants. Crowds of strikers had gathered near the Presnia Gates on October 19 and set about the familiar task of rousing their indifferent or timid comrades. Workers from the adjacent Grachev, Pal'm, and Sokov metalworks (employing 400, 180, and 150 men, respectively) were easily enticed into taking to the streets. Their employers were all too relieved to see the possibility of damage avoided. The Mamontov varnish factory (500 workers) had already struck, but the giant Prokhorov Trekhgornaia textile mill, which had recently shut down on administrative order, was once again in operation. The crowd approached the plant and demanded that the 6,000 workers come out to join them. Police were already on hand inside the factory and began shooting at the besiegers. They replied with a few revolver shots and a hail of bricks directed at the long facade of factory windows. Meanwhile, the Prokhorov workers had begun to leave the factory. They joined with the crowd, which swelled to 7,000 strong and began moving toward the university, singing the "Marseillaise" and crying "Long live the democratic republic!"[32]

In other cases, workers were less easily persuaded. Indeed, attempts to recruit them sometimes ended in violent clashes between the proselytizing strikers and recalcitrant members of their own professions.[33] Nor were all factory owners as amenable as the few in Presnia to seeing their workers lured into the street. On October 20, some 2,000 striking workers, mostly women from the tobacco firm of Dukat, approached the Bostandzhoglo tobacco factory in Basmannaia (V). Fifty watchmen and cabinetmakers wielding axes and spades attacked the unarmed crowd. Police and factory officials did nothing to interfere, creating the impression that the management had welcomed the assault.[34]

Crowds of workers continued to prowl the streets of industrial districts during the first weeks of November, trying to close down functioning enterprises. They often broke windows and did other damage to factory property, but rarely attacked individuals unless provoked. Police Chief Medem instructed district captains to put a stop to worker violence:

Groups of strikers and hooligans have been permitted to stalk the streets unimpeded, creating havoc and growing ever more daring as their numbers continue to swell. Such groups must be prevented from assembling and must be dispersed most energetically.

. . .

[You must] send out mounted detachments and have them behave in such a manner as to destroy any desire on the part of these hooligans ever to appear on the streets again.[35]

Curiously enough, the police themselves recorded few incidents of strike-connected violence.[36] There is no doubt, however, that red and black were guilty of similar misconduct. Crowds on both sides included large numbers of young boys and drunken workers.[37] The Black Hundreds destroyed private property, broke windows, and interfered with the pursuit of commerce on downtown streets, leaving the factory districts at the disposition of local strikers. The rightist crowds were far larger than the crowds of strikers, thanks largely to police recruitment. They were also more inclined to inflict personal injury. By October 22, the defenders of Tsar and country had become such a menace that Police Chief Medem finally told his captains to stop them from congregating.[38] On October 23, the City Council complained to Medem that police were still encouraging mob violence. The Baron insisted, however, that the press misrepresented his subordinates' behavior.[39]

Medem himself did not encourage these tactics.[40] Indeed, he was driven to condemn rightist fanatics for compromising the monarchist cause that he personally espoused:

Evil persons are trying at all costs to sow chaos in Moscow and to provoke mutual slaughter. To this end they have been distributing printed leaflets, endorsed by the so-called Russian People [russkie liudi], under the banner of "Faith, Tsar, and Fatherland," that urge honest people to take violent measures against the subversives [kramol'niki]. Only the most ferocious enemy of Russia would encourage such criminal actions. Let all be warned that I myself shall take care of the real subversives, but that summary justice [rasprava], especially with such blasphemous justification, will not be tolerated.[41]

Despite Medem's reassurances, the public continued to distrust the police. On October 21, police officers made the rounds of the Zamoskvorech'e (VI) and Gorodskaia (I) districts, recruiting participants for a patriotic demonstration. Thousands of the city's concierges worked as spies for the police, and they were therefore expected to show up in the line of duty.[42] As news of pogroms in other cities reached Moscow, panic gripped the Jewish community. Rumors spread that the homes of Jews and intellectuals had already been singled out for attack.[43] Crowds were seen running down Tver Street yelling "Beat up the Jews!"[44] As the police officers went busily about mobilizing the concierges for mob action, they were at the same time trying to carry out Medem's instructions to establish protective surveillance of Jewish residences. When they began taking down house numbers to this end, they only increased the terror of the Jewish population, now convinced of the realism of its fears, and fully as suspicious of the police as it was of the mob.[45]

A week after their first meeting with the City Council, concerned residents once again appealed to city officials to enforce law and order by authorizing a citizens' militia. At a special session on October 21, the council also heard numerous petitions demanding that the Cossacks be removed from their quarters in the Manège.[46] A group of barristers concluded their appeal with the warning that they would themselves take up arms and turn "to other organizations" for help with self-defense if the council refused to act. The council asked the Governor-General to move the Cossacks to a less central location, and Durnovo readily granted the request. The larger issues were harder to resolve. The council wanted Count S. Iu. Witte, now chairman of the Council of Ministers, to abolish the office of chief of police (gradonachal'nik) and put the city administration in charge of the police. The council further recommended that policemen be indicted for illegal conduct, and that the Secret Police be abolished. Witte referred the petitioners to D. F. Trepov, Assistant Minister of Internal Affairs in charge of the police. Trepov promised to look into police ties with the Black Hundreds in Moscow, but he disapproved of the plan to place city police in civilian hands. In any case, he said, he had no power to do so.

Even though it was clear that the council's request for control over the regular police force would not be met, the councilmen were still reluctant to accept a nonbureaucratic alternative. Some thought unarmed guards should be posted at public meetings, but few supported the idea of armed detachments. On October 25, the council finally voted against forming a militia, with only eight dissenting voices.[47]

In November, the council became increasingly conservative. On November 17, it elected as mayor the Octobrist leader N. I. Guchkov to replace Prince Golitsyn, who retired because of illness. On November 29, it refused to condemn the death penalty for the Sevastopol mutineers, the sailors of the Black Sea Fleet who on November 12 had defied their officers in the name of freedom of speech and the constituent assembly. "At the beginning of the liberation movement," remarked one councilman, Count S. L. Tolstoi, "we [the City Council] occupied a prominent place in its ranks. Now we have apparently abandoned this position."[48]

The underlying conservatism and political timidity of the City Council contributed to the eventual polarization of the opposition movement in Moscow. The council was in a position to bridge the widening gap between working-class and liberal politics by providing what might be called a civic alternative. The Moscow political community, from far left to right-of-center, more than once asked the council to legitimate and underwrite popular self-defense. The majority of petitioners wanted only to guarantee law and order and to protect private property. But even on these terms, the council refused to become politically involved. In refusing to play a creative role on the municipal level, the councilmen deprived the progressive forces of their only existing alternative to illegal activity and to partisan fractionalization.

Anticipating the council's final decision against forming a militia, the Union of Unions met on October 21 to consider taking independent action. Some members thought it futile to expect the existing institutions to solve the crisis. As one speaker put it, "In recent days it has become clear that many rights must be seized by society itself. Meetings used to be prohibited, but they continued to take place without permission and finally became legal; amnesty was not accorded, but seized. Thus we must also act on the question of self-defense. The Union of Unions must take the initiative." [49] Other speakers urged the Union of Unions to reject any notion of armed uprising. It must be careful to consider self-defense only in the strictest sense. [50] Still others remained critical of privately organized peacekeeping forces. In the end, the meeting reached no decision. Like the City Council, the Union of Unions contented itself with petitioning for removal of the Cossacks from the Manège. Its hesitancy, like the council's, reflected the typical liberal discomfort with violent forms of political action, even as a defense against violence.

Other professional groups, including many who were officially members of the Union of Unions, were not so put off by the thought of violence. Calling their own meeting on October 28, they formed an organization called the Moscow Committee for Self-Defense. [51] The committee announced its purpose on November 3:

Citizens! In recent days Russia has experienced the kind of horrors before which even Turkish bestiality pales. Wild crowds have destroyed homes, murdered passersby, and then torn them to pieces and thrown them into the water, or burned them alive. The majority of these crowds all over Russia are "dark people"—the benighted masses. They know not what they do.

Under the old order, the people had no legal protection against their oppressors. Those who benefited from that state of affairs are now busy inciting the ignorant . . . to vent their anger against persons who are trying to help the poor and uneducated make a better life. Once aroused, the mob even turns its rage gainst those who merely sympathize with the people's struggle and against those who are simply neutral, who stand aside but nevertheless refuse to join the Black Hundreds. Everyone is in danger! Life has become intolerable for all!

All who value freedom and happiness and care about the suffering of our people must help put an end to these horrors. Thousands of people are ready to lay down their lives for the cause. Our primary duty is to give them all the aid we can muster, especially financial assistance, so that fighters for the popular cause will be able to arm themselves against possible enemy attack. We must also strive to counter reactionary propaganda and make the benighted masses aware of the fact that a true popular government is in the interests of all classes. Last, we must get together ourselves, in our neighborhoods, on our own streets, and rally our own forces to prevent hooliganism and protect the innocent against violence.[52]

Many responsible citizens felt it was up to them to combat the reigning lawlessness. A group of merchants appealed to the police chief to protect them from bands of Black Hundreds who entered their shops and disrupted business. They complained that Cossacks refused to intervene when mobs went on nighttime window-breaking sprees on downtown streets. If the authorities continued to stand idly by, the storekeepers said, they would arm their clerks and see to their own defense. Shopkeepers on one central street eventually organized a permanent guard of 30 to 40 men to patrol the area on day and night shifts.[53]

Students, the group most vulnerable to attack on the streets, had already begun organizing their own defense before the end of the general strike. They openly collected money for arms at mass meetings. During the so-called siege of October 15–16, they turned the university into a makeshift fortress, complete with barricades and a military-like chain of command. Police reported that the students had accumulated as many as 300 revolvers.[54] This is undoubtedly an exaggerated figure, but it confirms the fact that the financial donations had already been put to use. The University Council officially closed the university on November 7, and it remained under armed guard.[55] Dormitories quickly emptied as many students returned home. A good 100 of them nevertheless remained in the buildings, which they used as an arsenal, field headquarters, and primitive explosives laboratory. They held shooting practice in the Engineering and Agriculture institutes, as well as in the university courtyards.[56]

The existence of special student self-defense squads, known as *boevye druzhiny*, had been common knowledge for some time. These small bands of students armed with revolvers had proudly escorted the Bauman funeral procession. In the days that followed, they were occupied in guarding mass meetings from attack. On October 23, for example, a large Black Hundred crowd besieged the Engineering Institute, where a meeting of students and 500 Brest railroad employees was in progress. The

hostile mob attempted to break down the gates, while throwing stones a
the windows and threatening to beat up anyone they could get thei
hands on. Students in the building's courtyard responded by firing int(
the air, but the assailants were undeterred. It was only when the student:
shot directly into the crowd that the attackers drew back. Six were killec
in the incident and at least 14 wounded.[57]

There is no evidence that students ever attacked first. To be sure, Bol
shevik leaflets distributed immediately after the October Manifesto, be
fore Bauman's funeral, had warned the proletariat not to rest on its lau
rels. The workers should arm themselves straightaway to prepare for the
overthrow of tsarism and the establishment of a truly popular constituen
assembly. "Long live socialism!" cried the Bolsheviks. "Long live the
armed uprising and the people's militia!"[58] After Bauman's murder, the
Mensheviks also endorsed the call for an armed uprising as the only re
course against Cossack brutality and Black Hundred lawlessness.[59] Bu
the vehemence of radical rhetoric in this period was unaccompanied by a
correspondingly aggressive plan of action.

The Social Democrats' commitment to insurrection did not prevent
them from recognizing that self-defense was a more important problem
for the time being than the insistence on ideological purity. As a first
move toward minimizing political differences on the left, the two Social
Democratic factions in St. Petersburg joined together on October 18 un
der the rubric of the United Federative Council (Federativnyi ob'edinen-
nyi sovet).[60] The Moscow Social Democrats followed their example, forming a local council of the same name and stressing their concern for issues
common to socialist and liberal groups alike. Their literature denounced
the government in moralistic terms for complicity in mob violence and
condemned municipal authorities for failing to ensure the safety of the
city's population.[61]

The Bolsheviks in particular distrusted their liberal allies for having
welcomed the constitutional compromise.[62] All the same, the united Social Democratic factions did not shrink from appealing to the class enemy
for the distribution of its more ample resources:

In looking for ways to finance the arming of the proletariat, we cannot limit our
search to the proletariat itself and persons sympathetic to its struggle. We must
demand aid from the bourgeois classes as well, and from their organizations, the
Dumas, zemstvos, bourgeois unions and parties. Life itself has provided us with a
most powerful argument, highly convincing to these classes: the organization and
arming of the "Black Hundreds" under the banner of patriotism and moderation
("freedom and the Tsar"), invariably assuming the form of plunder, robbery, Jewish and Armenian pogroms, and assaults on members of the intelligentsia, and
students. No matter how much the bourgeoisie fears the proletariat, part of it will

certainly understand that only the armed force of the proletariat, and none other, can protect society from rogues and robbers.[63]

The bourgeois classes hardly needed convincing; they had already taken the initiative. But it did not follow that they would turn to the working class to solve the problem for them. On the contrary; they tried desperately to persuade their own civic representatives to forestall this eventuality by acting on their own.

The Social Democrats differed from their allies to the right in their enthusiasm for measures that the more conservative groups saw as unavoidable but inherently undesirable. Where the Committee for Self-Defense spoke of social pacification, the Social Democrats talked of revenge. Where the Union of Unions decried adventurism, the United Federative Council envisioned an aggressive revolutionary strategy. For the time being, this was merely a theoretical belligerence. The Social Democrats were as yet unwilling to launch their followers on a foolhardy course of self-sacrifice. They even advised them to refrain from further public demonstrations, such as the Bauman funeral, to avoid falling victim to right-wing aggression.[64]

Organization Fever

The Moscow Social Democrats were in no position to follow up their bold rhetoric. The general strike had been losing support even before the October Manifesto was announced. It fell apart rapidly thereafter. The service and white-collar workers were the first to return to work. Most were already back on the job by the afternoon of October 18, when the Strike Committee officially terminated the strike. Train service resumed on most lines. Electricity, telephone, post and telegraph, and horse-drawn trams were soon back in operation. Pharmacy clerks and other city workers announced they would go back to work as soon as possible.[65] Many factory workers also went back to work in the week following the manifesto. Some individual strikes were not resolved, however, and new factories continued to join the movement even after the Social Democrats finally called off the strike on October 22.

Despite the persistence of violent conflict, labor leaders did not actively pursue the issue of self-defense in the wake of the manifesto. Instead, they turned their attention to the work of building a permanent labor movement. The strike itself created an interest in union organizing among many shop and factory workers. For two months after October 17, the government permitted virtual freedom of assembly. This made the establishment of legal trade unions a real possibility for the first time in Russian history. While on the one hand police were busy recruiting

neighborhood toughs to defend the principle of autocracy, on the othe
they tolerated a rash of openly political meetings. In theory, the polic
still had veto power over proposed public gatherings, but they rarel
used it. When the City Council informed Medem of their decision to al
low the Socialist Revolutionaries to meet on municipal premises, the
Baron chastized the councilmen for seeming to legitimize a subversive or
ganization.[66] And on one occasion, he vetoed a gathering of unemployed
workers. In at least one case, police even broke up a meeting of 2,00
concierges, presumably a move designed to protect their network o
neighborhood informers.[67]

These instances were exceptional in the two months or so after the Oc
tober Manifesto was published, a period that came to be known as the
Days of Freedom. There were over 400 officially approved public gather
ings between October 17 and December 8. People also met in factorie
and in private residences, without permission or publicity. Over half the
registered meetings were concerned with trade-union affairs. Man
formed the basis for union organization. Indeed, unions sprang up like
mushrooms after a rain, as the saying went.[68]

When the general strike ended, there were already 20-odd organiza
tions in existence that had taken the definite form of trade unions.[69] Dur
ing the Days of Freedom, another 50 groups, both white- and blue-collar
took the first steps toward unionization. Of these, perhaps 40 establishec
functioning organizations. Workers in other trades met without specific
goals in mind or without achieving concrete results. Still others decidec
to join existing unions. Two groups of retail employees, for example
joined forces after the October strike and formed an umbrella organiza
tion, the Moscow Union of Commercial and Industrial Employees, which
adopted the catchy informal title "Strength in Unity." The union attractec
seven additional groups during November.

The shop clerks in Strength in Unity showed an unusual degree of co
hesion. Most unions formed in this period were confined to narrowly de
fined trades. For example, the workers in the machine-building plants
and large textile mills did not organize successfully; but gold- and sil
versmiths, galloon- and braidmakers, tinsmiths, and gold thread spinners
each established separate associations. The reasons for this fragmentatior
are various. The prominent Menshevik labor organizer P. N. Kolokol'ni
kov offers two explanations, the absence of centralized leadership and the
rivalry between competing radical activists:

Such a mosaic [of small craft unions] reflected, on the one hand, the organizationa
fever of the Days of Freedom. Energetic individuals in each profession began set
ting up unions without knowing what was going on elsewhere, in other profes-

sions, and sometimes in other parts of the city. Thus, the territory of the purse-makers' union coincided with the Zariad'e [the area of small shops located behind the Kremlin]; it included about 100 workers who already knew each other well and met regularly in a certain favorite tavern. . . . The union of boxmakers or parquetry workers was the geographical offspring of the Lefortovo district. But another important cause of fragmentation was the party, or rather *fractional, affiliation of union organizers*.[70]

The woodworking trade suffered particularly from the effects of sectarian competition. The Bolsheviks, as we have noted, founded the joiners' union in September, as an outgrowth of the carpenters' strike. The membership came primarily from large furniture factories; workers at Shmidt in Presnia (area III) provided the union's central core. In November, Mensheviks and Socialist Revolutionary activists helped set up four independent unions as alternatives to the joiners' union: Mensheviks organized the turners and the toymakers; either Mensheviks or Socialist Revolutionaries organized the parquetry workers and the boxmakers.

There was no logical connection between the ideological affiliation of the trade unions and the occupations they represented. Although the Socialist Revolutionaries were not active in unions of industrial-type workers, they were popular in specific factories (the Prokhorov cotton mill, for example). It would be wrong to draw any conclusions about the character of workers who followed Menshevik or Bolshevik leadership. It is doubtful whether they understood the difference between the two factions (which, it must be recalled, had reunited as of October 18), and just as doubtful whether they selected their sponsors for ideological reasons. Some plant deputies at Prokhorov considered themselves Socialist Revolutionaries, others were close to the Mensheviks. "The fact is," recalls the Menshevik party organizer for the Presnia area, "that in the workshops and departments, votes were not cast for political positions, but for leading workers best known for their energy and practicality."[71] The worker-deputies may have been able to justify their own partisanship, but their followers had not judged them on that basis. They had voted for individuals they trusted. To delegate authority through democratic procedure was itself a political act, but it was not necessarily (and the sources suggest, rarely) accompanied by clear notions of the meaning of these actions or of their potentially far-reaching consequences.

The parties, for their part, did not discriminate on sociological grounds in their choice of targets. Several white-collar and service groups, despite their petty-bourgeois stigma, ended up in Bolshevik-led unions: waiters, office clerks and bookkeepers, bookshop employees. Some shop clerks fell under Menshevik influence (Strength in Unity, for example); others were liberal or Socialist Revolutionary. Socialist Revolutionaries also organized the chimneysweeps and the tavern employees. In the manufacturing sector, Bolsheviks cornered the metalworking trades (except for the Moscow-Brest shop workers, led by Mensheviks). Mensheviks dominated among the printers, ribbonmakers, tobacco workers, tea packers, and several woodworking groups. The Bolsheviks organized the bakers, candymakers (inconclusively), and joiners. The tailors followed the Mensheviks, the shoe- and bootmakers the Socialist Revolutionaries. Most of the unions established by the Mensheviks and Socialist Revolutionaries, however, were officially nonpartisan.

Another important source of union fragmentation was the artisan guild tradition. In 1905, workers with specific craft skills were the first to organize, just as they were first to strike in concert. The guild tradition persisted even among workers who had no relation to formal guild associations but practiced trades with a history of craft identity. Of the 23 artisan guild categories that existed in midcentury, 16 were represented in the trade unions that took form during 1905.[72] These 16, moreover, did not include the craft unions of other artisanal groups, such as tinsmiths, bronzesmiths, and velvet and embroidery workers, which were numerous but typically very small. Skilled workers distinguished among themselves with a fine eye. No doubt the exclusionary mentality of the guild tradition influenced the sectional character of many of these craft associations.[73]

Traditional patterns of group identification may have encouraged union organization among certain trades, but evidence shows that workers in the craft unions expressed a desire to break with the traditions and conditions of artisanal labor. Protests against the unfairness of piecework and against the obligation to live and eat on shop premises were common. Bakers and tailors were among the most vocal in lodging such complaints. The Union of Workers in All Guilds of the Clothing Industry declared its solidarity with the proletariat and demanded the abolition of piecework. Gold- and silversmiths likewise demanded the right to live on their own.[74]

The history of the precious-metal workers is instructive in this regard: it illustrates the transition from guild to trade-union principles involved in many of these fledgling organizations. In September, Bolshevik organizers helped the gold- and silversmiths conduct a successful strike, out of which came the nucleus of a trade union. In November, the smiths made overtures to the jewelers, who had their own organization, and invited them to join in a combined union of workers in the precious-metal trades. The two groups met in a tavern near the Fabergé factory (250 workers) in Miasnitskaia (area I). The jewelers did not understand why they should be obliged to exclude shop owners and foremen from the proposed union, since these had been part of the familiar guild association. Several days of argument were necessary to get them to agree to this condition. Although the combined union was not affiliated with any one political party, the charter included the Social Democratic minimum program as part of its demands. Their time-honored assumptions only recently shaken, the jewelers were in no position to understand the relevance of Social Democratic ideas to their own professional concerns. Again, it took energetic argument on the part of the gold- and silversmiths, or their leaders, to overcome the jewelers' resistance. Several thousand workers gathered in the Aquarium Theater on November 27 to celebrate the union's new, restructured constitution. They elected a board, which in turn chose delegates to the Moscow Soviet, and they concluded the meeting by singing the "Marseillaise." In name and symbol, this was a proletarian trade union, but, in fact, it was an amphibious creation: pointed in the direction of Social Democracy, perhaps, but still firmly rooted in the habits and assumptions of traditional social relations.[75]

Some of the strongest and largest Moscow unions in 1905 consisted of skilled craftsmen employed in factory settings. The ribbonmakers' union, for example, grew out of a strike committee formed at the Gandshin and Virts plant in Rogozhskaia (area V, 525 workers).[76] A strike at the Alekseev, Vishniakov, and Shamshin mill (500 workers, also in Rogozhskaia) generated the core of the Union of Workers in Gold Thread Production.[77] The joiners' union was centered at the Shmidt furniture factory (260 workers, in Presnia) and the bakers' organization at the main Filippov branch on Tver Street (385 workers). The tailors' union drew its strength from the larger shops.[78] The printers' union was centered at the Sytin plant (1,110 workers). This pattern reinforces the impression that the most militant and craft-conscious groups in the working class were artisanal trades undergoing the change from traditional to factory-type production.

That factory organization should have promoted militancy among the privileged factory strata appears, at first sight, paradoxical. Students of the Russian labor movement, such as S. Ainzaft, have argued that the small-shop organization of artisanal trades encouraged unionization because such workers lacked the framework for collective action supplied by the industrial plant itself. Indeed, the majority of factory laborers, as we have noted, did not join trade unions. When large metal works or textile mills went on strike, the workers formed plant committees, but these typically did not survive the particular conflict or transcend the individual enterprise. Tobacco workers constituted an exception to this rule. Largely unskilled and concentrated in a handful of substantial plants, they showed remarkable solidarity, followed the lead of interplant committees, sustained protracted strike actions, and established a viable trade union.

Yet the first workers to organize along professional lines that often coincided with traditional occupational categories were not the dispersed artisans, but the skilled workers who, like their unskilled fellows, found
themselves massed together in industrial plants. Although it is not always
clear whether such workers were ex-artisans or whether they had simply
learned their trade on the job or as factory apprentices, the available evidence (as we saw in Chapter Two) suggests that the bulk of them did not
have previous small-shop experience. If they formed trade unions, it was
not because they had learned the advantages of organization while employed in a traditional setting. Rather, the skilled industrial workers and
the small-shop artisans shared a sense of pride in their skills and a sense of
identification with a craft that predisposed them both to want to defend
their personal dignity and at the same time to think in collective terms.
Certain shared disadvantages, moreover, caused both groups to rankle at
their lot: the factory elite suffered along with the small-shop artisan from
the pressures and abuses of piecework and excessive overtime (factory
legislation notwithstanding).

But if the small-shop and factory-based craftsmen shared certain traits
and experiences that might have stoked their interest in trade unions, the
circumstances of factory work seem to have provided the decisive impetus
to organization. Despite the existence of small shop units within the
plant, the ultimate responsibility for management policy lay not with the
foreman, but with the firm's directors. The skilled worker tended to look
down on the common laborer, yet he could not deny that the two of them
were subject to the same managerial regime: security controls, surveillance, paydays, fines. This, along with the remoteness of factory owners, may have discouraged workers from identifying with their employers, an identification facilitated by the close personal relations typical of
old-fashioned artisan shops. The modest economic circumstances of many
master-artisans and subcontractors, as well as a tradition (though now
mostly theoretical) of upward mobility in the trade, also tended to blur
status distinctions in the small-shop context.

At the same time, factory workers enjoyed many advantages that the
artisans in small shops lacked. Enterprises under the jurisdiction of the
Factory Inspectorate were obliged by law to limit work hours, overtime,
and female and child labor. Their workers had recourse to official grievance procedures, at least in principle. Consequently, factory workers had
a clearer sense of their legal rights with respect to management, since factory legislation, however inadequate, was more rigorous and better en-
forced than the regulations governing artisanal labor.[79] Moreover, the
skilled factory worker was economically better off than the artisan, and
was thus in a better position to fight for his rights. The skilled factory

worker also exercised a position of leadership within the plant hierarchy. The industrial environment thus prepared the skilled worker to assume the initiative both in rousing his unskilled fellows and in mobilizing the more dispersed members of his trade.

It is also possible that the factory formed the cornerstone of the craft unions simply because it facilitated contact between radical activists and large numbers of skilled workers concentrated in one place. This explanation, like the others, must remain a matter of speculation. Social Democratic and Socialist Revolutionary rhetoric was almost always couched in terms of "working-class" or "proletarian" interests, and in the virtual absence of nonideological memoirs, we cannot say for certain what the workers themselves actually thought. Yet one fact is clear: the vast majority of trade unions in the manufacturing sector followed craft, not industrial, lines. The modern dimension of the worker's experience (the factory) may have been crucial in preparing him for innovative behavior (the planned strike, the labor union), yet traditional criteria still shaped the terms of his self-definition and his loyalties.

In addition to these structural and sociological considerations, timing helped determine the character of the new unions. Many of the organizations inaugurated in the Days of Freedom remained weak because they appeared after the fall strike wave had already peaked, and their existence was soon cut short by the outbreak of armed conflict in December. A long period of labor struggle was necessary to consolidate grass-roots support for working-class organizations. Solid, integrated unions usually did not grow out of the poststrike meetings. Only about 15 unions, in addition to the All-Russian Railroad Union, had 500 or more members by November, and most of them had been formed before the October strike (see Appendix B). Indeed, many of the unions that emerged after the strike were hardly more permanent than the meetings that ratified their existence:

These were mainly organizations of professional and political agitation. A group of the most energetic and conscious workers in each profession would work out a charter, usually based on a readily available model. They would announce a meeting that would draw several hundred participants; when the charter had been read and adopted, they considered the union to have been founded. It is clear that such organizations were not distinguished by great solidity, but under conditions prevailing in Moscow at the time, the unions played a significant political role.[80]

There was no central leadership to coordinate the trade-union movement in this period: to consolidate small units, prevent redundancy, and set nationwide policy.[81] Professional labor organizers felt the need for such a framework. Their first attempts at centralizing trade-union leadership dated back to the lull between the September and October strike movements. A series of meetings, known as the First All-Russian Conference of Representatives of Professional Unions, took place in Moscow on September 24, and October 1, 6, and 7.[82] The meetings produced the rudiments of an organization that helped instruct workers in the task of union organizing, but never exercised political leadership during 1905.

The conference was the brainchild of the organizer of the Kharkov Mutual Aid Society for Artisanal Laborers, A. A. Evdokimov, a former Social Democrat of Economist tendencies, now sympathetic to the liberation movement.[83] The so-called Economists represented the right wing of the Social Democratic movement. They emphasized trade-union work at the expense of revolutionary political organization. Some former Economists eventually found themselves in the liberal camp. It was thus natural for Evdokimov to cooperate with the predominantly liberal Museum for Assistance to Labor in launching his project. In fact, the museum's directors not only organized the conference, but personally presided over the meetings, which took place on the museum's premises.[84] Neither liberals nor bread-and-butter unionists like Evdokimov viewed labor unions as an instrument of revolutionary politics. They were interested in a stable, not a volatile, working-class movement.

The majority of conference members, however, were socialist activists. Twenty-five groups sent delegates: 19 of these were trade unions or mutual-aid societies, one was a group of watchmakers, and five were factory committees from large machine-building plants. Ten of the unions represented blue-collar workers. Seven of them were organized by the Social Democrats. These included the original groups in the short-lived Council of the Five Professions: bakers and joiners (Bolshevik-led); printers, tobacco factory workers, and machinists from the Moscow-Brest railroad shops (Menshevik-led). The other two, both metalworkers' unions (precious-metal workers and technicians), were under Bolshevik influence. The three non–Social Democratic blue-collar unions were the Moscow Union of Mechanical Workers (the remnants of the Zubatovite metalworkers' union) and two printers' organizations, one right-wing and one liberal.

All five of the individual factory committees were affiliated with the Social Democrats, four with the Bolsheviks, and the other with the Mensheviks. The watchmakers' political leanings are unknown.

The remaining nine organizations were predominantly white collar. These included the Socialist Revolutionary/liberal–sponsored All-Russian Railroad Union, All-Russian Union of Postal and Telegraph Employees, and Corporation of Workers and Low-Ranking Employees in the Moscow

City Administration. Of the six clerical and service workers' unions, three (of office workers and shop clerks) were liberal or Socialist Revolutionary, one (food shop employees) Menshevik, and one (waiters) Bolshevik; in one case (hairdressers), the affiliation is unknown.

In sum, the Social Democrats controlled nine unions and five factory committees, and the Socialist Revolutionaries and liberals seven unions, almost all in the white-collar and service categories;[85] two organizations had right-wing sponsorship, and the affiliation of two others is unknown. Of the seven leading conference organizers, three were Social Democrats and four were either liberals or nonrevolutionary trade unionists.[86]

Two basic issues occupied the delegates at these preliminary meetings. The first was the question of trade-union organization itself: how to increase membership and exercise leadership on a grass-roots level. This embroiled Menshevik and Bolshevik delegates in a sectarian debate over how much weight to give economic grievances as against demands of a political nature in building a workers' movement, a debate that remained unresolved. The second issue concerned the unification of the labor movement, which the delegates hoped to accomplish by calling a national congress for December 1905. Here liberals joined with the Mensheviks in opposing the Bolshevik plan to invite only proletarian organizations of a recognizably trade-union type. Given the scarcity of such organizations among factory workers and the prevalence of nonfactory workers in unions, such a restriction could only have proved self-defeating. The conference finally agreed to accept all organizations concerned with the rights and interests of wage labor, except those with Zubatovite affiliation (despite the presence of one such union at the founding meetings).[87]

The immediate outcome of the conference was the creation of the so-called Moscow Bureau of Professional Unions, charged with organizing the forthcoming congress. The bureau performed a useful function in guiding unionizing activity, but it did not exercise political leadership. The bureau consisted of representatives of 43 groups (39 unions and four factory committees) plus representatives of the political parties. It met eight times in 1905, but there were never more than 12 to 14 separate unions present at any single session.[88]

Eleven unions active in the October meetings attended bureau sessions. Most of these were among the city's largest, best-organized unions. Of this group four were white-collar unions: the Socialist Revolutionary/liberal–sponsored Corporation of Workers and Low-Ranking Employees in the Moscow City Administration, the Bolshevik Union of Waiters and Other Tavern and Hotel Employees (successor to the Waiters' Mutual Aid Society represented at the conference), the Menshevik Union of Commercial and Industrial Employees, "Strength in Unity" (incorporating the earlier Union of Employees in the Sale of Foodstuffs represented at the conference), and the liberal Union of Salaried Workers in Trade and Industry. The other seven were blue-collar unions: the Menshevik Union of Workers in the Printing Trade (successor to the Union of Moscow Printing and Lithography Workers represented at the conference), the Bolshevik Bakers' Union, the Menshevik Union of Workers in the Tobacco Industry, the Bolshevik Joiners' Union, the Menshevik Union of Moscow-Brest Railroad Shop Workers, the Bolshevik Union of Jewelers and Precious-Metal Workers, and the Bolshevik Union of Technicians. Thus, of the bureau's central core, five unions were led by Bolsheviks, four by Mensheviks, and two by liberals or Socialist Revolutionaries. Of the other 28 unions that took part in bureau meetings, the Social Democrats controlled nine (six blue-collar and three white-collar) and shared control of four with the Socialist Revolutionaries (two blue-collar and two white-collar). They also controlled all four of the factory committees. The Socialist Revolutionaries alone controlled only three unions, the liberals two; the rest were of unknown affiliation. The absence of delegates from the liberal- and Socialist Revolutionary-dominated All-Russian Railroad and Postal and Telegraph unions, both active in the conference, is another sign of the increasing importance of Social Democratic organizers in the labor movement leadership.

Like its parent body, the bureau was concerned primarily with practical questions of union organization. The assembled labor leaders again stressed the need to move away from traditional mutual-aid societies toward the creation of true trade unions. They deplored the narrow professional divisions characteristic of Moscow unions. They urged labor organizers to involve the rank and file in the conduct of union affairs by holding frequent general meetings. The bureau repeated the wish that nonproletarian groups be excluded from union membership, though such groups participated in the bureau's own deliberations. In addition, the bureau recommended that trade unions remain officially nonpartisan, though it approved of unions taking stands on specific political issues.[89] This decision represented a victory for the Mensheviks, who were in favor of developing a labor movement independent of party control.

The bureau chose an executive commission charged with the task of organizing the forthcoming national congress. The commission included the Kharkov organizer Evdokimov, the Social Democrats M. G. Lunts (Bolshevik) and P. N. Kolokol'nikov (Menshevik), the liberal lawyer and museum board chairman, N. K. Murav'ev, and the liberal municipal official and museum secretary, I. F. Gornostaev. It also included several union representatives: Mensheviks from the Union of Workers in the Printing Trade and from the ribbonmakers, Bolsheviks from the Union of Bookshop Employees and from the Bakers' Union, and a nonparty representative from the Menshevik-led Union of Commercial Employees.[90]

The commission met daily in the museum, where it received a stream of workers seeking guidance in the unfamiliar tasks of professional organization. "They came for instructions on how to organize; they came to find places to hold meetings and speakers to address them; they came looking for organizers and charters; they came to discuss party business and the affairs of the Moscow Soviet, which had not set up its own headquarters. They came from the city and from the surrounding countryside."[91] The commission also arranged for the publication of the *Bulletin of the Museum for Assistance to Labor* (*Biulleten' muzeia sodeistviia trudu*), which printed the texts of union charters, accounts of meetings, and announcements. It remains a primary source of information on the trade-union movement of 1905.

What relation did the establishment of centralized labor leadership in Moscow bear to the development of a politically educated working class? Most workers had joined the general strike in protest over the inequities and burdens of their daily existence. P. A. Garvi, who was intimately involved in grass-roots organizing throughout the revolution, quotes the opinion of a politically astute railroad worker-deputy. This informant cautiously evaluated the motives of his less-sophisticated fellows, but refrained from speculating on their understanding of events: "The ignorant working-class majority [*temnaia rabochaia massa*] joined the [general] strike, in order to achieve economic improvement. Only later were political demands added—after agitation."[92] His use of the passive voice suggests that the demands were neither repulsed nor actively endorsed.

The more honest of the participant-observers found it hard to decide in what way and to what extent the workers' state of mind, self-perception, and collective aspirations might have altered as the result of their experience. Yet none denied that change of some sort had occurred. As other social groups also went on strike, as intelligentsia organizers reached a wider audience, and as social conflict and repressive violence grew in scope and intensity, the political goals of the October movement no doubt took on a new meaning for the ordinary worker. The evidence amply demonstrates that popular exposure to political ideas increased dramatically during the fall events. Evidence also shows that a minority of workers were eager to take action within the shop or factory, in order to wrest economic concessions from management. Interest in forming committees, electing deputies, drawing up demands, reached a peak after the October Manifesto, indicating that workers interpreted that document as a license to take collective action.

Contact between the venturesome few and the experienced union organizers set in train two developments. In the first place, organizers encouraged interested workers to discuss the concrete problems common to their lot. The exchange of information and personal experience, the process that the American women's movement of our own time calls "consciousness raising," must have caused workers to reevaluate their situation. The sponsoring activist helped the group articulate its grievances and then logically demonstrated, in simple terms as the occasion demanded, that the problems facing his audience were social ones, and needed social solutions. Conflicts with management reinforced the embryonic sense of worker solidarity.[93]

The second development essentially grew out of the first: the organizers, having persuaded members of the initial core to their own way of thinking, then encouraged them to expand their contacts in other factories and among the passive majority in their own shops. Thus, the active involvement of a small number set off ripples that reached to the perimeter of the Moscow working class, in concentric circles of ever-decreasing understanding and initiative. At the center of each plant or profession were the tiny handful of individuals with complex, and perhaps ambitious, goals and long-term connections with the educated classes. Around them formed a more numerous group ready to respond to suggestion, and then others with little understanding of the rationale behind any undertaking, but not unwilling to follow the lead of the committed few.[94]

But the process of working-class organization and political education was uneven and contradictory. As we have seen, workers might take bold steps that suited intelligentsia purposes for reasons that clashed with intelligentsia ideas. Others might welcome those ideas in the excitement of the moment without altering their basic outlook. Activism did not always coincide with enlightenment. Certain groups that held fast to their conservative beliefs and respect for established authority mimicked the behavior of those who stood for the opposite principles. Even the concierges, for example, got together to promote their rights. The Bolshevik activist S. I. Mitskevich remembers that butchershop clerks from Okhotnyi Riad gathered for a meeting and were induced to listen to the Social Democrat I. I. Skvortsov-Stepanov, whom they received at first with hostility, but finally rewarded with a round of applause.[95]

On the other hand, the more volatile ranks of the working class showed a tendency to revert to passivity. The Moscow-Brest machine shops created their own, independent Social Democratic union. Yet even there, leaders could not always count on the sustained enthusiasm of the majority.[96] Workers everywhere, even among those sympathetic to the strike movements, were generally hostile to intelligentsia activists who brought the political message. During October, a group of radical young workers at the Mytishchi railroad-car works outside Moscow invited a Bolshevik spokesman to address their striking comrades. Another group of equally youthful workers greeted his appearance with scorn. Pelting him with stones and bricks, they are said to have cried, "Look, they [the radicals] have brought their God!" In the end, recalls a Bolshevik worker-activist who witnessed the scene, the orator won them over,[97] just as his colleague had charmed the butchers, though perhaps only for the moment.

The revolutionary crisis generated a thirst for action. It no doubt affected the collective psychology of Moscow workers who rose to the occasion. Just how is the question.

"During the revolution, there are weeks and days when the worker masses are spiritually regenerated, as if the scales had fallen from their eyes, and sudden insight turns yesterday's benighted slaves into decisive warriors."[98] Thus the gratified organizer confronted by the miracle of mass mobilization. To the historian, however, flashes of sudden insight pose more problems than they answer.

9

LABOR COUNCILS AND LABOR CONFLICTS

The Soviets

The most remarkable organizational product of the interaction between the revolutionary intelligentsia and the mass movement during 1905 were the soviets of workers' deputies. These district and citywide councils provided the radical parties a forum in which to address their factory-based constituency. The soviet guaranteed them a network that reached to the shop floor and the industrial outskirts. Through the soviets, workers were able to contribute to the decision making that governed the popular movement at crucial turning points in the year. In St. Petersburg, as we have noted, the central soviet took shape during the October general strike and was seen in the capital and throughout the Empire as the symbolic centerpiece of that movement. In Moscow, the socialist parties did not establish such an organization until late in November. Their purpose in doing so was twofold: to undermine the authority of the radical-democratic Strike Committee and to establish a central governing organ independent of the trade unions, which did not provide sufficient direction in political and tactical matters. Despite divergent conception of the role and significance of the soviet, all three radical parties cooperated in its creation and leadership.

The Moscow Strike Committee had relied on nonindustrial strikers for its primary political support. After the October Manifesto, when work had resumed, conflict within the committee became more intense. In early November, some of the Social Democratic members proposed a plan designed to weaken the committee by eliminating all professional and white-collar groups from its ranks. Not surprisingly, the motion was defeated—54 to 17, with 8 abstentions. Twelve Social Democratic delegates thereupon resigned.[1] The Strike Committee remained in existence throughout November as the self-proclaimed spokesman for non-blue-collar groups active in the opposition movement, but it gradually lost most of its following and eventually renounced all claim to political leadership. Once the soviet had been established, the committee was not adverse to sharing its remaining funds with its political rival.[2]

It was not, however, until the third week in November that Social Democrats convened the first meeting of what was to be the Moscow City Soviet of Workers' Deputies. At least 145, and possibly as many as 200, worker-deputies attended the opening session on November 21,[3] in a theater on Povarskaia Street in the Arbat (II). Two subsequent meetings took place in the Museum for Assistance to Labor, thus perpetuating the tradition whereby radical organizations made their nest in the shelter provided by the tolerant liberals who ran that institution. The soviet deputies represented less than 10 percent of Moscow's industrial enterprises.[4] Of the 72 firms that sent delegates, 21 were metal factories, 16 textile plants, and 15 enterprises in food preparation; the other 20 were from miscellaneous industries.[5] If one assumes that large plants were the most active, then this small number may have represented as much as half the city's industrial labor force.[6] In the absence of data, this must remain conjectural.

Mensheviks took the initiative in forming the Moscow Soviet.[7] N. I. Chistov from the Menshevik printers' union chaired the opening session. The delegates chose an executive committee consisting of eight workers from local city districts and six party leaders, two from each party.[8] All four of the Social Democrats belonged to the executive committee of the United Federative Council, the body the Bolshevik and Menshevik factions had created in October. The eight worker-delegates were also Social Democrats. The Socialist Revolutionaries consequently found themselves very much in the minority on the soviet's decision-making board. Like the executive commission of the Moscow Bureau, which did the actual work of the organization, a core of ten leaders from the three radical parties, the so-called Information Bureau, took charge of the soviet's affairs. The Social Democrats were thus in a position to lead meetings and determine ideology and tactics. The soviet's constituency, however, was politically independent. Even the Bolshevik M. I. Vasil'ev-Iuzhin, a member of the executive committee, concedes that the vast majority of worker-delegates at plenum meetings considered themselves nonparty.[9]

The first session met before the election procedure had been formally established. This was done five days later at a meeting of only 20 delegates. They instructed large firms to elect one delegate per 400 workers. Workers in smaller factories were advised to gather together to choose collective representatives. If this proved impossible, individual enterprises were to elect one delegate for every 50 workers to send to local district gatherings. These in turn would select a reduced number of deputies at the ratio of one per 500 workers.[10]

Liberal supporters of the soviet criticized the two-step procedure as undemocratic.[11] Indirect elections, however, were the only way for the soviet to reach workers in small shops without going through the unions. It also was a convenient way to involve nonunionized enterprises. Even where trades had already been organized, the soviet insisted on independent elections so as to give itself a clear line of authority. Only in cases where the factories were slow to act on their own did the soviet authorize existing unions to conduct elections, and then only if they were careful to involve all the workers and not merely their own members.

The Social Democrats also tried to bridge the gap between workers in small dispersed enterprises and the central city soviet by organizing local neighborhood councils. By early November, they had set up five such councils in the major working-class districts: Zamoskvorech'e (VI), Rogozhskaia (V), Lefortovo (V), Butyrki, in Sushchevskaia (IV), and Presnia-Khamovniki (III). They also started one in the downtown Gorodskaia district (I).[12] Unlike the district councils of St. Petersburg, which were never very strong, the Moscow councils not only continued operating after the formation of the central body, but often exercised considerable authority in their localities.[13] Since the Russian political system excluded the lower classes from participation in community management and civic affairs, the workers remained suspicious of elaborate institutional forms. They responded most readily to organizations such as the district councils, which corresponded most closely to the units of social life meaningful to them: in this case, large plants and working-class neighborhoods.

The original plan for a citywide council based on the Council of the Five Professions had called for the various trades to maintain their organizational independence within the proposed body.[14] Those trades that were most active in the September strike did not play an important part in the October movement, however. The original councils therefore lost their leadership role to the Strike Committee. By mid-November, moreover, they had transformed themselves into more permanent organizations of the trade-union type. In the effort to establish its independence, the soviet broke both with the trade unions and with the earlier strike committees.

This distrust of competing organizations was in part a function of sectarian rivalry. Because the Mensheviks were more active in trade-union affairs, the Bolsheviks wanted to keep unions as such from joining the soviet.[15] The two factions finally agreed to let unions with more than 500 members send an extra delegate to the soviet beyond those chosen directly in factory elections.[16]

Among the unions that voted to join the soviet during November were the Union of Technicians, the Union of Workers in the Mechanical Construction Guild, the Union of Workers in the Printing Trade, and the Corporation of Middle-Ranking Technicians Attached to the Moscow City Administration. The Moscow Bureau of Professional Unions was not directly represented, but it agreed to cooperate with the soviet.[17] Although the Social Democrats had criticized the Strike Committee for being nonproletarian, the soviet nevertheless granted advisory status to the All-Russian Union of Postal and Telegraph Employees and full voting rights to the Moscow Union of Commercial and Industrial Employees—"Strength in Unity." It also allowed the pharmacy clerks' union to join.[18] The policy of accepting union delegates helped deplete the ranks of the Strike Committee, now deserted by three important organizations: the union of printing workers, the corporation of middle-ranking technicians, and the union of commercial employees. The influx of predominantly white-collar associations did not, however, threaten the Social Democrats' political control or affect the symbolically working-class character of the soviet.

Intelligentsia revolutionaries were responsible for organizing the soviets in the first place, for determining their political complexion, and, on a district level, for exercising leadership in moments of conflict. Mensheviks took the lead in setting up professional councils and soviets, as they did in forming the central body. In order to mount a democratic revolution against the autocratic state and against the capitalist social order, the party had to command a broad working-class following. The Mensheviks viewed mass-membership organizations as a way to draw the working-class majority into political life and to teach it the need for further, revolutionary change. The Bolsheviks, on the other hand, feared that autonomous worker organizations might compete with party authority and distract the working class from the goal of socialist transformation. The European example showed that Social Democratic trade unions were fully compatible with the capitalist system and with bourgeois political domination. The Bolsheviks did not reject trade unions, but they made an effort to keep the ones they organized under the control of party activists and to impose their own political program on them.[19] During the October general strike, Bolsheviks participated in the St. Petersburg Soviet. Once the strike was over, they wanted the soviet officially to adopt the party platform, but the Mensheviks and Socialist Revolutionaries successfully resisted their maneuvers. The Bolsheviks' distrust of broadly based nonpartisan organizations was partly responsible for the delay in forming a Moscow soviet and for the soviet's contradictory attitude toward trade unions. Bolsheviks were active in the Moscow Soviet, but they never dominated the leadership.[20] In practice, the behavior of Bolshevik militants differed little from that of their Socialist Revolutionary and Menshevik colleagues in the wake of the October Manifesto. But at the same time, they kept up a steady barrage of rhetoric (sometimes endorsed by their less enthusiastic Menshevik colleagues in the United Federative Council) denouncing political compromise and challenging the regime to a final showdown. Their maximalist hyperbole might have echoed in vain if the government had not shown a similar interest in the failure of stable popular institutions and in the escalation of conflict between radical extremes.

Labor Organizations and the Working-Class Strike Movement

Unlike their comrades in Moscow, whose attention turned toward trade-union formation after October 17, industrial workers in the capital did not lose their enthusiasm for strike activity. Indeed, the contrast between Moscow and St. Petersburg reveals the clear limits of authority exercised by the innovative soviets in 1905. In both cities, the revolutionary intelligentsia pursued a policy of moderation and discouraged new attempts at large-scale confrontation. At the same time, Moscow Bolsheviks continued to nurture and popularize the idea of imminent armed uprising. But radical rhetoric was bolder than the actions of the rank and file, who confined themselves to meetings, trade-union affairs, and localized strike actions. Industrial conflicts flared up and died down, as we shall see, but no single cause or unifying issue captured the popular imagination. In St. Petersburg, by contrast, the workers did find such an issue. Soviet leaders were obliged to endorse their initiative, though they thought it an ill-timed enterprise. Even this prestigious body did not have the means to contain its following. This weakness was, in some sense, a paradoxical measure of the institution's success, but it showed that popularity was not the same as political power or political control.

The [St. Petersburg] Soviet of Workers' Deputies was an extremely primitive organization, basically not much more than a combination of factory meetings and given to reverting back into a meeting itself. This organ could successfully articulate the desires of the masses, but was in no position to indicate the limits of what was possible, or to contain and channel massive outbursts of enthusiasm. The executive committee, dominated by intelligentsia party activists, tried several times to play this moderating role, but was unsuccessful: its prudent advice was merely drowned in the fiery speeches of deputies, who transmitted the workers' eagerness for struggle direct from the factories.[21]

During the last week in October, workers in many St. Petersburg factories began a campaign to institute the eight-hour workday by direct action. They did so simply by walking off the job after eight hours of work. The soviet did not officially approve the idea until October 29. Having overcome their reluctance to sanction the campaign in the first place, revolutionary leaders soon found reason to believe it might serve as the basis for a broader strike movement focused on political issues. Sailors at the Kronstadt naval base had mutinied on October 26. The authorities quickly suppressed the rebellion and threatened to court-martial the ringleaders. On November 1, the soviet called for a general strike in support of the arrested sailors and in protest against the imposition of martial law in Poland. Over 100,000 St. Petersburg factory workers struck in response to the soviet's appeal.[22] But elsewhere enthusiasm was lacking. The soviet called on the soldiers of the Petersburg garrison to show solidarity with their military brothers at Kronstadt, but the troops remained indifferent. The Union of Unions declared its official sympathy with the movement, but none of its member unions responded. The Moscow Strike Committee, already in its death throes, also failed to answer the St. Petersburg Soviet's call. Liberals and Social Democrats took time out from their internecine struggle to agree that Moscow workers were not ready to launch a new strike so soon after the decline of the old.[23]

On November 7, the government announced that the mutineers were not being tried by court-martial and would not be subject to the death penalty, and it lifted martial law in Poland. The St. Petersburg Social Democrats promptly claimed that the political strike had been successful, but their claim rang hollow.[24] The fight for the eight-hour day had generated great enthusiasm in the factories. But by November 6, punitive wage cuts, the threat of lockouts, and the use of troops against strikers had all but defeated the movement. Six days later, the soviet advised the workers to abandon their effort.[25]

Nothing like the massive eight-hour-day campaign in St. Petersburg occurred in Moscow. Although a large number of Moscow's industrial workers struck at some time in November, the various strikes never cohered into a general movement. Moreover, the number of workers on strike fluctuated from week to week. The strike was extensive, but unstable and fragmented. By October 17, at least a third (and probably more, since the police were more conscientious in reporting the onset of strikes than in noting their termination) of the 33,300 Moscow factory workers who had struck since October 1 had already returned to work. Another 14,500 workers struck in the last two weeks of October, but by October 31 many of them were also back at work. During the first two weeks of November, the number of workers on strike exceeded 35,000; these were joined by another 9,000 toward the end of the month, but the rate at which workers joined the movement declined, and by the time of the soviet's first meeting on November 21, more than a third of the month's strikers were back on the job.

On November 21, therefore, the Moscow Soviet echoed the Strike Committee's earlier injunction against extending the strike movement. It urged the workers to concentrate instead on strengthening trade-union organization. The soviet approved the use of strikes only under two circumstances: where owners had retracted previously won rights, especially the right to elected deputies and to freely held meetings in the factories; and where conditions in a given enterprise were significantly worse than those in comparable firms.[26] The fight for the eight-hour day should be postponed, and government attempts to provoke a confrontation firmly resisted, until the task of union organization had been completed.[27]

Before the November strike movement completely disintegrated, however, it managed to involve 30 percent of Moscow's industrial working class. The most dramatic change in the strike movement after October 17 was the increased participation of textile workers. During the October general strike, textile workers accounted for 36 percent of all striking factory workers, and metalworkers for 28 percent; but relative to their respective shares in the city's work force, metalworkers were heavily overrepresented and textile workers slightly underrepresented. This relationship reversed itself in the weeks following the October Manifesto. Of the 14,500 workers who struck between October 18 and October 31, 11,700 were textile workers, or almost as many again as had joined the general strike. In November, textile workers constituted fully half the total strikers; metalworkers only 17 percent. The strike propensity of metalworkers was on the decline from earlier in the year, while that of the textile workers was on the rise (see appendix tables A.1 and A.2). Of the textile workers who struck in November, 90 percent were doing so for the first time in the year. The group of metal strikers, though smaller, contained a large core of consistently active workers: three-quarters had already quit work at least once before October 17. In both industries, large plants were more active than smaller shops, as they had been all along.

Workers from three other industries constituted the remaining third of November strikers. Those employed in food products manufacture were the most numerous contingent, followed by workers in leather and in minerals and chemicals. Strikes also occurred in the woodworking industry, but their extent cannot be determined. Almost all the striking workers in leather goods manufacture were employed by four large plants, all located in the southern corner of the Piatnitskaia district (VI): Dement (240 workers), Volk (300), Bakhrushin (400), and Til' (3,100).[28] The strike in the chemicals industry was also concentrated in big firms: the Nevskii tallow rendering works (400 workers, in Basmannaia, V), and two perfume factories, Rallé (500, in Sushchevskaia, IV) and Brokar (480, in Serpukhovskaia, VI). In the food products industry, the strike involved workers in a variety of large enterprises.[29] Workers also struck in many of the city's small sausage-making shops. Deputies from these dispersed enterprises met on November 8 to formulate demands, which included the nine-hour day, pay raises, the right to elect deputies, and the right to strike.[30] Along with the sausage makers, woodworkers were the only strikers in this period who were not concentrated in large enterprises.[31] Workers in printing and paper-goods production were largely inactive in November. The increased proportion of unorganized, politically inexperienced workers—mostly textile workers—among the November strikers helps account for the weakness of soviet influence over the strike movement.

The evidence at hand does not explain why the textile workers suddenly came to life in late October and November. We know that radical agitators and labor organizers used the leniency of the Days of Freedom to proselytize among the quiescent factory masses. Popular assemblies occurred in local taverns, on street corners, and in theaters, schools, and other public buildings throughout the city. The explosion of rhetoric surely reached into the furthermost corners of the industrial districts and undoubtedly elicited some kind of response. This is not to say that political ideas suddenly made an impression on the uninitiated. Indeed, the opposite was true: the vast majority of November strikers walked off the job to win better pay and improved work conditions. The willingness to act was itself an important step forward. But the boundaries of collective action remained narrow—the individual plant. And the motives were specific and concrete—the desire to obtain redress of grievances peculiar to that plant. The abstract slogans of the October strike were missing (along with the white-collar and professional groups that had supplied them), and the eight-hour-day movement caught on in only a few places. Only a minority of workers struck on matters of principle essential to the very existence of the labor movement.

The question of power relations in the workplace emerged as a focus of conflict in September and October. It continued to inspire a number of protests during November, especially in some of the larger plants. There is no evidence that the workers themselves understood the connection between workers' rights—the freedom to strike and to elect their own deputies—and the broader political issues at stake in 1905. But there is abundant evidence that questions of workers' rights and worker dignity evoked an immediate and passionate response on the shop floor. Metalworkers at both Gopper and Dobrov and Nabgol'ts, for example, struck after several of their number had been fired for active involvement in plant meetings and strike preparation. Bromlei metalworkers walked out after the factory management threatened to dismiss the entire work force for having instituted the eight-hour day on its own initiative.[32] All three strikes lasted into December. Two large perfume factories struck on November 7 in protest over the firing of deputies in one of the firms, where Bolshevik organizers were particularly active. The movement began at the Rallé plant in the north of the city and was supported by workers at Brokar, clear across town in the southernmost, Serpukhovskaia district.[33]

Not only in respect to the strike's motives, but also in getting its neighbors to join the strike, Rallé was the exception in November. When the perfume plant struck on November 7, nearby workers followed suit, in hopes of improving their own situation. Strikers from Rallé and a local textile mill joined forces to stop work at two metal factories. They also managed to interfere with operations at a crystal factory (Diutfua), where the worker-representatives were actually opposed to joining the strike. Many of the idled workers then gathered near the Rallé plant to listen to political speeches delivered by the ubiquitous "young man." They then constituted themselves the core of a neighborhood workers' assembly.[34] Police noted that the workers conducted themselves in an orderly manner; they had even gone so far as to shut local bars to prevent drunkenness.[35]

The violation of workers' rights also led to strikes in certain large textile mills. Two of the most publicized occurred in the giant Danilovskaia cotton mill, just outside the southern city limits, and at the centrally located Golutvinskaia cotton mill in northern Iakimanskaia (VI). Workers at Golutvinskaia first struck on November 4 to protest a case of retributive firing. To the demand for reinstatement of the dismissed workers, they added two others: the right to hold meetings on factory premises, and the recognition of elected deputies with immunity from police or management prosecution and the right to participate in decisions involving wages and employment. On November 10, the workers rejected the directors' counteroffer because it did not grant the deputies the full range of powers and protection the strikers demanded. To the earlier points, the workers now added a list of improvements in wages and work conditions. The symbolic issue of the eight-hour day figured among their demands, but most involved detailed and specific grievances. On November 12, the plant administration attempted to end the strike by dismissing the entire work force, but the workers simply refused to leave. Under normal circumstances, factory barracks provided management with avenues of control over their employees, but in cases of labor conflict, dormitories allowed the workers to resist dismissal and to prolong their strikes beyond the moment when management would have liked to lock them out.

After a week, the majority of Golutvinskaia workers (890 out of 950) finally accepted their terminal pay, left the plant, and set out for their respective villages.[36] None of the demands had been met when the factory began hiring new workers at the end of the month. As late as November 23, however, a small core of 14 workers still refused to accept dismissal. Seven of the intransigent were weavers by occupation (three on automatic looms, four on hand looms); four worked as spinners; two were office workers; and one was a canteen worker and a starosta. Twelve were between eighteen and thirty years old; two were about forty. None of them (all peasants by legal category) came from the same village, but three pairs came from the same *volosti*, the lowest provincial subdivisions, and two other pairs from the same *uezdy*, the next highest subdivisions. All but one were men.[37]

When faced with a lockout, workers had little choice but to give up the struggle. Factory owners now resorted to this powerful weapon more readily than they had during the October strike. The continuous working-class unrest of November was not linked to broad political aspirations, as articulated by an educated leadership. For this reason, perhaps, it alienated some progressive-minded conservatives who had been sympathetic to the October general strike because they had hoped the expansion of workers' civil rights would contribute to social stability. Some industrialists had expected political change to calm the troubled waters of economic discontent. The November strikes convinced them that this was not so. Factory owners now got together to join forces in opposing strike activity, and industrialist leaders consolidated their support for the Octobrist position.[38] At least 9,000 workers, almost all in textile plants, found themselves victims of lockouts. Small shop owners sometimes worked together to achieve the same effect. When furriers, for example, drew up a common set of demands, their employers formed a united front against them, and all shut their shops in anticipation of a strike.[39]

The tactic was usually successful. When, as at Gopper and Bromlei, workers struck to protest across-the-board firing, the effort was a meaningless gesture.[40] At the Kondrashev textile plant in Lefortovo (V), the workers returned to the closed factory and threw bricks at the building.[41] But in most cases, a lockout effectively put a stop to even this kind of spontaneous collective activity. The closing of several large plants deprived many workers of their wages, and in some cases, of lodgings as well. The dispossessed began returning to the countryside in droves, along with strikers who had tired of waiting for the resolution of drawn-out conflicts.[42]

In the meantime, as this rash of disconnected strikes was erupting in the factories, an unrelated series of strikes had begun to engage various groups of workers in nonmanufacturing professions. On November 5, for example, 350 telephone operators stopped work to protest the firing of 43 of their fellow employees. They also drew up a list of economic demands, but by mid-November had abandoned all but the central issue. The administration did not give in. The strike continued into December, with only 30 of the 400 telephone operators at their posts.[43]

Earlier, toward the end of October, waiters in taverns and restaurants had struck for improved work conditions. Most of the strikers were either unemployed or poorly paid waiters, who imposed their decision on the rest of the profession by gathering in crowds of 2,000 to 3,000 and literally forcing most restaurants to close their doors.[44] Domestic servants staged a massive walkout on November 8. A group of concierges also struck toward the middle of the month, refusing to sweep sidewalks and gutters until their wages had been increased and working conditions improved.[45] All these groups had formed unions, or were in the process of forming them at the time they struck. On October 23, for example, 8,000 waiters, meeting in the Engineering Institute and led by Bolshevik organizers, had voted to form a new union, the Union of Waiters and Other Tavern and Hotel Employees.[46]

Whereas the waiters' union boasted a considerable following, the union of concierges was no more than a paper organization, formally announced at a meeting on November 7.[47] So also with the Union of Domestic Servants, which was born in the November strike and held only a few meetings, though it was nominally represented on the Moscow Bureau of Professional Unions.[48] The three unions lasted only as long as members of these dispersed professions kept meeting and listening to the ideas of intelligentsia organizers. It was also at such gatherings that waiters and domestics agreed to strike, but the so-called unions had no control over the grass-roots movements.

Most of the newly constituted industrial labor unions were equally fragile: many were simply rebaptized factory committees. The strongest unions to emerge in November were those that had grown out of earlier strikes, no doubt because the individual factory committees had already learned to work together, and the workers had gotten practical experience in the election and functioning of worker-delegates. The unions of printers, bakers, tobacco workers, and tea packers all formalized their ex-

istence in the wake of extensive strikes. The Union of Workers in the Tobacco Industry acted as the spokesman of a long and well-organized
strike, which began in late September and lasted into November. The
union was led by members of the strike committees of the four principal
striking firms: Gabai, Dukat, Bostandzhoglo, and Reingart.[49] The committees themselves had been in operation since September. The union was
strong because the profession was concentrated in so few plants and because the workers had months of cooperation behind them.

The tea packers' and carpenters' unions organized a boycott of firms
that seemed to have shown particular disregard for workers' rights. In response to a union-led boycott of two furniture factories, factory owners
in that trade closed ranks; they held several meetings in November to
draw up industrywide guidelines for handling the workers' economic
demands.[50] Labor conflict in the tea-packing industry focused on the
Vysotskii plant, in Lefortovo, where the management had provoked a
strike on October 28 by refusing to recognize duly elected worker-deputies. The union demanded that workers in the railroad system and other
enterprises refuse to handle any of the firm's products, and that the public
refuse to buy them. A general meeting of workers in the district supported the boycott, which was sustained successfully until November
18.[51]

Among metal and textile workers, the process of electing and assembling worker-representatives had made even less progress than in other
occupations. The Social Democrats had formed a number of associations
among skilled workers in both industries (see Appendix B), but they did
not reach the mass of factory laborers. Even though workers in several
cases voted at plant meetings to support the program of the Social Democratic or Socialist Revolutionary Party, the November strikes in metal and
textile factories remained largely uncoordinated.[52] At best, striking workers in individual firms appealed to other factories for financial help, but
they did not frame their demands in terms that might have attracted
wider support.[53]

Although in late October the Social Democrats had tried to form a general metalworkers' union based on the old Zubatov organization, they did
nothing again until after the November strikes had already petered out.
Deputies from the firms of Zotov, Veikhel't, Guzhon, and Bromlei, all
connected with the Social Democrats,[54] drew up a charter on November
24. An official founding meeting took place on December 4, but the union
never actually functioned. Similarly, the Social Democrats tried to build
on the foundations laid by Zubatov in the textile industry. Delegates representing 21 factories attended the first organizational meeting of a pro-

jected Moscow union of workers in textile production on November 7. Although six or seven meetings followed, this union likewise never functioned.[55]

The Moscow Bureau of Professional Unions did not attempt to coordinate the diverse industrial strikes of this period by formulating unified lists of demands or by encouraging sympathetic strike action. Nor did the moribund Strike Committee or the new Moscow Soviet influence the November strikes.[56] The coordinating process was, in fact, confined largely to paper or to the meeting hall. Despite the creation of a host of worker organizations, the mass movement was less coherent than it had been in October. Without white-collar and professional groups to provide ideological structure, and without administrative and transport workers to cripple the economy, the November strike, for all its breadth, remained a local conflict focused on narrowly defined working-class issues.

The Protest Strike of Postal Employees

Two explicitly political campaigns stood out against this background of sporadic labor unrest: an attack on censorship and a protest mounted by postal and telegraph workers defending the right of government employees to unionize. Both were attempts to realize the guarantees of the October Manifesto. They attracted the support of liberals and socialists alike, equally concerned with the underlying civil rights issues. Neither campaign had any effect, however, on the ongoing strike movement, and neither inspired strike activity on the part of other educated groups.

The defense of freedom of the press was the combined effort of three organizations, representing management as well as clerks and factory workers: the Menshevik-led Union of Workers in the Printing Trade, the Bolshevik Union of Bookshop Employees, and a publishers' organization. Together they launched a boycott of publishers and printing firms that continued to submit material to the censor in advance of publication.[57] This cooperative venture was an example of what professional organizations could do once constitutional guarantees protected their existence. It was a characteristic strategy of the post-manifesto period: one that involved the exercise of public initiative within the framework of the law, and avoided physical confrontation.

The issue at stake in the postal strike likewise elicited broad public support, precisely because it concerned a question of civil rights, which touched on the interests of all social classes. The white-collar postal workers were a relatively cautious lot. They had been one of the least militant groups during the October general strike. They began to defend their rights only after these had been won by rather more flamboyant means than the majority of communications workers found attractive. Their outlook rapidly changed, however, when the government revoked their right to have a union. Since the postal-telegraph workers had scrupulously avoided collective action when it was illegal, they were all the more indignant to find themselves suddenly beyond the pale to which they had carefully confined themselves. Thus did the regime push its most timid subjects into a posture of unwilling, but seemingly unavoidable, antagonism to the autocracy and all it stood for.

The Union of Postal and Telegraph Employees adopted a charter and held its first formal meetings after the October Manifesto, though certain politically active members of the group had first thought of forming a union in July 1905, on the model of the All-Russian Railroad Union.[58] Blue-collar workers played only a small role in the union's leadership. Of the 22 most prominent activists later indicted for having instigated the November strike, only three were of working-class origin. All were low-ranking employees (mail carriers, dispatchers, couriers). Four of the others were young women in their twenties, two with titles of nobility; the rest had a variety of civil titles. The group's average age was thirty-three.[59] Information on a group of 19 postal employees detained on November 16 for participating in the union's first congress supports the observation that those most active in union affairs were persons holding responsible positions, of relatively mature age. The group's average age was thirty-four. Only four of them were not administrative personnel: one was a telephone operator, two were mail carriers, and one was a watchman.[60]

The union's original organizers were Socialist Revolutionaries, but the charter published on October 24 declared the organization to be free of specific party affiliation. The union limited its political position to supporting the demands for full civil rights and for the election of a popular government based on the four-point formula. Its main purpose, however, was the defense of the material, legal, and corporate interests of postal and telegraph employees.[61] Despite the unexceptional content of the charter, the Ministry of Post and Telegraph immediately declared that the union was illegal, denying that the provisions of the October Manifesto applied to government employees.[62] This move constituted the first official limitation of the manifesto's implied guarantees. The union took it as a direct political challenge.

Despite the ministry's stand, the union continued to hold public meetings, and plans went forward to hold an All-Russian Postal Union congress in Moscow beginning on November 15. The government reacted by firing three of the union leaders on the eve of the congress. The union in turn promptly dispatched a telegram to Count Witte, chairman of the Council of Ministers, giving the Ministry of Post and Telegraph 12 hours to retract its punitive decision. When no answer had arrived by the specified deadline, the postal congress officially announced the start of a nationwide strike to protest the firing. A series of economic demands accompanied the union's demand for its legal rights.[63] But the union had no sooner acted than the authorities, unwilling to tolerate the continued presence of the congress delegates any longer, sent the police to break up the opening day's evening session.

Not all post office employees received the strike call with equal enthusiasm. Telegraph workers showed the greatest resistance. Almost 100 of them continued to work through the night of November 15 under military guard; 30 to 40 were still at their posts by the next evening. The main post office closed the following morning, but workers in branch offices needed still further persuasion to quit. Typically, the task of spreading the strike fell to the younger postal workers, who grabbed whatever sticks and poles that came to hand and made the rounds of the city in groups, on foot or in postal wagons.

During the first week of the strike, the police did not interfere with union meetings. The period of tolerance ended on November 20, with the arrest of seven congress leaders. Three days later, police seized the post office, which had served as a general assembly hall. Mass meetings continued nevertheless in the Olympia and Aquarium theaters and in the Polytechnical Museum. The closing of the central post office only stimulated greater political fervor in the union delegates, who issued a general appeal for support, addressed to citizens, unions, and civic organizations. In it, they declared that their strike was directed primarily against the government, a government that "has cavalierly trampled on the basic rights of the people. Our victory is the victory of the entire people! Our defeat would be a direct blow to the cause of universal liberation."[64]

The union had previously refused to join either the Union of Unions, the Strike Committee, or the Moscow Soviet. It now suddenly announced its affiliation with the organizations representing Russia's laboring class— the St. Petersburg Soviet of Workers' Deputies and its local branches.[65] The Moscow Soviet, for its part, accepted the union on a nonvoting basis, despite its overwhelmingly white-collar membership.[66] This amounted to a recognition, on both sides, that "the proletarian cause" could not be equated simply with the economic and political interests of the industrial working class. Under the circumstances, the proletariat—as defined by its ideological mentors and represented by the soviet—had come to symbolize the fight for the political liberation of all classes. By this date, the liberally inclined Moscow Strike Committee had lost its authority, and the St. Petersburg Soviet had acquired a national reputation that far exceeded its actual powers, but generated widespread faith in its leadership potential.[67] To view the St. Petersburg Soviet at this point as the standard-bearer of the revolution was not an act of sectarian blindness, but a decision that reflected the apparent balance of power within the opposition movement.

In any case, the Moscow Soviet, at least, did not stand in splendid isolation from the moderate and liberal wing of the movement. It willingly met in the Museum for Assistance to Labor, as we have noted, and did not insist on the class purity of member associations. After joining the Moscow Soviet, the postal union continued to attract the support of many of the professional groups of liberal tendency that had taken part in the October strike.[68] The Moscow Bureau of Professional Unions pledged to resist attempts by private firms to offer their own staff as substitutes for striking postal workers. Clerks belonging to the Union of Commercial and Industrial Employees were particularly likely to be "volunteered" in this manner. Sympathy manifested itself in the form of material as well as moral support. By December, the strikers had received almost 25,000 rubles from a variety of groups, including the uneasy political associates on the left of the liberation movement: the Moscow Bolshevik Committee and the Socialist Revolutionaries (300 rubles each), the Kadets (3,000 rubles), and the Union of Unions.[69] Aid also came to the strikers in the form of free lodging, free meals, and credit coupons for food stores.

So universal was public dissatisfaction with government policy that conservatives who had hitherto taken no part in the 1905 political movement defended the essential justice of the postal workers' cause. Despite the inconvenience and financial loss occasioned by the work stoppage, the Moscow business community did not blame the striking employees. The fault lay, instead, with the authorities. On November 23, 16 factory owners and merchants sent an open letter to the Moscow Stock Exchange Committee, asking it to urge the ministry to meet the strikers' economic demands.[70] A week later the committee, representing the politically more conservative members of the city's business world, went even further than that: it not only sent a recommendation to that effect to Count Witte, chairman of the Council of Ministers, but promised the postal union that it would supplement the employees' salaries and help support the families of strikers (which pledge it fulfilled in the amount of 10,000 rubles) until the government finally improved the workers' economic situation. The Moscow City Board also found the postal employees' complaints justified. On December 2, it agreed that salaries were intolerably low, hours excessive, and living conditions poor.[71]

The government refused to compromise with the postal workers and tried instead to undermine the movement. The postal administration recruited strikebreakers from private firms and brought in postal employees from provincial centers in an effort to maintain normal service. The inexperience of many of the hastily assembled substitutes guaranteed that service remained at best confused. The strikers' efforts to interfere with postal operations only added to the chaos. Armed guards protected the substitutes as they entered the buildings. Unable to stop them, the strikers attacked the system's apparatus. They destroyed suburban telegraph lines, stopped mail wagons, emptied post boxes, prevented the transfer of mail from the railroad stations to the post offices. In response to a postal union appeal of November 18, railroad workers cooperated by sabotaging telegraph operations on their own independent network and impeding mail transport.[72] Assaults on individual mail carriers became more common as the strike progressed.

These obstructions seriously disrupted but did not shut down the postal system. Many regular employees refused to strike. According to official figures, 430 administrative employees in the telegraph division struck, and 313 continued working. Firemen collected mail under the guard of gendarme detachments. Volunteers recruited by the Union of the Russian People sorted local correspondence in the main post office. But the administration was not able to restore telegraph service, despite constant efforts to repair damage to the lines. And fewer and fewer regular postal employees appeared for work as the days wore on, which only increased the inefficiency of the 400 or so volunteers.

On November 20, police had arrested seven members of the postal union's central bureau. The union quickly elected replacements. Five days later, they too were arrested. The administration then fired 310 administrative personnel and 667 low-ranking employees (mail carriers, guards, and dispatchers) on November 27 and November 30. Despite the union's efforts to sustain morale, the strike collapsed.[73] Dismissed workers could regain their positions only if they pledged not to join organizations not explicitly authorized by the government.[74] By December 2, two-thirds of the fired administrative personnel had been reinstated on these terms, and five days later only 50 had not yet returned. Less than a third of the dismissed low-ranking employees had signed the pledge by December 2. The others returned to work only gradually and in insufficient numbers to permit the restoration of full mail delivery. Of the normal complement of 500 mail carriers, only 40 were working as of December 4.[75]

For all the widespread sympathy the postal strike had engendered, it did not have the same catalytic effect as the railroad strike had had in October. Professional groups did no more than contribute financial support to the movement. Factory workers had struck in large numbers in the weeks before the postal strike, but later in the month industrial strikes tapered off. The Moscow Soviet, of which the postal union was a member, refused to encourage factory workers to support the postal strikers with their own protests.

Despite its popularity in a variety of circles, the soviet realized its authority was tenuous. It had come into existence after the industrial strike wave had already peaked. Its leaders were dismayed at the movement's disorganization, but the situation was not in their control. By the soviet's second session, on November 27, the authorities had destroyed the postal union leadership, and had embarked on a campaign to cripple the mass movement and its representative organizations. A decree of November 29 gave local authorities the power to take extraordinary measures to prevent interference with postal, telegraph, or railroad services.[76] On secret instructions from Minister of Internal Affairs P. N. Durnovo, governors ordered the police to arrest the leaders of all "antigovernment" organizations.[77] Railroad, communications, and government employees guilty of instigating or engaging in strike activity, or of belonging to organizations that encouraged such behavior, now risked punishment of 16 months to four years in prison, plus loss of personal rights and property.[78]

On November 26, police arrested Khrustalev-Nosar', president of the St. Petersburg Soviet; on November 28, they arrested the leaders of the Union of Ticket Collectors of the Moscow-Brest Railroad; and on November 30, they raided the Museum for Assistance to Labor, nerve center of the Moscow labor movement, and seized pamphlets, papers, and money.[79] In response to the arrest of its chairman, the St. Petersburg Soviet issued a manifesto on December 2, asking people to withdraw their savings from state banks and to demand payment in gold. It also urged workers to refuse to accept wages in paper currency.[80] The day after this declaration of financial war on the government, police arrested 260 of the soviet's delegates, including members of the executive committee. The authorities closed the eight St. Petersburg newspapers that had published the manifesto and arrested their editors.[81]

The soviet leaders in Moscow had tried to avoid a confrontation with the government, which, they feared, could only destroy the last vestiges of the mass movement. During the Days of Freedom, organization for self-defense had taken second place to the development of worker organizations compatible with a stable social and political arrangement. But all the while, as we have seen, the Social Democrats had kept harping on the idea of armed revolutionary struggle, if only rhetorically.[82] The weakening of the October alliance permitted the socialists to emphasize issues that distinguished them from the liberals. In ascending order of feasibility, they demanded a constituent assembly, the establishment of a democratic republic, and the institution of a socialist society. Such demands were essentially agitational devices, rather than exhortations to action, and the call to armed struggle at first shared that characteristic.

In late November, the leaders of the Moscow Soviet realized the government was trying to provoke a showdown. Feeling that they were cornered, they decided to shift from a posture of cautious self-defense to a more desperate and radical strategy of violent counterattack. The idea of translating the slogan of armed insurrection into action began to take on a measure of reality.

10

CONFRONTATION

Mutiny

By late November, the revolutionary leaders saw their greatest hope, and the government's greatest liability, in the growing unrest in the armed forces. During the course of 1905, over 200 mutinies occurred. Most of these took place after the October Manifesto.[1] Indeed, sailors and soldiers throughout the Empire interpreted that document as a sign that the old rules no longer applied. Officers lost control over their men, who left their barracks, mingled with civilians, and acquainted themselves with current events.[2] A number of dramatic incidents occurred in the navy. Shortly after the manifesto was issued, sailors in the Black Sea Fleet stationed in Sevastopol attempted to obtain the release of those imprisoned after the June mutinies. Two weeks later, on November 12, the fleet was again disrupted by large-scale mutiny. Sailors at the Kronstadt naval base had mutinied, as we have noted, in late October; so had soldiers and sailors based in Vladivostok.[3] During November, the army alone experienced at least 125 mutinies or cases of unrest. Most engineering units and half the artillery units outside Manchuria and over half the infantry units in European Russia showed signs of insubordination.[4] The reserves were the most restless. Since the conclusion of the war with Japan in August, they had been eager to return home. The October Manifesto seemed to legitimize their right to show how much they resented the harsh army discipline, poor conditions, and delays in demobilization.

The mood of discontent spread to soldiers in the Moscow garrison during the last week in November. During the October strike, the officers of the troops quartered in the city kept their men confined to barracks, but after the manifesto, the soldiers regained their freedom of movement. Soldiers had participated in the Bauman funeral procession, and small groups in uniform appeared at public meetings in early November. The troops gained the impression that they, too, would benefit from the recent changes. A Moscow newspaper reported the following incident:

A group of soldiers in the Ekaterinoslav [grenadier] regiment—in a discussion with the regimental chaplain, Father Orlov—asked him to explain the meaning of the Manifesto of 17 October. Father Orlov stated categorically that the manifesto did not apply to the soldiers. The soldiers protested, declaring to the priest that they were citizens like all the rest. One of the soldiers, carried away in the argument, threw a pillow at Father Orlov.[5]

The first in the Moscow garrison to present military authorities with a formal set of demands were a group of soldiers in the third and fifth sapper battalions. The sappers, or military engineers, were better trained than ordinary recruits.[6] In presenting their demands, they followed the lead of the most highly educated among their noncommissioned officers: the draft volunteers, or *vol'noopredeliaiushchiesia*. Advanced schooling qualified these men to enjoy certain privileges once they had joined the army, based on their cultural superiority to the average noncommissioned officer who had risen through the ranks. The draft volunteers were usually city residents, and many continued to live outside the barracks, away from the recruits of peasant origin. Their freedom of movement and educational background gave them access to information and put them in contact with political events. They enjoyed the authority of rank but were not burdened by a commitment to a military career. It was the draft volunteers, unaided by outside left-wing activists, who took the initiative in organizing their subordinates.[7]

The discontented sappers gathered in the barracks mess hall on November 26 and drew up a list of grievances concerning the material conditions of military life. They also denounced the recent arrest of a fellow soldier for having engaged in political discussion. A representative of the battalion attended the November 27 meeting of the Moscow Soviet and declared the soldiers' readiness to support an armed insurrection under its leadership. The soviet hailed the sappers' enthusiasm for insurrection but did nothing to encourage their mutinous activity.[8]

On November 28, the Moscow chief of police asked the military authorities to remove the sappers from Moscow to prevent the spread of unrest. But contagion had already set in. Members of the Nesvizhskii infantry regiment and the third Pernovskii grenadier regiment met on November 29 and November 30 to formulate their own demands, which involved an array of political issues, as well as complaints about the organization of regimental life.[9] The most unsettling example of insubordination occurred in the Rostov grenadier regiment. Its activities filled the

military authorities with alarm and the revolutionary leadership with exaggerated expectations.

On November 30, when the Rostov grenadiers were called in to restore
order among the disgruntled infantrymen, they refused to take action.
Their unruly spirit was the product of ten days of intensive agitation
within the regiment. As in the case of the sappers, the key figures responsible for introducing revolutionary literature among the troops and for
stimulating the open expression of grievances were draft-volunteer noncommissioned officers. These men maintained contacts with revolutionary groups in the city, from whom they obtained propaganda pamphlets to
use in stirring up the troops.[10] Their task was made the easier because of
their position in the military hierarchy. Trained to obey directives from
above, the troops responded to the unorthodox appeal of their noncommissioned officers because the criticism of authority was sanctioned by
authority.

By the end of November, the Rostov noncommissioned officers had
organized three political circles. The Socialist Revolutionaries ran the
strongest of these groups (led by a clerk, S. Agafonov, and an under-
officer, N. Chernykh).* The other two were led by Social Democrats, but
they had little influence (the organizer was I. Ia. Shabrov, a draft volunteer later to head the regimental committee). The total membership of
these groups cannot have greatly exceeded 57, the number of men ultimately arrested and tried for their active part in the rebellion. On December 1, rations were cut. The Socialist Revolutionary group decided to
pass from propaganda to mobilization by calling an open meeting for the
next day. When the announcement fell into the hands of the military command, four ringleaders were immediately arrested: the aforementioned
Agafonov and Chernykh, plus V. Ul'ianinskii and a draft volunteer named
T. Serebriakov.[11]

The arrest forced the crisis to a head. Although one source says a group of
six or seven circle members hastily agreed to call the troops into action, it
seems unlikely that there was any collective decision. Ul'ianinskii, writing
some 20 years after the event, recalled that Agafonov simply refused to
submit to arrest and exhorted the soldiers to take up arms against their
commanding officers.[12] On either account, the Socialist Revolutionaries
appear to have been marginally more effective than their Social Democratic fellows in taking charge of the situation. A considerable number of

---

*Regular noncommissioned officers (*unter-ofitsery*) were enlisted men who had risen
from the ranks after acquiring combat experience or special training. The same require-
ments qualified draft volunteers to become under-officers. The rank carried no social or legal
privileges. *Entsiklopedicheskii slovar'*, 41 vols. (St. Petersburg: Brokgauz-Efron, 1890–
1904), vol. 34: 342–43.

soldiers responded to Agafonov's appeal and proceeded to hold a mass meeting. The commanding officers were excluded from the premises and stood idly by, observing the goings on, but taking no steps to restore order. There were no outsiders at the meeting, which selected a regimental committee to draw up demands and organize the defense of the dissidents. The committee distributed ammunition, saw that machine guns were placed in readiness, and assigned soldiers to guard duty.[13]

The committee's authority was consolidated in a fortuitous manner, one that illustrates the tenacious hold of traditional discipline on the average soldier. Having failed to persuade or compel the rebellious soldiers to obey orders, the regimental commander tendered his resignation. His telegram to Grand Prince Mikhael Aleksandrovich, the regiment's honorary commander, was intercepted by a member of the committee, who copied the text and distributed it among the troops. The soldiers were apparently convinced that the regimental commander had thereby officially designated the committee as his legitimate successor. In the words of Ul'ianinskii, "It was obvious that the regimental committee represented the same authority in the eyes of the soldier as had formerly been embodied in the regimental commander."[14] Nor had the exchange disturbed the tenor of military life: the soldiers conducted themselves with customary restraint and discipline. They executed the order to exclude officers from the barracks with the same matter-of-factness as they would have shown in executing the orders of those same officers.

On the next day, December 3, the committee called a meeting of the entire regiment to approve the list of demands. This was only a formality, since the committee had already sent the list to the newspapers the night before.[15] The Rostov grenadiers asked for pay raises, a two-year term of service, and improvements in medical aid, food, clothing, and barracks conditions (one bed for each soldier). They wanted to wear uniforms only when on duty and demanded that officers use polite address toward subordinates. The few general political demands were identical with those conventionally adopted by the revolutionary parties and other striking groups: amnesty for political prisoners and the calling of a constituent assembly. Other points, though concerned specifically with military life, in fact touched on political issues as well. The soldiers called for the right to free assembly and discussion in the military, and an end to the censoring of mail and barracks searches. They wanted their own regimental libraries and free access to books and newspapers; an end to the use of troops to quell civic disorders, to the death penalty, to military courts-martial (to be replaced by a peer court of honor), and to quotas in the military academies; the immediate return of troops from the Far East; and, of course, immunity from prosecution for the December 2 events. Shabrov, the committee chairman, and the two Socialist Revolutionaries, Agafonov and Chernykh, presented the list to the regimental commander. They warned that the soldiers would continue to disobey orders until all their demands were met.[16]

The Rostov soldiers persisted in calling their rebellion a strike, rather than an insurrection, as the intelligentsia militants would have it.[17] The troops showed little enthusiasm, moreover, for the abstract issues invoked by their leaders. Only the specific economic grievances elicited any discussion at the regimental assembly. By December 2, with the strike just one day old, the soldiers' mood had already begun to waver. It was clear that the mutiny would collapse if it did not spread to other regiments in the city. The Rostov rebels were strong only within the confines of their own barracks. Any group that ventured forth would easily fall into the hands of the officers, who were only waiting for a chance to reassume command.[18] At this critical moment, the Social Democratic militants outside the barracks deplored what they considered the irresolution of the Rostov leaders,[19] while the leaders awaited action from outside to save the troops from certain defeat.

The soldiers had no direct contact with party militants until the afternoon of December 2, when they were addressed by representatives of the Socialist Revolutionaries and the Bolsheviks. Their speeches did nothing to improve the sagging morale in the barracks.[20] The soldiers viewed these city types with derision. The language of revolutionary agitation was foreign to them, and they were offended by hostile references to the Tsar. The culminating indignity in the eyes of the assembled company was the appearance of a woman speaker, a Socialist Revolutionary party worker. To have to listen to a female, one that was, moreover, obviously Jewish, roused the audience to a peak of indignation. The soldiers considered themselves deeply insulted: "So this dame also wants to lecture us!" they sneered.[21]

Confidence in the regimental committee wavered. Enthusiasm for the strike declined even further when word spread that the soldiers drafted in 1901, whose term of service had been extended because of the Russo-Japanese war, were finally being demobilized. In the Rostov case, these draftees were the most experienced and authoritative men in the regiment. Many had become noncommissioned officers. Disgruntled over the extension of their term, these men had been more than ready to defy discipline and had played an active part in the strike. When they learned that the demobilization order would not apply to the Rostov grenadiers as long as the revolt continued, they began to agitate for an end to the strike.[22] Aware that their strike leaders had no power to release these draftees from duty, the Rostov soldiers were ready to submit to their com-

manding officers. On December 4, therefore, no one offered any resistance when the regimental commander arrested 57 outspoken leaders
of the revolt. The troops heard a speech praising the goodness of the Tsar
and the wickedness of subversive plotters, which they greeted with enthusiasm. The Rostov mutiny had come to an end. Twenty-eight of those
arrested were eventually sentenced; of these, 17 were draft volunteers
and six were under-officers.[23]

While the strike was still on, soldiers from other regiments had appeared at meetings in the Rostov barracks and indicated that their own
regiments were eager to join the movement. Such incidents allowed revolutionary newspapers to be optimistic about the prospects for a general
revolt in the Moscow garrison.[24] In reality such visitors were not representative of the mood of the majority; they were likely to be relatives or
acquaintances of Rostov soldiers who found themselves carried away by
the enthusiasm of the moment.[25]

During the three days of the Rostov rebellion, the expression of discontent in other companies limited itself to a few harmless incidents: on December 1, some 200 soldiers from the Nesvizhskii regiment entered the
quarters of the nearby Pernovskii regiment, where they persuaded 100
soldiers to join them in a march to the Sumskii dragoons. There they were
stopped by officers. After presenting a list of demands, the demonstrators
returned to their quarters, where their commanders talked them into
waiting until December 6 for a reply to their petition. On December 2,
meetings were also held in the Tavricheskii and Ekaterinoslavskii grenadier regiments.[26] The authorities responded by arresting a number of the
apparent ringleaders and depriving the restless troops of ammunition.

At a meeting on December 2, socialist organizers brought together representatives from four regiments (Rostov, Ekaterinoslavskii, Nesvizhskii,
Troitsko-Sergievskii), three sapper battalions, a Cossack regiment, and
the revolutionary parties.[27] It was the first and last time this self-styled
Soviet of Soldier Deputies met, for the collapse of the Rostov revolt
brought an end to all revolutionary activity in the Moscow garrison.

At the height of unrest, the military command had been ready to believe the worst. It hesitated to use force against the rebels for fear that
other regiments would refuse to take action against their fellows. The
Sumskii dragoons, for example, refused to march against the Rostov men,
who were armed with machine guns.[28] In the authorities' judgment, no
more than 2,000 soldiers in all could be deemed entirely reliable.[29] The
commander of the Moscow garrison was worried enough on December 2
to appeal for reinforcements.[30] They were not needed. Two days later, the
situation was under control.

Declaration of War

After the St. Petersburg Soviet's president was arrested on November 26, the soviet declared its resolve "to prepare for armed insurrection."[31] But the leaders took no practical steps in this direction. Indeed, they doubted the workers' readiness for such an undertaking and feared that premature action would undermine the gains so far achieved in the revolution. The St. Petersburg Soviet executive committee met for the last time on the afternoon of December 3. Even at this date, it could not decide on the proper response to the government's offensive. The Social Democratic United Federative Council favored a general strike. Representatives of the railroad and postal-telegraph unions supported the idea, but many on the executive committee lacked enthusiasm. Before the committee was able to resolve its differences, it found itself under arrest, along with 223 soviet deputies gathered for a plenum session. Workers elected other deputies to replace them, but the new soviet lacked the authority of the old.[32]

With the St. Petersburg Soviet in disarray, leadership of the workers' movement passed to Moscow, where the local situation was already one of growing agitation. Railroad workers had cooperated with the postal-telegraph strike by refusing to move the mail or to transmit telegrams of an "antisocial character," that is, any official message seen as threatening to the workers' movement.[33] Police arrested union leaders at the Moscow-Brest station on November 28, and two days later the administration dismissed five recalcitrant telegraphists on the Moscow-Kazan line.[34] On December 1, over 1,000 railroad workers gathered in the Kazan shops to protest the firing.[35] In response to the mood of growing resentment, worker-representatives from all Moscow rail lines met on December 3. They finally decided to call a general strike to support the principles at stake in the postal workers' movement.[36]

The leaders of the Moscow Soviet felt they had no choice but to go along. The workers would strike and the soldiers mutiny whether or not the soviet provided them with guidance. The absence of organized direction would only make the popular movement more vulnerable to defeat, and the soviet's prestige would suffer. Moreover, the imminence of Black Hundred mobilization, anticipated in conjunction with the ceremonial mass planned for the Tsar's nameday, December 6, argued the need for immediate action. Party leaders had no enthusiasm for a new general strike, however, and they feared that insurrection might well prove suicidal. They issued the strike call with reluctance and a sense of fatality. Even the Bolsheviks, whose pronouncements were the most uncom-

promising, demonstrated little optimism. One Bolshevik militant later recalled the situation in early December: "The beginning of government
repression, the increased conservatism of Kadet elements, Black Hundred pogroms, the growing unrest among the broad working-class masses
[*rabochie nizy*]—all these developments finally forced us Bolsheviks,
as well as the Mensheviks, the Socialist Revolutionaries, and the Soviet of Workers' Deputies to the point of explosion—to the December
tragedy." [37]

As he goes on to make plain, the authority of the revolutionary leadership was at best one-sided: ideology and organizational direction were
effective only when they coincided with the flow of popular energy, energy that could be mobilized more easily than it could be controlled.

Observing our growing influence in the soviet and in the factories, many of us
[Bolsheviks] . . . flattered ourselves with the hope that "the proletariat would follow us," whereas in fact the proletariat of that time—that complicated psy-
chic aggregate of semiconscious instincts, unexpressed thoughts, unformulated
needs—was only following the two laws that generally govern the movement of all
masses: the law of acceleration for free-falling bodies and the law of equal and
opposite reaction. [38]

The force to which the proletariat was instinctively reacting—to pursue the metaphor invoked by our Bolshevik memoirist—was the government campaign of repression. A Bolshevik envoy from the St. Petersburg
Soviet arrived in Moscow to address the Moscow Soviet at its December
4 meeting. Accounts of his message differ. One Moscow Bolshevik, M.
Liadov, later recalled him as saying that workers in the capital were ready
to strike over the arrest of their leaders and needed only the support of
workers in other cities to ensure their success. The Bolsheviks on the
Moscow Soviet were skeptical of the envoy's report, Liadov added, fearing that the St. Petersburg workers were too exhausted to launch a new
strike. [39] A second Moscow Bolshevik, M. I. Vasil'ev-Iuzhin, in his account, recalled the messenger himself as being uncertain of the workers'
mood in the capital, [40] and this version is consistent with the fact that the
St. Petersburg Soviet executive committee itself, on the brink of arrest,
had doubted the wisdom of calling a new strike. Still a third Bolshevik
account claims the envoy brought news of imminent insurrection in the
capital. [41] The Socialist Revolutionary V. Chernov tells still another tale.
He describes leaders in both cities as unwilling to take the initiative:
"The Moscow Soviet decided to declare a strike and transform it into
armed insurrection primarily because such a decision had been taken in
St. Petersburg; and in St. Petersburg the decision had been made because events in Moscow were 'leading up to an insurrection.'" [42]

At any rate, the collapse of the Rostov mutiny convinced the Moscow Soviet of the need for quick action. The proletariat must not fail to show solidarity with its most important ally in the upcoming struggle, the rebellious soldiery.[43] The soviet did not immediately declare a general strike and armed uprising, but merely urged the workers to prepare for the coming announcement. The coercive tactics of the government were a sign of weakness, said the soviet's December 4 resolution: "The government is making a new desperate attempt to keep power in its hands. In St. Petersburg the Soviet of Workers' Deputies is being arrested, newspapers shut down and confiscated, meetings dispersed."[44] But the soviet also recognized that the state was still strong enough to force its vulnerable adversary to a showdown:

The government . . . is making a desperate effort to rout the proletariat. . . . [It] has tried to provoke the proletariat with brazen tricks so as to draw it onto the streets to be shot down. Up until now the proletariat has patiently refused to fall for these tricks, answering with biting mockery and concerted preparation for the decisive battle. But all patience has its limits. The government's latest tricks are so criminal that they cannot be left unanswered. By means of massive force and arrests, the government is clearly preparing to infringe even those paper rights that the working class wrested from it in October. It [the government] is taking them back.[45]

Soviet leaflets at this juncture mixed hotheaded boasts of dealing the government a "decisive rebuff" with cautious phrases about "readiness." The rhetorical confusion and provocative bombast reflected the fear that the mass movement was not prepared to meet the government's challenge. Pessimism was rife even among Bolsheviks.[46] But the party, and by extension the soviet, was the prisoner of its own propaganda. Lenin had taken care to identify the Bolshevik party with the spirit of revolutionary maximalism and to tar its Menshevik rivals with the stain of "bourgeois parliamentarism," if only on the theoretical level. Months before the strike movement had reached its peak, Lenin had spoken of the need to prepare for insurrection.[47] In August, he coupled the slogan of armed uprising with the call to reject the government's timid constitutional concession, the Bulygin Duma. The existing regime must be destroyed, he said, in order to make way for a people's government, which alone could establish a genuinely democratic representative body.[48] Insurrection, moreover, could not but attract the support of the majority of progressive forces, outraged by the intensity of counterrevolutionary violence: "There are ever increasing numbers of people to whom all 'plans' and even revolutionary ideas of any sort are quite alien, but who nevertheless *see* and *feel* the necessity for an armed struggle when they witness the atrocities perpetrated by the police, the Cossacks, and the Black Hundreds against unarmed citizens."[49]

By September, Lenin felt sure that the days of individual terrorism were over, that the time had come for the masses to arm: "Military operations *together with the people*, are now commencing."[50] In early October, he applauded the September street fighting in Moscow as a sign that the working class was ready for violent confrontation. "The *method of the Moscow workers*," he wrote approvingly, "[is] the method of insurrection by the people."[51] The general strike pushed the revolution even further toward the inevitable climax by mobilizing the working class, exacerbating conflict between progressive and counterrevolutionary forces, and weakening the tsarist regime. The strike made clear that political compromise within the context of the present system would necessarily fail to satisfy the popular demand for an active role in political life. He was less optimistic a week or so later: "The revolution is *not yet* strong enough to deal the enemy a decisive blow," he acknowledged on October 13,[52] but the masses were gearing up for mortal combat, and the party must not fail to lead them to the final, decisive victory.

As we saw in the last chapter, many of the Social Democratic leaflets distributed during the October strike and following the Bauman funeral included exhortations to arm and prepare for insurrection, coupling the need for popular self-defense with the ultimate goal of transforming society. In the words of Vasil'ev-Iuzhin, the party had "too often insisted on the . . . necessity of armed uprising . . . to be able to abandon the idea with impunity at the first instance of government pressure. The working class would not forgive such faintheartedness."[53] The soviet nevertheless hesitated to act without testing the workers' temper. It therefore urged all factories to hold meetings on December 5 to discuss the proposed strike and uprising.[54]

From seven o'clock in the evening of December 5 until one o'clock the next morning, some 400 persons attended a Bolshevik party meeting in the Fiedler academy. The meeting opened with reports from factory representatives: "not district organizers, or professional party militants, but simple workers from the benches."[55] All said the working class was ready to strike.[56] The Bolshevik organizer for military affairs, A. N. Vasil'ev, calculated that the revolutionary forces could count on an armed strength of 900–1,000 organized men: 300 Bolsheviks, 300 Socialist Revolutionaries, 100 Mensheviks, and 300 others. Moreover, he estimated that only 4,000 of the 14,000 troops quartered in the city could be considered loyal to the government. He thus made it seem as though the workers stood a good chance of winning over the majority of soldiers and achieving some kind of military victory. By this date, however, unrest in the Moscow garrison had already quieted down, and such optimism was unwarranted.[57] It was not shared, moreover, by all members of the Moscow Bolshevik Central Committee. Despite the apparent enthusiasm of the rank and file, the committee was still split on the wisdom of launching an armed uprising. Two of its members, including the specialist in revolutionary warfare, remained skeptical of the troops' revolutionary temper and worried about the inadequacy of arms at the strikers' disposal.[58] Two other committee members, however, argued that the party had no choice but to assume responsibility for the uprising.[59]

While the Bolshevik debate was still in progress, representatives of 29 railroads had gathered in another part of the city to work out a unified program of economic and legal demands as guidelines for future struggle. They did not discuss the question of the general strike until the arrival of a representative of the St. Petersburg Bolshevik Central Committee, accompanied by M. Liadov, from the Bolshevik Central Committee in Moscow. The two Bolsheviks insisted on the need for armed uprising in connection with the coming political strike. They claimed the army was ready to join the workers, whom they pictured as eager for battle. The majority of railroad union delegates did not favor a political strike and were all the more skeptical about the wisdom of taking armed action. One worker suggested that only the unorganized masses thirsted for action, while their more sophisticated comrades realized the futility of such an undertaking.[60] Another participant reported:

The speakers [at the railroad union meeting] agreed that the strike was untimely, that the railroad workers were unprepared for it. All were sure that given the current political situation, a strike would inevitably turn into an armed uprising. The government was aware of this and was naturally trying to provoke just such an outcome. Underlining the poor preparation for armed conflict, one speaker expressed himself thus: "Our only arms, comrades, are Westinghouse regulators and brakes." In view, however, of the announcement by the Social Democratic representatives that the political strike of factory workers would take place even without the support of the railroads, we decided to announce our support of the general strike.[61]

In the end, the railroad delegates endorsed the strike, concluding that there was nothing to lose by taking the offensive, since the government was determined to destroy the union. But according to Liadov, the endorsement came only after the Bolsheviks had threatened to bypass the delegates and appeal directly to the railroad shop workers, among whom Bolshevik influence was strong.[62] Liadov returned to the Bolshevik party meeting with the decision wrested from the reluctant railroad conference. The news was decisive in overcoming the Bolshevik Central Committee's own doubts: the delegates voted, with only a few dissenting voices, to begin the general strike at noon on December 7.[63]

The Moscow Mensheviks, as one might suppose, were even less eager than the Bolsheviks to call for insurrection. At a conference of 250 Menshevik delegates held on December 4, only the representative of the printers' union was truly enthusiastic about the proposed offensive.[64] But though many agreed that the undertaking was doomed to defeat, they were reluctant to desert the movement.[65]

Despite their reservations, the Mensheviks were prepared to cooperate with the Bolsheviks to ensure that Social Democrats dominated the movement. Their joint body, the United Federative Council, met on the morning of December 6 to prepare for the meeting of the Moscow Soviet scheduled for later in the day. The council hoped to draw on the prestige of the Moscow Soviet and the resources and influence of the Socialist Revolutionaries, while maintaining effective control of the strike movement. The Mensheviks suggested that the Social Democrats present the soviet plenum with an organizational plan that would serve this purpose. To this end the council proposed that the soviet create a special information bureau to coordinate the strike. The proposal was adopted by the Moscow Soviet when it met that day. The two Social Democratic groups between them commanded seven of the seats on the new bureau, against only three for the Socialist Revolutionaries. The Social Democratic contingent was split four-three in favor of the Mensheviks and included a worker from each faction.[66]

The United Federative Council had also drafted the text of a strike announcement to put before the soviet's plenum, but the usual Social Democratic call to arms was too much for the Socialist Revolutionaries. Despite their greater experience with armed struggle and their traditional advocacy of extreme methods, the Socialist Revolutionaries feared the proletariat's isolation would spell defeat.[67] A new, more moderate draft was accordingly worked out by representatives of the three parties. It called for the declaration of a general strike and the exertion of all possible effort toward its transformation into an armed insurrection. To satisfy the Socialist Revolutionaries, the revised version included explicit reference to armed rebellion only as one of a final series of rhetorical exhortations.[68] The parties had papered over their differences, but they had hardly resolved them—or overcome their own ambivalence about the step they were endorsing. The December 6 soviet plenum meeting, which was attended by 120 persons, representing 91 enterprises, the railroad and postal unions, and the political parties, unanimously adopted the revised text.[69]

Despite the divergence of political goals and strategies, the radical-liberal alliance had survived the month of November. There were three reasons for its survival: the continuing strength of the counterrevolutionary elements in Moscow, the intensity of government repression, and the comparative moderation of left-wing activity. Busy increasing their popular base, Moscow radicals wished only to avoid violent conflict. The progressive forces shared not only a common enemy to the right, but also a similar concern for the constructive tasks of political organizing.

Now, however, the left lost the support of its moderate allies. The government had provoked the revolutionaries into making good the extremism of their rhetoric. This succeeded, where police repression and political compromise had both failed, in driving a wedge into the opposition movement. With the formal declaration of the new general strike and armed uprising, the Kadet Party openly dissociated itself from the tactics of the radical movement. P. N. Miliukov expressed his objections in an article written at the time:

The top officers must be certain that they are leading their soldiers to victory, not to the slaughterhouse. If they are not convinced of this, then the decision to call a political strike is wrong. In October, the political strike was a heroic civilian feat. It was doubtless a political mistake in November. Now, a political strike could turn out to be a crime—a crime against the revolution![70]

From Strike to Insurrection

On December 7, the first day of the strike, the executive committee of the Moscow Soviet issued a set of instructions to the workers:

1. All workers not yet participating in the strike should be taken from their work tomorrow, December 8.

2. Meetings should be held every morning in specially designated places, or on factory premises, to keep workers abreast of latest developments.

3. Local district soviets should meet daily in order to carry out the directives of the soviet executive committee.

4. General mass meetings are to be held daily.

5. The soviet newsletter will appear daily.

6. Factory guards are to remain on their posts under workers' supervision so as to ensure the safety of factory property. In the next few days, the soviet will organize its own guard service for the protection of property against theft and destruction.

7. Bars that do not serve alcoholic beverages may remain open, provided their owners allow them to be used as meeting places.

8. Food shops used by workers may remain open, provided they give credit.

9. During the period of the strike, workers will not pay rent. . . .

10. When the heating is turned off on factory premises, care must be taken to exclude workers' kitchens and living quarters.[71]

But by the time these instructions were issued, the factory workers had already shown their enthusiasm for the strike. As one observer noted, they struck without waiting for meetings. "Nothing comparable . . . had occurred during the October strike, when it had often been necessary 'to force the closing' [*snimat'*] of recalcitrant enterprises."[72] Why the strike should have been so popular in the factories is not clear. Perhaps there was a reluctance to return to work after Sunday's national holiday.[73] Perhaps the growing anger in Moscow's railroad shops had infected the general atmosphere. In any case, the industrial districts bustled with activity. Workers showed tremendous vitality in their own communities, but there was also a sense of unity that had been lacking in November.

The job of supervising and directing the strike fell to the district soviets. These local committees, as we have noted, came to life before the central soviet itself had been created. They constituted the only vital links between party leaders and rank-and-file supporters of the movement. Even now, the local assemblies did not wait to hear the views of the center before they took their own positions. For example, the 2,000 workers who flooded to a meeting of the Zamoskvorech'e soviet on December 8 passed a resolution demanding that the City Council, the zemstvos, and other civic organizations supply the strikers with money to purchase arms. Indeed, they thought the City Council should go even further: it should abdicate its authority and transfer its resources to the Moscow Soviet. As for the factory owners, the city soviet must compel them to dismiss their armed guards and to open their plants for use as popular gathering places. In case of a prolonged strike, the workers threatened to raid local grocery stores for provisions.[74] In fact, the day-to-day tasks before the district soviets were rather more benign than the purchase of arms or the plunder of food shops. In some areas, they played the part of economic watchdog: they made sure essential shops stayed open; they persuaded merchants to make credit available to strikers and not to raise prices.[75]

Workers in large firms (such as the Prokhorov mill in Presnia) played a central role in the soviets. Such plants also acted as independent units. Strikers took over the Sytin print shop, which they used to issue the first number of the soviet's newsletter, *Izvestiia moskovskogo soveta rabochikh deputatov*, on December 7. Sytin workers called for the overthrow of the City Council and its replacement by a popularly elected body. Other large plants also became centers of agitation; each of the tobacco factories, the Rallé perfume factory, and the Kushnerev printing plant drew large crowds.[76] Workers in still other large plants began fashioning arms. These included three textile mills, Prokhorov (6,000 workers), Tsindel' (2,400), and Mikhailov (1,265), the latter both in northern Zamoskvorech'e (VI);

the Bromlei machine works (1,500) in the lower Zamoskvorech'e; and the Sui candy factory (920) in Sushchevskaia (IV).[77]

The importance of giant factories as rallying points for striking workers and as centers of neighborhood leadership corresponds to their importance in the strike movement. The relative strike intensity among workers in plants of this scale was never as great as in December. In the course of the fall months, every metal and textile plant with 500 or more workers had been struck at least once. By December 19, half the textile workers and three-quarters of the metalworkers in plants of this size had struck more than once. The workers in metal plants with 1,000 or more workers had become increasingly militant over the months: one-third of them struck in October, more than half in November, and two-thirds in December. In the textile industry, the behavior of workers in large enterprises was more erratic. During the October strike, workers in mills with less than 500 hands had been the most active. Immediately after the manifesto, workers in a number of giant firms suddenly struck and then returned to work and did not strike again during November. In December, however, fully three-quarters of the textile hands in plants with 500 or more workers went on strike—a record proportion. The giants with 1,000 or more workers were particularly active: three out of five such firms in the Zamoskvorech'e (VI) struck; in Presnia-Khamovniki (III), all five giant mills closed their doors.

The increase in strikers from large-scale plants reflects the dramatic expansion of the workers' movement in December. No sooner had rail traffic halted on the Moscow lines (all except the Nikolaevskii, linking the two capitals, which escaped the strikers' control),[78] than thousands of factory workers walked off the job. By December 9, over 80,000 had gone on strike,[79] almost two and a half times as many as had participated in the October general strike, and almost twice the total for the month of November. The number of striking metalworkers was 55 percent greater than between October 1 and October 17, and the number of textile strikers was three times greater. Approximately half the workers in both industries were now on strike, along with 60 percent of the food industry labor force. Almost half the workers in mineral and chemical plants and two-thirds of those in leather factories also struck in December. After two months of relative inactivity, workers in the printing industry once again joined the strike movement in large numbers. At least as many printers struck in December as had participated in the September strike, and most were veterans of the earlier movement.[80]

Because of the steep rise in strike activity among workers employed in textile mills with 1,000 or more workers (up from 30 percent of their work force in November to over 80 percent in December), the December strike affected Presnia-Khamovniki (area III) more than any other area of the city. This quarter, as we have noted, was dominated by textile manufacture: mills employed two-thirds of the area's factory labor force; giant mills employed over 80 percent of the area's textile workers, almost twice the city average for textile worker concentration. Most of the giant plants in Presnia-Khamovniki had struck only fitfully before December. The 1,000 employees at the Moscow Lace Mill and the 3,000 at Giubner calico had struck briefly at the very end of October.[81] The 3,400 workers at the Zhiro silk mill had drafted demands in early October and been locked out by management; they had stopped work again in mid-November.[82] The 1,600 workers at the Dobrzhialovskaia canvas factory struck for the first time in the year on December 8.[83]

At Prokhorov, the largest of the mills, workers had struck in January but had remained calm throughout the summer and early fall.[84] On October 16, management had closed the firm in anticipation of a strike. Workers met two days later to discuss this possibility, but only half the assembly was for it. The engineers and solderers in particular refused to stop work,[85] a notable exception to the general pattern of metal shops taking the lead among textile workers. The next day, Prokhorov was forced to close temporarily, after an aggressive crowd of strikers from nearby factories engaged in a skirmish with police and pelted the factory windows with stones.[86] But work soon resumed and continued throughout November. The Zubatov union had a strong foothold in the mill, but by mid-November, the Socialist Revolutionaries had succeeded in winning over the Zubatov leaders and had acquired a large following in the plant.[87] Mensheviks were also popular, especially among the mechanics.[88] On December 7, the entire work force of 6,000 struck in response to the general strike call, without presenting any specific demands.[89] Until the very end of the December strike and insurrection, the Prokhorov factory served as the focal point of worker organization in the district.

As we have seen, the call for insurrection was hardly a popular move even among the revolutionary leaders, let alone the liberals. But the factory workers' strike nevertheless elicited a sympathetic response from a broad range of groups. Various organizations representing skilled and white-collar workers, including the now radicalized Union of Unions and the corporation of municipal employees, immediately announced their support for the strike.[90] Clerks in banks, shops, and pharmacies, tailors, municipal workers, and government employees joined the strike in large numbers.[91] Public halls drew a varied audience, as revolutionary activists organized meetings throughout the city:

All during the day [of December 7] the Polytechnical Museum was the scene of continuous meetings, with an endless succession of speakers and constantly changing crowds. Party agitators emphasized the necessity of turning the strike into armed insurrection, but warned against taking any practical steps toward this end without direction from the soviet executive committee. The meetings were attended mainly by workers and artisans, but several auditoriums also held meetings of government employees: clerks in the State Bank, in savings associations, in various branches of the judicial system, and customs officers.[92]

On the first day of the strike, policemen were few, and conflict occurred only when the strike spread to the downtown area:

The streets had been filled with crowds since early morning. Most stores were closed and boarded up. Striking shop clerks marched along Tver Street and other large avenues, forcing their fellows to quit work. Strikers in the Kuz'min fruit store shot and seriously wounded the owner when he refused point blank to close up shop. The closing of a restaurant in Carriage Row provoked a violent confrontation. In order to avoid such incidents, many shop owners are applying to the soviet for written permission to continue trade. On Sukharev Square, butchers barely restrained themselves from murdering a group of clerks who tried to get them to stop work; in the end, however, they were persuaded to leave their shops. In the same area, a speaker was attacked by hooligans, and two young seamstresses were beaten up as they made the rounds of nearby tailor shops.[93]

Admiral F. V. Dubasov, who had been appointed Governor-General on November 24, arrived in Moscow on December 4.[94] He did not waste time sizing up the situation: on December 7, he declared a state of emergency; on December 8, he followed up with an appeal to St. Petersburg for troop reinforcements.[95] On the evening of December 8, the first serious confrontation took place between the opposing sides. This incident, which came to be known as the Siege of the Aquarium Theater, impressed itself on the popular mind as an example of the government's disregard for legal guarantees and preference for violent measures. Later, when the government had truly outdone itself in the use of brute force, its behavior on this occasion came to be remembered for its relative restraint. It was still too soon after the October Manifesto, however, for the public to have lost its optimism. Moscovites responded with naïve indignation to official violations of the letter and the spirit of the manifesto. This attitude contributed to the rapid escalation of conflict during the early days of the December strike.[96]

Apart from the Polytechnical Museum, the Aquarium and Olympia theaters, side by side on Sadovyi Boulevard, between Arbat and Presnia, were the most popular meeting places in the city. Here revolutionary orators harangued the public with the familiar exhortations to armed struggle. Several thousand persons, including many armed *druzhinniki* (members of left-wing defense squads) were assembled in the Aquarium Theater on the night of December 8, when four companies of soldiers surrounded the buildings.[97] The officers refused to let anyone leave without being searched for weapons. Almost all the party leaders and most of the people with guns managed to slip out unnoticed through a back fence; many took refuge in a nearby school. At least 3,000 escaped in this manner. Those still trapped indoors debated for three hours whether to resist the indignity being forced on them. In the end, they submitted to the search. Fifty persons were detained and their revolvers confiscated; all were released the following day. A brief exchange of shots had occurred, and soldiers had used their whips on some of their captives: this was the violence involved in the Aquarium affair.[98]

The pattern of December 8 repeated itself the next day: during daylight hours workers met constantly in their factories, while on the downtown streets crowds of shop clerks, working-class youths, students, and curious residents gathered to talk and to listen to speeches, until being dispersed by troops or police. Flushed with indignation over the Aquarium incident, the druzhinniki became more zealous in their attempts to disarm individual policemen when they ran into them in the streets, but they were still not inclined to challenge the more formidable forces of the military. In only one incident did druzhinniki offer any resistance to the troops in their crowd-clearing activity. Indeed, the sentiment that predominated at factory meetings, even in those plants where the workers had begun to collect money for firearms, or to fashion their own crude weaponry with tools at hand, was the fear of provoking confrontation. Machinists in the Moscow-Brest railroad shops, for example, tried to control the irresponsible use of firearms. They insisted that no action be taken without explicit soviet authorization.[99]

As for the central leadership, few of its members had any military experience or any concrete plans for the conduct of the anticipated insurrection. When the United Federative Council met on December 7, it could only suggest that the armed bands continue their practice of disarming city policemen. Neither the council nor the Moscow Soviet's newly constituted Information Bureau had the opportunity to do more than enunciate this rudimentary plan of action. Police raided a bureau meeting on December 7, after the Socialist Revolutionaries had already left.[100] They arrested the seven Social Democrats and later that night caught the three Socialist Revolutionaries, along with the chairman of the Museum for Assistance to Labor, N. K. Murav'ev.[101] The Moscow Soviet was thus enfeebled from the start, though it did not immediately cease to issue directives. These served less to shape the course of events than to describe the consequences of initiatives taken elsewhere.

As on the previous evening, the worst of the violence on December 9 came after the fall of darkness. Some 300 to 400 people had gathered on

Strastnaia Square when they were approached by dragoons sent to clear the area. The crowd was friendly and urged the soldiers to join their meeting. The dragoons responded with gunfire. They wounded several persons and killed one young man who had sought shelter in a tram pavilion. Once the troops had left, his companions set fire to the pavilion, shouting "Scoundrels! Murderers!" They retreated only at the appearance of firefighters. They then proceeded up Tver Street to Triumphal Square, where they joined up with another crowd. Together they began to pull down telegraph poles and to pile them into the street, along with barrels, boards, and metal scraps, tied up with telegraph wire.

The building of the first barricades was an impulsive gesture. Groups of politically active workers and druzhinniki had set the example, but they did so on the spur of the moment. Party and soviet leaders had said nothing of barricades. As P. N. Kolokol'nikov, a Menshevik member of the soviet executive committee, wrote later: "In the first days of the movement, local meetings and demonstrations were organized in a spontaneous manner. The building of barricades was initiated from below, not from above. The slogans of the Federative Council and the soviet executive committee only served to sanction retrospectively what had already occurred."[102]

People suspected that government-sent provocateurs also lent eager hands to the enterprise, which was certain to provoke energetic reprisals.[103] Indeed, dragoons stationed in houses surrounding the square and along Tver Street began shooting at the crowd as soon as the barricades had been erected. The druzhinniki fired back, and at least one person in the crowd was killed and several were wounded. At eleven o'clock the soldiers began taking down the barricades. For two hours thereafter they kept up a continuous hail of rifle fire into the surrounding streets.[104]

Despite the reaction of the troops, the Social Democrats did not try to convert defensive barricade building into an aggressive strategy. The United Federative Council encouraged peaceful attempts to win the soldiers' sympathy, in the hope that sufficient numbers might yet be persuaded to join the strikers and armed conflict still be avoided.[105] Workers were eager for any rumor of discontent among the soldiers, but the facts were not encouraging. Troops from the Alexander barracks on Bol'shaia Serpukhovskaia Street, for example, began to resist orders, but the promise of an extra ration of soap and a glass of vodka brought them quickly under control.[106]

The Social Democratic leaders recognized that their power to influence events was at best tenuous. As early as December 6, the soviet executive committee had divided itself into two sections of 12 members each, one to assume active direction and the other to be held in reserve. Not all dis-

tricts were represented in the active half, and the few times it met, attendance did not exceed five or six delegates. The executive committee lost
touch with the opinions of the district organizations, and became almost
entirely dependent on the United Federative Council for direction.[107] But
the council itself met for the last time on the evening of December 9,
when it conceded that "in view of the difficulty of maintaining contact between the [soviet] executive committee and the masses, the local soviets
must assume direct leadership of the struggle."[108]

Meanwhile, the Moscow Soviet had issued no tactical guidelines to
govern the activities of the armed self-defense squads, the *boevye druzhiny*. The druzhinniki contented themselves with theoretical discussion
and small practice sallies, concentrated on capturing arms from individual
policemen.[109] The squads continued to act entirely on their own initiative
in December, even though a special committee had been constituted in
early November to coordinate their activities. This so-called Coalition
Council (soviet) of Druzhiny met only twice after its formation: once on
December 9, when it failed to issue any directives, and again on December 16, when it called for an end to fighting on the very eve of Presnia's
destruction by tsarist forces.[110]

Armed bands had first made their appearance during the September
printers' strike, and students had begun organizing similar units during
the October 14 siege of the university. By the time of Bauman's funeral,
membership in the university bands exceeded 200 persons.[111] Social
Democratic and Socialist Revolutionary militants helped organize the
druzhiny, but they worked on their own with no official blueprint to guide
them. Only in mid-October did the Bolsheviks finally speak in specific
terms of the form of organized action appropriate to the circumstances of
urban revolution. On October 15, *Rabochii*, a short-lived Social Democratic paper, under Bolshevik editorship, commented: "In order to carry
out an uprising, one must have a distinct combat organization—detachments of armed men, organized in the manner of military outfits. Without
such detachments it is impossible to stage an uprising that will not degen-
erate into a disorderly rebellious outburst [*bunt*]."[112] Such brigades, said
Rabochii, should be used to seize arms, raid arsenals and banks, and take
over communications services; they should destroy bridges and roads,
build barricades, and engage the enemy in the streets: "Popular uprising
should take the form of street warfare in which the troops are surrounded
on all sides by the insurgents and each house is turned into a fortress,
becoming an ambush for the troops, so that danger threatens them from
every balcony and window and their movement is blocked at every step
by a mass of proliferating barricades." The Bolsheviks did not offer any
other specific instructions on the formation and deployment of the bri-

gades until early in December.[113] By then the majority of squads had already been set up.

The largest single unit was the Free District Druzhina. This umbrella organization, formed after Bauman's funeral, had at least 500 members, the bulk of them either professionals of one sort or another (about 200) or bank employees (200); at least 50 students and 50 skilled workers were also in the unit. In addition, there were several smaller bands of students, craftsmen, and others, with 470 members altogether.[114] As many as 16 factories had their own units: seven in area III (Presnia-Khamovniki), three in area IV, four in area V, and two in area VI.[115] Other workers gathered into free-floating druzhiny. About 500 men all told belonged to these factory and free-floating groups.

Finally, there were said to be approximately 450 railroad shop workers and administrative employees organized into seven druzhiny. The largest, on the Moscow-Kazan line, had 200 members, half blue-collar and half administrative staff.[116] These railroad druzhiny were funded by the Moscow Strike Committee, which spent over 26,000 rubles during November and December for the purchase of arms. This indicates that only the most radically inclined groups were still active in the committee. But from the amount of money available, it is also clear that the Social Democrats and Socialist Revolutionaries were not alone in supporting worker self-defense. The railroad workers were the best armed of all the bands. They mainly policed railroad property and rarely engaged in street fighting. On some lines (such as Iaroslavl, Kazan, Kursk, and Windau) workers gained control and assumed full administrative functions. Witnesses agreed that the strikers observed admirable discipline in heeding their union leaders and in protecting railroad property from willful damage or looting.[117] The railroad druzhinniki did not, however, manage to prevent people from running off with the contents of the hundreds of freight cars stuck in city depots. Indeed, it is quite possible they deliberately ignored or even took part in the looting.[118]

Despite the difficulty in pinning down the exact number of druzhinniki, it is clear that no more than 1,000 people actually participated in armed action at any one time. The most generous estimate, including replacements and substitutes, still does not exceed 2,000 squad members for the entire course of the insurrection.[119] To meet a threat of this size, the government mobilized an impressive show of military might. Magnified by the scale of repression, the uprising took on tremendous symbolic proportions.

11

THE DECEMBER UPRISING

The Partisan Tactic

In the turbulent days of December, the authorities first tried to handle the armed bands roaming the streets the way they had dealt with the leaders of the working-class movement: by arresting enough of them to destroy their organization. But the druzhinniki were by definition a leaderless bunch: the nerve center of the rebellion was hard to find, and replacements were waiting in the wings. And now that uprising was the order of the day, the revolutionaries were more likely to meet the government head on than allow themselves to be rounded up in peaceful fashion. Their honor now hung in the balance.

The first large-scale confrontation between druzhinniki and government forces centered on the Fiedler academy, located just beyond Chistyi Pond in the Iauzskaia district (II). This was one of the main centers of druzhina activity. The director of the school, forty-two-year-old Ivan Ivanovich Fiedler, was a liberal from an upper-class family. An engineer by training, he had served as city councilman from 1901 to 1905.[1] Since October he had allowed revolutionary groups to meet on the premises. There was hardly a day in November when 200 to 300 persons did not assemble there.[2] In early December, armed bands consisting largely of students used the school as a base of operations. The druzhinniki would leave at night in groups of ten or fifteen on exploratory expeditions and return in the daytime. The place began to resemble a "revolutionary camp," according to one participant.[3] The occupants held regular shooting practice and attended special classes on the theory of street fighting and on the care of the wounded. High school and university students rubbed shoulders with worker and intelligentsia druzhinniki. Socialist Revolutionaries and Social Democrats spent time in heated political discussion. The Secret Police learned of their activities through an agent who worked as liaison between the Moscow Bolshevik Committee and the druzhiny.[4] The regular police, however, had no idea of what was taking place in the academy.[5]

On the evening of December 9, over 100 armed druzhinniki were inside the school, along with at least 500 participants in a railroad union meeting.[6] At eight o'clock, a squad of dragoons and a squad of gendarmes suddenly surrounded the building.[7] The captain and his officers entered to confront a stairway bristling with pointed guns. The defenders of this academic fortress, it must be remembered, were almost all under the age of thirty, most no older than twenty-one, and none possessed the least military experience. Of the 99 people later arrested and tried for their part in the Fiedler incident, at least half came from educated middle-class or lower middle-class families. Along with 35 students, there were six railroad administration employees (the oldest group, at an average age of twenty-nine), 17 railroad machine shop workers, and 26 factory workers, most in their late teens. Most of the other 15 people were of non-working-class background.[8] Few of the women carried guns; female students joined the first-aid units organized by a young doctor named N. G. Kotik.

The captain had instructions to disarm the druzhinniki, take them into custody, and eventually release them. But the young people refused to surrender their guns. They distrusted the captain's promise of leniency, and they did not want to lose the large cache of arms in their possession. Moreover, the captives found it hard to take the situation seriously. The officers were educated men. They chatted easily with the students and with Fiedler, who interceded on the revolutionaries' behalf with paternal concern.[9]

But stubbornness only condemned the besieged to passivity. During the next four hours, the druzhinniki discussed tactics while the captain waited for artillery reinforcements. Someone suggested they throw bombs at the troops and attempt to escape in the ensuing confusion. No one took responsibility for a decision, however, and nothing was done. At midnight, two light artillery guns were moved in, and the captain once again offered to let those willing to surrender leave the building unharmed. The young people again rejected the offer, and the artillery went into action. To this point, the occupants of the school had been well protected in the upper stories and the central staircase, but now artillery fire began to shatter the building's façade, and the upper floors became vulnerable. The guns were situated out of the aim of the sharpshooters, who were thus relatively helpless against their opponents.

Once the shelling began in earnest, Fiedler urged the young people to give in. They would not be persuaded. When Fiedler appealed to the officers to show restraint, they arrested him, and the exchange of bombs, grenades, and gunfire continued. When the druzhinniki themselves finally asked to surrender, the soldiers refused to negotiate. One of the two students sent to talk with the besiegers remembered this refusal as a shock: "In our naïveté," he wrote, "we had expected they would treat us even now as equals."[10] The exchange of gunfire resumed. The women at last began waving white flags. Some of the men soon joined them in offering to give themselves up.

The officers agreed to let the druzhinniki leave their firearms in the vestibule and promised not to harm them when they left the building. But the unarmed young men and women had no sooner reached the waiting soldiers when they attacked them with open swords. Some were wounded; some tried to escape through the windows of adjoining apartments. The wanton cruelty of the apparently drunken troops made the most vivid and shocking impression on participants and witnesses. In all, 20 of the besieged were wounded, seven or eight killed, and over 100 led off to prison. In the building, soldiers found 13 bombs, 18 rifles, and 15 revolvers.[11] In revenge for the siege of the Fiedler academy, a group of Socialist Revolutionaries bombed the Moscow Secret Police headquarters that same evening.

The officers initially approached the situation as if it were a simple police action, rather than a military confrontation. There was reason to view the problem at Fiedler's as a case of generational conflict, or of youthful hotheadedness, rather than of class warfare. The druzhinniki refused to negotiate, however, out of fear, pride, and more than a touch of naïve arrogance. At the same time, they realized they were militarily overpowered. When the revolutionaries did agree to parley with the enemy, they sent their most respectable members—Fiedler, Kotik, and student druzhinniki—to deal with the officers. They did not appeal to the troops themselves, who turned out in the end to be their worst enemies. The siege was a turning point for both sides: the government began to rely more on military tactics, and the revolutionaries realized that conflict had reached serious proportions.

On the morning of the next day, December 10, vast crowds filled the streets and squares along the outer boulevards, while troops cordoned off Tver Street and stationed artillery on Strastnaia Square. Druzhinniki politely disarmed individual officers and policemen as they met them in the street, and exchanged occasional shots with military patrols. It was not until afternoon that soldiers began systematically shooting into the crowds. Heavy artillery fire swept the wide boulevards radiating out from Strastnaia Square and penetrated the side streets as far as Kudrinskaia Square on the outer ring. People filled the outer boulevards and responded to the shooting by feverishly building barricades from Kudrinskaia on the west all the way north to Sukharevskaia-Sadovaia. Druzhinniki, concierges, workers, students, upper-class women, and even "gentlemen in beaver collars" gathered fruit stands, telephone poles, iron house gates, and other loose objects, which they piled across the streets every hundred feet or so.[12]

The barricades consisted of anything from simple wires stretched across the street to elaborate fortresses constructed of overturned trams or railway carriages. House gates, grating, and fences, sign boards, empty barrels, baskets, crates, charcoal or flour sacks, sawed-off telephone and telegraph poles, trees cut down from the sidewalks—all this was piled onto the barricades, tied together, and reinforced by wires. The *druzhinniki* themselves only supervised the construction. Little boys, adolescents, and sometimes adult residents (often under threats from the *druzhinniki*) did the actual work. Armed *druzhinniki* protected the barricades by shooting at approaching soldiers. . . . They followed the partisan tactic, refusing to confront troops or police, quickly fleeing after shooting began through convenient doorways and back courtyards.[13]

Soldiers and firemen dismantled the structures, but people quickly rebuilt them as soon as they were torn down.

While the central boulevards witnessed scenes of bloody conflict, the factory districts remained unaffected. Large meetings were held in factories and halls in Lefortovo and Rogozhskaia (V), where thousands of workers heard the militant exhortations of Social Democratic orators. Police did not interfere. On December 10, some 1,500 workers gathered in the Polytechnical Museum (II), and on the same day 5,000 to 6,000 workers from the Renomé candy factory and other nearby plants staged a peaceful demonstration around the Butyrskaia Prison (IV). In Presnia (III), a massive crowd set out from the Prokhorov factory and marched through the district, brandishing red flags. Prokhorov workers were eager to join the barricade building on downtown streets, but a Cossack division prevented them from reaching Kudrinskaia Square, gateway to the center of the city. The Prokhorov deputies told their comrades to concentrate on defending their own neighborhood. The Cossacks did not use force in turning back the demonstration. Elsewhere, however, in Khamovniki, dragoons attacked a crowd of 5,000 workers who had appealed to soldiers in nearby barracks to join them in the street.[14]

By late afternoon of December 10, the fever of barricade building had spread to Presnia:

The streets overflowed with people. Many were just curious bystanders. But the majority of residents helped put up barricades. Old women, for example, dragged sleds and bed frames; concierges carried gates and wood. Throughout Presnia resounded the rumble and crash of telegraph poles and street lamps falling to the ground, as though an entire forest were being felled. Workers tore off house gates and piled them in the streets. Occasionally house owners and concierges tried to stop them, but they retreated when threatened by *druzhinniki*.[15]

The situation in the Zamoskvorech'e (VI) was similar:

The streets of Zamoskvorech'e had an excited, holiday air; crowds of people gathered on street corners in an attitude of expectation. Here and there they built barricades, less from considerations of strategy than from the need to find some occupation. The builders were mainly working-class youths, joined by an occasional solid citizen—artisans and shopkeepers could be seen dragging broken benches, two-legged stools, and other superfluous household objects onto the altar of revolution. Cossacks were concentrated in the center of the city and did not appear. Police uniforms vanished. Simonovo became something of an autonomous republic: the police evaporated, as they did everywhere else, and full power fell into the hands of the local soviet delegates. A significant portion of the working-class population (mainly family members) hurriedly evacuated the area, and the highways were filled with columns of people leaving for home in the countryside [*ukhodivshie k sebe na rodinu*], as far away from trouble as possible.[16]

The Governor-General did not have sufficient armed strength to control the insurrection. On December 11, he telegraphed St. Petersburg with a request for more troops. "The situation is becoming very serious," he said. "The ring of barricades around the city continues to tighten. The troops are obviously inadequate to deal with the situation."[17] He also appealed for police reinforcements. The police chief, for his part, complained that "despite the state of emergency in Moscow, various union organizations continue to hold meetings in the city, not only in buildings assigned by the city administration, but also in other locations. Revolutionary elements use these meetings for agitational purposes. Under conditions now prevailing in Moscow, police find it impossible to maintain surveillance."[18]

Meetings were most numerous at the district level. Indeed, in areas blocked off by barricades, they were immune from police interference. In one part of the Zamoskvorech'e, for example, all police had disappeared after December 7, and by December 10 the workers had taken over. "They established patrols to protect the residents and entirely controlled the area. They used eating houses and tea rooms for party gatherings and mass meetings. A general cafeteria was opened, as well as something resembling a hotel, where party activists and *druzhinniki* spent the nights."[19]

If the workers themselves were quick to jump into the fray, their leaders were not always ready to lead them. The former Bolshevik activist A. V. Sokolov recalls the following scene from an interparty meeting at the 500-worker Bari metal plant to the southeast of Moscow on December 9:

Bolshevik, Menshevik, and Socialist Revolutionary organizers argued until they were hoarse over what methods should take precedence in popular movements in general and in the Russian revolution in particular—"mass agitation" or "vanguard action." While this was going on, the crowd of workers assembled in the factory dining room sat and waited for directions from their leaders. They waited for an hour, then two, while the leaders continued to argue, the subject of the argument becoming ever more obscure. "The devil with you," cried one of the worker-delegates at last. "The workers are already beginning to leave."[20]

No doubt many left for the streets, where the conflict continued to intensify, without either side showing evidence of planned action. The armed bands sniped at the troops, who tried to reach the unseen enemy by firing into the crowds. Many unarmed persons were wounded. Incidents such as the following were common on the main downtown streets:

A crowd approached the police chief's house on Tver Boulevard [between the Tver and Arbat sections] and began shooting at the windows. After several warnings, troops responded with shrapnel shell. They shot in the direction of the Old Triumphal Gates, as well as along the boulevards. . . . They killed several persons and wounded many others. . . . The shooting continued with interruptions from one to four P.M. The distraught crowd reassembled each time and shot back at the troops, who then returned fire from the bell tower of the Strastnyi Monastery and from the First Women's High School building. Shots injured quite a few curious onlookers. Patrols completely surrounded Tver Street and blocked all access to the side streets, but the curious still made their way into the street and fell victim to the firing.[21]

During the night of December 10, police and firemen dismantled or burned barricades, only to find them reassembled the next morning. The entire outer ring of boulevards, from the Smolensk market on the southwest to the Red Gates on the east, had become a battlefield, laced with debris and telephone wire. Each of the major squares was a center of troop concentration or an artillery emplacement. The soldiers directed their gunfire into the surrounding area along the broad radiating streets. From their position in Kudrinskaia Square, for example, they were able to shoot both toward the Smolensk market in Arbat and toward Devich'e Pole in Khamovniki.[22]

In most cases, the druzhinniki did not provoke the soldiers to attack, but merely confined themselves to the defense of barricades. Near the Red Gates (at the juncture of areas II, IV, and V), for example, the rebels defended their position from the shelter of doorways, but soldiers succeeded in seizing their barricade and burning it to the ground. The Kushnerev printers' druzhina was more successful in repulsing a Cossack attack, and workers in the Miusskii tram park machine shops (in area IV,

near the Brest station) managed to fend off continual assault from the rela
tive safety of overturned tram cars.[23]

Occasionally, the druzhinniki became more aggressive. The pharmacy
clerks' union had its headquarters in Carriage Row, the street between
the Petrovskii barracks and Carriage Square in Sretenskaia (II). Here a
group of 45 armed men, members of the pharmacy clerks' druzhina,
backed by a crowd of almost 400 unarmed persons, was trying to dislodge
a group of 20 gendarmes concealed in a doorway when reinforcements appeared with artillery. The druzhinniki held firm, and the street remained
under the pharmacy clerks' control. In such enclosed spaces, blocked off
by a dense network of barricades, the druzhinniki were able to resist considerable force.[24]

As the fighting spread, fewer people came to meetings in the center of
the city, and factory workers stopped holding public demonstrations.
Dragoons began surrounding factories in the outlying districts, and many
workers simply left for home.[25] Those who stayed behind became increasingly militant. It was not long before workers in the Zamoskvorech'e
had covered the neighborhood with barricades. In this case, they were
led to do so by Social Democratic organizers. The Social Democrats
spread the word by addressing crowds of 5,000 to 6,000 workers that congregated in the Tsindel' cotton mill in the southeast corner of Piatnitskaia.
By afternoon, workers from the Sytin printing plant and the Mikhailov
wool mill had completely blockaded the streets around Sytin. Bromlei
metalworkers seized nearby Kaluzhskaia Square. On the instructions of
the local soviet, they extended the web of assembled debris along the major streets radiating out from the square toward the south and west. Mid-
way between these two centers of worker activity—Sytin and Bromlei—
Serpukhovskaia Square was crowded with Cossacks, busy firing into the
mouths of converging streets. In the evening drunken troops deliberately
set fire to the centrally located Sytin plant, which had published the soviet's daily newsletter and whose workers had demonstrated such exem-
plary zeal in the construction of barricades. The troops kept firemen from
putting out the blaze, which consumed the entire building in the course
of the night, in dramatic climax to the day's growing violence.[26]

By December 12, the authorities had lost control of all the railroads,
except the Nikolaevskii, connecting Moscow with St. Petersburg.[27] The
rest of the network, said one administrator, was "in the hands of the mutineers' fighting squads, which act in concert with the strikers to keep away
all well-intentioned employees."[28] On the evening of December 12, the
strikers attempted to capture the crucial Nikolaevskii line. A crowd of
2,000 strikers, including several hundred armed men, gathered in the ad-

acent Iaroslavl station. From that convenient vantage point, the druzhinniki fired at the soldiers guarding the Nikolaevskii station, but could not
drive them away. The link between Moscow and the capital remained
open.[29]

The Social Democrats had so far encouraged mass meetings and public
demonstrations as a means of mobilizing popular support. They had urged
the strikers to show restraint in the hope of winning the armed forces over
to the side of revolution. But the troops had remained loyal. Worse still,
from the Social Democrats' point of view, the government was becoming
more aggressive. The Bolsheviks, in prompt response to changing circumstances, issued new tactical guidelines. Strikers and their sympathizers must from now on remain indoors. "Avoid going to mass meetings," read the Bolshevik proclamation, which appeared in the soviet's
newsletter of December 11.[30] "We will soon see them in the free state,
but now we must fight and do nothing but fight. The government under-
stands this very well and only makes use of our meetings to slaughter and
disarm us." It was time for the partisan tactic. The masses must retire,
while small groups of armed men led the assault on government forces.

Main rule—*do not act in crowds*. Act in small groups of not more than three or
four persons. There should be as many of these groups as possible, and each of
them should learn to attack quickly and disappear quickly. One hundred Cossacks
can easily shoot down crowds of a thousand persons. You will confront a hundred
Cossacks with one or two marksmen. It is easier [for the troops] to hit one hundred than to hit one, especially if that one shoots unexpectedly and disappears
mysteriously. The police and the army will be powerless if all Moscow is covered
with these small elusive detachments.

The druzhinniki were warned against a repetition of the mistake that
had resulted in the disastrous siege of Fiedler's academy:

Do not occupy fortified places. The troops will always be able to take them or
simply to destroy them with artillery. Our fortresses should be courtyards and
other such places from which it is easy to take aim and *from which it is easy to
escape*. If [the troops] take the spot, they will find no one and will lose many men.
They cannot seize them all. To do so they would have to fill every house with
Cossacks.

The directive's Bolshevik authors pictured partisan warfare as an extended campaign of terrorist attacks on individual members of the armed
forces, preferably high-ranking officers. They suggested that the insurgents spare foot soldiers and ordinary policemen, who might still be made
to sympathize with the revolution. Most of this advice merely described
the habits of existing bands. Even the formal suggestion to proceed with

barricade building, issued by the Social Democrats on December 9, had come after the first structures had already appeared.[31] Only district party leaders had any real effect on the course of events.[32]

From December 12 to December 17, the pattern of conflict was similar. Troops continued to clear away the rubble, but the police were able to regain control of the streets only in the Zamoskvorech'e.[33] A good part of the city was still blocked off.[34] Though under continuous bombardment, people worked in the open to repair barricades. "Simple women—workers' wives, maid servants, and others—work on the barricades on an equal basis with the men. They are tireless. They saw down trees, smash telegraph poles, tear up kiosks, break up horse-drawn tram cars, build barricades and obstacles, defend them, and stand fast before cannons and machine guns."[35]

Food stores were open in the mornings, and residents were able to purchase supplies. The bombardments usually began at noon. Random sniper shots confused the soldiers. They could not locate the enemy or distinguish him from the rest of the population. Witnesses as always disagreed about which side usually initiated the shooting. The revolutionaries, at least, were convinced that government provocateurs deliberately stirred the soldiers to action:

It was enough for a single shot to be fired from a particular house for artillery to be drawn up immediately and the bombardment to begin. Revolver shots from windows were in most cases the work of provocateurs, since the *druzhinniki* shoot from concealed positions that allow them to flee through convenient exits. The shooting is answered by devastating artillery fire trained on the whole house. The guilty and the innocent suffer equally.[36]

Government propaganda exaggerated the strength of the opponent and played on the prejudices of the soldiers by picturing the insurrection as the work of Jewish conspirators. A liberal supply of vodka added to the soldiers' confusion. The troops began to see all civilians as their enemy and often shot at random into crowds. This behavior only increased the populace's sympathy for the strikers.[37] The respectable liberal legal journal *Pravo* (which provides an invaluable daily chronicle of events in Moscow) characterized the behavior of the troops as "ferocious in the extreme."[38]

The government, on its side, was convinced that residents of the battle-torn areas were abetting the revolutionaries. To counteract the strong-arm methods of the druzhinniki, Governor-General Dubasov declared that property owners would be held responsible for any shooting from the windows of their houses on pain of fines or imprisonment and the confiscation of their property. In addition to using regular troops for counter-insurgency, Dubasov organized voluntary militias, with the cooperation of the reactionary Union of the Russian People and under the direction of the police. The volunteers helped destroy barricades and walked the streets in bands of 40, armed with rifles. Many members of the police force abandoned their regular uniforms and posts to participate in this effort, and some even joined the Black Hundreds.[39]

Property owners in the first Khamovniki precinct took steps toward organizing a system of self-defense, an enterprise enthusiastically supported by the local police, endorsed by the Governor-General, and sponsored by the most reactionary member of the City Council, A. S. Shmakov. They circulated a hectographed announcement with the following text:

Today's extraordinary situation calls for peaceful individuals to undertake their own self-defense. We cannot and must not continue to tremble for our lives and for those of our families. In our helplessness and disarray we become the victims of evildoers. Today's meeting of property owners and apartment tenants has therefore selected a commission of public safety for our district. With the Governor-General's permission, it will organize an armed guard under an officer's command. At least 6,000 rubles a month will be necessary to maintain this outfit, and donations should be given as soon as possible to the treasurer, Ananii Klavdievich Zhiro [owner of the giant Zhiro silk mill]. Property owners should contribute in proportion to their tax bracket, and tenants should use their own judgment.

Citizens, this is a serious affair! The danger is great and terrible! Let us unite, and may the evildoers themselves experience the same terror they have caused us to feel. In the name of the love we bear our wives and children, and for the sake of saving our own selves, let us be strict and implacable in the belief that we are right to recognize the necessity for armed self-defense. Onward, and may God be with us![40]

Liberal councilmen, meanwhile, accused the authorities of promoting lawlessness and violence. The government itself, not the revolutionaries, was responsible for the greatest damage to life, property, and social stability. By December 14, for example, Councilman N. M. Kishkin was in no mood to mince words:

Moscow has been under fire for five days. . . . Why? They say that an armed uprising is taking place. . . . The streets are barricaded, but the barricades are undefended . . . ; there is shooting at individual policemen and officers, but armed insurrection as such, that is, deliberate attacks on public and state buildings, has not occurred. On the other hand, we have seen how troops destroyed the Fiedler academy, the Sytin printing plant, and the Prokhorov factory, and we witness the bombardment of streets on which there are only pedestrians. . . . A week ago the revolutionaries presented us with armed uprising on paper, the same paper on which they also declared a democratic republic. But now we have merely partisan warfare. The troops shell buildings, but the Governor-General denies he has given the order to do so. . . . We are issued the strictest orders, which are immediately violated by the authorities. . . . It is clear that the troops are not under the administration's control.[41]

The council agreed that the city administration ought to have more say in the deployment of the police and the military. It was reluctant, however, to suggest some alternative measure of its own devising or even to petition the authorities for an extension of its powers in police matters. During the week of most intense conflict, the council met almost continuously. The result was a lot of talk—with the conservative councilmen excoriating the insurgents and the liberals deploring government policy—but no action.[42]

In general, the Moscovites caught in barricaded sections of the city seem to have been favorable to the insurgents. Public opinion turned against the troops because of the extent to which uninvolved residents had suffered in the fighting.[43] All accounts of the uprising agree that the druzhinniki succeeded in keeping the peace and in gaining the trust of the local residents, even in areas where the revolutionaries were not in complete control. The pharmacy clerks' druzhina, for example, had secured a foothold in Carriage Row:

Citizens often showed up at the *druzhina* headquarters with requests for assistance; a fire might have started in a certain courtyard, or hooligans been at work in another. The *druzhina* dispatched patrols to investigate all such appeals. For this reason, the population respected and sympathized with the *druzhina*, warning it of the enemy's approach, reporting on the location of wounded bodies found on the streets, and providing the squad with ample provisions. . . . Neighborhood residents, as well as the *druzhina*'s enemies, vastly exaggerated the squad's strength and fighting ability.[44]

In areas controlled by local soviets, such as the Presnia district, the workers maintained order and eliminated the threat of mob violence.[45] Inhabitants viewed the soviets as guardians of their own safety and respected their authority. Merchants, for example, were known to appeal to them for permission to bring certain items into an area.[46] Vandalism was minimal. Factories were generally unharmed by their occupiers. Workers regarded only gun shops and the food supply trains in the depots as legitimate targets for plunder. Even an outspoken critic of the revolutionaries and their tactics had to admit that they conducted themselves well:

The inhabitants of Presnia were impressed most of all by the unexpected circumstance that from the day the strike began and the *druzhinniki* assumed the protection of the district, theft was reduced almost to zero. Later, when these voluntary sentinels had left and hooligans began taking advantage of the weakness of police surveillance, it was difficult for certain [reactionary] members of the press to equate the revolution with the expropriation of property; the poor simply would not believe it.[47]

The cooperation of local residents, or at least their neutrality, was essential to the success of the partisan tactic, which depended on the squads' having access to private property. Property owners often found themselves subjected to simultaneous threats from both sides, and citizens were usually in no position to resist either the forceful demands of the armed bands or the contrary orders of the police. One landlord recalled his dilemma:

Once six armed deputies appeared and demanded a room in one of my houses for use as a meeting place. They forbade me to enter the room myself and threatened to kill me if I disobeyed. What should I have done? Take the room and God be with you. . . .

Then the concierge came to say that the police insisted we lock the front gate. So I said, go ahead, lock up.

A half-hour later back he comes. "Sir, the *druzhinniki* say that if I dare lock up they will kill me on the spot." So then I said, "Forget it. Let the police come and lock it themselves if it's so important to them." One can't send a man to his death. Thus we were always being threatened, either by the police or the *druzhinniki*.

Near my house was a barricade made of chopped wood and various things piled up. I told the concierge to drag it a bit farther away. As soon as he had done so, an armed revolutionary appeared out of nowhere and threatened him with a revolver, but at that very moment he was himself struck down by a shot from a soldier's rifle.[48]

Many nonpolitical residents and students who were not involved in the fighting volunteered to serve in medical brigades. Concerned medical personnel had established emergency first aid service as early as October. In November, the All-Russian Medical Personnel Union organized a central bureau and district brigades centered around local hospitals.[49] Private donations covered the expense of medical supplies, and people offered their apartments as makeshift clinics to supplement the overflowing hospitals. The brigades displayed the Red Cross and went unarmed. The soldiers generally respected their freedom of movement until the last days of the insurrection. Barricades and street fighting soon interrupted contact between the Red Cross units and the Medical Union's bureau. After December 9, the medical brigades, like the armed bands, were obliged to act on their own. The bureau was reduced to collecting casualty figures.[50]

On December 12, Dubasov outlawed the voluntary medical brigades, claiming that the Red Cross had been used as cover for armed attacks on soldiers; the troops were now to shoot all unofficial medical personnel in the area of conflict. In the same announcement, he warned that anyone on the streets after six in the evening would be searched by police and arrested if found with unauthorized firearms. To prevent large crowds from serving as cover for snipers, Dubasov further instructed soldiers and police to fire at groups of more than three persons gathered on the street. Anyone caught pulling down telegraph or telephone poles would be arrested and risked imprisonment. If they resisted, they would be shot on the spot. Arrests now increased, as did the number of wounded bystanders. On December 14, Dubasov prohibited all meetings, public and private. By the evening of the fifteenth, the streets had become empty.[51]

By December 12, the district revolutionary leaders had lost contact with other parts of the city and had ceased to receive instructions from any central organizations.[52] Downtown and in the Zamoskvorech'e, the skirmishes between troops and druzhinniki continued unabated until December 16. In the Rogozhskaia district and the adjoining Simonovskii region, neither troops nor police ever attacked the barricades or assaulted the druzhinniki. Workers controlled the Simonovskii region but took no offensive actions. Plans to seek the support of the soldiers in the nearby Krutitskii barracks came to naught when the workers found themselves confronted by armed guards.[53] An unnatural calm reigned in the Rogozhskaia area, where several factories had organized druzhiny. The government forces simply refused to engage in conflict. Even the Kursk railroad druzhina remained inactive. Eventually, workers who were eager to fight went to the Zamoskvorech'e or to Presnia.[54] It was in Presnia that the confrontation between the government forces and the revolutionaries reached its climax, bringing the revolutionary conflict of 1905 to a dramatic and bloody close.

The Battle for Presnia

While shooting raged in other parts of the city, Presnia remained relatively calm and felt itself to be a world apart.[55] Local leaders had only a vague idea of what was happening elsewhere. On December 11, Socialist Revolutionary and Social Democratic party militants set up a combat committee to provide political and military direction. The committee consisted of two Bolsheviks, Z. Ia. Litvin-Sedoi, an auto technician (age twenty-nine), and Z. N. Dosser, a lawyer (twenty-three); one Menshevik, P. A. Garvi, no professional training (twenty-four); and three Socialist Revolutionaries, V. I. Zommerfel'd (Martynov), a former Moscow University student (age unknown), S. D. Dmitriev, a weaving supervisor at Prokhorov and a former Zubatovite (twenty-eight), and I. I. Baulin, an engraver at Prokhorov (twenty-eight).[56]

Despite the difficulty of crossing between the downtown and Presnia,

Zommerfel'd's mother braved the dangers. Throughout the insurrection, the young revolutionary received a daily visit from his intrepid parent, and none of his comrades found the event at all odd or ridiculous.[57] Had they been capable of laughter, they might have been incapable of revolution. This touching and humorous detail underscores the homespun character of 1905 in Moscow: many party activists were exceedingly young and inexperienced; the radical youth often had strong personal ties to respectable society; the revolution, and even the insurrection, remained in some sense a family affair. It occurred on home ground, it involved one's close friends and relatives, it disturbed one's daily life. For Moscow residents, 1905 was not a remote spectacle or an alien threat, but an upheaval in which many of the contestants were intimately familiar.

These circumstances no doubt encouraged public tolerance for many aspects of the revolution that were unquestionably destructive of life, property, and tranquility. If this tolerance involved a certain condescension toward the revolution's self-appointed helmsmen (an attitude that may have veiled an underlying fear of the social forces unleashed in the turmoil), the revolutionaries took themselves dead seriously. In December, the revolutionaries pinned their ambitions on the ability of the armed bands to win popular support and in some undefined way to produce a crisis of confidence in the monarchy, if not to achieve outright military victory. But they had not the means for such a victory. Presnia boasted seven factory-based fighting squads, along with one attached to the Moscow-Brest railroad shops, more than any other industrial area; but even in Presnia their numbers were not impressive. Estimates on the membership in these squads range from about 200 to 600 men at any given moment. The variations reflect not only the scarcity of evidence on the subject, but also the fact that the number of armed men in Presnia changed constantly as druzhinniki from other parts of the city moved in when conflict died down in their own districts.[58] The weapons at their disposal, moreover, were few and far between. Most came from the Mamontov plant, where the owner, disturbed by the high level of crime in the vicinity, had received police permission to arm his workers so they could defend themselves.[59] The guns thus obtained entered the service of revolution in December.

The Presnia factory druzhiny continued to operate as individual units until the very last days of the siege.[60] The Bolshevik Litvin-Sedoi was the only person on the Combat Committee with any military experience, and none of its members offered any tactical suggestions.[61] There was no sustained shooting in Presnia before December 13, when soldiers attacked the Prokhorov plant.[62] The druzhinniki made isolated attempts to disarm small groups of policemen and officers encountered along the borders of the district. They occasionally exchanged fire with Cossacks or police patrols and managed to steal some guns from the private apartments of individual policemen.[63] They spent most of their time patrolling the area, though on several occasions they attacked police stations. This increased their prestige and raised the strikers' morale, since it was clear that the local authorities could do nothing to stop them.[64] As late as December 14, the district police captain acknowledged that the streets were in the hands of the druzhinniki. He was unable to prevent workers from assembling in the factories or from collecting arms. Armed revolutionaries guarded the print shops, so that official proclamations could not be published.[65]

The center of political activity in Presnia was the 6,000-worker Prokhorov cotton mill. In November, Prokhorov workers began holding large meetings in the factory dining room and in the nearby Mamontov plant. Socialist Revolutionary slogans were very popular among the audience. On November 6, the plant elected 54 leaders. Eighteen of them (including the only six women chosen) worked in the weaving department, and 18 others in the printing shop; nine were mechanics, and the rest worked in finishing, spinning, and dyeing. Their average age was twenty-five and a half years.[66] The engravers and mechanics (both metalworking trades) represented the top of the wage-skill hierarchy in textile mills. The engravers had been unionized since the late 1890's, when the Social Democrats had organized a calico printers' strike at the Giubner mill. The Union of Engravers and Calico Printers had sent delegates to the Moscow Bureau meetings in November 1905. But in the Prokhorov mill, it was not they but the weavers who had been the most restless group since the 1890's. The weavers, as we have seen, were second only to the metalworkers in the textile-mill hierarchy: most were men who were on the whole more literate, more highly skilled, and better paid than other textile operatives. The Prokhorov strikes of May 1895 and January 1898 both originated in the weaving department, among male weavers.[67] The Zubatov textile union had attracted a considerable following among weavers in various Moscow mills.[68] In January 1905, the striking Prokhorov weavers were joined by workers from the spinning, printing, and mechanical sections, but in October, as we have noted, the mechanics voted against striking.[69] When the Golutvinskaia mill struck in November, the weavers had held out longer than other workers against management pressure. Thus, the group that pushed things to a head in December represented one of the most privileged sectors of the textile labor force—and one, moreover, with a history of collective protest.

Nine of the 54 workers elected on November 6 (along with one other person) represented the factory in the Moscow Soviet. All ten were men: two weavers, four printers, two finishers, and two of unknown trades.

Half were Social Democrats and half Socialist Revolutionaries (including Dmitriev and Baulin, who became members of the Presnia Combat Committee). A committee of 10 persons organized the factory druzhina in December: seven of the plant's soviet deputies (three Social Democrats and four Socialist Revolutionaries), plus three other November 6 deputies (all Socialist Revolutionaries, including two other former Zubatovites). Socialist Revolutionary workers also took charge of barricade building. The Socialist Revolutionary Party consolidated its influence by sending five intelligentsia organizers to advise the workers. They acted in cooperation with the Bolshevik Litvin-Sedoi.[70]

The factory druzhina was composed of 35 workers.[71] At its core were the plant's ten soviet deputies. Thirty druzhinniki, along with 32 other Prokhorov workers, were eventually indicted for taking part in the uprising. Only one was a woman. In addition, six nonworkers were arrested at the plant: two women, both in their twenties, one a Socialist Revolutionary Party member, the other a governess; and four men, three in their late teens and one twenty-seven years old.[72]

The authority of the deputies soon replaced that of the factory management. The workers and party organizers in the leadership committee set up their headquarters in the plant's kitchen and proceeded to regulate all aspects of factory life. They organized Red Cross brigades and armed patrols.[73] Local residents and workers in other enterprises came to the Prokhorov deputies for guidance and instructions. The physical organization of the plant itself enabled the deputies to control the workers' activity. "The fact that the vast majority of Prokhorov workers lived in dormitories on the factory premises played an enormous role in the armed uprising," writes a Soviet historian. "The leaders demanded that workers who did not participate in the *druzhiny* or in armed exercises should take part in patrols and guard duty on factory grounds. . . . They assigned these duties on a military basis: even those reluctant to follow orders were forced to do so."[74] But most of the workers were willing volunteers. Many of the uncooperative—especially women—simply ran away to the countryside. Those who remained were able to hold out because the factory owner, N. I. Prokhorov, continued to supply them with food, out of humanitarian concern.[75]

P. A. Garvi says that Prokhorov "still acted the liberal."[76] The industrialist not only fed the workers, but allowed them to use plant premises for their own purposes. Without this sympathetic treatment, the Prokhorov workers would have been out on the street or home in their villages. The radical inclinations of N. P. Shmidt, the furniture factory owner, may likewise account for the importance of that enterprise as a center of worker organization. Bourgeois connivance was nothing to be sneered at.

The humbler members of educated society also lent a helping hand tc
revolution. The Presnia soviet, for instance, met in the private clinic of a
psychiatrist who had been active in politics since early in the year.[77] This
soviet was closely linked to the district Combat Committee. I. I. Baulin,
one of the Socialist Revolutionary Prokhorov deputies, was the soviet's
president. Its secretary was also a member of the committee—the Menshevik P. A. Garvi, who set the agendas and was, in his own words, the
organization's "actual leader."[78] Garvi described the soviet's role in his
memoirs:

In fact, the soviet had to function as a kind of local government: merchants would
appeal to it for permission to transport kerosene into the district; discussion would
arise over whether to permit the sale of groceries in food shops, and so on. But as
a plenum, the soviet mainly served the purpose of transmitting information and
maintaining ties between the striking enterprises. It was not an administrative
center [i.e., did not make decisions that guided the strikers' actions]. The Combat
Committee was in charge of the fighting. It actually depended more on the parties
than on the soviet for guidance.[79]

The authority of the Presnia soviet remained intact until the area came
under fire from the tsarist forces. In other areas, the strikers' mood began
to falter as early as December 12, and the flight of workers to the countryside increased. Although most factories remained on strike, some attempted to resume operations. An organizer describes the mood in the
Zamoskvorech'e on December 15:

People gather in small groups, discussing events, but no one knows what to do.
The suggestions of militant individuals are met with skepticism. The streets are
completely calm. The great majority of stores are open, and cabs appear everywhere. In several bakeries, white bread is once more being sold. Hardly any factories are back at work. But today a group of workers at no other than the Tsindel'
cotton mill [one of the most politically active plants in the area] were urging the
deputies to end the strike by tomorrow. A large majority forced them to be silent.
In general, the deputies and the organized workers are at a complete loss for
where to go and are afraid to admit even to themselves that the strike is "lost."
. . . At the Til' and Zhemochkin [leather] factories and in various small enterprises separate groups are secretly returning to work. But incomparably more
striking is another phenomenon: that is, the epidemic flight to the countryside.
Crowds of people go through the streets on foot with white knapsacks over their
shoulders.[80]

Workers in the outlying factory districts who retained strong ties with
the countryside were returning home. The battle seemed lost, and, as
one observer noted, the Christmas season was approaching. "Christmas
was a great holiday for Russian factory workers. It was no more possible

for them to pass up the usual celebration—at home, among their families, at local fêtes—than for a flock of birds to skip an annual migration to warmer climes. This completed the dissipation of the *druzhina* forces— in any case none too strong—and wrought disorganization in the leadership."[81] The druzhinniki abandoned their barricades on the boulevards; the districts were no longer in communication; and many leaders disbanded their groups. When military reinforcements arrived from the capital on December 15, the balance of forces shifted decisively.

The last meeting of the Moscow Soviet took place that same day, in the Tsindel' cafeteria, on the initiative of the Mensheviks.[82] The meeting was far from full. Only about 90 persons were present; some districts were unrepresented, and others sent only a few deputies. Those assembled felt unable to decide on what course they should now follow in the absence of so many members, and they left the problem for the executive committee to resolve. All the same, the deputies were still in a combative mood, though many admitted that the workers' spirit was flagging. No one spoke in favor of ending the strike, not even the Mensheviks who had first suggested the possibility two days earlier. The Socialist Revolutionaries, the railroad workers, and the Bolsheviks were still eager to hold out. The Mensheviks agreed to go along only because they did not want the movement to collapse in disorganization.

The deputies soon realized, however, that their own intransigence was not widely shared. That evening, the Mensheviks once again proposed that work be allowed to resume. The next day, December 16, the Bolsheviks voted to end the strike on December 19. The executive committee of the Moscow Soviet followed suit, issuing the official announcement on December 18.[83] The declaration reflected the back-to-work trend in the factories and the exhaustion of most of the city.[84]

Although Presnia had been spared the severe barrage of artillery fire during the first week of the strike, even there, by December 14, the morale of organized workers had begun to deteriorate. Druzhinniki kept soldiers and police off the streets, but the workers nevertheless realized they could not hope to achieve any sort of victory. The rest of the city had already capitulated, and workers elsewhere were returning to their benches. Some Presnia workers even approached the mayor with an offer to surrender. But others were unwilling to give up, continuing to build barricades as late as December 15.[85]

The Semenovskii regiment, under the command of Colonel G. A. Min, arrived in Moscow on December 15. The next morning it began the bombardment of Presnia. Min received instructions from Major-General S. M. Sheideman, quartermaster-general of the Moscow Military District, and from Lieutenant-General G. K. von Shtakel'berg: he was to root out the druzhinniki still hidden in Presnia and "ruthlessly destroy them."[86] Min was in constant communication with Governor-General Dubasov, who was therefore aware of the situation at all times.[87]

In their uncompromising attitude toward the rebels, the military authorities were only fulfilling the Tsar's own orders. On December 13, the Council of Ministers recommended that troops act "decisively and mercilessly against anyone offering armed resistance." Those who were not shot down should be court-martialed and if necessary executed on the spot. Count Witte, chairman of the Council of Ministers, asked Nicholas to have the Minister of War put this policy into effect as soon as possible. On December 15, the minister instructed district military commanders to use force against armed insurgents.[88] Later, governors and police chiefs received orders to the same effect from the Minister of Internal Affairs, P. N. Durnovo: police and gendarmes were to show no mercy in dealing with rebels; they were to use armed force and were under no circumstances to negotiate with the revolutionaries.[89]

By the evening of December 16, most of the druzhina captains had ordered their followers to disperse. When the artillery barrage began in earnest the next morning, the government troops encountered only scattered shooting in the streets.[90] The soldiers nevertheless kept up a constant barrage of gunfire directed at windows and doorways that might conceal rebel snipers. The plan of attack focused on the major centers of druzhina activity. The troops besieged the Prokhorov, Mamontov, and Shmidt factories, where workers were still entrenched behind their barricades. The soldiers set fire to numerous plants, including Shmidt and Mamontov, and destroyed at least 15 buildings.[91] Flames soon encircled the entire area. The authorities maintained that artillery fire had caused the destruction, but witnesses accused the soldiers of arson.[92]

At Prokhorov, the workers refused to surrender: 410 held out until December 19.[93] Nine were immediately tried by field court-martial and shot in the factory courtyard.[94] Most were released; the ringleaders were tried and sentenced the following year. The Socialist Revolutionary workerdeputy and former Zubatovite S. D. Dmitriev was among those who recanted and testified against their comrades.[95] When the soldiers searched the plant, they found 23 rifles and shotguns, 13 revolvers, 16 explosive charges, and one sack of ammunition.[96]

By December 18, party leaders had managed to escape from the area into the center of the city.[97] Aided by local residents, the soldiers cleared Presnia of barricades. Although the druzhinniki were now gone, the bombardment continued throughout the day, killing many residents who had taken no part in the fighting.[98] As many as 700 revolutionaries and civilians died, and as many as 2,000 were wounded, in the course of December, compared with fewer than 70 men killed in the police and the military combined.[99] Of the 1,011 noncombatants reported to have received hospital care, almost 100 were children under fifteen years of age (most of them boys) and over 100 were women. In addition, the hospitals reported treating 13 druzhinniki. Many more undoubtedly escaped notice, since they were often cared for by Red Cross brigades in private homes.[100]

Postmortems

The December uprising represented the last spasm of repressive violence and the last attempt at revolutionary self-defense. Throughout the autumn, strikers had protected themselves against assault by government forces and hostile social groups. The partisan tactic, for all its terrorist pedigree, was not an offensive strategy, but a continuation of self-defense. The insurgents did not assault the bastions of power, but limited themselves primarily to fending off armed attack. Popular support for the rebels grew out of widespread indignation at the government's use of exaggerated force. This sympathy was sustained by the responsible manner in which rebel leaders exercised their authority on the district level. Enthusiasm for the positive goals of the insurrection is more difficult to detect; indeed, it is doubtful whether the abstract goals appended to the revolutionary appeal had much meaning for the participants themselves.

The ferocious military assault extinguished the last vestiges of popular resistance. It also won the enmity of the city's population. Even progressives who had been eager to credit the government's good intentions were now sorely disabused of their illusions. Other liberal city councilmen joined Kishkin in denouncing the government's extreme response to the December events. And Miliukov, who had earlier condemned the strike declaration as a crime against the revolution, now saw the government as pitted against the whole of Russian society. Its paranoid brutality had deprived it of moral and political authority.[101]

Another liberal, Peter Struve, was no less hostile to the uprising than Miliukov. In fact, Struve denied that an insurrection had actually occurred in Moscow. Rather, intellectuals playing at revolution had erected "sham barricades . . . in alliance with terrorized concierges and enthusiastic boys off the streets." These theatrical antics stood out against the "daring and heroic struggle of fanaticized *workers*, who had doomed themselves to destruction." The pathetic demonstration had, however, been "enough to provoke the senseless and pitiless destruction of houses, and the slaughter of the movement's participants, as well as of innocent individuals on a scale unprecedented in our history."[102] The so-called uprising was not in fact a popular movement, but a conflict of extremes, both of them politically unrepresentative and morally irresponsible: the radical intelligentsia on the one hand, and the government bureaucracy on the other. The state, Struve concluded, was no less the enemy of society than the rebels it was so eager to suppress.[103]

If the Moscow workers were "daring and heroic" in Struve's view, it was because they were the victims of their own naïve enthusiasm, the holy fools of revolution, the dupes of party ideologues. But Struve was over-eager to credit the revolutionary intelligentsia with responsibility for the December events. Lenin, who was no less eager to assume responsibility, had to admit that the mass movement had stolen a march on its political mentors. "The organizations *failed to keep pace* with the growth and range of the movement," he acknowledged in 1906. "From a strike and demonstrations to isolated barricades. From isolated barricades to the mass erection of barricades and street fighting against the troops. Over the heads of the organizations, the mass proletarian struggle developed from a strike to an uprising."[104]

The move from strike to uprising was not, of course, entirely spontaneous. If Lenin meant to suggest that the December insurrection was a naïve and spontaneous popular outburst, he was doing himself and his organization less than justice. Without months of Bolshevik propaganda, without dedicated students and party activists (without, too, the provocative impact of government policy), it is doubtful whether 1905 would have terminated as it did. If Lenin is here seeking to justify the Bolshevik line as the natural expression of popular sentiment, he is contradicting one of his own basic principles. The party does not tailor its strategy to the spontaneous urges of the working class. Rather, Lenin's remark underlines a central fact about 1905. Party activists were capable of drawing Moscow workers into the trade-union movement and into the strike movement. They publicized their ideas in the factories and in the shops. They elicited a tremendous response, not only among the factory elite and sometimes also among the rank and file, but among white-collar and artisanal groups as well. But the parties never controlled the form and direction of popular involvement. They did not manipulate the crowd for purposes of power politics, or to satisfy grandiose fantasies of personal self-importance. Precisely the breadth and intensity of popular unrest made this impossible. The workers had their own goals, which to a certain extent coincided with those of the revolutionary leadership. But, as Lenin acknowledged with a mixture of pride and chagrin, the working class demonstrated a remarkable degree of autonomy. Struve may rightly decry the ideological self-deception that sections of the radical intelligentsia practiced on themselves, but he does not give the working class the credit it deserves.

The pathways of political authority were particularly devious in 1905.

Intelligentsia militants did not have the power to control their constituency. Indeed, the more formal the institution through which they strove to do so, the less successful they were. Centralized organizations, as we have noted, had the weakest impact on the course of events, a fact that party leaders of course deplored. Intelligentsia militants had greater effect at the district and factory levels. The local soviets were the forum through which the parties exercised their influence; but they possessed an authority that the parties alone did not wield. Combining the functions of strike committee, community center, and police force, the soviet form of organization evolved from an organ of revolutionary propaganda and intelligentsia dominance into a center of popular local administration.

This evolution surpassed the expectations of the soviets' sponsors, but it was due in part to their own long-term efforts that such a development was possible. Persistent agitation, in the context of universal unrest, had helped alter the outlook and behavior of the working class, even of those untutored multitudes who responded but feebly to direction and understood but dimly the import of their own actions. And, of course, years of education had produced a small core of workers who knew what they wanted and were able to whittle away at the passive majority from within the fraternal boundaries of class. Some such process, surely, caused the indifferent mass to dwindle in size as the year wore on. The penumbra surrounding the organized nucleus continued to grow. Participation in the soviets far outstripped membership in the political parties. Participation in the December strike was even more extensive.

It is easy to ignore the oblique effects of underground activity and even open campaigning on the workers' mood and capacity for action, because the mechanism of cause and effect is all but invisible to the historian's eye. This difficulty opens the door to facile assumptions about the direct impact of party strategy on the mass movement, assumptions that confuse ideology with agency. Lenin, for one, did not make this mistake. The subsequent Bolshevik claim to have "governed . . . the soviet, as an insurrectionary organ, as an organ of popular power,"[105] does not withstand scrutiny. If the claim is meant to suggest a sectarian monopoly over organizational affairs and the decision-making process, it is simply an empty boast, a reflection of post-1917 politics, not of historical reality. At the time, the Bolsheviks were no more in command of the situation than the other radical parties. Their views were not dominant, and their own actions often contradicted their theories. In fact, the three socialist groups cooperated effectively in December, and all participated in the same organizations.[106] If the claim is meant merely to suggest that control over the soviet (even if a tripartite control) resulted in control over the mass movement, it falls under the weight of contrary evidence.

Undue attention to the events of December has a way of diverting our attention from the more profound and also more obscure social processes at work in 1905. The Bolsheviks focused their propaganda and subsequent analysis on the uprising, for strategic and theoretical reasons of their own. Mensheviks and Socialist Revolutionaries joined them in tactical and later theoretical arguments over its wisdom and degree of success. Contemporaries likewise were captured by the lurid pathos of this culminating episode of the revolution. The historian must not fall prey to a similar fascination. The preoccupation itself is a symptom of the gap between ideology and social reality that pervaded the politics of 1905 in all its many varieties.

The December uprising, and in particular the battle over Presnia, came to symbolize the tragedy of 1905: the defeat of democratic aspirations by the repressive state. This symbolism accurately reflects the way in which the *idea* of the proletariat came to stand for the revolution as a whole. In the face of autocratic obstinacy, moderate slogans rang hollow and moderate strategies lost their appeal. Focus on the December events, however, obscures both the sociological and the political reality of the revolution. The unskilled factory work force was not representative of the majority of striking workers in 1905. The textile masses struck in large numbers in January, with no sense of collective purpose or common identity; they bypassed the strike movements of the fall, which involved skilled trades and white-collar workers in well-coordinated actions; and they remained largely impervious to trade-union activity. During the October strike, the factory workers' movement coincided with the efforts of the educated classes to achieve institutional reforms in the autocratic system. In these two weeks of greatest political significance for the revolution, Presnia-Khamovniki was at its most quiescent. In October, society demanded access to the political process. By striking, petitioning, and organizing when such activity was illegal, it wrested its civil rights from the government *iavochnym poriadkom*, by direct action. After the October Manifesto, political activity had become, in principle at least, a legal mode of expression. The organizational efforts of November—party building and trade-union formation—were no longer revolutionary acts, but legitimate forms of collective action.

The working-class strikes of November did not challenge the existing legal and political system; they concentrated on social injustice and on defending the rights won in October. The same was true for the various protests of service and white-collar groups in this period. By the end of the month, however, it became clear that the government not only did not intend to honor the promises of the October Manifesto, but was determined to destroy the mass movement that had fueled the revolution. The government pushed for confrontation, and thereby diverted the working class from its economic concerns and prevented the labor movement from consolidating its institutional gains.

One is left with the impression that the incorporation of the working class into the general polity was as fearful a prospect to the regime as it was to the Bolshevik Party. A viable constitutional system was impossible without some form of lower-class participation. The Bolsheviks feared such an outcome might cause the proletariat to abandon its revolutionary aspirations. Lenin's party did not share the Menshevik dream of a mass labor movement working from within to transform bourgeois society into true social democracy. The regime, for its part, clearly viewed the constitutional alternative as a threat to the stability of the bureaucratic system, the hallowed bulwark against social unrest and the latent violence of the "gray" masses. The government focused its repressive strategy on the workers' movement and forced the radical intelligentsia to make good its most extravagant claims. In so doing, it not only interrupted the solid work of trade unionism, but also damaged the politically moderate and socially heterogeneous movements that favored a compromise solution to the crisis.

The government itself contributed to the view of the December insurrection as a revolt of the unwashed masses. The state could not extinguish political life in privileged circles, but it could, with relative impunity, isolate and destroy autonomous activity among the working class. It could do so because the working class was not integrated (socially or geographically) into the urban community, and because an active working class was a potential threat even to the educated classes that viewed its cause with sympathy and welcomed its alliance in the interests of reform. Cut off from the rest of the city, the workers in Presnia were bound to go down in defeat. The public responded in outrage to the government's repressive bacchanalia—in the spirit of the cross-class solidarity that had all along characterized the revolution. This destruction signaled the fate of society as a whole, as long as the autocratic regime remained in place and unmodified. But as a symbol, Presnia misrepresents the revolution. The real triumph of the working class in 1905 was not its desperate heroism in the face of overwhelming force, but its ability to take part in the political process along with the larger community. Despite the ephemeral nature of many of the organizations generated in the course of revolutionary conflict and despite the effectiveness of the repression that followed the revolution, the lessons of this experience were not entirely lost.

Appendixes

A

SOME BASIC STATISTICS

TABLE A.1
Factory Strike Movement in Moscow, January–December 1905

Branch of industry[a]		Number of strikers (percent of period's total strikers)						
				October				
	January	September	1–17	18–31	1–31	November	December
Textiles N = 63,500(41%)	14,400 (39%)	2,000 (8%)	12,100 (36%)	11,700 (81%)	23,800 (50%)	23,000 (50%)	36,000 (44%)
Metal, machine N = 30,500(20%)	10,300 (28%)	10,000 (38%)	9,200 (28%)	500 (3%)	9,700 (20%)	7,800 (17%)	14,300 (17%)
Food, tobacco, alcohol, tea N = 25,800(17%)	6,700 (18%)	5,000 (19%)	5,700 (17%)	900 (6%)	6,600 (14%)	9,200 (20%)	15,500 (19%)
Printing N = 12,500(8%)	3,000 (8%)	6,000 (23%)	3,600 (11%)	—	3,600 (8%)	—	5,900 (7%)
Minerals, chem. N = 8,200(5%)	1,400 (4%)	—	1,000 (3%)	650 (5%)	1,650 (3%)	1,750 (4%)	4,000 (5%)
Leather N = 6,900(5%)	1,000 (3%)	3,100 (12%)	500 (2%)	300 (2%)	800 (2%)	4,600 (10%)	4,500 (6%)
Paper N = 6,400(4%)	200 (1%)	—	1,200 (4%)	400 (3%)	1,600 (3%)	—	1,700 (2%)
Total N = 153,800	37,000 (101%)[b]	26,100 (100%)	33,300 (101%)[b]	14,450 (100%)	47,750 (100%)	46,350 (101%)[b]	81,900 (100%)

SOURCE: Factory File.

NOTE: These figures show the number of workers who struck at least once during each month. Those remaining on strike from the previous month are counted along with new strikers, but workers who struck on more than one occasion in the same month are counted only once. The division into months is to some extent arbitrary, since the successive strike waves did not begin and end with precision, but this schema allows one to compare the peaks of strike activity by drawing a cross section of strikers for each period. The month of October is subdivided to show the number of workers on strike between October 1 and October 17, the period leading up to and including the general strike. The figures for October 18–31 do not include holdovers from October 1–17 in order to show the degree of renewed strike activity after the October Manifesto.

[a] The woodworking, construction, and apparel industries are not included in Tables A.1–A.3 because work force and strike data are inadequate.

[b] Percentage totals more than 100 because of rounding.

TABLE A.2

Strike Propensity of Moscow Factory Workers During the Five Major Phases of the 1905 Strike Movement

Branch of industry	Index of strike propensity						
				October			
	January	September	1–17	18–31	1–31	November	December
Textiles	.95	.20	.88	2.00	1.22	1.22	1.07
Metal and machine	1.40	1.90	1.40	.15	1.00	.85	.85
Food, tobacco, alcohol, and tea	1.06	1.12	1.00	.35	.82	1.18	1.12
Printing	1.00	2.88	1.38	—	1.00	—	.88
Minerals and chemicals	.80	—	.60	1.00	.60	.80	1.00
Leather	.60	2.40[a]	.40	.40	.40	2.00[a]	1.20[a]
Paper	.25	—	1.00	.75	.75	—	.50

SOURCE: Based on percentages in Table A.1.

NOTE: The concept of strike propensity comes from Robert Goetz-Girey, Le Mouvement des grèves en France, 1919–1962, vol. 3 of Henri Guitton and Alain Barrère, eds., L'Economique (Paris, 1965). The index of strike propensity is obtained by dividing the percentage of all striking workers in any period employed in a given industry by the percentage of the total industrial work force constituted by the workers in that same industry.

[a]The high strike propensity for leather workers is due to the strike at the giant Til' tannery in the Zamoskvorech'e, whose 3,100 workers constituted 45 percent of the entire industry's work force.

TABLE A.3

Extensiveness of Strike Participation by Moscow Factory Workers According to Plant Size

Branch of industry	Index of extensiveness for plants with:			
	Under 100 workers	100–499 workers	500–999 workers	1,000 and more workers
Textiles	.50	.76	1.13	1.23
Metal and machine	.55	1.09	1.20	1.36
Food, tobacco, alcohol, and tea	.82	.89	1.22	.96
Printing	1.00	1.28	1.18	.59
Minerals and chemicals	.64	1.21	.95	—
Leather	.52	1.06	—	1.22
Paper	1.04	2.00	0	0

NOTE: The index of extensiveness measures the proportion of workers in each category involved at least once during the year in strike activity. It is obtained by dividing the percentage of all strikers in a particular industry employed by firms of a given size by the percentage of the industry's total work force employed by firms of the same size.

There were no mineral or chemical factories with 1,000 or more workers and no leather factories with 500–999.

B

MOSCOW TRADE UNIONS, 1905

The names of the largest and most solidly constituted unions at the end of the year are set in large and small capitals. All dates are 1905 if no year is specified; and political affiliation or influence is always stated when known. The following abbreviations are used in the list:

PU Participant in the All-Russian Conference of Representatives of Professional Unions in Moscow

MB Participant in meetings of the Moscow Bureau of Professional Unions

SC Member of the Moscow Strike Committee

MS Member of the Moscow Soviet of Workers' Deputies

The sources for the unions' participation in the bodies listed above are as follows: PU, *BMST*, no. 1: 3, Milonov, *Kak voznikli*, pp. 165–67; MB, Muzei: *Materialy*, pp. 66–67; SC, *PkP*, p. 33, *Pravo*, no. 42 (Oct. 31): 3484; MS, diverse sources included in the notes.

Apart from the largest, best-known unions, it is not possible to tell whether many of the unions listed below actually functioned beyond the date of their formation. The list includes all unions that adopted a name or charter and all groups that participated in PU and MB sessions, whether or not they called themselves unions. Groups that met with the intention of forming unions, but never did so, as far as we know, are listed separately at the end of each section.

It is not possible to identify all the unions that were members of the Moscow Soviet. When evidence of membership exists, this is indicated on the list below; but some unions on the list not so designated may also have sent delegates to the soviet.

1. Textiles

Union of Engravers and Calico Printers (Soiuz graverov i raklistov), MB.
Founded in 1898–99 in Prokhorov and Tsindel' cotton mills; SD sponsors.[1]

UNION OF RIBBONMAKERS; also UNION OF RIBBON-WEAVERS (Soiuz lentochnikov; Soiuz lentochnykh tkachei), MB.
Founded in Aug.–Sept.; centered in Gandshin-Virts factory; Menshevik sponsors; 800 members.[2]

Union of Braidmakers and Galloonmakers (Soiuz tkachei-basonshchikov i galun-shchikov), MB.[3]

Union of Workers in Textile Production (Soiuz rabochikh tekstil'nogo proizvodstva), MB.

Founded in early Nov. as outgrowth of Zubatov organization; SD sponsors; met seven or eight times in Nov.–early Dec. (first meeting, Nov. 7, drew representatives from 21 factories).[4]

Union of Dyers and Dressers (Soiuz krasil'no-appreturnogo proizvodstva).

Founded in early Nov.; Bolshevik, Menshevik, and SR sponsors; Nov. 18–20 meetings in Khishin silk mill (335 workers, in Basmannaia, V) drew 54 deputies from 18 factories; Dec. 4 meeting of 500 in Aquarium Theater.[5]

Union of Workers in the Velvet Guild (Soiuz rabochikh bakhromnogo tsekha).

Met Nov. 8; no more than a strike committee.[6]

Union of Workers in Gold Thread Production (Soiuz rabochikh zolotokanitel'nogo proizvodstva).

Met Nov. 13 as outgrowth of strike at the Alekseev, Vishniakov, and Shamshin ribbon factory in Rogozhskaia, V; Bolshevik sponsors; officially nonparty.[7]

Union of Embroidery Workers (Soiuz rabochikh vyshival'shchikov).

Met four or five times in Nov.–Dec.; maximum meeting attendance 500.[8]

2. Metal and Machine

MOSCOW UNION OF JEWELERS AND PRECIOUS-METAL WORKERS (Soiuz rabochikh po obrabotke blagorodnykh metallov), PU, MB, MS.

Founded in Sept.; Bolshevik sponsors; mid-Nov., gold and silver workers joined with jewelers and adopted a charter that included the SD minimum program; officially nonparty; Nov. 28 selected delegates to Moscow Soviet; over 500 members; maximum meeting attendance 4,000–5,000.[9]

Moscow Union of Mechanical Workers (Moskovskii soiuz mekhanicheskikh rabochikh), PU (as Zubatov organization).

Remaining members of the former Zubatov Society of Workers in Mechanical Production, along with delegates from the Zotov (300 workers), Veikhel't, Guzhon, and Bromlei metal factories, met eight times in Nov.–Dec.; SD sponsors; Nov. 24, charter drawn; Dec. 4, official founding meeting.[10]

Union of Workers in Bed Manufacture in the Krymov and Kuchkin Metal Factories (Soiuz krovatnogo proizvodstva Krymova i Kuchkina), MB.

Formed to lead October strike; actually a factory committee, like others at Dobrov and Nabgol'ts (PU), Bromlei (PU), Gopper (PU), Grachev (PU), Gantert (160 workers, MB), and the suburban Bonaker factory (350 workers, MB) and Mytishchi railroad-car works (1,500 workers, PU and MB).[11]

Union of Artisanal Workers in the Bronze Guild (Soiuz rabochikh mednogo tsekha remeslennykh zavedenii), MB.

Met four times in Nov.–Dec.; maximum meeting attendance 400.[12]

Workers in Watchmaking (Chasovshchikov-rabochikh).

Represented as a group in MB, but no evidence of a formal organization existing.[13]

Union of Technicians (Soiuz tekhnikov), PU, MB, SC, MS.

Founded Oct. 30 as outgrowth of liberal Mutual Aid Society for Russian Technicians in Moscow, established Aug. 1905; Bolshevik sponsors; Nov. 10, resolved to join Moscow Soviet; 150 members.[14]

Union of Workers in the Mechanical Construction Guild (Soiuz rabochikh slesarno-stroitel'nogo tsekha), MS.

Founded Nov. 6; Bolshevik sponsors; officially nonparty; Nov. 27, joined Moscow Soviet; Dec. 6 meeting of 1,000.[15]

Union of Workers in the Metal-Rolling Guild (Soiuz rabochikh metallo-tkatskogo tsekha).

Nov. 8 meeting; Bolshevik sponsors.[16]

Union of Jewelry, Silver, Engraving, and Bronze Journeymen (Soiuz iuvelirnykh, serebrianykh, gravernykh i bronzovykh podmaster'ev).

Met four times in mid-Nov.–Dec.; Bolshevik sponsors; maximum meeting attendance 200.[17]

Union of Workers in Mechanical and Surgical Instrument Production (Soiuz rabochikh mekhanicheskogo, khirurgicheskogo i instrumental'nogo proizvodstva).

Met twice in late Nov.–early Dec.[18]

Union of Blacksmiths (Soiuz kuznetsov).

Met twice in Nov.–Dec.; maximum meeting attendance 500.[19]

Union of Tinsmiths (Soiuz paial'shchikov).

Founded early Dec.; 200 members; led two strikes.[20]

3. Food, Tobacco, Tea

BAKERS' UNION (Soiuz bulochnikov), PU, MB.

Preliminary meetings in March; founded during Sept. strike; Bolshevik sponsors; met at least eight times in Nov.–Dec.; 1,770 members, mainly from Filippov Tver Street bakery and other large enterprises.[21]

UNION OF WORKERS IN THE TOBACCO INDUSTRY (Soiuz rabochikh tabachnoi promyshlennosti), PU, MB, MS.

Founded as outgrowth of Dukat strike (Sept. 24–early Nov.); centered at Dukat and Gabai; Menshevik sponsors; officially nonparty (ex-Zubatovites cooperated); as many as 2,000 members; both Dukat and Gabai organizations sent delegates to the Moscow Soviet.[22]

UNION OF TEA PACKERS (Soiuz chaerazvesochnikov), MB.

Founded after October strike by Mensheviks, in Gubkin-Kuznetsov factory, in Lefortovo, V, where SRs were also strong; officially nonparty; charter became model for other unions; Nov. 13 meeting of 900 and Dec. 6 meeting of 3,000; as many as 2,000 members.[23]

Union of Candymakers (Soiuz konditerov), MB.

Founded Nov. 6 as outgrowth of Zubatov organization (800 representatives of 28 factories and shops attended founding meeting); Bolshevik sponsors.[24]

Sausage Makers' Union (Soiuz kolbasnikov).

Met Nov. 8 to formulate strike demands; Nov. 26, proposed union charter published in VP.[25]

4. Printing

Moscow Typographers' Assistance Fund (Vspomogatel'naia kassa tipografov v Moskve), PU.

Founded in 1869; right-wing sponsors; run by director of Mamontov publishing house; 800 members.[26]

Mutual Aid Society of Printing Workers (exact Russian title unavailable).

Founded in 1903; Zubatovite sponsors; meetings continue into July 1905.[27]

Union of Moscow Printing and Lithography Workers for the Struggle to Improve Conditions of Labor (Soiuz moskovskikh tipo-litografskikh rabochikh dlia bor'by za uluchenie uslovii truda), PU.

Founded after 1903 printers' strike; Menshevik sponsors; 400 members; reformed as the legal Union of Workers in the Printing Trade after the October general strike.[28]

Fund for Assistance to Workers in the Printing Trade (Fond sodeistviia rabochim pechatnogo dela), PU.

In existence summer through Sept.; left-liberal sponsors; officially nonparty.[29]

UNION OF WORKERS IN THE PRINTING TRADE (Soiuz rabochikh pechatnogo dela), MB, SC, MS.

Founded Oct. 19 as legal outgrowth of the Union of Moscow Printing and Lithography Workers for the Struggle to Improve Conditions of Labor (8,000 attended founding meeting); Menshevik sponsors; 4,000 members; at least 15 meetings during Days of Freedom; Nov. 15, withdrew from Strike Committee to join Moscow Soviet; Dec. 4, joined by Proofreaders' Union.[30]

Proofreaders' Union (Soiuz korrektorov), MS.

Joined the Union of Workers in the Printing Trade on Dec. 4.[31]

5. Chemicals, Leather, Paper, Apparel

UNION OF MALE AND FEMALE TAILORS (Soiuz portnykh i portnikh), MB.

Founded before May; Menshevik sponsors; officially nonparty; Nov. 1, charter adopted; maximum meeting attendance 3,000; 1,200 members (1,000 male, 200 female), mostly from large shops.[32]

Union of Shoemakers and Bootmakers (Soiuz sapozhnogo i bashmachnogo dela), MB.

Founded before May; SR sponsors; maximum meeting attendance 1,000-plus.[33]

Pursemakers' Union (Soiuz koshelechnikov).

Founded in May; as of Jan. 1906, "all members to a head had gone home to the country."[34]

Union of Workers in Dyeing and Dry-Cleaning Establishments (Soiuz rabochikh krasil'nykh i piatnovyvodnykh predpriiatii), MB.

Met more than once in late Nov., early Dec.; maximum meeting attendance 500.[35]

Glovemakers' Union (Soiuz perchatnikov), MB.

Nov. 27 meeting of 300.[36]

Union of Journeymen Tailors (Soiuz portnykh podmaster'ev), MB.[37]

Union of Workers in Slipper Manufacture (Soiuz rabochikh tufel'nogo proizvodstva), MB.[38]

Union of Tailors in the Railroad Guild (Soiuz rabochikh portnykh zhelezno-dorozhnogo tsekha).

Founded mid-Nov. to represent 500 strikers in shops with railroad contracts.[39]

Moscow Union of Workers in All Guilds of the Clothing Industry (Moskovskii soiuz rabotnikov vsekh tsekhov po izgotovleniiu odezhdy).

Nov. 20 meeting adopted charter, declared solidarity with proletariat, and demanded abolition of piecework.[40]

Union of Workers in Perfume Production (Soiuz parfiumernykh rabochikh).

Nov. 23 meeting of 1,000 adopted SD program.[41]

Union of Workers in the Leather Luggage Trade (Soiuz rabochikh proizvodstva kozhevenno-dorozhnykh veshchei).

Dec. 4 meeting.[42]

Union of Workers in Military Saddle and Harness Production (Soiuz rabochikh shorno-voenno-amunichnogo proizvodstva).

Dec. 4 meeting of 2,000-plus.[43]

Meetings that did not result in unions: candlemakers' guild, Nov. 19; furriers' guild and cardboard-box makers, Nov. 27; brushmakers, Nov. 29.[44]

6. Wood and Construction

JOINERS' UNION (Soiuz stoliarov), PU, MB.

Founded in Sept. in the Shmidt furniture factory, in Presnia, III; Bolshevik sponsors; 1,500–1,700 members, mainly from furniture factories.[45]

Union of Workers in the Turners' Guild (Soiuz rabochikh zontochno-tokarnogo tsekha), MB.

Founded in Nov. by Mensheviks as an alternative to the Bolshevik joiners' union.[46]

Electricians' Union (Soiuz elektromonterov), MB.

Founded in late Nov.; SD sponsors; maximum meeting attendance 400.[47]

Union of Industrial Construction Workers (Soiuz promyshlenno-stroitel'nykh rabochikh), MB.

Founded Nov. 3; radical-architect sponsors; intended as central union to coordinate sectional craft unions (plumbers, plasterers, painters, marble cutters); four meetings in Nov.–Dec.[48]

Union of Marble Cutters (Soiuz mramorshchikov).

Founded Oct. 29; four meetings in late Oct.–early Dec.; maximum meeting attendance 1,000.[49]

Union of Workers in Toy Factories (Soiuz rabochikh fabrik igrushek).

Nov. 9 meeting of 18 persons from 10 enterprises; alternative to the Bolshevik Joiners' Union; Menshevik sponsors.[50]

Union of Parquet-Floor Layers (Soiuz parketnikov).

Alternative to the Bolshevik Joiners' Union; either Menshevik or SR sponsors.[51]

Union of Boxmakers (Soiuz iashchechnikov).

Alternative to the Bolshevik Joiners' Union; either Menshevik or SR sponsors; met two or three times in Nov.[52]

Painters' Union (Soiuz maliarov).

Founded in late Nov.[53]

UNION OF PLUMBING AND HEATING MECHANICS (Soiuz slesarei po vodoprovodnym rabotam i otopleniiu).

Founded Dec. 5 (500 attended founding meeting); maximum meeting attendance 1,000; 500 members.[54]

Union of Icon Painters (Soiuz tserkovnykh zhivopistsev).

First proposed by Mensheviks in summer; founded Dec. 6; officially nonparty.[55]

7. Service and White-Collar

Moscow Society of Merchants' Shop Assistants (Moskovskoe obshchestvo kupecheskikh prikazchikov).

Founded in 1861; Monarchist sponsors (Gov.-Gen. Grand Duke Sergei was an honorary member); included owners as well as employees, mainly in large fabric stores.[56]

Moscow Mutual Aid Society of Commercial Employees (Moskovskoe obshchestvo vzaimopomoshchi kommercheskikh sluzhashchikh), PU.

Founded in 1889; leaders in 1905 were left-liberals close to the Kadet Party; members mostly bookkeepers in Moscow banks.[57]

Moscow Waiters' Mutual Aid Society (Moskovskoe obshchestvo vzaimopomoshchi ofitsiantov), PU.

Founded in 1902 by city councilman V. I. Ger'e; included restaurant owners, but no women; April–May, Bolsheviks took over society; Oct. 23, reorganized as the Union of Waiters and Other Tavern and Hotel Employees.[58]

UNION OF OFFICE CLERKS AND BOOKKEEPERS (Soiuz kontorshchikov i bukh-galterov).

Founded in Feb.; left-liberal sponsors (chief organizer S. N. Prokopovich); May, joined Union of Unions; Bolsheviks later gained influence within union; 950 members at end of year.[59]

Moscow Union of Employees in the Sale of Foodstuffs (Moskovskii soiuz sluzha-shchikh v torgovle s'estnymi pripasami), PU.

Founded after March strikes in two factories; Menshevik sponsors; Oct. 19, joined with Moscow Union of Commercial Employees to form Moscow Union of Commercial and Industrial Employees—"Strength in Unity"; 300 members.[60]

Moscow Hairdressers' Union (Moskovskii soiuz parikmakherov), PU.

First attempts at organization began in April; Nov. 13, official founding meeting; at least one meeting in Dec.[61]

Moscow Union of Salaried Workers in Trade and Industry (Moskovskii soiuz naemnykh rabotnikov torgovli i promyshlennosti), PU, MB.

Founded in May; left-liberal sponsors; Union of Unions platform.[62]

Moscow Union of Commercial Employees (Moskovskii soiuz torgovykh sluzha-shchikh), MB.

Founded by Menshevik sponsors; Oct. 19, joined with Moscow Union of Employees in the Sale of Foodstuffs to form Moscow Union of Commercial and Industrial Employees—"Strength in Unity."[63]

Second Moscow Union of Commercial Employees (Vtoroi moskovskii soiuz tor-govykh sluzhashchikh), PU.

SR sponsors.[64]

Union of Bookshop Employees (Soiuz naemnykh rabotnikov knizhnogo dela), MB.

First meeting Oct. 14; Bolshevik sponsors; Nov. 5 meeting adopted charter and declared solidarity with printers' union; maximum meeting attendance 250.[65]

Union of Employees in Credit Establishments (Soiuz sluzhashchikh v kreditnykh uchrezhdeniiakh), MB, SC.

Oct. 15 meeting adopted charter; liberal influence; included employees in the state sav-ings association; represented at Oct. 28 meeting of the Moscow Committee for Self-Defense.[66]

MOSCOW UNION OF COMMERCIAL AND INDUSTRIAL EMPLOYEES—"STRENGTH IN UNITY" (Moskovskii soiuz torgovo-promyshlennykh sluzhashchikh—"v edinenii sila"), MB, SC, MS.

Founded Oct. 19 to combine Moscow Union of Employees in the Sale of Foodstuffs and Moscow Union of Commercial Employees; Menshevik sponsors; officially nonparty. Nov. 6, union organized as federation of sectional unions—Nov. 15, 1,000 hardware store em-ployees voted to join; Nov. 17, music shop employees joined; Nov. 20, 2,000 employees in retail metalware shops voted to join; Nov. 21, 2,000 employees in dry goods and gro-cery stores voted to join; Nov. 26, employees in stationery, notions, toy stores joined; Dec. 1, employees in furrier shops joined; Dec. 4, 100 cashiers voted to join. Maximum "Strength in Unity" meeting attendance 5,000; 2,500 members at end of year.[67]

UNION OF WAITERS AND OTHER TAVERN AND HOTEL EMPLOYEES (Soiuz ofitsian-tov i drugikh gostinykh i traktirnykh sluzhashchikh), MB.

Founded Oct. 23; Bolshevik sponsors; reorganization of Waiters' Mutual Aid Society (8,000 attended founding meeting).[68]

UNION OF TAVERN EMPLOYEES (Soiuz sluzhashchikh v pivnykh), MB.

Founded Oct. 23; SR sponsors; 500 members from factory-owned taverns.[69]

News Vendors' Union (Soiuz gazetchikov), MB.

Met six times Nov.–Dec.; maximum meeting attendance 200.[70]

Jnion of Lumberyard Employees (Soiuz sluzhashchikh v lesopromyshlennykh predpriiatii), MB.

Founded in Oct.; non-Bolshevik.[71]

Union of Employees in Insurance and Transport Establishments (Soiuz sluzhashchikh v strakhovykh i transportnykh uchrezhdenii), MB.

Nov. 4 meeting of 450; Dec. 5 meeting of 1,500.[72]

Shop Association of Tavern Clerks (Soiuz arteli prikazchikov v pivnykh), MB.

Founded Nov. 6; same SR sponsors as Union of Tavern Employees; 250 members from independent taverns.[73]

Union of Domestic Servants (Soiuz domashnei prislugi), MB.

Initiated by members of the liberal Union for Women's Equality; reorganized in mid-Nov. by Bolshevik sponsors; maximum meeting attendance 1,500; 300 members; occupational groups represented included governesses, nursemaids, housekeepers, cooks, lackeys, coachmen, chambermaids, and porters; functioned primarily as an employment office for out-of-work maids.[74]

Union of Butchershop Employees (Soiuz sluzhashchikh v miasotorgovliakh).

Founded Nov. 6 by anti-Black Hundred butchershop employees.[75]

Gardeners' Union (Soiuz sadovnikov), MB.

Founded Nov. 13 by employees of suburban nurseries; met at least once more in Nov.[76]

Union of Concierges (Soiuz dvornikov).

Met Nov. 7; Nov. 23 meeting of 2,000 dispersed by police.[77]

Window Washers' Union (Soiuz protirshchikov stekol).

Founded in Nov. by a liberal lawyer; met at least once in Dec.[78]

Society of Cooks (Obshchestvo povarov).

Charter adopted Nov. 20.[79]

Chimneysweeps' Union (Soiuz trubochistov).

Founded late Nov.; SR sponsors; Dec. 3 meeting of 500.[80]

Meetings that did not result in unions: bath attendants, Nov. 1, 6, 14; cabdrivers, Nov. 5; employees in tearooms and taverns without alcoholic beverages, Nov. 18, 26; office clerks in printing and publishing firms, Nov. 20; funeral parlor employees, Nov. 26; deliverymen, Nov. 30, Dec. 2; employees in icon shops, Dec. 1; psalm readers, Dec. 1 (attendance 300); cloakroom attendants and ticket takers in private theaters, Dec. 5 (attendance 300).[81]

8. Communications and Transport

Union of Railroad Workers, Attached to the Moscow Committee (Bolshevik) of the RSDWP (Soiuz zheleznodorozhnykh rabochikh, pri moskovskom komitetom RSDRP).

Founded in February; April, renamed Union of Railroad Employees of the Moscow Network, Attached to the Moscow Committee of the RSDWP. (Soiuz zheleznodorozhnykh sluzhashchikh moskovskogo uzla, pri moskovskom komitetom RSDRP).[82]

ALL-RUSSIAN UNION OF RAILROAD WORKERS AND EMPLOYEES (Vserossiiskii zheleznodorozhnyi soiuz sluzhashchikh i rabochikh), PU, SC.

Founded in April; predominantly SR leaders; officially nonparty; May, joined Union of Unions.[83]

All-Russian Union of Postal and Telegraph Employees (Vserossiiskii pochtovo-telegrafnyi soiuz sluzhashchikh), PU, MS.

First conceived July; Oct. 22, charter adopted; SR and left-liberal sponsors; officially nonparty; mid-Nov., first congress; Nov. 23, congress joined Moscow Soviet.[84]

UNION OF MOSCOW-BREST RAILROAD SHOP WORKERS (Soiuz rabochikh master-skikh Brestskoi zheleznoi dorogi), MB.

Founded before Sept.; Menshevik sponsors; over 600 members, mostly shop workers, some linemen.[85]

Union of Moscow-Kazan Railroad Shop Workers (Soiuz rabochikh masterskikh Kazanskoi zheleznoi dorogi), MB.

Member-union of the All-Russian Union of Railroad Workers and Employees; met independently at least three times in Nov.[86]

Union of Moscow-Brest Railroad Employees (Soiuz sluzhashchikh Moskovsko-Brestskoi zheleznoi dorogi).

Oct. 23 meeting of 1,000 adopted charter; may have been part of the Union of Moscow-Brest Railroad Shop Workers.[87]

Union of Ticket Collectors of the Moscow-Brest Railroad (Soiuz sluzhashchikh kontrolia Moskovsko-Brestskoi zheleznoi dorogi).

Supported postal-telegraph strike in Nov.; may have been part of the All-Russian Union of Railroad Workers and Employees.[88]

Union of Telephone Operators and Employees (Soiuz telefonistok i telefonnykh sluzhashchikh).

Founded Nov. 4; run by delegates' council of 35 men and 12 women; mass meetings throughout Nov.[89]

9. Municipal and Government Employees and Skilled Professions

Corporation of Employees in the Moscow City Administration (Korporatsiia sluzhashchikh po moskovskomu gorodskomu upravleniiu).

First meeting Jan.; July, charter drafted; Sept., charter adopted; Union of Unions-type association.[90]

Pharmacy Clerks' Union (Soiuz farmatsevtov), MB, MS.

Founded May; strong SD influence; officially nonparty; member of Union of Unions; represented at Oct. 28 meeting of Moscow Committee for Self-Defense.[91]

CORPORATION OF WORKERS AND LOW-RANKING EMPLOYEES IN THE MOSCOW CITY ADMINISTRATION (Korporatsiia rabochikh i nizshikh sluzhashchikh v moskovskoi gorodskoi uprave), PU, MB.

First meeting in April; officially founded in July; sponsored by nonparty municipal civil servant and labor specialist I. F. Gornostaev; Oct. 9, charter adopted; Nov. 13 meeting of 1,000; Nov. 22 meeting of 4,000–5,000 voted to support SR program over Kadet and SD positions.[92]

Corporation of Middle-Ranking Technicians Attached to the Moscow City Administration (Korporatsiia srednikh tekhnikov pri moskovskom gorodskom upravlenii), SC, MS.

Oct. 12, voted to join general strike; Nov. 5, voted to leave Strike Committee and join Moscow Soviet; Nov. 20, adopted SD program.[93]

Corporation of Doctors Employed by the City (Korporatsiia sostoiashchikh na sluzhbe u goroda vrachei).

Oct. 12, supported hospital workers' cause; Dec. 3 meeting supported postal-telegraph strike; liberal influence.[94]

Corporation of Hospital Workers (no exact name).

Mid-Oct., agitating for improvement in conditions; represented at Oct. 28 meeting of Moscow Committee for Self-Defense.[95]

Corporation of Employees in the Moscow Provincial and District Boards (Korporatsiia sluzhashchikh v moskovskoi gubernskoi i u'ezdnoi upravakh).
Unofficial group represented at Oct. 15 meeting in City Council chambers; represented at Oct. 28 meeting of Moscow Committee for Self-Defense.[96]
Corporation of City Engineers (no exact name).
Represented at Oct. 28 meeting of Moscow Committee for Self-Defense.[97]

Union of Unions members with branches in Moscow: Academics' Union [included professors and junior university instructors]; Agronomists' and Statisticians' Union; All-Russian Union of Engineers and Technicians (Vserossiiskii soiuz inzhenerov i tekhnikov); All-Russian Union of Medical Personnel [medical doctors]; Lawyers' Union; Union of Educators in Middle Schools (Soiuz deiatelei srednei shkoly); Union of Journalists and Writers; Veterinarians' Union.[98]

Meetings that did not result in unions: Employees of the Moscow Provincial Zemstvo, Oct. 12, 18, Dec. 2; the Central Group of Municipal Personnel, during Oct. strike; higher technical personnel of the city administration, Oct. 19, Dec. 13 (statement to City Council); clerks for the Justice of the Peace, Nov. 3; middle-level medical, veterinarian, and nursing personnel, Nov. 23 (SD program), Nov. 28; office clerks of the circuit court, Dec. 1.[99]

Notes

Notes

Complete authors' names, titles, and publication data for the works cited in short form in these Notes will be found in the Works Cited, pp. 291–97. All journals and newspapers cited herein are from 1905 unless otherwise specified. The following abbreviations are used in the Notes:

BMST   *Biulleten' Muzeiia Sodeistviia Trudu*

MV   *Moskovskie vedomosti*

OpO   *Obshcheprofessional'nye organy 1905–07 gg.*, vyp. 1 (Moscow, 1926)

PDMP   *Professional'noe dvizhenie moskovskikh pishchevikov v gody pervoi revoliutsii*, sb. 1 (Moscow, 1927)

PkP   *Prilozhenie k Pravu*, no. 45–46 (Nov. 20, 1905)

RS   *Russkoe slovo*

RV   *Russkie vedomosti*

Stachka   L. M. Ivanov, ed., *Vserossiiskaia politicheskaia stachka v oktiabre 1905 goda*, part 1

TsGAOR   Tsentral'nyi gosudarstvennyi arkhiv Oktiabr'skoi revoliutsii

TsGIAL   Tsentral'nyi gosudarstvennyi istoricheskii arkhiv SSSR v Leningrade

VP   *Vecherniaia pochta*

Chapter 1

1. To cite only one example of the official version of 1905: N. N. Iakovlev, *Narod i partiia v pervoi russkoi revoliutsii* (Moscow, 1965), pp. 382–86. Soviet scholarship presents material that challenges these conclusions, but the general interpretation remains in force.

2. This generalization is true of the vast majority of textile workers, but of a smaller majority of food workers. The food industry also included a significant number of small-shop craftworkers.

3. S. I. Mitskevich notes the widespread but nonsectarian appeal of the revolutionary movement among the professional intelligentsia: "There were significant strata of the intelligentsia that did not understand the meaning of party differences

and were not interested in exploring them: they sympathized with the revolutionary movement 'in general' and were ready to assist any one of the revolutionary parties. *Revoliutsionnaia Moskva*, p. 328.

4. Quotes in Ivanov, "Preemstvennost'," p. 65.

5. Quoted in V. I. Romashova, "Obrazovanie postoiannykh kadrov rabochikh v poreformennoi promyshlennosti Moskvy," in L. M. Ivanov et al., eds., *Rabochii klass i rabochee dvizhenie v Rossii, 1861–1917* (Moscow, 1966), p. 53.

6. Reginald E. Zelnik, *Labor and Society in Tsarist Russia: The Factory Workers of St. Petersburg, 1855–1870* (Stanford, Calif., 1971), p. 43.

7. Quote from 1886 in S. N. Prokopovich, *K rabochemu voprosu v Rossii* (St. Petersburg, 1905), p. 87; see also p. 88 for discussion.

8. This interpretation is based on Zelnik (cited in note 6, above), pp. 29, 137–38.

9. For the reaction of skilled workers, see Timofeev, pp. 5–6.

10. Prokopovich (cited in note 7, above), pp. 95–96, 98–99.

11. Andrzej Walicki, *The Controversy Over Capitalism* (Oxford, Eng., 1969), pp. 54–55, 60–61.

12. *Ibid.*, pp. 165, 170, 177.

13. "Naturally, in Soviet [scholarly] literature, the question of whether or not there was a working class in Russia does not exist. This question was resolved long ago: in theoretical terms by the work of Marxists, and on a practical plane, by the actions of the proletariat, which carried out the socialist revolution." These are the words of the leading Soviet labor historian, L. M. Ivanov ("Preemstvennost'," p. 65). This attitude does not, however, characterize Soviet scholarship of the 1920's. Two historians who emphasized the importance of artisanal and nonmanufacturing workers in the strike and trade-union movements of 1905 are Nikitin, pp. 95–104, and Ainzaft, *Pervyi etap*, pp. 53–55.

14. A full exposition of this position may be found in Adam B. Ulam, *The Unfinished Revolution: An Essay on the Sources of Influence of Marxism and Communism* (New York, 1960). See, for example, pp. 6–10, 43, 63–64; also, p. 188: "the spirit of revolutionary Marxism is the exploitation of the anarchism inherent in backwardness." In this same vein, Keep, p. 150, sees 1905 as "a spontaneous and chaotic upheaval, with many anarchic features."

15. Joan W. Scott, "The Glassworkers of Carmaux, 1850–1900," in Stephan Thernstrom and Richard Sennett, eds., *Nineteenth-Century Cities: Essays in the New Urban History* (New Haven, Conn., 1969), pp. 3–5, outlines the two major current interpretations of the origins of popular unrest: (1) as a product of social dislocation, and (2) as a consequence of the workers' integration into the larger community. For the hypothesis that integration promotes stability, see Clark Kerr and Abraham Siegel, "Interindustry Propensity to Strike—An International Comparison," in A. Kornhauser et al., eds., *Industrial Conflict* (New York, 1954), pp. 191–94.

16. E. J. Hobsbawm, *The Age of Revolution, 1789–1848* (New York, 1962), p. 252.

17. *Ibid.*, p. 253. See also George Lichtheim, *A Short History of Socialism* (New York, 1970), p. 36.

18. P. H. Noyes, *Organization and Revolution: Working-Class Associations in the German Revolutions of 1848–1849* (Princeton, N.J., 1966), pp. 26–27.

19. Frederick D. Marquardt, "A Working Class in Berlin in the 1840s?," in Hans-Ulrich Wehler, ed., *Sozialgeschichte Heute: Festschrift für Hans Rosenberg zum 70. Geburtstag* (Göttingen, 1974), pp. 191–210. Quote, p. 201.

20. Noyes (cited in note 18, above), pp. 73, 193–98.

21. Marquardt (cited in note 19, above), pp. 194–95.

22. William H. Sewell, Jr., "The Working Class of Marseille Under the Second Republic: Social Structure and Political Behavior," in Peter N. Stearns and Daniel J. Walkowitz, eds., *Workers in the Industrial Revolution: Recent Studies of Labor in the United States and Europe* (New Brunswick, N.J., 1974).

23. Scott, *Glassworkers*. Quote, p. 98.

24. See E. J. Hobsbawm, "Lenin and the Aristocracy of Labor," in *Revolutionaries* (New York, 1973), pp. 121–29.

25. E. J. Hobsbawm, "The Labour Aristocracy in Nineteenth-Century Britain," in *Labouring Men: Studies in the History of Labour* (London, 1964), pp. 273, 274, 280, 286.

26. *Ibid.*, p. 282.

27. *Ibid.*, pp. 288–89.

28. *Ibid.*, pp. 300–301. For a detailed study of this change, see Hinton.

29. "Absolutism in Russia must be overthrown by the proletariat. But in order to be able to overthrow it the proletariat require[s] a high degree of political education, of class consciousness and organization. All these conditions cannot be fulfilled by pamphlets and leaflets, but only by the living political school, by the fight and in the fight, in the continuous course of the revolution." Rosa Luxemburg, *The Mass Strike, the Political Party and the Trade Unions* (1906; New York, 1971), p. 31.

30. "Labour Traditions," in *Labouring Men* (cited in note 25, above), p. 371.

Chapter 2

1. Buryshkin, pp. 252, 261, for organizations in the business community. On printers, see Orlov, p. 219.

2. On retail corporations, see Verkhoven', p. 51.

3. *Obzor po g. Moskve*, p. 114; S. I. Iakubovskaia, "Spetsial'nye vysshie shkoly," in *Istoriia Moskvy*, vol. 5: 446, 448, 453, 460.

4. In 1903–4, the students at Moscow University came from the following backgrounds: 27% noble, 21% merchants and honored citizens, 17% middle strata (source does not specify Russian categories), 14% civil servants, 11% clergy, 5% peasant by legal category, and 5% military and other. See Burch, pp. 321–22.

5. Jürgen Kocka has defined the white-collar/blue-collar distinction in the German context: "*Angestellte* [or sluzhashchie], in contrast to *Arbeiter* [rabochie], were engaged in work of nonmanual, or at least not exclusively manual character; they usually received salaries, not wages; in spite of increasing overlapping the average white-collar worker earned more than the average blue-collar worker; in terms of industrial relations *Angestellte* enjoyed well-defined privileges which *Arbeiter* did not have (vacations, better conditions under company pension and insurance plans, more job security, frequently more contact with the employer and management)." "The Problem of Democracy and the Lower Middle Classes in the First Third of the Twentieth Century," paper presented at the XIV International

Congress of Historical Sciences, San Francisco (Aug. 22–29, 1975), p. 4. For further discussion, see Jürgen Kocka, *Angestellte zwischen Faschismus und Demokratie: Zur politischen Sozialgeschichte der Angestellten: USA 1890–1940 im internationalen Vergleich* (Göttingen, 1977), pp. 34–39.

6. K. Muromskii, *Byt i nuzhdy torgovo-promyshlennykh sluzhashchikh* (Moscow, 1906), pp. 8, 17.

7. Of the 85,500 entrepreneurs and self-employed workers listed in the census, 34,500 were so-called *khoziaeva-odinochki*, or independent entrepreneurs without hired labor. Some 14,000 of these were artisans. Members of this group were often poor, economically insecure, and dependent on orders from large shops, though they did not work under the authority of any single employer. Technically they do not belong to the category of wage labor, but in terms of status, social habits, and standard of living they are, in fact, part of the working class. For a definition of this group, see Oliunina, p. 48. Statistical data from *Perepis' Moskvy*, part 1, vyp. 2: Table 7, pp. 116–59. I would like to thank Victoria E. Bonnell for providing me with a copy of this table.

8. Breakdown of civil servants in *VP*, no. 300 (Dec. 5); estimates of postal and telegraph workers drawn from Bazilevich, pp. 136, 139–241.

9. *VP*, no. 300 (Dec. 5).

10. *Spravka o khode rabot po uregulirovaniiu rabochego voprosa v Moskovskom gorodskom upravlenii* (Moscow, 1906), pp. 4–28.

11. Verkhoven', p. 52.

12. Pushkareva, *Zheleznodorozhniki* (1975), p. 45.

13. *Ibid.*, pp. 34–35; Rostov, pp. 124–25.

14. Pushkareva, *Zheleznodorozhniki* (1975), pp. 35, 43–44. See also Bogdanov, pp. 5–7; Pushkareva, "Zheleznodorozhniki" (1959), p. 29.

15. Pushkareva, *Zheleznodorozhniki* (1975), pp. 39, 51, 54–57.

16. Compare the following sources (*T* = total number of workers included in the category of factory labor): *Obzor po g. Moskve*, pp. 107–9: *T* = 87,000; Gornostaev, part 2: *T* = 95,000; *Spisok fabrik*: *T* = 99,600; Pogozhev, *Uchet chislennosti*, Appendix table 3, pp. 107–18: *T* = 105,100. Internal breakdowns of the work force by branch of industry also differ from one source to another.

17. Pogozhev, *Uchet chislennosti*, p. 1.

18. On Moscow, see I. F. Ugarov, "Formirovanie i sostav moskovskogo proletariata nakanune revoliutsii 1905–1907 gg.," *Voprosy istorii*, no. 8 (1975), pp. 31–44. On St. Petersburg, see Semanov, pp. 10–57; and Shuster, pp. 5–58. See Shuster, p. 8, for an intelligent and nonideological discussion of the impossibility of forming neat statistical categories, and on the error of seeing artisanal and industrial enterprises as two distinct forms of production: precapitalist as against capitalist, nonproletarian as against proletarian. Shuster, p. 6, also gives a critical rundown of the major published sources of labor statistics.

19. See the example of Kanatchikov, pp. 66–67.

20. This exclusion is cited by Shuster, p. 7, among others. For the Artisan Board's jurisdiction, see *PDMP*, p. 21. On similar exclusions in the garment industry, see Oliunina, p. 16.

21. Pazhitnov, *Problema*, pp. 184–85.

22. *Ibid.*, p. 135.

23. Oliunina, pp. 172, 176; data collected in 1910. See Belousov, p. 8, on citified artisans who retained peasant status.

24. Pazhitnov, *Problema*, p. 167, gives 37,400 in 1896, 70,000 in 1910.

25. *Perepis' Moskvy*, part 1, vyp. 2: Table 7. The figures cited here exclude white-collar workers, owners (including independents, the *odinochki*), and working family members. They cover only wage laborers, a group that includes apprentices.

26. These data come from two published sources: Gornostaev; and Pogozhev, *Adresnaia kniga*. Strike reports have been used for information about workers in small firms that are either not mentioned in the handbooks or not identified by payroll size.

27. The handbooks together list a total of 1,700 factories and shops in the city of Moscow, but identify only 70% by number of workers employed. They designate almost all the firms of unspecified size as artisanal. It is thus safe to assume they were small shops. The percentage of firms of identified size in a given industry depends on the importance of large firms in that sector: thus, almost 80% of textile firms included by name are identified by payroll size, compared with 66% of metalworking and 45% of woodworking enterprises.

28. A thorough inspection of the archives, were this possible, might show that the police were actually more precise than this in their reporting.

29. Semanov, p. 25. The importance of textile production in the central industrial region is underlined by the data for Moscow Province outside the city of Moscow. There, textile workers made up 70% of all factory workers, compared with 40% inside Moscow. The figures for metalworkers are 9% and 20%, respectively. For Moscow Province, see Pogozhev, *Adresnaia kniga, passim*; and Pogozhev, *Uchet chislennosti*, Appendix table 3, pp. 107-18.

30. For Moscow, *Spisok fabrik* and Pogozhev, *Adresnaia kniga*, agree in relative proportions, though not in base figures. On St. Petersburg, see Semanov, p. 38. In 1906, only 25% of the textile workers in France worked in plants of this scale. See Peter N. Stearns, *Lives of Labor: Work in a Maturing Industrial Society* (New York, 1975), p. 156.

31. For St. Petersburg, Semanov, p. 38, gives the proportion as 61%; and *Spisok fabrik*, pp. 310-18, gives it as 75% (calculations mine).

32. Quoted in Hinton, p. 24.

33. Verkhoven', p. 33.

34. *Perepis' Moskvy*, part 2, vyp. 1: Table 7, pp. 118-19, 140-41.

35. Semanov, p. 33.

36. Calculations based on *Spisok fabrik*, pp. 280-92, 310-18, show 9% of St. Petersburg metalworkers in shops with fewer than 100 workers, compared with 38% in Moscow. The figures from this source are not complete, but they are comparable.

37. Sanburov, p. 31.

38. Timofeev, pp. 4, 51; Kanatchikov, p. 80.

39. Belousov, p. 15; Timofeev, pp. 33-34.

40. Belousov, p. 16. For a description of the work conditions and authority re-

lations in Moscow's gold and silver workshops, see Mamontov, pp. 180–83. On the authority of masters in tailoring shops, see Oliunina, pp. 242, 275–76.

41. For a description of metal-plant shop organization in St. Petersburg, see Surh, pp. 79–82.

42. Timofeev, pp. 5, 6, 11; Sanburov, pp. 104–6; Rashin, p. 590; Kanatchikov, pp. 17–19.

43. Timofeev, pp. 8–10. In January 1905, workers in the Moscow-Brest railroad machine shops included in a list of demands presented to the administration the demand that masterovye not be obliged to perform unskilled labor (chernaia rabota). See Trusova, Nachalo, p. 276.

44. Timofeev, pp. 12–13.   45. Ibid., pp. 51–64.
46. Verkhoven', pp. 38–39.   47. Hinton, pp. 96–97.

48. Kanatchikov, pp. 8–68, especially, for seniority, p. 18. For a sensitive discussion of Kanatchikov's memoirs, see Reginald E. Zelnik, "Russian Bebels: An Introduction to the Memoirs of Semen Kanatchikov and Matvei Fisher," part 1, Russian Review, vol. 35.3 (1976): 249–89. The plants at which Kanatchikov worked were of the following sizes: List (440 workers), Bromlei (1,500), Mytishchi (1,500), and Vartse and McGill (260).

49. Workers could be fined for crossing the plant without permission (Timofeev, p. 67).

50. Mitskevich, "Na zare," p. 26.

51. Mitskevich, Na zare, contains several examples of such movement: E. I. Nemchinov, "Vospominaniia," pp. 159, 174, goes from the Moscow-Brest shops to the Mytishchi railroad-car works in 1898; M. I. Petrov, "Moi vospominaniia," p. 189, goes from Veikhel't to Bromlei in 1894; between 1892 and 1894, A. D. Karpuzi, "Na perevalakh," pp. 196–99, goes from Dobrov and Nabgol'ts to Veikhel't to Gopper to Guzhon; and F. I. Ignatov, "Iz besedy," pp. 211–12, works at the Nizhni Novgorod shops until 1893, then transfers to Guzhon, then to the Moscow-Kursk shops in 1895.

52. These figures are from the Factory File. The census gives cotton mill workers as 25% of all textile workers, wool workers as 28%. The File counts 5,000 more textile workers than are included in the census all together, and has 20,200 cotton mill workers to the census's 14,500.

53. Pazhitnov, Ocherki istorii (1958), p. 94.

54. Pogozhev, Adresnaia kniga, pp. 9–89, sections on textiles.

55. Rozhkova, p. 222.

56. Pazhitnov, Ocherki istorii (1955), p. 197. In the Prokhorov Trekhgornaia factory, 80% of spinning workers but only 66% of weavers were women (Lapitskaia, p. 49).

57. Perepis' Moskvy, part 2, vyp. 1: Table 7, pp. 124–25, 146–47. For Moscow Province, see Koz'minykh-Lanin, pp. 20, 26. The proportion of women in the European textile industry was even higher in this period: in Britain (1911), 65%; in France (1906), 55%; in Germany (1905), 50%. (Stearns [cited in note 30, above], p. 30.)

58. Koz'minykh-Lanin, p. 22.

59. Shestakov, *Rabochie*, p. 46; Lapitskaia, p. 49.

60. Shestakov, "Materialy," p. 169. See also I. M. Koz'minykh-Lanin, *Gramotnost' i zarabotki fabrichno-zavodskikh rabochikh moskovskoi gubernii* (Moscow, 1912), pp. 14–15.

61. On the male-female literacy rate in textiles, see I. M. Koz'minykh-Lanin, *Ukhod na polevye raboty fabrichno-zavodskikh rabochikh moskovskoi gubernii* (Moscow, 1912), Tables 1 and 2; and for the specific case of the Tsindel' factory, Shestakov, "Materialy," p. 157. For the rate among engravers and printers, see Shestakov, *Rabochie*, p. 46; and Rashin, p. 586. The figure for metalworkers is from Sher, *Istoriia*, p. 32.

62. Rozhkova, p. 222; Shestakov, "Materialy," pp. 167–69; Koz'minykh-Lanin, *Gramotnost'* (cited in note 60, above), p. 12.

63. Koz'minykh-Lanin, p. 56. See also statistics quoted in Sher and Svavitskii, p. 20.

64. Koz'minykh-Lanin, pp. 46, 51. The same pattern holds for the garment industry, a purely artisanal trade (Oliunina, p. 217).

65. G. von Schulze-Gaevernitz, *The Cotton Trade in England and on the Continent*, tr. Oscar S. Hall (London, 1895), p. 96; Pazhitnov, *Ocherki istorii* (1958), p. 89. Surh, p. 52, gives a worker-spindle ratio of 16.6 : 1,000 for the Empire, and of 8.1 : 1,000 for St. Petersburg.

66. Pazhitnov, *Ocherki istorii* (1958), p. 91.

67. *Statistika bumagopriadel'nogo i tkatskogo proizvodstv za 1900–1910 goda* (St. Petersburg, 1911), p. 51.

68. For textile workers, Shestakov, *Rabochie*, p. 44; Shestakov, "Materialy," p. 158; Rozhkova, p. 229; Sanburov, p. 365. For metalworkers and mechanics in textile mills, Sanburov, pp. 53, 54, 365, and Rozhkova, p. 229, respectively.

69. *Perepis' Moskvy*, part 1, vyp. 1: Table 8, p. 139.

70. Belousov, p. 8.

71. *Perepis' Moskvy*, part 1, vyp. 2: Table 2, p. 10.

72. Koz'minykh-Lanin, *Ukhod* (cited in note 61, above), Tables 1, 2, 4.

73. Johnson, pp. 64–65.

74. *Ibid.*, p. 62. Also true of artisans (Oliunina, p. 176).

75. Belousov, p. 14.

76. For example, see Kanatchikov, pp. 3–8.

77. Johnson, pp. 37–38, 40–50.

78. The following discussion is based on Robert E. Johnson, "The Nature of the Russian Working Class: Social Characteristics of the Moscow Industrial Region, 1880–1900," Ph.D. dissertation, Cornell University, Ithaca, N.Y., 1975, Chaps. 2–4.

79. *Ibid.*, p. 247.

80. On heavy drinking among tailors, for example, see Oliunina, pp. 239–41.

81. Kanatchikov, pp. 18–19, 80.

82. Only 5.3% of the Tsindel' textile workers had severed all ties with the countryside in 1900 (Shestakov, "Materialy," p. 161).

83. Timofeev, pp. 27–31; Lapitskaia, pp. 43–46.

250   NOTES TO PAGES 34-37

84. For descriptions of life in the communal apartment (the living *artel'*), see Kanatchikov, pp. 8–14; and Timofeev, pp. 15–16, 24–27. Lapitskaia, p. 53, describes how dormitories were used to control workers.

85. To quote the Presnia Menshevik leader P. A. Garvi (p. 653): "The workers in enterprises such as Prokhorov, where they live in factory 'dormitories' and eat at management expense, sustained the [December] general strike longer than the workers in enterprises that did not provide room and board."

86. Sher and Svavitskii. See also Sher, *Istoriia.*

87. Sher, *Istoriia*, pp. 17, 32; Sher and Svavitskii, p. 20.

88. Sher and Svavitskii, pp. 6, 8–9.

89. Calculations for printers based on the Factory File, which covers 148 firms with a total of 12,500 workers. This total is twice as high as the figure given by the Factory Inspectorate for 1905: 79 firms with 7,442 workers (Sher, *Istoriia*, p. 12). The 1902 census, however, lists 8,000 printers in Moscow (*Perepis' Moskvy*, part 2, vyp. 1: Table 7, subsections 144–46). Orlov, pp. 216, 226, a Soviet study, reports 180 private printing firms and 41 others in Moscow in 1905, but does not offer a figure for the number of workers employed.

90. Sources disagree on the distribution of printing workers by plant size. The Factory Inspectorate calculated that 63% (of a base of 7,442 workers) were concentrated in factories with 100 or more workers. According to Sher, *Istoriia*, pp. 12, 14, the 1902 census gives the proportion as only 40%, on a base of 12,000. This is more than the total in *Perepis' Moskvy*, part 2, vyp. 1: Table 7, which does not indicate the number or size of shops. The Inspectorate's figure is high because it excluded small shops from its count. This discussion relies on the Factory File, because, as I have explained, the File identifies each enterprise individually.

91. A comparison of figures in *Spisok fabrik*, pp. 150–55, 162–67, shows a similar distribution of workers in Moscow as in St. Petersburg, but in Europe, large printing plants were less common. Sher, *Istoriia*, pp. 15–16, compares the state of the printing industry in Moscow with that in Berlin and Germany as a whole in this period.

92. Orlov, pp. 128, 149, 190, 199, 214.

93. *Ibid.*, pp. 227–29. The pattern of hiring and training new workers from outside to operate machines that performed the tasks formerly done by hand rather than downgrading the handicraftsmen is not uncommon. For the case of late-nineteenth-century France, see, for example, Scott, p. 4 and elsewhere. On the social effects of mechanization in the British metal industry during the First World War, see Hinton, pp. 59–62.

94. Orlov, p. 190.

95. Sher and Svavitskii, pp. 11–12, 24–25.

96. Orlov, pp. 215–17, 222–23.

97. Sher and Svavitskii, pp. 23, 31, 32.

98. Petrov (cited in note 51, above), p. 187, describes the production system at Veikhel't.

99. Oliunina, pp. 119–201, 206, 218.

100. On the hours of work, see *ibid.*, pp. 190, 192; and Nemchinov, p. 160.

101. *PDMP*, p. 21.

102. *PDMP*, pp. 21, 33.

103. *PDMP*, pp. 27, 33-35.

104. Sher and Svavitskii, pp. 47-48; Lapitskaia, pp. 53-61; Oliunina, pp. 197-99.

105. I. Evsenin, *Pervye stranitsy iz istorii bor'by rabochikh fabriki "Einem"* (Moscow, 1926), pp. 5-8, 13-14; *PDMP*, p. 30.

106. Factory File data for candy workers agree completely with figures in *PDMP*, p. 31.

107. *PDMP*, pp. 44-45.

108. *PDMP*, p. 190.

Chapter 3

1. Rashin, p. 354. My estimate for Moscow.

2. *Perepis' Moskvy*, part 1, vyp. 1: Table 2, p. 111.

3. Rashin, p. 195, for St. Petersburg; Verkhoven', pp. 30-33, for Moscow.

4. Pogozhev, *Uchet chislennosti*, pp. 76, 80.

5. Calculations based on figures in Verkhoven', pp. 30, 33.

6. Koz'minykh-Lanin, pp. 20, 26, 29, 33.

7. *Ibid.*, pp. 23, 28.   8. *Ibid.*, p. 30; Orlov, p. 218.

9. Sher, *Istoriia*, p. 12.   10. Iakovlev, p. 268.

11. That is, male employment rose 3.6% between 1902 and 1903, female 116%, causing women to go from 4% to 8% of the metal-industry work force. On employment by sex, see Koz'minykh-Lanin, p. 26.

12. On wages, see Koz'minykh-Lanin, pp. 51-52.

13. *Rabochie zavoda*, p. 22.

14. Iakovlev, p. 268.

15. Koz'minykh-Lanin, pp. 1, 6, 11, 29, 39, 42-44, 51.

16. Orlov, pp. 213-14; Sher and Svavitskii, p. 12.

17. Iakovlev, p. 312, states emphatically: "There is absolutely no basis for attributing to the [Russo-Japanese] War a depressing effect on the nation's economy." In Iakovlev's view, earlier interpretations made the mistake of confusing the political and social effects of the war, which were negative, with its economic effects, which were not. A. Finn-Enotaevskii, *Sovremennoe khoziaistvo Rossii (1890-1910 gg.)* (St. Petersburg, 1911), pp. 211-12, for example, says the war reversed the trend of economic recovery begun in 1903. This is also the position of M. S. Balabanov, "Promyshlennost' v 1904-1907 gg.," in Martov et al., vol. 4, part 1: 37, 44. The Soviet economic historian S. G. Strumilin, *Ocherki ekonomicheskoi istorii Rossii i SSSR* (Moscow, 1966), p. 449, holds that in general the war stimulated production, except in certain industries: organic products, chemicals, wood, and silk textiles.

18. Even Iakovlev, p. 311, seems to suggest that the generally positive effect of the war was not felt in Moscow. More research is certainly needed on the war's impact on specific industries, both in terms of production and in terms of the reorganization of the work force.

19. Koz'minykh-Lanin, pp. 28, 51.

20. Iakovlev, pp. 322, 330.

21. *Ibid.*, p. 321, for prices; Koz'minykh-Lanin, p. 6 for employment, pp. 42–43, for wages. The contraction of the wool labor force in Moscow Province in 1904 seems illogical. None of the sources explains why this should be so in a time of expanded production. Finn-Enotaevskii (cited in note 17, above), p. 212, says textile workers throughout the Empire worked fewer hours in 1904 than in 1903. His interpretation is unpopular among Soviet scholars, as we have seen. His figures for the cotton industry, moreover, do not reflect the situation in Moscow Province, where production and employment both were up in 1904. Pazhitnov, *Ocherki istorii* (1955), p. 182, says wool production was up almost 20% in 1904 over 1903, and says nothing of a shrinking labor force or of sudden changes in production techniques.

22. Iakovlev, p. 311; Koz'minykh-Lanin, p. 11.

23. Koz'minykh-Lanin, pp. 29, 56.

24. This conclusion is based on changes in the prices of four basic commodities—the cheapest varieties of bread and meat, potatoes, and peat, the least expensive of the fuels—as reported in *Svodnyi biulleten'* for 1901–5.

25. I have calculated the real wages of factory workers by comparing changes in consumer prices with the wage fluctuations in Moscow Province as given in Koz'minykh-Lanin, p. 56. Sher, *Istoriia*, pp. 160–61, says the printers' standard of living remained the same between 1903 and 1905.

26. Koz'minykh-Lanin, pp. 46, 51, reports the tendency for lower wages to prevail in smaller firms. Even metalworkers in small shops took a pay loss between 1903 and 1905. Oddly enough, textile workers in small factories gained some in 1904 and 1905—without, however, rising from the bottom of the industry pay scale.

27. For craft wages, see *Svodnyi biulleten'* for 1901–5; and the statistical summary in *Statisticheskii ezhegodnik*, part 8: Table 3, pp. 112–13.

28. Balabanov (cited in note 17, above), p. 41, cites in particular the woodworking industry as suffering from high unemployment as a result of the war. This agrees with Strumilin (cited in the same note), p. 449, who notes that the woodworking industry as a whole suffered in 1904. Annual wages for carpenters in Moscow were lower in 1904 than they had been in 1901. See *Svodnyi biulleten'* for 1901–5.

29. This can be inferred from data in Koz'minykh-Lanin, pp. 23, 28.

30. Timofeev, p. 5.

31. The chasti were further broken down into precincts (*uchastki*). For a good description of Moscow in the late nineteenth century, see Hanchett, Chap. 1.

32. Belousov, pp. 18, 35–37. Belousov offers a vivid description of the artisan quarter at the end of the nineteenth century.

33. *Ibid.*, p. 68; Hanchett, pp. 36–37. Kanatchikov, p. 12, describes the habits of one such worker. Oliunina, p. 241, speaks of tailors drinking the clothes off their own backs.

34. The population density figures in this section are from *Statisticheskii atlas*, pp. 5, 9. Calculations mine. The population in areas I and II was 10% noble and clergy and 8% honored citizen and merchant, compared with citywide averages of 6% and 5%, respectively (*Perepis' Moskvy*, part 1, vyp. 1: Table 8, p. 139).

35. *Statisticheskii atlas*, Table 35, pp. 64–65.

36. For residential patterns of the student population, see Burch, pp. 315, 339. For the legal status of students at Moscow University, see Chap. 2, note 4, above.

37. For death statistics, see *Svodnyi biulleten'* for 1902, p. 104; and for 1905, p. 100. In certain quarters of area I, literacy reached 88% for men and 62% for women.

38. Of all the peasant women in the area, a quarter were domestic servants, compared with 14% citywide (*Perepis' Moskvy*, part 1, vyp. 1: Table 8, pp. 137–39; *Statisticheskii atlas*, pp. 61–62).

39. I. Verner, *Zhilishcha bedneishego naseleniia Moskvy* (Moscow, 1902), pp. 4, 19.

40. Hanchett, pp. 34–35; *Perepis' Moskvy*, part 1, vyp. 1: Table 8, pp. 137–39. On the working-class family in Moscow at the end of the nineteenth century, see Johnson, pp. 53–61.

41. In the second Lefortovo precinct, literacy was as low as 66% for men and 32% for women.

42. Area III had 42% women in the peasant category, compared with 37–39% in the other industrial areas.

43. Lapitskaia, pp. 59–61.

44. Garvi, pp. 637, 646.

45. The statute gave the vote to two categories of city residents: property owners whose houses were evaluated for tax purposes at no less than 3,000 rubles, and merchants and industrialists who qualified for membership in the first guild by virtue of paying annual taxes of at least 500 rubles. See N. Karzhanskii, *Kak izbiralas' i rabotala moskovskaia gorodskaia duma*, 2d ed. (Moscow, 1950), pp. 12–13.

46. Voting statistics for the 1904 City Council elections were published every other day or so between Nov. 24, 1904, and Dec. 17, 1904, in *Russkie vedomosti*: see nos. 327, 329, 331, 333, 336, 338, 341, 343, 345, 347, 349, and 350.

47. Verkhoven', pp. 35–36. See also Buryshkin, pp. 58, 112–203, for major industrial families in Moscow.

48. *Moskovskaia gorodskaia duma, 1897–1900* (Moscow, 1897).

49. *Spravochnaia kniga*, pp. 40–46.

50. *Statisticheskii ezhegodnik*, part 10: Table 1, pp. 145–46.

51. *Ibid.*, Table 2, pp. 147–52.

52. The office of gradonachal'nik replaced the more restricted one of police commissioner on January 1, 1905. N. P. Eroshkin, "Administrativno-politseiskii apparat," in *Istoriia Moskvy*, vol. 5: 667–68. The Factory Inspectorate, however, was ultimately responsible to the Ministry of Finance. See Laverychev, *Tsarizm*, p. 160, on the conflict between the Ministries of Finance and Internal Affairs for control of the Inspectorate. Further discussion of this conflict may be found in Schneiderman, pp. 34–39.

53. *Statisticheskii atlas*, Table 36, pp. 65–66.

54. *Statisticheskii ezhegodnik*, part 13: Table 4, p. 166. The dvorniki swept the yard, did odd jobs, guarded the premises against intruders, and like the French concierge, kept an eye on the activity of tenants in rented buildings.

55. Eroshkin (cited in note 52, above), p. 664.

56. Verkhoven', p. 38; Johnson, p. 23; Kanatchikov, p. 71.

57. A. S. Nifontov, "Gorodskie raiony kapitalisticheskoi Moskvy," in *Istoriia Moskvy*, vol. 4: 268.

Chapter 4

1. Bukhbinder, p. 200. On SD infiltration of Sunday schools and workers' courses, see Schneiderman, pp. 90-92.

2. Wildman, pp. 37, 46-47, 50-55, 78. See also Mitskevich, "Na zare," pp. 20-21.

3. The plants represented were the metal factories of Guzhon (2,500 workers), Veikhel't (800), List (440), Bromlei (1,500), Dobrov and Nabgol'ts (1,020), Gopper (600), and Grachev (400); the Brest (1,200), Kursk (1,650), and Kazan (2,500) railroad shops; and the Mikhailov (1,265) and Filippov (235) wool textile mills (Schneiderman, p. 73; Vasin, p. 36; see also Mitskevich, "Na zare," p. 24).

4. Of seven worker members of the Workers' Union arrested in 1898, three worked in the Kazan railroad shop, two as carpenters, one as a painter; one was a carpenter in a machine factory; and two were machinists in textile mills. Only one was an unskilled factory worker. (Ivanov, *Rabochee dvizhenie* [1961-63], part 1: 658-61.) Patternmakers tended to respond to SD agitation, as did machinists and turners, who were especially active (*ibid.*, pp. 341, 403-4).

5. Police report on Workers' Union contacts, *ibid.*, p. 362. This collection contains numerous documents on the union's activities.

6. Johnson, pp. 144-45.

7. Surh, pp. 50-65.

8. Johnson, pp. 128-29.

9. See leaflets in Ivanov, *Rabochee dvizhenie* (1961-63), part 1: 343-46.

10. *Ibid.*, pp. 355-58, 362-63.

11. *Ibid.*, pp. 412-13.

12. *Ibid.*, pp. 59-62, 348-49; *ibid.*, part 2: 52-61; Ivanov, *Rabochee dvizhenie* (1975), p. 34.

13. M. Rakovskii, "Zubatov i moskovskie gravery (1898-1899 gg.)," *Istoriia proletariata SSSR*, no. 2 (1930): 199-202. Note that this SD-sponsored engravers' organization was considered an artisans' association (*ibid.*, p. 201).

14. Johnson, pp. 143-45.

15. Surh, pp. 65-67.

16. *Ibid.*, pp. 59-61.

17. See report of Workers' Union central committee, in Ivanov, *Rabochee dvizhenie* (1961-63), part 1: 411. See also Wildman, p. 55.

18. Mitskevich, "Ocherki istorii moskovskoi partiinoi organizatsii," in N. Ovsiannikov, ed., *Na zare rabochego dvizheniia v Moskve* (Moscow, 1919), pp. 20-39.

19. Vasin, p. 67.

20. Ivanov, *Rabochee dvizhenie* (1961-63), part 2: 61-66, 291-93.

21. Nemchinov, p. 162.

22. *Ibid.*, pp. 174-75.

NOTES TO PAGES 58-63

23. Schneiderman, pp. 103, 104. For an individual example, see "Iz besedy," pp. 211–12.

24. On the student movement in 1900–1901, see N. Cherevanin, "Dvizhenie intelligentsii," in Martov et al., vol. 1: 277–78. See also Burch, p. 111; and Gusiatnikov, pp. 42–55. On the street violence, see Ivanov, *Rabochee dvizhenie* (1975), pp. 34–36.

25. "During the student unrest of February 1901, many workers took part in the demonstrations, but this was a spontaneous action, and the Moscow [SD] Committee did not manage to become involved in it, nor to lead it, nor even to issue a single proclamation during the unrest" (Mitskevich, *Revoliutsionnaia Moskva*, p. 283).

26. Schneiderman, pp. 99–100.

27. Quoted in Laverychev, *Tsarizm*, pp. 130–31.

28. Bukhbinder, pp. 171, 173; Schneiderman, pp. 101–2, 105, 108–9.

29. I. Kh. Ozerov, *Nuzhdy rabochego klassa v Rossii* (Moscow, 1905), p. 14.

30. Ozerov, *Politika*, pp. 274, 278. This argument was presented in 1903 against the idea of mutual aid societies (Laverychev, *Tsarizm*, p. 163).

31. From *What Is to Be Done?* Quoted in Schwarz, pp. 287–88.

32. Ozerov, *Politika*, pp. 106, 205–6; Ainzaft, *Zubatovshchina*, pp. 51–59. See also Laverychev, *Tsarizm*, p. 142. The council had originally been created to facilitate official control over the unions. See Schneiderman, pp. 114–15, 145.

33. The four metal factories known to have been affected by Zubatov organizers were Guzhon, Zotov, Bromlei, and Gakental' (Shchap, p. 19; Milonov, *Kak voznikli*, p. 110). Information on engravers and others from Rakovskii (cited in note 13, above), pp. 203, 230; and Ainzaft, *Zubatovshchina*, pp. 57–58. See also F. Bogdanov-Evdokimov, "Zubatovshchina v Moskve," *Vestnik truda*, no. 9 (Nov. 1923): 237; and Schneiderman, p. 146.

34. Schneiderman, pp. 152–53.

35. Laverychev, *Tsarizm*, pp. 151, 155, 156, 158.

36. Schneiderman, pp. 146–49. This plant was also known as the Guzhon mill, after its director, who also ran the steel mill of that name.

37. Ainzaft, *Zubatovshchina*, pp. 63–64, 66, 68. See also Laverychev, *Tsarizm*, pp. 152–53, 159; and Schneiderman, pp. 185–87.

38. The starosta system was first proposed in 1901 (Ozerov, *Politika*, p. 271). For the starosta statute of June 10, 1903, and its application at the Prokhorov Trekhgornaia textile plant, see Gornostaev, part 2: 24–29.

39. Ivanov, *Rabochee dvizhenie* (1975), pp. 178–82. See also Schneiderman, pp. 187–89. Schneiderman's figure of 15,000 strikers must be exaggerated, since there were barely that many printing workers in Moscow.

40. Sher, *Istoriia*, pp. 136–50, on SD union before 1905.

41. *Ibid.*, pp. 127–36. In 1902, the SD activist from Moscow N. E. Bauman admitted: "We consider it our duty at this point to speak the naked truth, however lamentable it might be: in Moscow, revolutionary Social Democracy has ceded to police socialism" (quoted in Mitskevich, *Revoliutsionnaia Moskva*, p. 302).

42. This is the view of Ainzaft, *Zubatovshchina*, p. 74.

43. See statement by P. Struve in Galai, p. 176. For a discussion of the consti-

tutionalist and democratic trends within the movement at the end of 1904, see Emmons, pp. 45-86.

44. Maevskii, pp. 37-38. See also Emmons, p. 47. Quote from *Memoirs of Count Witte*, p. 230.

45. M. Taganskii, "Moskovskaia gorodskaia duma i ee obshchestvennaia rol' v sobytiiakh poslednego vremeni," in *Tekushchii moment* (Moscow, 1906), p. 11. See also Sef, p. 44.

46. Maevskii, pp. 38-39. On the announcement of the campaign, see Schwarz, pp. 33-34. See also Emmons, pp. 74-76.

47. Gusiatnikov, pp. 135-37. Accounts of the Dec. 5 and 6 demonstrations in Moscow may be found in the SR paper *Revoliutsionnaia Rossiia*, no. 57 (Dec. 25, 1904) and no. 58 (Jan. 20, 1905).

48. The Gapon organization enjoyed greater independence from police control than the Zubatov movement in Moscow did. For an excellent discussion of the Gapon movement in St. Petersburg, see Surh, pp. 114-93. For a full account, see Walter Sablinsky, *The Road to Bloody Sunday: Father Gapon and the St. Petersburg Massacre of 1905* (Princeton, N.J., 1976).

49. Surh, pp. 130-44 *passim*, 166-75 *passim*. See also Schwarz, pp. 59-61, 67.

50. Surh, pp. 220-32. See also L. S. Kuznetsova, "Stachechnaia bor'ba rabochikh Peterburga v ianvare 1905 goda," *Voprosy istorii*, no. 1 (1955): 11-25.

51. Official strike figures for 1900-1905 compiled by V. E. Varzar; quoted in Iu. Z. Polevoi, "Rabochee i sotsial-demokraticheskoe dvizhenie v Moskve vo vtoroi polovine 90-kh i nachale 900-kh godov," in *Istoriia Moskvy*, vol. 5: 83. Total figures for the industrial working class in Moscow Province in 1905 may be found in Koz'minykh-Lanin, p. 33.

52. "Ianvarskoe rabochee dvizhenie 1905 g.: materialy fabrichnoi inspektsii," *Istoriia proletariata SSSR*, no. 1 (1930): 250. On Jan. strikes in Moscow, see Nevskii, "Ianvarskie zabastovki"; Trusova, *Nachalo*, pp. 226-321; Tsukerman, pp. 97-105; Shchap, pp. 31-32; and Maevskii, p. 53.

53. For a general characterization of the dynamics of the January movement, see Anweiler, p. 37. Although there had been student demonstrations in the streets in Moscow in Dec. 1904, no such incidents occurred in Jan. 1905. In the way of negative evidence, neither *Revoliutsionnaia Rossiia*, nos. 58, 59 (Jan. 20, Feb. 10), nor the documentary collection on the early period of the revolution (Trusova, *Nachalo*, pp. 226-321) mentions any student activity. On the positive side, one can find several references in the documents to the failure of any public demonstrations to take place (see Trusova, pp. 245, 291). In February, students in cities throughout the Empire voted to go on strike (that is, not to attend classes) until September (Gusiatnikov, pp. 145-50).

54. Argument for the continuity of *popechitel'naia politika*, in Laverychev, *Tsarizm*, p. 190.

55. Schwarz, p. 77; Schneiderman, p. 61.

56. Schwarz, pp. 89-94; Surh, pp. 294-98. One of the lawyers was G. S. Nosar', later (under the name Khrustalev-Nosar') president of the St. Petersburg Soviet (Surh, pp. 325-30).

57. Schwarz, pp. 113, 123; Surh, pp. 305-6, 314.

58. Surh, pp. 114-16, 119-22; Dan, p. 287; Schwarz, pp. 114-19.

59. D. Kol'tsov, p. 200; Schwarz, pp. 124-25; Surh, pp. 312-13.

60. Dan, pp. 287-89.

61. Statement by G. A. Krestovnikov in May 1905, quoted in Laverychev, *Tsarizm*, pp. 198-99.

62. Sef, p. 26; Laverychev, *Tsarizm*, p. 199; Laverychev, *Po tu storonu barrikad*, p. 31.

63. On the assassination of Grand Duke Sergei, see Harcave, pp. 126-27. On the Mukden defeat, see Michael T. Florinsky, *Russia, a History and an Interpretation*, vol. 2: 1274. On the rescript, see Harcave, pp. 120-30; Dan, pp. 308-9; and Maevskii, pp. 56-57. Text in Lazerevskii, pp. 30-31.

64. By May 1905, seven professional unions had come into existence. The groups organized were (1) engineers and technicians, (2) clerks and bookkeepers, (3) schoolteachers, (4) medical doctors, (5) writers, (6) pharmacy clerks, and (7) railroad employees and workers (Kirpichnikov, p. 2).

65. Mitskevich, *Revoliutsionnaia Moskva*, pp. 290-92, discusses the political spectrum within the Medical Society.

66. *Ibid.*, pp. 343-45.

67. Maevskii, pp. 57-59. The 14 member unions of the Union of Unions were (1) academics, (2) lawyers, (3) agronomists and statisticians, (4) medical doctors, (5) veterinarians, (6) railroad personnel, (7) writers, (8) zemstvo members, (9) engineers, (10) clerks and bookkeepers, (11) schoolteachers, (12) pharmacy clerks, (13) the union for women's equality, and (14) the union for Jewish equality (Kirpichnikov, pp. 6-7). Most groups in the liberation movement did not include the vote for women in their demand for universal suffrage. The Union of Unions and later the Kadets were deeply divided on this issue. Marxists and SRs were the least ambivalent in their commitment to women's equality. See Richard Stites, *The Women's Liberation Movement in Russia* (Princeton, N.J., 1978), pp. 199-206.

68. Sef, p. 47; Keep, p. 162.

69. Sef, pp. 53-54, 56, 67; Laverychev, *Po tu storonu barrikad*, pp. 34-39. For the statement calling for a national assembly with decision-making power and a list of signatories, see *Pravo*, nos. 30 and 32 (Aug. 2 and Aug. 14): 2461-62, 2586.

70. Dan, pp. 310-311.

71. Trepov continued to be the police chief of St. Petersburg as well (see Harcave, p. 168).

72. Kirpichnikov, p. 11.

73. Dan, pp. 313-18; Sef, p. 59; Kirpichnikov, pp. 10, 14.

74. Mitskevich, *Revoliutsionnaia Moskva*, pp. 354-55.

75. *Ibid.*, pp. 352-53.

76. *Ibid.*, pp. 369-70.

77. Maevskii, pp. 63-65.

78. *Ibid.*, pp. 69-71; Harcave, p. 152.

79. Harcave, pp. 156-58.

80. *Ibid.*, p. 162. Florinsky (cited in note 63, above), p. 1176. For the complete text of the Aug. 6 decree, see Lazarevskii, pp. 122–92. For interpretation, see articles by V. M. Gessen and N. M. Lazarevskii in *Pravo*, no. 33 (Aug. 21). See also Dan, pp. 326–34.

81. I. V. Gessen, "V dvukh vekakh: zhiznennyi otchet," *Arkhiv russkoi revoliutsii*, vol. 22 (Berlin, 1937): 202.

82. For the text of the Moscow City Council's Aug. 9 resolution on the Tsar's decree, see *Pravo*, no. 32 (Aug. 14).

83. See article by V. M. Gessen in *Pravo*, no. 31 (Aug. 6).

84. See Dan, p. 335.

85. *Pravo*, no. 34 (Aug. 28): 2808–9. The professors present at the first meeting were V. I. Vernadskii, M. Ia. Gertsenshtein, A. A. Manuilov, and Prince E. N. Trubetskoi. Others in attendance included Princes Petr D. Dolgorukov, Pavl D. Dolgorukov, and D. I. Shakhovskoi, and City Councilman N. N. Shchepkin.

86. Keep, p. 216.

87. Mitskevich, *Revoliutsionnaia Moskva*, p. 384.

88. *Memoirs of Count Witte*, p. 230.

89. Police reports of general meetings before Sept. 15, when classes resumed: Sept. 1 (4,000 present), Sept. 2 and 3 (n.a.), Sept. 5 (4,000), Sept. 6 (1,500), Sept. 7 (4,000), Sept. 8 (2,000), Sept. 9 (n.a.), Sept. 11 (2,000), Sept. 12 (4,000), Sept. 13 (200). (*Stachka*, pp. 37–38; Latysheva, pp. 195, 202–3, 219; Tikhomirov, pp. 59–60; Syromiatnikov, pp. 197–98.)

90. Keep, pp. 217–18. For the conservative reaction, see *Stachka*, p. 39.

91. Texts of the Sept. 11 political platforms may be found in *Stachka*, pp. 38–39. Voting figures appear in Tikhomirov, pp. 60–61.

92. *Stachka*, p. 39; Latysheva, pp. 219, 222.

93. For example, a gathering on Sept. 19 drew over 3,000 persons (*Stachka*, p. 40).

94. *Ibid.*, p. 41; Latysheva, pp. 195, 216. Manuilov, professor of political economy, was among the early supporters of the Zubatov movement in Moscow.

95. Rector's report to Gov.-Gen., Sept. 22, in Syromiatnikov, p. 199.

96. Rector's report to Gov.-Gen., Sept. 24, and professor's account in Latysheva, pp. 226, 236.

97. *Pravo*, no. 38 (Sept. 25): 3194. The rector said that he had come to this decision "in view of the continuous intrusion of outsiders into the university and the systematic violation of the [University] Council's regulations, and also because of the imminent danger of bloody confrontation. . . . The Police Chief has pointed to the growing workers' movement of recent days, which undoubtedly is being nourished by the mass meetings." (Rector's report to Gov.-Gen., Sept. 22, in Syromiatnikov, p. 199.)

Chapter 5

1. "In the course of 1905 up until September, [Moscow] was the center of the bourgeois-liberal movement (zemstvo-municipal congresses) and the center of the radical-intelligentsia movement leading to the organization of the 'Union of

Unions,' but the workers' movement in Moscow lagged behind in comparison
with the movement in many other centers of . . . Russia" (Mitskevich, *Revoliutsionnaia Moskva*, pp. 381–82).

2. Sher, *Istoriia*, pp. 110–17.
3. Ivanov, *Rabochee dvizhenie* (1975), pp. 178–80.
4. Sher, *Istoriia*, pp. 121–26.
5. *Ibid.*, pp. 136–51. Quotation on p. 151.
6. *Ibid.*, pp. 151–60.
7. Ionov, p. 64.
8. Surh, pp. 366–67.
9. Grinevich, pp. 26–27; Sher, "Moskovskie pechatniki," pp. 25, 42–45. In
the summer of 1905, a group of printers founded a legal organization called the
Fund for Assistance to Workers in the Printing Trade, but it never functioned
(Sher, *Istoriia*, p. 160).
10. Orlov, pp. 215, 222.
11. Ionov, p. 65, claims the Sytin strike was begun by Zubatovites, but no
other source supports him. Perhaps he means to suggest that ex-Zubatovites were
active; their printers' union certainly was not.
12. The workers wanted a 30% raise for those currently earning 9–20 rubles a
month, 20% for those earning 20–30 rubles, 15% for those earning 30–45 rubles,
and 10% for those earning more than 45 rubles. *Pravo*, no. 40 (Oct. 9): 3344–45.
13. Sher, *Istoriia*, pp. 162–65.
14. Since the figures on the various strikes in Moscow during 1905 are compiled from several sources, they are not footnoted individually, except when a particular source is especially relevant. The most important of the sources used were
as follows.
   Unpublished archival documents: TsGAOR, *F.* 63: *op.* 1, *d. 773, d. 785; op.* 2,
d. 773 (vol. 4); *op.* 14, *d. 773* (vol. 7), *d. 912; op.* 25, *d. 773* (vols. 3, 3 *pr.*, 6 *pr.*,
8, 10, 11), *d.* 870; *op.* 26, *d. 773* (vol. 2).
   Published documents from archival sources: *Stachka*; Sidorov; Leskova and
Kogan.
   Newspaper accounts: *Bor'ba*, nos. 1–9 (Nov. 27–Dec. 7); *Izvestiia moskovskogo soveta rabochikh deputatov*, nos. 1–6 (Dec. 7–12), reprinted in Nevskii,
Sovetskaia pechat', pp. 107–50; *Novosti dnia*, nos. 8008–8031 (Sept. 19–Oct.
24); *Pravo*, nos. 30–40 (Aug. 2–Oct. 9); *RV*, nos. 267–302 (Oct. 12–Nov. 16); *RS*,
nos. 274–328 (Oct. 19–Dec. 23); *VP*, nos. 218–303 (Sept. 1–Dec. 20).
   The most important secondary source was Tsukerman.
15. Sher asserts that the majority of printing plants had struck by Sept. 21
("Moskovskie pechatniki," p. 49). He may have based this on the statement of a
representative of the printers' council, who claimed, in a report to the Oct. 2
meeting of the Representatives of the Five Professions, that 110 printing enterprises, employing 10,000 workers, had taken part in the strike during September
(*BMST*, no. 1: 12). According to my own calculations, however, half the printing
workers (employed by two-thirds of the city's printing plants) never struck at all
during September. The figures for Sept. 24 agree with the estimate for Sept. 25 in

MV, no. 263 (Oct. 4) of 50 striking plants and a total of 5,900 strikers. The same figures appear in a police report to the Ministry of Internal Affairs dated Sept. 26: TsGAOR, *F*. 63, *op*. 25, *d*. 773 (vol. 3 *pr*. [1905], p. 1).

16. Strike propensity measures the activity of a group of workers or area relative to the participation of other groups or areas. To obtain this measure, one divides the percentage of workers on strike belonging to a particular group by the percentage of the total city work force employed by the industry or area in question. The concept of strike propensity comes from Robert Goetz-Girey, *Le Mouvement des grèves en France, 1919–1962*, vol. 3 of Henri Guitton and Alain Barrère, eds., *L'Economique* (Paris, 1965), pp. 103–9. Reginald E. Zelnik suggested this source.

17. *Pravo*, no. 38 (Sept. 25): 3212.

18. *Ibid.*, no. 39 (Oct. 1): 3269. See also list of demands and discussion in Sher, *Istoriia*, pp. 171–74.

19. On the disadvantages of piecework, see Timofeev, pp. 37, 47–49. See also Oliunina, pp. 234–36, on tailors. On the effect of shortages in materials, see Ivanov, *Rabochee dvizhenie* (1961–63), part 1: 52.

20. Sher, *Istoriia*, p. 174.

21. *Ibid.*, p. 175.

22. *Stachka*, p. 63.

23. Lenskii, p. 323; see also *BMST*, no. 1: 12; and Sher, *Istoriia*, p. 168.

24. Sher, "Moskovskie pechatniki," pp. 52–54. See also Kolokol'nikov, "Otryvki," sb. 2: 228; and Sher, *Istoriia*, p. 169.

25. Ozerov, pp. 261–68; Lenskii, p. 323.

26. Printers' union leaflet issued between Sept. 27 and Sept. 29, in *Stachka*, pp. 72–73. See also report by the printers' council representatives in *BMST*, no. 1: 12.

27. The activity of both SRs and SDs was closely connected with radical student groups. The SRs were no longer active in the bakery industry by 1905 (Iliukhin, p. 104).

28. Milonov, *Kak voznikli*, pp. 161–62.

29. The museum's chairman, N. K. Murav'ev, was a lawyer specializing in labor problems and a member of the Union of Liberation. His assistant, M. G. Lunts (M. Grigor'evskii), was a Bolshevik labor organizer. The museum's secretary, I. F. Gornostaev, was a member of the Moscow City Board sympathetic to the liberation movement. Other museum board members were P. I. Kedrov, a liberal medical doctor and SR sympathizer, and V. N. Bobrinskaia, a member of the Union for Women's Equality and later of the Kadet Party. Advisory members of the board were S. M. Bleklov, statistician; V. E. Ignat'ev, medical doctor; Kh. S. Letsentsov, lawyer; P. M. Shestakov, editor of *Russkie vedomosti*; and two SDs, the lawyer M. A. Mebel' and the engineer B. A. Peters. (See Milonov, *Kak voznikli*, p. 163; Ainzaft, "Professional'noe dvizhenie," p. 218; and *OpO*, pp. 93–94.) Mitskevich, *Revoliutsionnaia Moskva*, p. 358, says Murav'ev was close to the SDs.

30. "1905 god: god nastupleniia proletariata," in *PDMP*, pp. 18–22. See text in Trusova, *Revoliutsionnoe*, pp. 312–13; also pp. 315–16 for police report on

NOTES TO PAGES 82-87

strike. For meetings in the museum building, see Mitskevich, *Revoliutsionnaia Moskva*, pp. 359–60.

31. *PDMP*, pp. 25–27.

32. *Ibid.*, p. 24.

33. *Ibid.*, p. 32.

34. *Ibid.*, p. 37. The wage differences involved for master bakers were as follows: 15–18 rubles at the pre-April level; 25–35 rubles promised in the April agreement; 20–25 rubles offered in Sept. (*ibid.*, p. 27; see also Iliukhin, pp. 106–8).

35. Iliukhin, p. 109. *PDMP*, p. 38, estimates the number of bakeries participating in the September strike as "over 40," based on Secret Police statistics. This figure is corroborated by Nikitin, p. 88, who estimates the number of firms on strike in the food industry as a whole at 44. This would include the two candy factories and the two tobacco-packing plants that are known to have gone out.

36. See SD bulletin issued after Sept. 29, in *Stachka*, p. 91; and the police report of Sept. 29, in TsGAOR, *F.* 63, *op.* 2, *d.* 773, vol. 4, p. 2.

37. Podkopaev, p. 185.

38. Ivanov, *Rabochee dvizhenie* (1961–63), part 1: 651–53; Nevskii, "Ianvarskie zabastovki," pp. 10–11.

39. Podkopaev, p. 188.

40. "1905 god" (cited in note 30, above), p. 40.

41. Podkopaev, pp. 188–89.

42. The 1902 census lists 18,500 woodworkers of various kinds (see *Perepis' Moskvy*, part 1, vyp. 2: Table 7, Group III, and also subsections 147, 152, and 154). Although the Factory File identifies only 98 enterprises with a total of 6,400 woodworkers, this sample most likely includes all the city's larger firms. None of the 98 enterprises employed as many as 500 workers; 16 were in the 100 or more category, with a total of about 3,000 workers, and 24 were in the 50–100 category, with a total of about 2,000 workers. The vast majority of woodworkers thus labored in the smallest shops.

43. Milonov and Rakovskii, pp. 91–92.

44. *OpO*, p. 103, for the Bolshevik link.

45. Milonov and Rakovskii, pp. 92–94. See also report in *BMST*, no. 1: 13.

46. My own data plus information given in Milonov and Rakovskii, p. 96.

47. Mamontov, pp. 185–89.

48. For SD penetration and labor unrest in the 1890's, see Vasin, p. 55; and Ivanov, *Rabochee dvizhenie* (1961–63), part 1: 341–61, 397–415.

49. The following material on the spread of the strike in the metal industry is drawn from *Stachka*, pp. 58–59, 65–67, 70, 74; and the police reports in TsGAOR, *F.* 63, *op.* 25, *d.* 773, vol. 3 *pr.*, pp. 41, 50, 146, 151, 292.

50. Mamontov, pp. 193–94.

51. Zaiats, pp. 91–92. See also Spektor, p. 6; and Tsukerman, pp. 128–31.

52. Spektor, pp. 6–8.

53. Tsukerman, pp. 131–33, supplemented by my own data. See also Zaiats, p. 94. For January, Nevskii, "Ianvarskie zabastovki," pp. 8–12.

54. TsGAOR, *F.* 63, *op.* 1, *d.* 773, pp. 99, 149.

55. Lenskii, pp. 317, 322.

56. *Pravo*, no. 40 (Oct. 9): 3346.

57. TsGAOR, *F.* 63, *op.* 1, *d.* 773, p. 151.

58. *Pravo*, nos. 39 and 40 (Oct. 1, Oct. 9): 3267–70, 3346. See also report from the Tver district police chief to the Secret Police, Sept. 25, on street clashes of Sept. 23 in *Stachka*, pp. 59–60.

59. *Pravo*, no. 40 (Oct. 9): 3347; also report from Secret Police to the Gov.-Gen., Sept. 25, concerning that day's incidents in *Stachka*, pp. 60–61.

60. *Pravo*, no. 39 (Oct. 1): 3272.

61. TsGAOR, *F.* 63, *op.* 1, *d.* 773, p. 157.

62. *Ibid.*, *op.* 25, *d.* 773, vol. 3 *pr.*, p. 12. Their addresses did not appear in the record.

63. *Ibid.*, p. 91.

64. *Pravo*, no. 39 (Oct. 1): 3272.

65. *MV*, no. 263 (Oct. 4); police report in *Pravo*, no. 40 (Oct. 9): 3348.

66. For contrasting reports of police and the factory's owner, see *Pravo*, nos. 39 and 40 (Oct. 1, 9): 3271, 3360–61; and report from the Moscow Secret Police to the Gov.-Gen., Sept. 27, in *Stachka*, p. 71.

67. Report from the chief of police to the Ministry of Internal Affairs, Sept. 27, in TsGAOR, *F.* 63, *op.* 25, *d.* 773; vol. 3 *pr.*, pp. 71–72.

68. These two factories, owned by the brothers A. V. and K. V. Zibrekht, were in the Sushchevskaia district (IV); one had 72 workers and the other 82 (Milonov and Rakovskii, p. 93). See also report from the first Sushchevskaia precinct police captain to the Moscow Secret Police, Sept. 27, in *Stachka*, pp. 73–74.

69. Delegates came from the List plant in Butyrki and the Til'mans factory. The bicycle factory was Meller's "Duks" with 170 workers: *Pravo*, no. 39 (Oct. 1): 3273–74; report from the chief of police to the Gov.-Gen., Sept. 30, in *Stachka*, pp. 91–92.

70. The so-called Moscovite's Diary, recounting a scene that supposedly occurred on Sept. 25, pictures the crowds as composed of hooligans (*MV*, no. 265, Oct. 6).

71. Tikhomirov, p. 70: diary entry for Sept. 29, 1905.

72. Liberal analysis in Lenskii, p. 317.

73. Tikhomirov, p. 70.

74. His position reflected the views of the right-wing newspaper *Moskovskie vedomosti*, which enthusiastically cited his remarks. The paper's editor-in-chief was V. A. Gringmut, who later founded the Russian Monarchist Party. (See Tikhomirov, p. 72.) Shmakov's chief liberal opponent in the City Council was N. N. Shchepkin.

75. *MV*, no. 259 (Sept. 21).

76. Lenskii, p. 232; police report in TsGAOR, *F.* 63, *op.* 2, *d.* 773, vol. 4, p. 132.

77. Lenskii, p. 323.

78. *Ibid.*, p. 324.

79. TsGAOR, *F.* 63, *d.* 773, vol. 4, pp. 299, 306, 355, 360; *Stachka*, pp. 330, 338.

80. Mamontov, pp. 189-90.

81. Milonov and Rakovskii, pp. 94-95.

82. Kolokol'nikov, "Otryvki," sb. 2: 229, sb. 3: 217. See also Garvi, p. 553.

83. *OpO*, p. 103.

84. *BMST*, no. 1: 12-15.

85. "Izvlecheniia," pp. 75-76.

86. Leaflet of the Menshevik-sponsored Union of Moscow Printing and Lithography Workers, dated between Oct. 2 and Oct. 6, in *Stachka*, pp. 403-4.

87. On Oct. 2, a similar crowd had accompanied Trubetskoi's coffin to the railroad station in St. Petersburg (Surh, pp. 400-401).

88. One former Menshevik organizer sees the absence of the SD parties as a sign of their exclusion from the mainstream of the liberation movement at this time (Garvi, pp. 534-36).

89. *MV*, no. 263 (Oct. 4).

90. *MV*, no. 265 (Oct. 6).

91. Garvi, p. 546.

Chapter 6

1. "Izvlecheniia," p. 76.

2. On the crucial role of professional/white-collar/intelligentsia groups in leading and supporting both the railroad union and the general strike as a whole, see N. Cherevanin, "Proletariat," in N. Cherevanin, V. Gorn, and V. Mech', eds., *Obshchestvennye sily i ikh bor'ba v russkoi revoliutsii* (Moscow, 1907), pp. 45-46, 48-51.

3. The Kazan shops had 2,500 blue-collar workers, the Kursk shops 1,650, and the Brest shops 1,200. On these strikes, see Nevskii, "Ianvarskie zabastovki," pp. 10-12. Pereverzev, p. 39, says the Windau and Briansk shops also struck, and Nevskii says some workers in the Riazan-Ural and Iaroslavl shops were involved as well.

4. Rostov, p. 131; Romanov, no. 10: 33-34.

5. On SD influence, see Chapter 4; and A. Shestakov, "Vseobshchaia oktiabr'skaia stachka 1905 goda," in Pokrovskii, vol. 2: 276. Police reports on these strikes, as well as text of the workers' demands, may be found in Trusova, *Nachalo*, pp. 252-54, 264-67, 273-76.

6. Quoted in Pushkareva, *Zheleznodorozhniki* (1975), p. 99. The Moscow-Kazan line was one of three private lines in Moscow. The Windau-Riabinsk and Kiev lines were the other two. (J. N. Westwood, *A History of Russian Railways*, London, 1964, p. 143.)

7. Text of workers' petition to Moscow Gov.-Gen. in Trusova, *Revoliutsionnoe*, pp. 234-35.

8. This is the opinion of V. V. Romanov, the then vice-chairman of the railroad union and a Bolshevik sympathizer (Romanov, no. 10: 55).

9. *Ibid.*, no. 7: 88.

10. Pushkareva, *Zheleznodorozhniki* (1975), pp. 86, 92.

11. *Ibid.*, p. 89.

12. Reports on February strikes and texts of workers' demands in Trusova, *Nachalo*, pp. 291-312 *passim*.

13. *Ibid.*, p. 294.

14. Romanov, no. 10: 57-59.

15. *Ibid.*, no. 7: 88.

16. Pushkareva, *Zheleznodorozhniki* (1975), pp. 95-96, 98, 100.

17. *Ibid.*, p. 101; Romanov, no. 11a: 22, 26, no. 7: 89, 93.

18. Romanov, no. 11a: 25-26, no. 7: 89-96. See also Bogdanov, p. 25.

19. Bogdanov, p. 31; Rostov, p. 136.

20. The seven original members of the central bureau and their affiliations were chairman, V. N. Pereverzev, director of commercial service of the Moscow-Iaroslavl line, SR; vice-chairman, V. V. Romanov, road service engineer on the Moscow-Windau line, SD-Bolshevik; I. I. Bednov, telegraph technician at Moscow-Kazan station, SR; Voronin, bookkeeper, SR or nonparty; K. D. Namitnichenko, lawyer in the Moscow-Kursk administration, SD-Menshevik; L. I. Grishin, Brest shop worker, SD-Bolshevik (later withdrew); unnamed worker, anarchist.

The members coopted in July were M. I. Bogdanov, pension fund director and student lawyer, nonparty; Zhenishek, engineer, nonparty; I. I. Trofimov, accountant, nonparty; G. N. Bruevich, bookkeeper, nonparty; I. Pechkovskii, Moscow-Kazan machinist, SR; G. B. Krasin, engineer, politics unknown.

These lists are based on Pereverzev, p. 43; and Rostov, pp. 137, 140. The two sources agree on the members, except for Krasin, who is named by Pereverzev, and Pechkovskii, who is named instead by Rostov. Pereverzev also names a certain Zalugovskii in connection with the July group. The sources also agree on the political orientation of the bureau members, except for Voronin, whom Pereverzev calls SR and Rostov calls nonparty. Mitskevich, *Revoliutsionnaia Moskva*, p. 391, calls Krasin and Namitnichenko Bolshevik sympathizers. Additional details (some contradictory) in Pushkareva, *Zheleznodorozhniki* (1975), p. 111.

21. Romanov, no. 11a: 43.

22. Even Pushkareva admits this: see *Zheleznodorozhniki* (1975), pp. 120-25, 127.

23. For the text of the union resolutions, see Romanov, no. 11a: 29-30; and Pereverzev, p. 42.

24. Romanov, no. 11a: 44-46.

25. At the so-called Third RSDWP (Bolshevik only) Congress in April 1905, L. B. Kamenev said: "Unless Social Democracy takes the present movement in hand, we are running the risk that the worker will enter the revolutionary movement with only bourgeois-democratic demands, without advancing a political platform of his class. . . . The spontaneous mass movement of the working class will not carry us on its shoulders, or, rather, it isn't *us* it will carry." (Quoted in Schwarz, p. 133.)

26. Pushkareva, *Zheleznodorozhniki* (1975), pp. 109, 125. The Bolsheviks offered a sociological justification for the existence of this union that accorded ill

with the class analysis they applied in criticism of the All-Russian Railroad Union. The Moscow Bolshevik Committee stated: "Railroad employees, by their socio-economic position, belong to the great proletarian family. They have no property, but earn the necessities of life through the sale of their labor to capital, to the owners of railroad enterprises." (Quoted in Mitskevich, *Revoliutsionnaia Moskva*, p. 356.)

27. Romanov, no. 6: 52; Rostov, p. 143; Pereverzev, p. 46.

28. Romanov, no. 11a: 42, no. 6: 26–28; Pushkareva, *Zheleznodorozhniki* (1975), pp. 120–25; Pereverzev, p. 46.

29. Pereverzev, p. 47.

30. At the July congress, representatives of the Polish railroads wanted the union to add a demand for Polish national autonomy to its political program, and the SRs and liberationists supported their motion. The SDs were unable to defeat the motion because of the combined vote of delegates from the Vilna and Polish railroads. The SDs therefore "resigned" from the union, though they did not leave the congress. When the issue was submitted to local committees nation-wide, the SD position against Polish autonomy won out, the Poles resigned, and the union survived as a coalition of SR and SD groups. (See Rostov, pp. 142–43; and Pereverzev, p. 48.)

31. Kirpichnikov, p. 10.

32. Trusova, *Revoliutsionnoe*, pp. 226–27.

33. Romanov, no. 6: 32–34.

34. *Ibid.*, no. 7: 70; Pereverzev, p. 48; Pushkareva, *Zheleznodorozhniki* (1975), pp. 136–37.

35. Rostov, p. 150; D. Kol'tsov, p. 232.

36. Pushkareva, *Zheleznodorozhniki* (1975), pp. 145–46.

37. M. N. Pokrovskii, *Russkaia istoriia v samom szhatom ocherke*, vol. 3: *Izbrannye proizvedeniia* (Moscow, 1967), p. 409.

38. Garvi, pp. 547, 551.

39. *BMST*, no. 1: 14; Muzei: *Materialy*, p. 76; Garvi, p. 550.

40. Pushkareva, *Zheleznodorozhniki* (1975), p. 148, says the Oct. 2 meeting of the Council of the Five Professions called for a general strike, but there is no mention of this in the protocol of that meeting (see *BMST*, no. 1: 12–15).

41. Rostov, p. 151.

42. Bogdanov, p. 31; Pereverzev, p. 50. Pushkareva does not mention this epi-sode in her discussion of the strike's origins (*Zheleznodorozhniki*, 1975, pp. 148–49).

43. Pushkareva, *Zheleznodorozhniki* (1975), p. 149, says the Bolsheviks issued the strike call the evening of Oct. 6 and the union's central bureau did so "at the same time," thus giving the impression that the union did not take the initiative. This impression contradicts Bogdanov's view (p. 31). In her thesis ("Zhelezno-dorozhniki," 1959, p. 167), Pushkareva claims that on Oct. 3 the Moscow Bolshe-vik Committee called for a general strike to begin Oct. 7, but she does not repeat this assertion in her book. There (p. 148) she gives the impression that the Bolshe-viks supported the All-Russian Railroad Union's strike plan from the very begin-

ning of the month, but the leaflet to which she refers was not issued until some-time after Oct. 6, perhaps even as late as Oct. 13. This may be confirmed by checking her own reference to *Stachka*, p. 415.

44. Schwarz, p. 138; Surh, pp. 408–9, 412–14. See *Stachka*, pp. 422–23, for Moscow Bolshevik leaflet.

45. *Stachka*, p. 423. See also Schwarz, pp. 132–34, on Bolshevik use of the insurrection slogan.

46. Romanov, no. 6: 52.

47. Pushkareva, *Zheleznodorozhniki* (1975), pp. 150–51; Pereverzev, p. 51.

48. Pereverzev, p. 51.

49. Information on the propagation of the railroad strike compiled from the re-ports in *MV* and *PkP*.

50. See *Novosti dnia*, no. 8016 (Oct. 8).

51. *PkP*, p. 2; Pereverzev, p. 52.

52. Account published by the railroad union, in *PkP*, p. 11.

53. *PkP*, p. 12.

54. Recalled by the Bolshevik organizer A. V. Sokolov, pp. 42–43.

55. Surh, p. 416.

56. Milonov and Rakovskii, vyp. 1: 102.

57. Milonov, *Kak voznikli*, p. 123.

58. *Rabochie zavoda*, pp. 40–41.

59. Tsukerman, pp. 139–40.

60. *Ibid.*, pp. 146, 150.

61. Oct. 10 police report in *Stachka*, pp. 421–22.

62. Garvi, pp. 556–57.

63. For a description of this process, see SD Bulletins nos. 2 and 9 in *Stachka*, pp. 432–33, 438–39.

64. Example in *Novosti dnia*, no. 8025 (Oct. 18). See also SD Bulletin no. 9 in *Stachka*, pp. 438–40.

65. *Novosti dnia*, no. 8025 (Oct. 18); Antoshkin, p. 34; Tsukerman, pp. 145, 147; TsGAOR, *F.* 63, *op.* 14, *d.* 912, p. 272.

Chapter 7

1. Maevskii, pp. 80–83.

2. Surh, pp. 402–15.

3. Miliukov, p. 78; Keep, pp. 228–30.

4. For use of the term soviet, see above, p. 78n.

5. G. S. Krustalev-Nosar', "Istoriia soveta rabochikh deputatov," in *Istoriia soveta rabochikh deputatov g. S. Peterburga: stat'i* (St. Petersburg, 1906), p. 147. For a breakdown of the Petersburg working class, see Semanov, pp. 31, 32, 34.

6. Surh, pp. 424–25.

7. Anweiler, pp. 46–47, 55–58, 67; Surh, pp. 427–29, 444–45.

8. *PkP*, p. 33; *Pravo*, no. 42 (Oct. 31): 3484. See Appendix B for the unions on the Strike Committee.

9. Garvi, p. 561.

10. *VP*, no. 277 (Nov. 12).

11. Kolokol'nikov, "Otryvki," sb. 3: 216-17.

12. Pereverzev, p. 52.

13. Kolokol'nikov, *Professional'nye soiuzy*, p. 27.

14. Ainzaft, "Professional'noe dvizhenie," p. 169.

15. *OpO*, p. 130.

16. *MV*, no. 214 (Aug. 7).

17. Ainzaft, "Professional'noe dvizhenie," pp. 172-75; *MV*, no. 208 (Aug. 1).

18. *MV*, no. 258 (Sept. 20).

19. Ainzaft, "Professional'noe dvizhenie," p. 175.

20. *Ibid.*, pp. 175-76.

21. The following account is based on reports in *PkP*, p. 6; *MV*, no. 271 (Oct. 12); and *RV*, no. 267 (Oct. 12).

22. *RV*, no. 267 (Oct. 12).

23. *PkP*, p. 43; *RV*, no. 269 (Oct. 14); *MV*, no. 273 (Oct. 14). Text of statement in *PkP*, p. 42; and *MV*, no. 273.

24. *PkP*, p. 20; *MV*, no. 273 (Oct. 14).

25. The following account is based on Ainzaft, "Professional'noe dvizhenie," pp. 180-83; and I. Zil'berg, *Professional'noe dvizhenie sluzhashchikh farmatsevtov v period pervoi russkoi revoliutsii* (Moscow, 1930), pp. 11, 18.

26. Ainzaft, "Professional'noe dvizhenie," p. 184; Surh, p. 382.

27. Ainzaft, "Professional'noe dvizhenie," p. 185. The sequence of events I have presented follows contemporary accounts appearing in the press: *PkP*, p. 7, citing the report of *Russkie vedomosti*. Ainzaft's chronology seems to differ slightly: he speaks of a raid occurring on the evening of October 10, that is, after the strike declaration.

28. Ainzaft, "Professional'noe dvizhenie," pp. 185-86.

29. *PkP*, pp. 7, 21; *MV*, no. 271 (Oct. 12). According to Ainzaft, "Professional'noe dvizhenie," p. 185, Moscow had 56 pharmacies all told. About 40 of them struck (Zil'berg [as cited in note 25 above], p. 19).

30. *Stachka*, p. 434.

31. *Novosti dnia*, no. 8021 (Oct. 14).

32. Quoted in Ainzaft, "Professional'noe dvizhenie," p. 172.

33. Statement published in *Bor'ba*, no. 6 (Dec. 3), reprinted in Sidorov, p. 597.

34. *Novosti dnia*, no. 8021 (Oct. 14).

35. *MV*, no. 271 (Oct. 12).

36. Police report of Oct. 13 in TsGAOR, *F*. 63, *op*. 14, *d*. 773, vol. 7, p. 71.

37. *PkP*, pp. 6, 21.

38. *PkP*, pp. 25, 34, 65; *MV*, no. 272 (Oct. 13).

39. *RV*, nos. 269, 270 (Oct. 14, 15); Laverychev, *Po tu storonu barrikad*, pp. 36, 41.

40. *PkP*, p. 44. The resolution was passed at a meeting on Oct. 13.

41. Telegram from Ass't. Min. of Internal Affairs D. F. Trepov to the Moscow Gov.-Gen., Oct. 13, in *Stachka*, p. 432.

42. *MV*, no. 274 (Oct. 15). The text was printed in the newspapers after the notice was posted.

43. *PkP*, pp. 52−53; *Novosti dnia*, no. 8022 (Oct. 15).

44. *PkP*, pp. 55−56; *RV*, no. 270 (Oct. 15).

45. *MV*, no. 274 (Oct. 15).

46. *PkP*, pp. 57−58.

47. For accounts of the following incidents, see *PkP*, pp. 64−66.

48. *RV*, no. 275 (Oct. 20).

49. Delegates from the following groups were present (see *PkP*, pp. 69−70; and Garvi, pp. 563−64):

Business organizations and corporate governing bodies: Artisans', Merchants', and Small Tradesmen's societies; Moscow Grain Exchange; marshals and deputies of the nobility; Moscow Stock Exchange Committee; Moscow Stock Exchange Society.

Government and public institutions: Agricultural, Engineering, and Technical institutes; Moscow District Board; Moscow Provincial Zemstvo Board; Moscow Railroad Administration; Moscow University.

Newspapers: *Novosti dnia*; *Russkie vedomosti*; *Russkoe slovo*.

Political groups: Central University Student Organization; Moscow Strike Committee; Peasants' Union; Social Democratic Party; Socialist Revolutionary Party; Union for Jewish Equality; Union for Women's Equality; Union of Unions; Union of Zemstvo Constitutionalists.

Professional organizations: Agricultural, Technical, and Pedagogical societies; associations of lawyers, lawyers' assistants, and barristers; unions of agronomists, engineers, journalists, medical doctors, pharmacy clerks, professors, teachers, and veterinarians.

Trade unions: All-Russian Union of Railroad Workers and Employees; Corporation of Employees in the Moscow City Administration; Corporation of Workers and Low-Ranking Employees in the Moscow City Administration; group of employees in the Moscow Provincial and District boards; Union of Moscow Printing and Lithography Workers (SD).

50. Garvi, pp. 559−61, 565−66.

51. *PkP*, p. 71. Muromtsev had the backing of S. A. Levitskii and M. G. Komissarov. Shchepkin's position was supported by 11 councilmen.

52. *PkP*, pp. 69−72.

53. Quoted in Garvi, p. 567.

54. *MV*, no. 275 (Oct. 16).

55. Hans Rogger, "The Formation of the Russian Right, 1900−1906," *California Slavic Studies*, vol. 3 (1964): 80−83.

56. *MV*, no. 273 (Oct. 14).

57. The text also appeared in *Moskovskii listok* and *Russkii listok* (N. K. Kol'tsov, p. 12).

58. *RV*, no. 270 (Oct. 15), editorial. This liberal daily was published by Alexander Chuprov, professor of economics at Moscow University, and Vasilii Skalon, chairman of the board of the Moscow District Zemstvo.

59. N. A. Rozhkov, "Vospominaniia o 1905 gode," in N. Rozhkov and A. Sokolov, *O 1905 gode: vospominaniia* (Moscow, 1925), p. 20.

60. Garvi, pp. 554–55.
61. Imperial Decree of Oct. 13 in Lazarevskii, pp. 222–27.
62. Sokolov, p. 42.
63. *PkP*, pp. 54, 64–65; *MV*, no. 274 (Oct. 15).
64. Sokolov, pp. 43–44.
65. *PkP*, pp. 76–77.
66. Text of Gov.-Gen.'s statement in *MV*, no. 275 (Oct. 16); and *PkP*, p. 76.
67. Letter to the editor of *Russkie vedomosti*, quoted in N. K. Kol'tsov, p. 19.
68. *MV*, no. 275 (Oct. 16). The text had the Metropolitan's advance approval (Tikhomirov, p. 81).
69. *PkP*, p. 77.
70. *PkP*, pp. 69, 72; *MV*, nos. 274, 277 (Oct. 15, 18); Garvi, p. 568.
71. Surh, pp. 429, 439.
72. Sokolov, p. 43.
73. The following account is from *Novosti dnia*, no. 8025 (Oct. 18).
74. Councilman M. Ia. Gertsenshtein at Oct. 17 Council meeting, quoted in *RV*, no. 273 (Oct. 18).
75. Sokolov, p. 44.

Chapter 8

1. Miliukov, p. 49.
2. *Ibid.*, pp. 49–50, 52.
3. See the Kadet Party resolution of Oct. 18 in *PkP*, pp. 95–96.
4. On Kadet–Union of Unions politics, see Miliukov, pp. 74–77. The text of the Union of Unions resolution of Oct. 17 is in *PkP*, pp. 96–97; and the resolutions of the Strike Committee of Railroad Workers and Employees and of the Moscow Strike Committee are in *PkP*, pp. 96, 114, and *RV*, no. 275 (Oct. 20). On the SD-SR role in drafting the Strike Committee statement, see Garvi, pp. 573–80.
5. *RS*, no. 274 (Oct. 19). See also no. 276 (Oct. 21).
6. Surh, p. 435.
7. Resolutions in *PkP*, pp. 95–97, 98, 101, 114; and *RV*, no. 275 (Oct. 20).
8. Garvi, p. 581.
9. *PkP*, p. 130; *RS*, no. 274 (Oct. 19).
10. *RS*, no. 274 (Oct. 19); *RV*, no. 274 (Oct. 19); police account in *Stachka*, p. 466.
11. *Stachka*, p. 466.
12. *RV*, no. 274 (Oct. 19).
13. *Novosti dnia*, no. 8026 (Oct. 19).
14. *RS*, no. 274 (Oct. 19); *RV*, nos. 274, 275 (Oct. 19, 20); *PkP*, p. 131.
15. *RS*, nos. 275, 276 (Oct. 20, 21); *RV*, no. 275 (Oct. 20); report of the second Tver precinct police captain to the police chief, Oct. 19, in TsGAOR, *F.* 63, *op.* 1, *d.* 785, p. 33; see also p. 279.
16. *RS*, nos. 275, 276 (Oct. 20, 21).
17. *RS*, no. 276 (Oct. 21).

18. Letter from a tutor in a textile training institute, in *RS*, no. 277 (Oct. 22).
19. Telegram from the police chief to police captains, quoted in Leskova and Kogan, pp. 56–57.
20. Report of the second Tver precinct captain to the police chief, Oct. 19, in TsGAOR, *F.* 63, *op.* 1, *d.* 785, p. 32.
21. *RS*, no. 274 (Oct. 19); *RV*, no. 274 (Oct. 19); *PkP*, p. 135; SD Bulletin no. 12, Oct. 17–19, in *Stachka*, p. 451.
22. *RV*, nos. 275, 276 (Oct. 20, 21).
23. Details in Garvi, p. 586.
24. *PkP*, pp. 132–33, quoting from *Russkoe slovo*; *RV*, no. 276 (Oct. 21). See also Vasil'ev-Iuzhin, "Moskovskii sovet," part 1: 113.
25. *RS*, no. 281 (Oct. 26); *RV*, no. 276 (Oct. 21); *PkP*, pp. 133–34. See also police report in *Stachka*, pp. 569–70. On Nov. 4, the City Council reported that its investigation of this incident showed the shooting had not been initiated by the students: *RS*, no. 291 (Nov. 5).
26. *RV*, nos. 278, 279 (Oct. 23, 24).
27. N. K. Kol'tsov, pp. 22–34; *RS*, no. 278 (Oct. 23).
28. Account from *RV*, no. 278 (Oct. 23), quoted in N. K. Kol'tsov, pp. 28–29. See also *Novosti dnia*, no. 8030 (Oct. 23).
29. *RS*, no. 278 (Oct. 23).
30. Miliukov, p. 53. See also Garvi, p. 571. Mitskevich, *Revoliutsionnaia Moskva*, p. 383, describes the right-wing groups as composed primarily of shopkeepers and tavernkeepers and the "lumpenproletariat" (that is, the traditional urban poor, typically the unemployed and the down-and-outs), but also including workers "in small artisanal enterprises."
31. N. K. Kol'tsov, p. 26, citing *Novosti dnia*, no. 8030 (Oct. 23).
32. *RS*, no. 275 (Oct. 20); *RV*, no. 276 (Oct. 21).
33. For example, conflict occurred among carpenters in the third Sushchevskii precinct (IV) on Oct. 18: *RV*, no. 275 (Oct. 20).
34. *VP*, no. 255 (Oct. 21).
35. Police circulars of Nov. 12 and Nov. 14, quoted in Leskova and Kogan, pp. 94, 96.
36. The police log of telephone reports for Oct. 18–Nov. 30 shows only 14 separate incidents of coercive behavior by strikers trying to stop work in various factories, and only half of these involved property damage. None entailed personal injury. See Leskova and Kogan, pp. 56–105. Similarly, in none of the four incidents I have found in other contemporary sources did the workers direct their violence against individuals. See, for example, *RS*, no. 298 (Nov. 12).
37. See *RS*, no. 298 (Nov. 12).
38. Telegram from police chief to police captains, Oct. 22, and report of an estimated 10,000-person right-wing crowd on Oct. 23 in Leskova and Kogan, pp. 71, 73.
39. *RV*, no. 279 (Oct. 24).
40. *VP*, no. 258 (Oct. 24), editorial.
41. Announcement by police chief, Oct. 28, sent to police captains for public distribution, quoted in Leskova and Kogan, p. 78.

42. *RV*, no. 277 (Oct. 22); *PkP*, p. 134.

43. *RV*, no. 279 (Oct. 24). For an example of such a rumor reported to police on Oct. 25, see Leskova and Kogan, p. 75.

44. Leskova and Kogan, p. 73, citing an incident noted on Oct. 23.

45. Telegram from police chief to police captains, Oct. 21, in *ibid.*, p. 67; *RS*, no. 278 (Oct. 23).

46. My account of this session and of the delegation to the Gov.-Gen. is based on *RV*, no. 277 (Oct. 22).

47. *RS*, no. 281 (Oct. 26).

48. See *Stenografīcheskie otchety*, p. 898, for Nov. 17 mayoral election, and pp. 912-14, for the Nov. 29 council meeting, the discussion of the Sevastopol resolution, the protest and resignation of one councilman, A. D. Armand, and the Tolstoi quotation in the text. On the Sevastopol mutiny, see Harcave, pp. 221-22.

49. Speech by G. Bleklov, quoted in *RS*, no. 277 (Oct. 22).

50. Speech by G. Mandel'shtam, quoted in *ibid.*

51. Participants in the Oct. 28 meeting are listed in *RV*, no. 284 (Oct. 29). The groups represented were the Moscow Strike Committee, the Museum for Assistance to Labor, the Moscow Technical Society, the Central University Student Organization, the Union for Women's Equality, committees of employees of the Provincial Zemstvo Board and of workers and employees in the Moscow City Administration, the Corporation of City Engineers, and the unions of agronomists and statisticians, of bank employees (presumably the Union of Employees in Credit Establishments), of engineers, of hospital medical personnel, of junior university instructors (presumably part of the Academics' Union), of lawyers, of medical doctors (the Union of Medical Personnel), of pharmacy clerks, of railroad employees, and of veterinarians.

52. Text in *Novosti dnia*, no. 8042 (Nov. 4).

53. *RS*, nos. 277, 279, 284 (Oct. 22, 24, 29).

54. Report from Secret Police to Police Dept., Oct. 22, quoted in Syromiatnikov, pp. 203-4.

55. *RS*, nos. 292, 294 (Nov. 6, 8).

56. Secret Police report, Nov. 17, in Sidorov, p. 577.

57. *RS*, no. 278 (Oct. 23); *RV*, no. 279 (Oct. 24); report of the Engineering Institute Council in *Stachka*, p. 473.

58. SD Committee (Bolshevik) leaflet dated between Oct. 18 and Oct. 20 in *Stachka*, pp. 456-58.

59. Leaflet dated Oct. 19 in *Stachka*, pp. 459-60. Garvi, p. 584, recalls the Mensheviks' endorsement of insurrection as a momentary lapse in their resistance to such a tactic.

60. *Pravo*, no. 42 (Oct. 31): 8483-84. On party unification in October, see Schwarz, pp. 235-42, 345.

61. Leaflet dated between Oct. 19 and Oct. 22 in *Stachka*, pp. 460-62.

62. Moscow Bolshevik Committee leaflet dated between Oct. 18 and Oct. 20 in *ibid.*, p. 457.

63. SD central committee leaflet of Oct. 27, in *Voennye voprosy v resheniiakh KPSS, 1903-1917 gg.: sbornik dokumentov* (Moscow, 1960), p. 64.

64. *Pravo*, no. 42 (Oct. 31): 3483; SD leaflet of Oct. 22–23, in *Stachka*, pp. 471–72.

65. *RV*, no. 274 (Oct. 19).

66. For Medem's objection, which seems to have come after the fact, see his letter to D. D. Dubakin, dated Oct. 29, in TsGAOR, F. 63, *op.* 14, *d.* 784, vol. 3, p. 1.

67. The two incidents took place on Dec. 2 and Nov. 23, respectively; the case of the unemployed workers is documented in TsGAOR, F. 63, *d.* 784, part 1, p. 20, and that of the concierges in TsGAOR, F. 63, *op.* 14, *d.* 784, vol. 3, p. 10, and *RS*, no. 310 (Nov. 24).

68. Garvi, p. 593.

69. As far as I am able to determine, there were at least 26 trade-union-like organizations in existence as of Oct. 22, involving the following groups: printers, precious-metal workers, technicians, ribbonmakers, calico printers, bakers, tobacco workers, joiners, tailors, bootmakers and shoemakers, pursemakers, wallpaper factory workers, retail employees (four associations), office clerks and bookkeepers, bank clerks, waiters, railroad workers and employees, Brest machine shop workers, post and telegraph workers, municipal employees (three groups), and pharmacy clerks. See Appendix B for a full list of Moscow trade unions in 1905.

70. Kolokol'nikov, "Otryvki," sb. 3: 227. Italics in original. The boxmakers' and parquetry workers' unions seem to have been two separate organizations. See Appendix B.

71. Garvi, p. 599.

72. List of artisan guilds in Pazhitnov, *Problema*, p. 184.

73. These arguments about the influence of guild tradition on the development of trade unions in 1905 appear in Ainzaft, *Pervyi etap*, p. 55. Soviet historians of the 1920's were sensitive to the importance of artisans in the early labor movement. See also Kolokol'nikov, "Otryvki," sb. 3: 224–25, 227.

74. *VP*, no. 292 (Nov. 27); Mamontov, p. 188.

75. Mamontov, pp. 194–97.   76. Milonov, *Kak voznikli*, p. 115.

77. *OpO*, p. 110.   78. *OpO*, p. 113.

79. On the inadequacy of the legislation regulating conditions of artisanal labor, see Oliunina, pp. 272–82.

80. Sher, "Moskovskie pechatniki," p. 63. Sher was a Menshevik organizer.

81. Kolokol'nikov, "Otryvki," sb. 3: 230.

82. Minutes of meeting, in *BMST*, no. 1: 2–5.

83. *Ibid.*, p. 2. The precise name of Evdokimov's organization was Kharkovskoe obshchestvo vzaimnogo vspomozheniia zanimaiushchikhsia remeslennym trudom.

84. Milonov, *Kak voznikli*, p. 158.

85. *BMST*, no. 1: 3; Milonov, *Kak voznikli*, pp. 165–67. For participating unions, see Appendix B. The five plants that sent separate delegations were the Mytishchi railroad-car works (Bolshevik), Grachev metal (Menshevik), Dobrov and Nabgol'ts metal (probably Bolshevik), Bromlei metal (probably Bolshevik), and Gopper metal (probably Bolshevik).

86. The SDs were the Bolsheviks M. G. Lunts and I. I. Skvorstov-Stepanov, and the Menshevik P. N. Kolokol'nikov. The others were N. K. Murav'ev and S. N. Prokopovich, both liberals, and the trade unionists A. A. Evdokimov from Kharkov and I. Z. Zheludkov from St. Petersburg. (Milonov, *Kak voznikli*, p. 172.)

87. *Ibid.*, p. 176; Ainzaft, "Professional'noe dvizhenie," pp. 219–22; Kolokol'nikov, "Otryvki," sb. 2: 232.

88. Oct. 27, Nov. 3, 10, 16, 17, 24, and Dec. 1, 8. See *BMST*, no. 1: 5–7, and no. 2: 4–7; Muzei: *Materialy*, pp. 66–70; *OpO*, pp. 103–10, 120–22; and Milonov, *Kak voznikli*, pp. 180–82. For participating unions, see Appendix B.

89. *BMST*, no. 1: 6; Muzei: *Materialy*, p. 69; Milonov, *Kak voznikli*, p. 178.

90. Ainzaft, "Professional'noe dvizhenie," p. 222.

91. Kolokol'nikov, "Otryvki," sb. 3: 230.

92. Garvi, p. 574.

93. Mitskevich, *Revoliutsionnaia Moskva*, p. 359.

94. *Ibid.*, pp. 352–53.   95. *Ibid.*, p. 414.

96. Garvi, pp. 551–52.   97. Nemchinov, pp. 175–76.

98. Garvi, p. 557.

Chapter 9

1. *VP*, nos. 269, 274, 275 (Nov. 4, 9, 10).

2. *VP*, no. 299 (Dec. 4); *RS*, no. 321 (Dec. 5).

3. The date Nov. 21 is confirmed by Vasil'ev-Iuzhin, "Moskovskii sovet," part 1: 98–99, who cites the one-day error in contemporary newspaper reports.

4. Figures from Pogozhev, *Adresnaia kniga*, and Gornostaev.

5. *RS*, nos. 309, 312 (Nov. 23, 26). The *RS* account cites the number of deputies present as 180, but the figure of 145 is given in the account of the Nov. 24 meeting of the Moscow Bureau of Professional Unions, printed in the information bulletin of the Museum for Assistance to Labor. That source also gives the breakdown of 72 factories used in the text. Unfortunately, the bulletin does not identify the individual factories involved, and I have not found this information elsewhere. (See Muzei: *Materialy*, p. 68.) The Soviet historian N. N. Demochkin claims that the Moscow City Soviet eventually had 250 deputies: see his "Partiia i sovety v 1905 g.," *Voprosy istorii KPSS*, no. 1 (1965): 77.

6. The Soviet historian V. Nevskii contends that the 200 soviet deputies represented the majority of Moscow workers: "Sovety v 1905 godu," in Pokrovskii, vol. 3, part 1: 46. This is probably an exaggeration. The figure would be valid only if each of the 200 deputies represented at least 500 workers, giving the soviet organizational ties with as many as 100,000 workers, or 60% of the industrial labor force. But at a ratio of 1:400, the ratio the soviet itself decided on for the larger firms, the total number represented would have been about 80,000, or less than half the factory work force.

7. Schwarz, pp. 342–46.

8. The two Bolsheviks were V. L. Shantser and M. I. Vasil'ev-Iuzhin; the two Mensheviks were I. A. Isuf and someone named Isakovich, and the two SRs were V. Rudnev and V. Zenzinov.

9. Vasil'ev-Iuzhin, "Moskovskii sovet," part 1: 92, 100–101; Garvi, p. 606.

10. Vasil'ev-Iuzhin, "Moskovskii sovet," part 1: 105; report on Nov. 27 meetin
from *Novaia zhizn'*, no. 24 (Nov. 29), reprinted in Sidorov, pp. 585–86. See als
Anweiler, p. 53.

11. See editorial in *VP*, no. 286 (Nov. 21).

12. Robert M. Slusser, "The Moscow Soviet of Workers' Deputies of 1905,"
Ph.D. dissertation, Columbia University, 1963, p. 152. Reports of meetings o
four of the above-mentioned district soviets are to be found in Sidorov, as follows

Lefortovo: Nov. 11 meeting of representatives from 50 factories, with a total o
18,000 workers, elected 34 delegates to the city soviet (pp. 571–72: report from
Moskovskaia gazeta, no. 4, Nov. 13).

Gorodskaia: 64 workers present on Nov. 17 (p. 580: report from *Moskovskaic
gazeta*, no. 9, Nov. 19).

Butyrki: 100–120 workers present on Nov. 28 (pp. 587–88: report from *Bor'ba*,
nos. 2, 3, Nov. 29, 30).

Presnia-Khamovniki: 600 present on Nov. 21 and 23 (p. 592: report from
Vpered, no. 1, Dec. 2).

There is also a report of a Nov. 28 meeting of deputies in the Sokol'niki district,
at the northern end of Meshchanskaia (IV), attended by 52 workers from 11 factories (p. 594: report from *Vpered*, no. 2, Dec. 3).

13. Kolokol'nikov, "Otryvki," sb. 3: 222; Garvi, p. 602.

14. See resolution quoted in Lenskii, p. 326. The original plan was a Menshevik idea (Schwarz, p. 342).

15. This opinion is offered by the Menshevik P. A. Garvi: *Vospominaniia*,
p. 606.

16. Vasil'ev-Iuzhin, "Moskovskii sovet," part 1: 106.

17. *RS*, nos. 292, 298, 302, 312, 314 (Nov. 6, 12, 16, 26, 28).

18. Vasil'ev-Iuzhin, "Moskovskii sovet," part 1: 106; Kolokol'nikov, "Otryvki,"
sb. 3: 222.

19. Mitskevich, *Revoliutsionnaia Moskva*, p. 358.

20. For the Bolshevik attitude toward the soviets, see Anweiler, pp. 76–79;
and Schwarz, pp. 344–45, 349–50.

21. Voitinskii, p. 215.

22. Surh, pp. 460–64.

23. For the text of the St. Petersburg Soviet's appeal and the Moscow reaction,
see *VP*, no. 269 (Nov. 4). On St. Petersburg, see Voitinskii, pp. 238, 246–47.

24. Voitinskii, pp. 248–66; Trotsky, pp. 166–86. For details of the political
strike and the eight-hour-day campaign, see Surh, pp. 470–86.

25. Keep, p. 238.

26. Vasil'ev-Iuzhin, "Moskovskii sovet," part 1: 103.

27. This argument appears in *Novaia zhizn'*, no. 20 (Nov. 24), quoted in
Sidorov, p. 582.

28. Nikitin, pp. 97–98.

29. These included three wine warehouses and two sugar refineries in various
parts of the city, each employing over 500 workers; two candy factories in the
northern districts (IV); the Dukat tobacco plant (900 workers in Presnia, III); and a

number of firms in the Basmannaia district (V): Bostandzhoglo (1,550 workers) and Reingart (300), both tobacco, and Bogay (250 workers) and Vysotskii (900), tea.

30. *VP*, no. 278 (Nov. 13). There were about 900 sausage makers in Moscow *Perepis' Moskvy*, part 1, vyp. 2: Table 7, subsection 99a).

31. On the woodworkers' movement in November, see Milonov and Rakovskii, pp. 104–13.

32. O. P. Zaporozhskaia, "Revoliutsionnoe dvizhenie rabochikh-metallistov Moskvy v 1905–1907 gg." (dissertation, Moscow State Pedagogical Institute, 1955), pp. 207–13; *VP*, nos. 274, 294 (Nov. 9, 29). On Gopper, TsGAOR, *F.* 63, *op.* 25, *d.* 773, vol. 10, pp. 177–500 *passim*; *RS*, no. 296 (Nov. 10); Sidorov, pp. 404–5. On Dobrov and Nabgol'ts, TsGAOR, *F.* 63, *op.* 25, *d.* 773, vol. 10, pp. 189, 204, 332, etc.; *RS*, no. 305 (Nov. 19); Trudy, pp. 96, 98, 99, 104. On Bromlei, TsGAOR, *F.* 63, *op.* 25, *d.* 773, vol. 10, pp. 134, 264, 380, 445; *VP*, nos. 274, 294 (Nov. 9, 29); *RS*, no. 296 (Nov. 10); Sidorov, pp. 397, 404, 405.

33. For the demands of the Brokar workers, see Sidorov, pp. 567–68. On the general situation, see Nikitin, pp. 96–97.

34. TsGAOR, *F.* 63, *op.* 25, *d.* 773, vol. 10, p. 121.

35. Leskova and Kogan, p. 86.

36. The Golutvinskaia workers' demands are listed in Sidorov, pp. 565–66. The general situation is described in Tsukerman, pp. 169–72.

37. TsGAOR, *F.* 63, *op.* 25, *d.* 773, vol. 10, p. 410.

38. Laverychev, *Po tu storonu barrikad*, pp. 43–47; Sef, pp. 77–95.

39. *RS*, no. 301 (Nov. 15).

40. See the appeal of the striking Gopper workers in *Bor'ba*, no. 3 (Nov. 30).

41. *RS*, no. 298 (Nov. 12).

42. *RS*, no. 302 (Nov. 16).

43. *VP*, nos. 279, 300 (Nov. 14, Dec. 5); *RS*, nos. 283, 298, 303, 317 (Oct. 28, Nov. 12, Nov. 17, Dec. 1). The demands of the telephone workers included a six-hour workday; hourly pay to be replaced by monthly salary, with a minimum wage of 40 rubles a month; abolition of overtime and fines; workers to be paid for time on strike; annual paid vacation; and worker-delegates to have power to approve hiring and firing decisions and to regulate worker-management relations. Complete list in *RS*, no. 283 (Oct. 28).

44. *Novosti dnia*, nos. 8030, 8031 (Oct. 23, 24).

45. Nikitin, pp. 102–3; *VP*, nos. 256, 277 (Oct. 22, Nov. 12); *RS*, nos. 286, 295, 297 (Oct. 31, Nov. 9, Nov. 11). On the concierges, see also local police report of Nov. 21 in TsGAOR, *F.* 63, *op.* 25, *d.* 773, vol. 10, p. 403.

46. *Novosti dnia*, no. 8031 (Oct. 24).

47. TsGAOR, *F.* 63, *d.* 784, part 1, p. 5.

48. On the first union meeting, see *RS*, no. 296 (Nov. 10).

49. The union's 10 leaders were all workers, three from Gabai, five from Dukat, and one each from Bostandzhoglo and Reingart. Two of the Gabai leaders and two of the Dukat leaders were also elected to represent the union on the Moscow Soviet. (*PDMP*, pp. 189–90.)

50. Milonov and Rakovskii, pp. 108–12.

51. Nov. 4 meeting of workers in Lefortovo reported in *RS*, no. 292 (Nov. 6) for general situation, see *PDMP*, p. 46.

52. Examples of workers voting to support the SR party: five textile factories, Prokhorov Trekhgornaia (6,000 workers), Timashev machine embroidery (265), Zak cotton (140), Simono silk (1,000), Sapozhnikov silk (300), all in different parts of the city; one metal factory, Nosenkov (320); one chemical plant, Nevskii tallow rendering works (400); and two tea plants, Popov (500) and Gubkin-Kuznetsov (550). These represent only the cases reported in newspaper accounts. See *VP*, nos. 274, 276, 279 (Nov. 9, 11, 14); and *RS*, nos. 288, 290, 304, 308, 310 (Nov. 2, 4, 18, 22, 24).

Examples of factory meetings supporting the SD party resolutions are numerous; to cite only one, Bromlei workers on Nov. 11. Report in *Moskovskaia gazeta*, no. 5 (Nov. 15), cited in Sidorov, pp. 574-75.

53. Examples of such appeals are those by Gopper workers printed in *Bor'ba*, no. 3 (Nov. 30), and by Bromlei and Kerting workers in *ibid.*, no. 6 (Dec. 3).

54. See Shchap, pp. 49-52; and Kolokol'nikov, "Otryvki," sb. 3: 227. All but the Zotov workers had been members of the SD Workers' Union in the 1890's (see Chap. 4, note 3).

55. See Zaiats, p. 96. Menshevik organizers also tried to start a textile union in the Lefortovo district; one meeting was held on Nov. 28; *VP*, no. 295 (Nov. 30). On textile union organization, see also Spektor, pp. 3-15.

56. Nikitin, p. 95.

57. *RS*, nos. 291, 296, 300 (Nov. 5, 10, 14).

58. Background in Bazilevich, pp. 48-54, 133-40. The following account of the union's actions and the strike draws largely on this source, pp. 187, 225-41, and on Tunnel', pp. 26-51.

59. TsGIAL, F. 1289, *op.* 8, *d.* 134, pp. 33, 34. The three leading spokesmen for the union were P. N. Miller, expeditor, age 39; K. V. Parfenenko, distribution official, 23; and N. G. Dvuzhil'nyi, senior mechanic in the electrical engineering department, 30.

60. TsGAOR, F. 102, *op.* O.O. *d.* 2100/1905, pp. 75, 76.

61. Charter in *VP*, no. 258 (Oct. 24).

62. First announcement by the Ministry of Post and Telegraph on Oct. 31, supported by the Council of Ministers; additional circular by the Ministry dated Nov. 3. See texts in Sidorov, p. 111, and Tunnel', pp. 23-24.

63. These economic demands, first formulated on Oct. 24 (see Nikitin, p. 99), included the following: a minimum wage of 50 rubles for postal and telegraph administrative employees, of 35 rubles for mail carriers, and of 30 rubles for couriers and dispatchers; a rent allowance to be determined at 40% of salary; gradual wage increases; a six-hour day for administrative staff and an eight-hour day for mail carriers and dispatchers; special pay for night and holiday work; a month's annual vacation and a pension after 25 years' service. (See Bazilevich, p. 42.)

64. Text in Tunnel', p. 52.

65. Resolution, *ibid.*, p. 55.

66. Vasil'ev-Iuzhin, "Moskovskii sovet," part 1: 106.

67. Surh, p. 500.

68. Among them, several groups of railroad employees (the Union of Ticket Collectors of the Moscow-Brest Railroad, and a number of employees of the Kursk, Nizhii Novgorod, and Muromsk lines), the All-Russian Union of Engineers and Technicians, the All-Russian Union of Medical Personnel, the Corporation of Doctors Employed by the City, employees in state savings associations, and the veterinarians' union (see Bazilevich, p. 229).

69. See the Union of Unions' statement in support of the postal strike in Bor'ba, no. 3 (Nov. 30).

70. RS, no. 310 (Nov. 24).

71. RS, nos. 317, 319 (Dec. 1, 3).

72. Text of the Nov. 18 appeal in Sidorov, p. 115.

73. See the union's appeal of Nov. 28 in Bazilevich, ibid., pp. 43–44.

74. Text of the pledge in Bor'ba, no. 4 (Dec. 1).

75. Bazilevich, pp. 232–43; RS, no. 321 (Dec. 5).

76. Imperial Decree of Nov. 29 in Lazarevskii, pp. 279–81.

77. Governors' telegram in RS, no. 318 (Dec. 2).

78. Imperial Decree of Dec. 2 in Lazarevskii, pp. 281–88.

79. RS, no. 317 (Dec. 1); VP, no. 296 (Dec. 1).

80. Vasil'ev-Iuzhin, "Moskovskii sovet," part 2: 93. On the St. Petersburg Soviet's manifesto, see Harcave, p. 232; text in Sidorov, pp. 25–26.

81. VP, no. 298 (Dec. 3); Surh, p. 510.

82. Examples of calls to armed uprising are to be found in the following SD leaflets: three issued in October and early November, reprinted in Stachka, pp. 459–62, 482–83; 11 issued in October and six in November, reprinted in G. D. Kostomarov, N. Rodionova, and M. Zimina, eds., Listovki moskovskikh bol'shevikov v pervoi russkoi revoliutsii (Moscow, 1955), pp. 300–306, 317–18, 324–49. Texts of two additional November pamphlets in Sidorov, pp. 561–64, 572–74. Some of these leaflets were issued by the Bolshevik Moscow Committee and some by the Bolshevik-Menshevik United Federative Council.

Chapter 10

1. Bushnell, pp. 44–45.

2. Ibid., pp. 69, 71. See also Allan K. Wildman, The End of the Russian Imperial Army: The Old Army and the Soldiers' Revolt (March-April 1917) (Princeton, N.J., 1980), p. 48.

3. For documents on naval mutinies, see Sidorov, pp. 191–342.

4. Bushnell, p. 73. See also Harcave, pp. 203, 220–23.

5. Moskovskaia gazeta, no. 8 (Nov. 18), quoted in Bushnell, p. 70.

6. Trotsky comments on the connection between social origin and political awareness in the military: "The same fact can be observed in all revolutionary movements in our army: the most revolutionary are sappers, engineers, gunners, in short, not the gray illiterates of the infantry, but skilled, highly literate, technically trained soldiers. To this difference at the intellectual level corresponds one of social origin: the vast majority of infantry soldiers are young peasants, whereas the engineers and gunners are recruited chiefly from among industrial workers." (1905, p. 208.)

7. Vasil'ev-Iuzhin, "Moskovskii sovet," part 1: 114–15. See also Vasil'ev-Iuzhin, "Revoliutsionnoe dvizhenie," pp. 418–19. For more on the vol'nooprede-liaiushchiesia, see *Voennaia entsiklopediia*, 18 vols. (St. Petersburg, 1911–15), vol. 7: 29–30. For a description of the draft volunteers, see Wildman (cited in note 2, above), pp. 28–29.

8. Ul'ianinskii, p. 37; Mel'nikov, pp. 270–72; Vasil'ev-Iuzhin, "Moskovskii sovet," part 1: 119; Sidorov, pp. 585–87, 609.

9. Mel'nikov, pp. 273–75; Sidorov, p. 612.

10. Ul'ianinskii, p. 39.

11. Mel'nikov, p. 289; Ul'ianinskii, p. 40; Shabrov, pp. 124–25.

12. Shabrov, p. 126, claims the SRs acted as a group; Ul'ianinskii, p. 41, provides the alternate version.

13. Ul'ianinskii, p. 42.

14. *Ibid.*, p. 43.

15. It was published in *RS*, no. 319 (Dec. 3).

16. Ul'ianinskii, pp. 44–45, 47.

17. N. A. Snegul'skii [Saur], "Vosstanie grenaderov," in *Na barrikadakh*, p. 175.

18. Ul'ianinskii, p. 46.

19. Sokolov, p. 52.

20. Ul'ianinskii, p. 47, says that the militants were deceived about the effectiveness of their speeches. See Mel'nikov, p. 284, for quotes of such overblown interpretations.

21. Shabrov, p. 129; Ul'ianinskii, p. 47.

22. Ul'ianinskii, p. 48.

23. Mel'nikov, p. 287; Ul'ianinskii, pp. 50–51; *Byloe*, vol. 1, no. 5 (May 1906): 310–11. Excerpt from the military tribunal's prosecution of the Rostov rebels in Sidorov, pp. 620–41.

24. Mel'nikov, p. 283.

25. Ul'ianinskii, p. 46.

26. Sidorov, p. 612; Mel'nikov, pp. 276–77.

27. Mel'nikov, p. 285; Vasil'ev-Iuzhin, "Revoliutsionnoe dvizhenie," pp. 422–23.

28. Mel'nikov, p. 281; Ul'ianinskii, p. 44.

29. Kokhmanskii, pp. 195–96. As of Nov. 13, there were 17,000 soldiers in the Moscow garrison, 9,000 of whom were infantrymen in the process of demobilization (Bushnell, p. 216).

30. Sidorov, pp. 443, 613.

31. Quoted in Trotsky, p. 221.

32. Surh, pp. 509–12.

33. *RS*, nos. 313, 316 (Nov. 27, 30).

34. *RS*, nos. 316, 317 (Nov. 30, Dec. 1).

35. *RS*, nos. 319, 320 (Dec. 3, 4).

36. Kokhmanskii, pp. 5–6.

37. Sokolov, p. 48.

38. *Ibid.*

39. Liadov, p. 130. These memoirs of a Bolshevik active in 1905 were first published in 1926.

40. Vasil'ev-Iuzhin, "Moskovskii sovet," part 2: 98.

41. S. Chernomordik, quoted in Iaroslavskii, p. 124.

42. Chernov, p. 259.

43. Vasil'ev-Iuzhin, "Moskovskii sovet," part 2: 96.

44. Text of the Moscow Soviet's Dec. 4 resolution in *ibid.*, p. 97, and in Sidorov, p. 645.

45. "Pravitel'stvo zhazhdet krovi," *Vpered*, no. 4 (Dec. 6), quoted in Vasil'ev-Iuzhin, "Moskovskii sovet," part 2: 132-33.

46. On the pessimism expressed by "Marat" (V. L. Shantser) and other Bolsheviks, see Sokolov, p. 52.

47. "Revolution Teaches" (July 13, 1905), in V. I. Lenin, *Collected Works*, vol. 9 (Moscow, 1962), pp. 146-55.

48. "The Boycott of the Bulygin Duma and Insurrection" (Aug. 3, 1905), *ibid.*, pp. 179-87.

49. "Black Hundreds and the Organization of an Uprising" (Aug. 16, 1905), *ibid.*, p. 204. Italics in the original.

50. "From the Defensive to the Offensive" (Sept. 13, 1905), *ibid.*, pp. 246-51. Italics in the original.

51. "The Political Strike and the Street Fighting in Moscow" (Oct. 4, 1905), *ibid.*, p. 354. Italics in the original.

52. "The All-Russian Political Strike" (written Oct. 13, published Oct. 18, 1905), *ibid.*, p. 394. Italics in the original. See also "The Denouement Is at Hand" (Nov. 3, 1905), pp. 447-54, and "Between Two Battles" (written Nov. 2, published Nov. 12, 1905), pp. 456-64.

53. Vasil'ev-Iuzhin, "Moskovskii sovet," part 2: 99.

54. *Ibid.*, pp. 97, 99; Iaroslavskii, p. 125.

55. The quote is from Liadov, p. 133. He says that 800 persons were present, contradicting Kokhmanskii, p. 8.

56. This mood is reported by all sources. For example, Vasil'ev-Iuzhin, "Moskovskii sovet," part 2: 102-3; Liadov, p. 133; Kokhmanskii, p. 9; and Iaroslavskii, pp. 123-29. See also Levin, p. 1.

57. Liadov, pp. 131-32. The figure of 1,000 armed men in the self-defense squads is accepted as accurate by Iaroslavskii, p. 88. See the comments on unwarranted optimism in Iaroslavskii, p. 129, and Kokhmanskii, p. 196.

58. The two committee members were L. N. Kudriavtsev (Evgenii) and R. S. Zalkind (Zemliachka). (Kokhmanskii, p. 9; Liadov, p. 133; Sokolov, p. 53; and Iaroslavskii, p. 126.)

59. The two committee members were M. I. Vasil'ev-Iuzhin and A. V. Sokolov (Vasil'ev-Iuzhin, "Moskovskii sovet," part 2: 103).

60. Kokhmanskii, p. 10.

61. *Ibid.*, p. 11.

62. Liadov, p. 130.

63. On the effect of the railroad conference resolution on the Bolshevik meeting, see Kokhmanskii, p. 9.

64. *Ibid.*, pp. 7-8.

65. V. Zenzinov, *Perezhitoe* (New York, 1953), p. 226.

66. Vasil'ev-Iuzhin, "Moskovskii sovet," part 2: 104-5, 110-18. The three non-working-class Mensheviks on the bureau were I. A. Isuf and Isakovich, both of whom sat on the soviet's executive committee, and V. Sher, a printers' union organizer. Their two Bolshevik counterparts were M. I. Vasil'ev-Iuzhin and V. L. Shantser, also soviet executive committee members. One of the three SRs was V. N. Pereverzev, representing the railroad union. According to Kokhmanskii, p. 140, the SRs first wanted to form a 10-member Coalition Council consisting of two representatives from each of the following groups: the soviet executive committee, the railroad union, and the Bolshevik, Menshevik, and SR parties. The SDs supposedly rejected this idea at the soviet's Dec. 6 meeting. They wanted the Coalition Council reduced to an informational organ and the soviet executive committee itself to lead the strike. None of the proposed leadership bodies existed long enough to influence events. Only the soviet executive committee took any action at all. The details are in fact trivial, except as indications of conflict among the rival parties. Evidence on the inaction of central organs abounds: see, for example, Iaroslavskii, p. 195.

67. Chernov, p. 281; Vasil'ev-Iuzhin, "Moskovskii sovet," part 2: 104-5. Vasil'ev-Iuzhin had drafted the announcement.

68. Quoted in Vasil'ev-Iuzhin, "Moskovskii sovet," part 2: 107, 130.

69. See accounts from Bor'ba, no. 8 (Dec. 6), and Zhizn' (n.d.) reprinted in Kokhmanskii, pp. 13-15. For the text of the soviet's appeal, see Kokhmanskii, pp. 15-17, and Vasil'ev-Iuzhin, "Moskovskii sovet," part 2: 128-30. For the text of the railroad union's endorsement, printed in Bor'ba, no. 9 (Dec. 7), see Kokhmanskii, pp. 17-18, and Iaroslavskii, pp. 133-34.

70. Miliukov, p. 82.

71. Kokhmanskii, p. 23.

72. Garvi, p. 624.

73. Mitskevich, Revoliutsionnaia Moskva, p. 447.

74. Kokhmanskii, p. 152.

75. Ibid., p. 141; L. Geller and N. Rovenskaia, eds., Peterburgskii i moskovskii sovety rabochikh deputatov 1905 goda (v dokumentakh) (Moscow-Leningrad, 1926), pp. 113-15.

76. Kokhmanskii, p. 31.

77. Smaller factories where workers made weapons were the metal plants of Dill' (90 workers) and Vinter (180) in the Zamoskvorech'e and of Blok (170) in Sushchevskaia (IV): ibid., pp. 22-23.

78. The Nikolaevskii was immediately placed under armed guard (Sidorov, p. 723).

79. Contemporary accounts and Soviet historians follow the estimate published in the Moscow Soviet newsletter for Dec. 8 (Izvestiia moskovskogo soveta rabochikh deputatov, no. 2), in accepting the figures of 100,000 strikers for the first day of the strike and 150,000 by the next day. (See Kokhmanskii, p. 20; and Trudy, pp. 106, 110, editorial notes.) These figures include railroad workers. My estimate for the same period includes only factory workers. Contemporary estimates probably included strikers in the suburbs, who by my calculations numbered at least 9,000.

80. One contemporary account (Kokhmanskii, p. 20) gives the total number of striking printing workers as 10,000. I have precise information on only 6,000, but the number may have been higher.

81. Tsukerman, p. 150; VP, no. 252 (Oct. 18).

82. Tsukerman, p. 178; also Leskova and Kogan, p. 95.

83. TsGAOR, F. 63, op. 14, d. 912, p. 110.

84. Tsukerman, pp. 99–102.

85. Novosti dnia, no. 8025 (Oct. 18).

86. RS, no. 275 (Oct. 20).

87. Antoshkin, p. 25; VP, no. 280 (Nov. 15).

88. Garvi, pp. 597, 599.

89. TsGAOR, F. 63, op. 14, d. 912, p. 56; F. 63, op. 25, d. 773, vol. 10, p. 621; Tsukerman, pp. 181–82.

90. Sidorov, pp. 598, 652–53; Kokhmanskii, pp. 11–13; Pravo, no. 50 (Dec. 18): 4009.

91. Levin, p. 5; Pravo, no. 50 (Dec. 18): 4009–12, 4017–26 passim, 4038–39. For the statements of the Corporation of Workers and Employees in the Moscow City Administration and a group of senior technical personnel read at the City Council meeting of Dec. 13, see Stenograficheskie otchety, pp. 999–1000. In fact, the pharmacy clerks' union had earlier declared its intention to strike for demands specific to the profession. The announcement, made on Dec. 1 and published in Bor'ba, no. 6 (Dec. 3), appears in Sidorov, p. 597.

92. Kokhmanskii, p. 32.   93. Ibid., p. 25.

94. RS, no. 321 (Dec. 5).   95. Iaroslavskii, pp. 135–36.

96. On this "naïve" belief in legality, see Levin, p. 4.

97. The size of the crowd was estimated at 12,000 (Pravo, no. 50 [Dec. 18]: 4017). There were approximately 200 men in the military force (Sidorov, p. 723).

98. Kokhmanskii, pp. 34–38.

99. Ibid., p. 40.

100. Vasil'ev-Iuzhin, "Moskovskii sovet," part 2: 110–11, 114–19; Iaroslavskii, p. 195.

101. Iaroslavskii, p. 136; Kokhmanskii, p. 24.

102. Kolokol'nikov, "Otryvki," sb. 3: 232.

103. Kokhmanskii, pp. 44–47.   104. Ibid., pp. 45–46.

105. Ibid., p. 141.   106. Ibid., pp. 41–42.

107. Ibid., pp. 141–42.   108. Ibid., p. 142.

109. Abramovich, p. 152.

110. The council's composition was as follows: one representative from the Moscow Committee of the SD Party (Bolshevik); two from the Moscow Group of the SD Party (Menshevik); two from the Moscow Committee of the SR Party; one from the Central University Organization; and one each from four self-defense groups: "Free District," "University" (students), printers, and "Caucasian" (students). (See Kokhmanskii, pp. 167–74.) The total lack of planning and the isolation of this central organization from the district organizations are confirmed by Obninskii, p. 39.

111. Kokhmanskii, p. 163; Iaroslavskii, p. 93.

112. The quotes in the text are from *Rabochii*, no. 3 (Oct. 15), reprinted in *Moskovskoe vooruzhennoe vosstanie*, pp. 4–5. *Rabochii* was an illegal paper printed in Moscow by the SD Central Committee; only four members appeared between August and the end of October (see note in Sidorov, p. 921).

113. See Sidorov, pp. 600–601, for the druzhina constitution issued by the Bolsheviks.

114. These druzhiny were as follows: the "Georgian" (25 members); the "Bear" (25); two printers' bands (75); a bakers' band (20); the "Caucasian" students (150); several independent student bands (140); and a pharmacy clerks' band (35): Kokhmanskii, p. 165; Iaroslavskii, p. 86; *Moskovskoe vooruzhennoe vosstanie*, pp. 108–11; D. D. Gimmer, "Dekabr'skoe vooruzhennoe vosstanie," in Chernomordik, sb. 1: 140; Tylkin, *ibid.*, p. 173.

115. The 7 factories in area III were Prokhorov cotton (6,000 workers, 35 squad members), Dukat tobacco (900 workers, 25 members), Genner sugar (600 workers, unknown number of members), Mamontov varnish (500 workers, 15 members), Grachev metal (400 workers, 15 members), Shmidt furniture (260 workers, 40 members), and Pal'm metal (180 workers, unknown number of members). The three factories in area IV were Kushnerev printing (900 workers, 60 squad members), Miusskii tram park shops (800 workers, 50 members), and Gabai tobacco (600 workers, 35 members). The 4 factories in area V were Guzhon metal (2,500 workers, 40–50 squad members), Gubkin-Kuznetsov tea (550 workers, 40 members), Gakental' metal (540 workers, 10 members), and Perepud metal (270 workers, 10 members). The 2 factories in area VI were Tsindel' cotton (2,400 workers) and Sytin printing (1,110 workers), both with squads of unknown size. For data on factory squads, see Kokhmanskii, p. 103; Antoshkin, pp. 49, 56; Sedoi, p. 62; Garvi, p. 640; M. M. Avdeev, "Boevaia druzhina zavoda Guzhona," in *Na barrikadakh*, p. 61; M. V. Vinogradov, "Boi u Miusskogo parka," *ibid.*, pp. 56, 58; *1905*, pp. 102–13; M. Popov, "Vospominaniia o dekabr'skom vosstanii 1905 goda," *Proletarskaia revoliutsiia*, no. 12(47) (1925), pp. 111, 115; M. Akhun and A. Makovskii, *Voennaia i boevaia rabota bol'shevikov v 1905–1907 gg.* (Leningrad, 1941), p. 81.

116. Besides the Kazan brigade there were brigades for Kursk (40 men), Brest (25), Iaroslavl (70), Kiev (36), Riazan (40), and Windau (37); Kokhmanskii, pp. 121–22, 167; *Moskovskoe vooruzhennoe vosstanie*, p. 89.

117. Kokhmanskii, pp. 123–24, 126, 166–67; Obninskii, p. 38.

118. *Pravo*, no. 50 (Dec. 18), *passim*.

119. Iaroslavskii, p. 88.

Chapter 11

1. See *Spravochnaia kniga*, p. 45.

2. *1905*, pp. 116–17, 126.

3. B. A. Dunaev, "V iunosheskie gody," in Chernomordik, sb. 2: 39.

4. *Ibid.*, pp. 39–40; *Moskovskoe vooruzhennoe vosstanie*, p. 103.

5. *1905*, pp. 120, 124.

6. Klimkov, p. 16, says there were over twice that number of druzhinniki—approximately 250.

7. Sidorov, pp. 723–24.

8. *Moskovskoe vooruzhennoe vosstanie*, pp. 99–106.

9. *Ibid.*, p. 97; Abramovich, p. 156 (the author, at the time a twenty-four-year-old Moscow University student, was among the 99 arrested after the siege); *1905*, p. 127; Kokhmanskii, p. 51.

10. Abramovich, p. 160.

11. See accounts of witnesses at the trial in *1905*, pp. 120–32. See also Kokhmanskii, pp. 53–56; Abramovich, pp. 160–64; and *Moskovskoe vooruzhennoe vosstanie*, pp. 99–106.

12. Kokhmanskii, pp. 61–63; Obninskii, p. 34; *Dekabr'skie dni v Moskve: zapiski druzhinnika* (St. Petersburg: Zemlia i volia, 1906), p. 7; M. Nikolaev, *Vospominaniia nachal'nika boevoi druzhiny: dekabr' 1905 g. na Presne* (Moscow, 1926), p. 27. The participation of "gentlemen in beaver collars" is from Levin's account, p. 7.

13. *Moskovskoe vooruzhennoe vosstanie*, p. 22.

14. Kokhmanskii, pp. 64–67, 152, 155.

15. Participant's account quoted in *ibid.*, pp. 68–69.

16. Sokolov, p. 54, describing Dec. 9. Simono was in the southeastern corner of Rogozhskaia.

17. Storozhev, p. 109. For an estimate of the troops on hand, see Kokhmanskii, pp. 195–96.

18. Police Chief Medem to Gov.-Gen. Dubasov, Dec. 12, in Storozhev, p. 110.

19. N. Morozov-Vorontsov, ed., *Zamoskvorech'e v 1905 g.: sbornik vospominanii, dokumentov i fotografii* (Moscow, 1925), p. 55.

20. Sokolov, pp. 54–55.

21. *Pravo*, no. 50 (Dec. 18): 4026.

22. *Ibid.*, pp. 4029–30.

23. Kokhmanskii, pp. 75, 77, 78; Obninskii, p. 36.

24. Tylkin, p. 174; Kokhmanskii, pp. 76–77.

25. Kokhmanskii, p. 156.

26. *Ibid.*, pp. 78–81, 152, 156; Klimkov, p. 29; Levin, p. 11.

27. Sidorov, p. 765.

28. *Ibid.*, pp. 682–83.

29. *Pravo*, no. 50 (Dec. 18): 4032.

30. Proclamation of the Combat Organization of the Moscow Bolshevik Committee, *Izvestiia moskovskoga soveta rabochikh deputatov*, no. 5 (Dec. 11). All the following quotations are from this document. Reprints can be found in Nevskii, *Sovetskaia pechat'*, pp. 134–36, and Sidorov, pp. 665–66.

31. Kokhmanskii, p. 142.

32. See Iaroslavskii, p. 183, for his admission that Presnia was run by local druzhina leaders, not by the Central Committee.

33. Kokhmanskii, p. 85.

34. On the barricaded areas as of Dec. 12, see *Pravo*, no. 50 (Dec. 18): 4033; for Dec. 13, see Kokhmanskii, p. 89; and Sidorov, p. 724.

35. *Pravo*, no. 50 (Dec. 18): 4037.

36. Newspaper account quoted in Kokhmanskii, p. 86.

37. *Ibid.*, pp. 199–202; *Pravo*, no. 50 (Dec. 18): 4034.

38. *Pravo*, no. 50 (Dec. 18): 4030, 4042.

39. Kokhmanskii, pp. 98–99; Klimkov, p. 30; *Pravo*, no. 50 (Dec. 18): 4024.

40. Statement read at the Dec. 13 City Council meeting (*Stenograficheskie otchety*, p. 1008).

41. *Ibid.*, p. 1017.

42. City Council meetings for Dec. 13–Dec. 16, and Dec. 20, *ibid.*, pp. 996–1096.

43. Kokhmanskii, p. 90; *Pravo*, no. 50 (Dec. 18): 4043.

44. Tylkin, p. 175. See also Kokhmanskii, p. 208, on residents helping to feed *druzhinniki*.

45. Kokhmanskii, p. 99; Levin, p. 6; N. V. Nasakin-Simbirskii, *Ocherki moskovskoi revoliutsii* (St. Petersburg: Kluba obshchestvennykh deiatelei v pol'zu bezrabotnykh, 1906), p. 32.

46. *RS*, no. 327 (Dec. 22).

47. Obninskii, p. 44. Because of the author's known disapproval of the armed uprising and of what he felt were the illusions of the revolutionaries, his word in this matter is especially significant: he clearly would not have wanted to contribute to the revolutionary mythology.

48. Report of F. V. Ezerskii in Nasakin-Simbirskii (cited in note 45, above), p. 45.

49. According to Klimkov, p. 31, there were 24 brigades. For a description of the organization of the voluntary Red Cross service, see *Bor'ba*, no. 3 (Nov. 30) cited in Sidorov, pp. 588–89. For the Medical Union announcement, see *ibid.*, pp. 650–51.

50. Kokhmanskii, pp. 184–88.

51. G. Kostomarov, V. Simonenko, and A. Drezin, eds., *Iz istorii moskovskogo vooruzhennogo vosstaniia: materialy i dokumenty* (Moscow, 1930), pp. 200–205; Storozhev, p. 110; *Pravo*, no. 50 (Dec. 18): 4043.

52. S. Chernomordik, "Piatyi god v Moskve," in Chernomordik, sb. 1: 41; I. I. Kuz'min, "V Butyrskom raione," in *Na barrikadakh*, p. 51.

53. V. M. Savkov, "V Sokol'nikakh i v Zamoskvorech'i," in Chernomordik, sb. 1: 57–58.

54. I. M. Golubev and P. G. Terekhov, "1905 god v Rogozhskom raione," in *ibid.*, pp. 240–43. A similar calm prevailed in Lefortovo (Ts. S. Bobrovskaia [Ts. S. Zelikson], "Iz revoliutsionnogo proshlogo," in *Na barrikadakh*, p. 148).

55. Garvi, p. 648.

56. See Sedoi, p. 62; F. Averbukh, *1905 god na Presne* (Moscow, 1925), p. 30; Garvi, pp. 613–14; and Kokhmanskii, p. 102.

57. Garvi, p. 614.

58. Sedoi, p. 62; Garvi, p. 640; Antoshkin, pp. 49, 56; Kokhmanskii, p. 103. The following figures can be found: 200–300 men, in Garvi, p. 639; 400–600, in *Moskovskoe vooruzhennoe vosstanie*, p. 56; and 300–400, in Averbukh (cited in note 56, above); p. 33. Iaroslavskii, p. 87, cites Sedoi for figures on Presnia, ranging from 350 men at any given time to 700 or 800 for the entire period. Although Iaroslavskii, p. 181, is skeptical about the size of factory *druzhiny* as given in

Kokhmanskii, p. 103, he offers no precise alternative figures. For the migration of druzhiny from other areas, see Kokhmanskii, p. 177. See also Savkov, p. 58; and Golubev and Terekhov, p. 243 (cited in notes 53 and 54, above).

59. Garvi, p. 637.
60. Iaroslavskii, p. 201.
61. Sedoi, p. 63.
62. Iaroslavskii, pp. 180-85, 188; Kokhmanskii, pp. 102-3, 109; Pravo, no. 50 (Dec. 18): 4038, for Dec. 13 attack on the Prokhorov mill.
63. 1905, p. 106.
64. Garvi, pp. 640-41; 1905, pp. 105-6; Moskovskoe vooruzhennoe vosstanie, pp. 23, 56-57.
65. Telegram from the Presnia police captain to Police Chief Medem, Dec. 14, in Sidorov, p. 684.
66. Antoshkin, pp. 25, 41-43, 53; Moskovskoe vooruzhennoe vosstanie, pp. 82-83.
67. Ivanov, Rabochee dvizhenie (1961-63), part 1: 59-62, part 2: 57-61.
68. Schneiderman, pp. 146-47, 152.
69. Tsukerman, pp. 99-102.
70. The SRs were V. I. Zommerfel'd from the district Combat Committee, S. G. Mukhina, M. I. Sokolov, and two men identified only as Chestnov and Rivkin (Antoshkin, p. 50; Moskovskoe vooruzhennoe vosstanie, p. 81).
71. Moskovskoe vooruzhennoe vosstanie, pp. 71-72.
72. Ibid., pp. 82-85; Antoshkin, p. 46.
73. Kokhmanskii, pp. 106, 108; Moskovskoe vooruzhennoe vosstanie, pp. 66-67; 1905, p. 104.
74. Antoshkin, pp. 53-54.
75. Pravo, no. 51 (Dec. 24): 4128.
76. "Liberal'nichavskii eshche vladelets fabriki" (Garvi, p. 599).
77. Ibid., p. 624. Mitskevich, Revoliutsionnaia Moskva, p. 337, mentions this same doctor. A physician by training, Mitskevich conducted his own revolutionary agitation in the clinic of another psychiatrist (ibid., p. 330).
78. Garvi, p. 602.
79. Ibid., p. 647.
80. Quoted in Kokhmanskii, pp. 160-61. Tsindel' had 2,400, Til' 3,100, and Zhemochkin 400 workers.
81. Obninskii, p. 40.
82. Mitskevich, Revoliutsionnaia Moskva, p. 434.
83. Kokhmanskii, p. 148; Vasil'ev-Iuzhin, "Moskovskii sovet," part 2: 126; Kolokol'nikov, "Otryvki," sb. 3: 233. Texts of announcements ending strike in Sidorov, pp. 712-15. See also Liadov, p. 149.
84. Pravo, nos. 50, 51 (Dec. 18, 24): 4045, 4118, 4119.
85. Kokhmanskii, pp. 109-10; Pravo, no. 50 (Dec. 18): 4045-46.
86. Min's report on the storming of Presnia in Sidorov, pp. 729-35. Quote on p. 730.
87. Ibid., p. 864n.
88. Dec. 15 report of S. Iu. Witte to Nicholas II on the Council of Ministers'

meeting of Dec. 13, *ibid.*, pp. 156–57. Secret circular from Min. of War A. F. Rediger to district military commanders, Dec. 15, *ibid.*, p. 157.

89. Min. of Internal Affairs P. N. Durnovo to governors and police chiefs, Dec. 21, *ibid.*, pp. 161–62.

90. *Ibid.*, pp. 688–89; Levin, p. 18.

91. Kokhmanskii, pp. 113–14.

92. *Pravo*, no. 51 (Dec. 24): 4128; Storozhev, pp. 134–35.

93. Sidorov, pp. 719, 743–45, 750, 864n; *Pravo*, no. 51 (Dec. 24): 4123, 4128.

94. Antoshkin, p. 71.   95. *Ibid.*, p. 76.

96. Sidorov, p. 864n.   97. Garvi, pp. 662–74.

98. Kokhmanskii, p. 115.

99. Official reports listed 52 policemen and officers and 14 concierges in police employ killed. Among the troops, 9 soldiers and 1 officer were killed, and 51 soldiers and 3 officers were wounded. Reports printed in *Pravo*, no. 52 (Dec. 31): 4215–16, and *RS*, no. 327 (Dec. 22). *Pravo*, no. 51 (Dec. 24): 4130, estimates the final number of civilians wounded at 2,000 and the dead at 670, not including those unregistered by hospitals and cemeteries.

100. The list of individual victims was compiled by the Medical Union Bureau from the reports of 47 hospitals, and was published in *VP*, no. 303 (Dec. 20). The source does not indicate how many of these casualties were merely wounded, and how many died. People treated by Red Cross brigades in private houses were not included in the official counts. One cannot hope to arrive at accurate figures, but one may be skeptical of such extravagant claims as the one in *Pravo*, no. 50 (Dec. 18): 4030, that 8,000 city residents had been wounded as of Dec. 11.

101. P. N. Miliukov, *God bor'by: publitsisticheskaia khronika 1905–1906* (St. Petersburg, 1907), pp. 170–71, 177–78.

102. P. Struve, "Dva zabastovochnykh komiteta," *Poliarnaia zvezda*, no. 3 (Dec. 30): 225. Italics in original.

103. P. Struve, "Zametki publitsista: o moskovskikh sobytiiakh," *ibid.*, no. 4 (Jan. 5, 1906), p. 281.

104. V. I. Lenin, "Lessons of the Moscow Uprising" (Aug. 1906), in *Collected Works*, vol. 11 (Moscow, 1962): 172.

105. Mitskevich, *Revoliutsionnaia Moskva*, p. 435.

106. Lenin himself acknowledged this. See "The Victory of the Cadets and the Tasks of the Workers' Party" (April 1906), in *Collected Works*, vol. 10 (Moscow, 1962): 252.

Appendix B

Much of the information on the union meetings is drawn from TsGAOR, F. 63, d. 784, part 1, and TsGAOR, F. 63, op. 14, d. 784, vol. 3. These files are cited in the following short forms in the Appendix notes: TsGAOR, part 1; TsGAOR, vol. 3.

1. Kolokol'nikov, *Professional'nye soiuzy*, p. 15; *OpO*, p. 120; Rakovskii, pp. 199–202.

2. Kolokol'nikov, *Professional'nye soiuzy*, p. 39; Sviatlovskii, p. 135; Milonov, *Kak voznikli*, p. 115; Zaiats, pp. 91–92; Spektor, pp. 6–8.

3. Sviatlovskii, p. 119.

4. *BMST*, no. 2: 16; Muzei: *Materialy*, p. 78; *OpO*, p. 112; Zaiats, p. 96. Meetings: *RS*, no. 292 (Nov. 6); *VP*, no. 295 (Nov. 30); TsGAOR, part 1, vol. 3.

5. Spektor, pp. 13–14. Meetings: TsGAOR, part 1.

6. *BMST*, no. 2: 17; *OpO*, p. 113. Meeting: *VP*, no. 273 (Nov. 8).

7. Kolokol'nikov, *Professional'nye soiuzy*, p. 16; *BMST*, no. 2: 9–10; *OpO*, p. 110.

8. Meetings: *VP*, no. 268 (Nov. 3); TsGAOR, part 1, vol. 3.

9. Mamontov, pp. 185–97; Kolokol'nikov, "Otryvki," sb. 3: 228.

10. Shchap, pp. 49–52; TsGAOR, part 1, vol. 3.

11. Krymov employed 100 workers; the number employed by Kuchkin is not listed in the handbooks or mentioned in available sources. *OpO*, p. 120; *BMST*, no. 1: 3; Milonov, *Kak voznikli*, p. 165.

12. Shchap, p. 44; *OpO*, p. 120.

13. *OpO*, p. 98.

14. *OpO*, pp. 98, 127; Muzei: *Materialy*, p. 78. Meetings: *VP*, no. 266 (Nov. 1); *RS*, nos. 290, 298, 319 (Nov. 4, 12, Dec. 3).

15. Kolokol'nikov, *Professional'nye soiuzy*, p. 16. Meetings: *BMST*, no. 2: 9; *RS*, no. 314 (Nov. 28); TsGAOR, part 1, vol. 3.

16. Kolokol'nikov, *Professional'nye soiuzy*, p. 35; *Bor'ba*, no. 3 (Nov. 30).

17. *BMST*, no. 2: 13; *OpO*, pp. 111–12. Dec. 8 meeting: TsGAOR, part 1.

18. Shchap, pp. 43–44; TsGAOR, part 1, vol. 3.

19. *Ibid.*

20. *Ibid.*

21. Kolokol'nikov, *Professional'nye soiuzy*, p. 39; Sviatlovskii, p. 135; Muzei: *Materialy*, p. 70; *OpO*, pp. 97, 106–107; *BMST*, no. 1: 24–27 (charter). Meetings: *RS*, nos. 290, 307 (Nov. 4, 21); TsGAOR, part 1, vol. 3.

22. Kolokol'nikov, *Professional'nye soiuzy*, p. 39; *OpO*, pp. 97, 106; *BMST*, no. 1: 23–24 (charter); *PDMP*, p. 190. Meetings: *RS*, no. 284 (Oct. 29); *VP*, no. 272 (Nov. 7); *Bor'ba*, no. 2 (Nov. 29); TsGAOR, part 1, vol. 3.

23. Kolokol'nikov, *Professional'nye soiuzy*, p. 39; *OpO*, pp. 106, 111; *BMST*, no. 2: 10–12. Meetings: *RS*, no. 290 (Nov. 4); TsGAOR, part 1, vol. 3.

24. *BMST*, no. 2: 16–17; *OpO*, pp. 112–13. Meetings: *VP*, nos. 266, 273 (Nov. 1, 8); *RS*, nos. 290, 307 (Nov. 4, 21).

25. *OpO*, p. 106; *VP*, nos. 278, 291 (Nov. 13, 26).

26. *OpO*, p. 97; Milonov, *Kak voznikli*, p. 165.

27. Sher, *Istoriia*, pp. 127–36; Ionov, p. 64.

28. Grinevich, p. 26; *OpO*, p. 96; Sher, *Istoriia*, pp. 136–60.

29. Grinevich, p. 27; Sher, *Istoriia*, p. 160; *OpO*, p. 96. Milonov, *Kak voznikli*, p. 117, erroneously calls this organization The Fund for the Improvement of Labor Conditions of Printing and Lithography Employees.

30. *OpO*, pp. 105–6; *BMST*, no. 1: 19–23, no. 2: 14–16; Kolokol'nikov, *Professional'nye soiuzy*, p. 39. Meetings: *RS*, nos. 296, 318 (Nov. 10, Dec. 2); *RV*, no. 275 (Oct. 20); TsGAOR, part 1, vol. 3.

31. *RS*, no. 321 (Dec. 5).

32. Sviatlovskii, pp. 120, 135; Kolokol'nikov, *Professional'nye soiuzy*, pp. 15, 39; *BMST*, no. 2: 17–18; Muzei: *Materialy*, p. 77; *OpO*, p. 113. Meetings: *RS*, nos. 300, 305, 314 (Nov. 14, 19, 28); *VP*, nos. 269, 274 (Nov. 4, 9); TsGAOR, part 1, vol. 3.

33. Kolokol'nikov, "Otryvki," sb. 3: 227; Grinevich, p. 26; Sviatlovskii, p. 120; *OpO*, p. 120. Meetings: *RS*, no. 307 (Nov. 21); *Bor'ba*, nos. 3, 9 (Nov. 30, Dec. 7); TsGAOR, part 1.

34. Kolokol'nikov, "Otryvki," sb. 3: 227; Muzei: *Materialy*, p. 70; Milonov, *Kak voznikli*, p. 127. Meetings: TsGAOR, part 1.

35. Meetings: TsGAOR, part 1, vol. 3.

36. Kolokol'nikov, "Otryvki," sb. 3: 227; *OpO*, p. 120. Meeting: *Bor'ba*, no. 3 (Nov. 30).

37. Mentioned only as participant in Moscow Bureau.

38. *OpO*, p. 120; Milonov, *Kak voznikli*, p. 127.

39. *BMST*, no. 2: 19–20

40. Meeting: *VP*, no. 292 (Nov. 27).

41. Meeting: *RS*, no. 310 (Nov. 24).

42. Meeting: *VP*, no. 297 (Dec. 2).

43. Meetings: *RS*, no. 318 (Dec. 2); TsGAOR, part 1, vol. 3.

44. Meetings: TsGAOR, part 1.

45. Kolokol'nikov, *Professional'nye soiuzy*, p. 39; Sviatlovskii, p. 135; *OpO*, pp. 97, 107, 119; Milonov, *Kak voznikli*, p. 126. Meetings: *RS*, nos. 304, 317 (Nov. 18, Dec. 1); *Bor'ba*, no. 3 (Nov. 30); TsGAOR, part 1, vol. 3.

46. Kolokol'nikov, "Otryvki," sb. 3: 227; *OpO*, pp. 119, 127; Milonov, *Kak voznikli*, p. 126. Meetings: *RS*, no. 318 (Dec. 2); TsGAOR, part 1.

47. This union is also referred to as the Union of Workers in Electric Lighting (Soiuz rabotnikov po elektricheskomu osveshcheniiu) and the Union of [Workers in] Electric Technology Enterprises (Soiuz elektro-tekhnicheskikh predpriiatii); it is possible that more than one union existed among electricians. Shchap, p. 46; Kolokol'nikov, *Professional'nye soiuzy*, p. 16. Meetings: *Moskovskaia gazeta*, no. 9 (Nov. 19); *RS*, no. 309 (Nov. 23); *Bor'ba*, nos. 2, 8 (Nov. 29, Dec. 6); TsGAOR, part 1, vol. 3.

48. *BMST*, no. 2: 17; *OpO*, p. 113. Meetings: *VP*, no. 275 (Nov. 10); *RS*, no. 319 (Dec. 3); *Bor'ba*, no. 9 (Dec. 7); TsGAOR, part 1.

49. *BMST*, no. 2: 18–19. Meetings: *RS*, nos. 284, 285, 308 (Oct. 29, 30, Nov. 22); TsGAOR, part 1, vol. 3.

50. *BMST*, no. 2: 18; *OpO*, p. 113; Milonov, *Kak voznikli*, p. 126. Meeting: TsGAOR, part 1.

51. Kolokol'nikov, "Otryvki," sb. 3: 227; *OpO*, p. 119.

52. *Ibid.* Meetings: TsGAOR, part 1.

53. Meetings: *Bor'ba*, no. 4 (Dec. 1); TsGAOR, part 1, vol. 3.

54. Muzei: *Materialy*, pp. 76, 91–92. Meetings: TsGAOR, vol. 3.

55. *BMST*, no. 2: 18; *OpO*, p. 113. Meetings: TsGAOR, part 1.

56. *OpO*, p. 97; Milonov, *Kak voznikli*, p. 118.

57. *Ibid.*

58. Kolokol'nikov, *Professional'nye soiuzy*, p. 39; *BMST*, no. 2: 7–9; *OpO*, p. 110.

59. Kirpichnikov, pp. 2, 6; Grinevich, p. 25; *BMST*, no. 1: 16–17; *OpO*, p. 105; Milonov, *Kak voznikli*, p. 120; Galai, p. 246. Meetings: *RS*, nos. 288, 314 (Nov. 2, 28); *VP*, nos. 294, 297 (Nov. 29, Dec. 2); *Bor'ba*, no. 9 (Dec. 7).

60. Grinevich, pp. 17, 25; Milonov, *Kak voznikli*, p. 166; *OpO*, p. 97.

61. Ainzaft, "Professional'noe dvizhenie," pp. 196–97; *OpO*, p. 97; Dec. meeting: TsGAOR, part 1.

62. *OpO*, p. 97; Milonov, *Kak voznikli*, p. 119.

63. *OpO*, p. 97; Milonov, *Kak voznikli*, p. 166; *RS*, no. 314 (Nov. 28). Although the union had already joined "Strength in Unity," Muzei: *Materialy*, p. 67, lists it as an independent participant in the MB meetings.

64. Milonov, *Kak voznikli*, p. 166.

65. *BMST*, no. 2: 12–13; *OpO*, p. 111. Meetings: *VP*, no. 275 (Nov. 10); *RS*, no. 303 (Nov. 17); TsGAOR, part 1, vol. 3.

66. *BMST*, no. 2: 19; *OpO*, pp. 105, 114. Meetings: *RV*, 284 (Oct. 29); *RS*, nos. 308, 317, 318 (Nov. 22, Dec. 1, 2); *VP*, no. 298 (Dec. 3); *Bor'ba*, no. 2 (Nov. 29).

67. Kolokol'nikov, *Professional'nye soiuzy*, p. 39; Muzei: *Materialy*, pp. 78, 85–87; *OpO*, pp. 104–5; *BMST*, no. 1: 15–16; Vasil'ev-Iuzhin, "Moskovskii sovet," part 1: 106; Kolokol'nikov, "Otryvki," sb. 3: 222. Meetings: *VP*, nos. 273, 288, 294, 298, 299 (Nov. 8, 23, 29, Dec. 3, 4); *RS*, nos. 296, 303, 314, 318, 321 (Nov. 10, 17, 28, Dec. 2, 5); TsGAOR, part 1, vol. 3.

68. Kolokol'nikov, *Professional'nye soiuzy*, p. 39; *BMST*, no. 2: 7–9; *OpO*, p. 110. Meetings: *Novosti dnia*, nos. 8030, 8031 (Oct. 23, 24); *RS*, nos. 279, 303 (Oct. 24, Nov. 17).

69. Kolokol'nikov, *Professional'nye soiuzy*, p. 39; *BMST*, no. 2: 10; *OpO*, p. 111. Meetings: *RS*, nos. 284, 293, 301, 308 (Oct. 29, Nov. 7, 15, 22); *VP*, no. 294 (Nov. 29); TsGAOR, part 1, vol. 3.

70. Meetings: *VP*, nos. 280, 289 (Nov. 15, 24); *Bor'ba*, no. 3 (Nov. 30); TsGAOR, part 1, vol. 3.

71. Milonov, *Kak voznikli*, p. 120; *OpO*, p. 120.

72. Meetings: *RS*, no. 291 (Nov. 5); TsGAOR, part 1, vol. 3.

73. *BMST*, no. 2: 10; *OpO*, p. 111.

74. *BMST*, no. 2: 13–14; *OpO*, p. 112. Meetings: *RS*, nos. 296, 311 (Nov. 10, 25); *VP*, nos. 280, 282 (Nov. 15, 17).

75. Meetings: *RS*, nos. 293, 305, 314 (Nov. 7, 19, 28); *Bor'ba*, no. 2 (Nov. 29).

76. Milonov, *Kak voznikli*, p. 135; *OpO*, p. 116. Second meeting: TsGAOR, part 1.

77. Meetings: TsGAOR, part 1, vol. 3.

78. *BMST*, no. 2: 19, *OpO*, p. 114. Dec. 8 meeting: TsGAOR, vol. 3.

79. E. Ignatov, "Iz istorii obshchestva povarov moskovskogo promyshlennogo raiona," in *Materialy po istorii*, sb. 2: 172. Meeting: TsGAOR, part 1.

80. Kolokol'nikov, "Otryvki," sb. 3: 227. Meetings: *RS*, nos. 318, 319 (Dec. 2, 3); TsGAOR, part 1, vol. 3.

81. *RS*, nos. 289, 293, 307, 310, 318 (Nov. 3, 7, 21, 24, Dec. 2); TsGAOR, part 1, vol. 3.

82. Pushkareva, *Zheleznodorozhniki* (1975), p. 109.

83. Bogdanov; Pereverzev; Pushkareva, *Zheleznodorozhniki* (1975); Romanov; Rostov. Meetings: *RS*, no. 291 (Nov. 5); TsGAOR, part 1, vol. 3.

84. Tunnel'; Bazilevich; Milonov, *Kak voznikli*, p. 133; *OpO*, p. 98; Vasil'ev-Iuzhin, "Moskovskii sovet," part 1: 106; *VP*, no. 258 (Oct. 24), charter. Meetings: *RS*, nos. 306, 310, 313 (Nov. 20, 24, 27); *Bor'ba*, no. 2 (Nov. 29).

85. Muzei: *Materialy*, p. 77; *OpO*, p. 98. Meetings: TsGAOR, part 1.

86. Muzei: *Materialy*, p. 76; *OpO*, pp. 120, 127. Meetings: *VP*, no. 274 (Nov. 9); *RS*, nos. 301, 313 (Nov. 15, 27).

87. Oct. 23 meeting, *VP*, no. 272 (Nov. 7); Nov. 13 meeting of Brest employees and shop workers, *RS*, no. 300 (Nov. 14).

88. Bazilevich, p. 229.

89. *BMST*, no. 2: 12. Meetings: *RS*, nos. 283, 318 (Oct. 28, Dec. 2); *Bor'ba*, nos. 3, 4, 5 (Nov. 30-Dec. 2); TsGAOR, part 1.

90. Milonov, *Kak voznikli*, pp. 128-29; Ainzaft, "Professional'noe dvizhenie," pp. 169, 176-79.

91. Ainzaft, "Professional'noe dvizhenie," pp. 180-86; Kolokol'nikov, "Otryvki," sb. 3: 222; *RV*, no. 284 (Oct. 29).

92. *BMST*, no. 1: 3; Muzei: *Materialy*, pp. 87-89 (charter); *OpO*, p. 130; Milonov, *Kak voznikli*, pp. 128-29; Ainzaft, "Professional'noe dvizhenie," pp. 169-76. Meetings: *RS*, nos. 282, 288, 309, 322 (Oct. 27, Nov. 2, 23, Dec. 6); *VP*, no. 279 (Nov. 14); *Bor'ba*, no. 9 (Dec. 7).

93. Meetings: *MV*, no. 272 (Oct. 13); *RS*, nos. 292, 307 (Nov. 6, 21); TsGAOR, vol. 3.

94. *RV*, no. 267 (Oct. 12); *RS*, no. 321 (Dec. 4).

95. *RV*, nos. 267, 284 (Oct. 12, 29).

96. *PkP*, pp. 69-70; *RV*, 284 (Oct. 29).

97. *RV*, no. 284 (Oct. 29).

98. Kirpichnikov, pp. 2, 6; *RS*, nos. 277, 290 (Oct. 22, Nov. 4); *VP*, nos. 268, 281 (Nov. 3, 16); *Bor'ba*, no. 9 (Dec. 7); Galai, pp. 234-36.

99. *PkP*, pp. 33, 42; *MV*, no. 273 (Oct. 14); *RV*, no. 269 (Oct. 14); *RS*, nos. 275, 290, 310, 318, 319 (Oct. 20, Nov. 4, 24, Dec, 2, 3); TsGAOR, part 1.

Works Cited

Abramovich, M. "Moskovskie druzhinniki v 1905 g.," *Krasnaia nov'*, no. 9, 1925.

Ainzaft, S. *Pervyi etap professional'nogo dvizheniia v Rossii (1905–1907)*. Vyp. 1. Ed. V. Iarotskii. Moscow-Gomel', 1924.

————. "Professional'noe dvizhenie v 1905 godu," in Iu. K. Milonov, ed., *Moskovskoe professional'noe dvizhenie v gody pervoi revoliutsii*. Sb. 1. Moscow, 1926.

————. *Zubatovshchina i gaponovshchina*. 4th ed. Moscow, 1925.

Antoshkin, D. V. *Fabrika na barrikadakh: Trekhgornaia manufaktura v 1905 g.* Moscow, 1931.

Anweiler, Oskar. *The Soviets: The Russian Workers, Peasants, and Soldiers Councils, 1905–1921*. Tr. Ruth Hein. New York, 1974. Originally published in German in 1958.

Bazilevich, K. V. *Ocherki po istorii professional'nogo dvizheniia rabotnikov sviazi, 1905–1906*. Moscow, 1925.

Belousov, I. A. *Ushedshaia Moskva: zapiski po lichnym vospominaniiam s nachala 1870 godov*. Moscow, [1927].

Bogdanov, M. *Ocherki po istorii zheleznodorozhnykh zabastovok v Rossii*. Moscow, 1907.

Bukhbinder, N. A. "K istorii zubatovshchiny v Moskve, po neizdannym protokolam zubatovskikh soveshchanii," *Istoriia proletariata SSSR*, no. 2, 1930.

Burch, Robert Jean. "Social Unrest in Imperial Russia: The Student Movement at Moscow University, 1887–1905," Ph.D. dissertation, University of Washington, Seattle, 1972.

Buryshkin, P. A. *Moskva kupecheskaia*. New York, 1954.

Bushnell, John. "Mutineers and Revolutionaries: Military Revolution in Russia, 1905–1907," Ph.D. dissertation, Indiana University, Bloomington, 1977.

Chernomordik, S., ed. *Piatyi god*. 2 sb. Moscow, 1925.

Chernov, V. M. *Pered burei: vospominaniia*. New York, 1953.

Dan, F. "Obshchaia politika pravitel'stva i izmeneniia v gosudarstvennoi organizatsii v period 1905–1907 gg.," in Martov et al., listed below, vol. 4, part 1.

Emmons, Terence. "Russia's Banquet Campaign," *California Slavic Studies*, vol. 10 (1977).

Galai, Shmuel. *The Liberation Movement in Russia, 1900–1905*. Cambridge, Eng., 1973.

Garvi, P. A. *Vospominaniia sotsialdemokrata*. New York, 1946.

Goetz-Girey, Robert. *Le Mouvement des grèves en France, 1919–1962*, vol. 3 of Henri Guitton and Alain Barrère, eds., *L'Economique*. Paris, 1965.

Gornostaev, I. F., ed. *Fabriki i zavody g. Moskvy i ee prigorodov: adresnaia i spravochnaia kniga o fabrichno-zavodskikh, glavnykh remeslennykh i torgovo-promyshlennykh predpriiatiiakh i drugie spravochnye svedeniia*. Moscow, 1904.

Grinevich, V. *Professional'noe dvizhenie rabochikh v Rossii*. 2d ed. Moscow, 1922.

Gusiatnikov, P. S. *Revoliutsionnoe studencheskoe dvizhenie v Rossii, 1899–1907*. Moscow, 1971.

Hanchett, Walter S. "Moscow in the Late Nineteenth Century: A Study in Municipal Self-Government," Ph.D. dissertation, University of Chicago, 1964.

Harcave, Sidney. *The Russian Revolution of 1905*. London, 1964.

Hinton, James. *The First Shop Stewards' Movement*. London, 1973.

Iakovlev, A. F. *Ekonomicheskie krizisy v Rossii*. Moscow, 1955.

Iaroslavskii, E. M. *Vooruzhennoe vosstanie: dekabr'skoe vosstanie*. Vol. 3, part 2 of Pokrovskii, listed below.

Iliukhin, A. F. "Professional'noe dvizhenie moskovskikh bulochnikov v 1905–1907 godakh," in *Professional'noe dvizhenie moskovskikh pishchevikov v gody pervoi revoliutsii*. Sb. 1. Moscow, 1927.

Ionov, I. N. "Zubatovshchina i moskovskie rabochie v 1905 g.," *Vestnik moskovskogo universiteta*, Series 9, Istoriia, no. 3 (March–April 1976).

Istoriia Moskvy. Vols. 4 and 5. Moscow: Akademiia nauk SSSR, 1954–55.

Ivanov, L. M. "Preemstvennost' fabrichno-zavodskogo truda i formirovanie proletariata v Rossii," in Ivanov et al., eds., *Rabochii klass i rabochee dvizhenie v Rossii, 1861–1917*. Moscow, 1966.

———., ed. *Rabochee dvizhenie v Rossii v XIX veke: sbornik dokumentov i materialov*. Vol. 4. Moscow, 1961–63.

———. *Rabochee dvizhenie v Rossii v 1901–1904 gg.: sbornik dokumentov*. Leningrad, 1975.

———. *Vserossiiskaia politicheskaia stachka v oktiabre 1905 goda*. Part 1. Moscow-Leningrad: Akademiia nauk SSSR, 1955.

"Iz besedy s Mariei Aristarkhovnoi Ignatovoi (po ee lichnym vospominaniiam)," in Mitskevich, ed., *Na zare*, listed below.

"Izvlecheniia iz protokola vtorogo obshchego sobraniia deputatov rabochikh razlichnykh professii v Moskve 4-go oktiabria 1905 g.," in Muzei: *Materialy*, listed below.

Johnson, Robert E. *Peasant and Proletarian: The Working Class of Moscow in the Late Nineteenth Century*. New Brunswick, N.J., 1979.

Kanatchikov, S. I. *Iz istorii moego bytiia*. Vol. 1. Moscow-Leningrad, 1929.

Keep, J. L. H. *The Rise of Social Democracy in Russia*. Oxford, Eng., 1963.

Kirpichnikov, S. D. *Soiuz soiuzov.* St. Petersburg, 1906. Signed S.D.K.

Klimkov, V. *Raspravy i rasstrely: pis'ma, ocherki i nabroski spetsial'nogo korrespondenta gazeta "Rus'" ("Molva").* Moscow, 1906.

Kokhmanskii, P. V., ed. *Moskva v dekabre 1905 g.* Moscow, 1906.

Kolokol'nikov, P. [K. Dmitriev]. "Otryvki iz vospominanii," in *Materialy po istorii,* listed below, sb. 2 and sb. 3.

————. *Professional'nye soiuzy v Moskve.* N.p., n.d.

Kol'tsov, D. "Rabochee v 1905–1907 gg.," in Martov et al., listed below, vol. 2, part 1.

Kol'tsov, N. K. *Pamiati pavshikh: zhertvy iz sredy moskovskogo studenchestva v oktiabr'skie i dekabr'skie dni.* Moscow, 1906.

Koz'minykh-Lanin, I. M. *Deviatiletnii period (s 1 ian. 1901 g. po 1 ian. 1910 g.) fabrichno-zavodskoi promyshlennosti moskovskoi gubernii.* Moscow, 191[?].

Lapitskaia, Sima Markovna. *Byt rabochikh Trekhgornoi manufaktury.* Moscow, 1935.

Latysheva, O. I. "Moskovskii universitet v revoliutsionnoi bor'be v period pervoi russkoi revoliutsii 1905–1907 gg.," dissertation, Moscow State University, 1956.

Laverychev, V. Ia. *Po tu storonu barrikad: iz istorii bor'by moskovskoi burzhuazii s revoliutsiei.* Moscow, 1967.

————. *Tsarizm i rabochii vopros v Rossii, 1861–1917.* Moscow, 1972.

Lazarevskii, N. M., ed. *Zakonodatel'nye akty perekhodnogo vremeni 1904–1906 gg.* St. Petersburg, 1907.

Lenskii. "Moskovskie dni," *Pravda: ezhemesiachnyi zhurnal iskusstva, literatury i obshchestvennoi zhizni,* Sept.–Oct. 1905.

Leskova, L. I., and K. S. Kogan, eds. "'Dezhurnye' dnevniki moskovskogo gradonachal'stva, 25 sentiabria 1905 g.-12 ianvaria 1906 g.," in *Materialy po istorii revoliutsii 1905–07 gg.* Trudy Gosudarstvennogo istoricheskogo muzeia. Vyp. 41. Moscow, 1967.

Levin, K. N. "Vooruzhennoe vosstanie v Moskve," in *Tekushchii moment: sbornik.* Moscow, 1906.

Liadov, M. [M. N. Mandel'shtam]. *Iz zhizni partii v 1903–1907 godakh: vospominaniia.* Moscow, 1956. Originally published in 1926.

Maevskii, E. "Obshchaia kartina dvizheniia," in Martov et al., listed below, vol. 2, part 1.

Mamontov, N. "Dvizhenie rabochikh po obrabotke blagorodnykh metallov v Moskve (po lichnym vospominaniiam)," in *Materialy po istorii,* listed below, sb. 5.

Martov, L., P. Maslov, and A. Potresov, eds. *Obshchestvennoe dvizhenie v Rossii v nachale XX-go veka.* 4 vols. St. Petersburg, 1909–14.

Materialy po istorii professional'nogo dvizheniia v Rossii. Sb. 1–5. Moscow, 1924–27.

Mel'nikov, A. B. "Revoliutsionnoe dvizhenie v Moskovskom garnizone v period dekabr'skogo vooruzhennogo vosstaniia," *Istoricheskie zapiski,* no. 49, 1954.

Memoirs of Count Witte. Tr. and ed. Abraham Yarmolinsky. New York, 1921.

Miliukov, P. *Political Memoirs, 1905–1917.* Ed. Arthur P. Mendel. Tr. Carl Goldberg. Ann Arbor, Mich., 1967. Originally published in Russian in 1955.

Milonov, Iu. K. *Kak voznikli profsoiuzy v Rossii*. Moscow, 1929.

Milonov, Iu. K., and M. Rakovskii. *Istoriia moskovskogo professional'nogo soiuza rabochikh derevoobdelochnikov*. Vyp. 1. Moscow, 1928.

Mitskevich, S. I. "Na zare rabochego dvizheniia v Moskve," in Mitskevich, ed., *Na zare*, listed below.

————. *Revoliutsionnaia Moskva (1885–1905)*. Moscow, 1940.

————, ed. *Na zare rabochego dvizheniia v Moskve: vospominaniia uchastnikov moskovskogo rabochego soiuza (1893–1895 gg.) i dokumenty*. Moscow, 1932.

Moskovskoe vooruzhennoe vosstanie po dannym obvinitel'nykh aktov i sudebnykh protokolov. Vyp. 1. Moscow, 1906.

Muzei sodeistviia trudu. *Biulleten'*, no. 1 (Nov. 16, 1905); no. 2 (Nov. 26, 1905). Reprinted in *Obshcheprofessional'nye organy*, listed below.

————. *Materialy po professional'nomu dvizheniiu rabochikh*. Vyp. 1. Moscow, 1906. Reprinted in *Obshcheprofessional'nye organy*, listed below.

Na barrikadakh: iz vospominanii uchastnikov moskovskogo dekabr'skogo vooruzhennogo vosstaniia 1905 goda. Moscow, 1955.

Nemchinov, E. I. "Vospominaniia starogo rabochego," in Mitskevich, ed., *Na zare*, listed above.

Nevskii, V. I. "Ianvarskie zabastovki 1905 g. v Moskve," *Krasnaia letopis'*, no. 2–3, 1922.

————, ed. *Sovetskaia pechat' i literatura o sovetakh*. Vol. 3 of M. N. Pokrovskii, ed. *1905: materialy i dokumenty*. 8 vols. Moscow, 1925–28.

Nikitin, S. "Moskovskoe stachechnoe dvizhenie v 1905–7 gg.," in Iu. K. Milonov, ed., *Moskovskoe professional'noe dvizhenie v gody pervoi revoliutsii*. Sb. 1. Moscow, 1926.

Obninskii, V. *Novyi stroi*. Part 1. Moscow, 1909.

Obshcheprofessional'nye organy 1905–07 gg. Vyp. 1. Moscow, 1926.

Obzor po g. Moskve za 1905 god. Moscow, 1907.

Oliunina, E. A. *Portnovskii promysel v Moskve i v derevniakh moskovskoi i riazanskoi gubernii: materialy k istorii domashnei promyshlennosti v Rossii*. Moscow, 1914.

Orlov, B. P. *Poligraficheskaia promyshlennost' Moskvy: ocherk razvitiia do 1917 goda*. Moscow, 1953.

Ozerov, I. Kh. *Politika po rabochemu voprosu v Rossii za poslednie gody*. Moscow, 1906.

Pazhitnov, K. A. *Ocherki istorii tekstil'noi promyshlennosti dorevoliutsionnoi Rossii: khlopchatobumazhnaia, l'no-pen'kovaia i shelkovaia promyshlennost'*. Moscow, 1958.

————. *Ocherki istorii tekstil'noi promyshlennosti dorevoliutsionnoi Rossii: sherstianaia promyshlennost'*. Moscow, 1955.

————. *Problema remeslennykh tsekhov v zakonodatel'stve russkogo absoliutizma*. Moscow, 1952.

Perepis' Moskvy 1902 goda. Vyp. 1 and 2. Moscow, 1904, 1906.

Pereverzev, V. N. "Pervyi vserossiiskii zheleznodorozhnyi soiuz 1905 goda," *Byloe*, 4 (32), 1925.

Podkopaev, I. F. "Moskovskie tabachniki v revoliutsionnom i professional'nom dvizhenii v 1905–1908 godakh," in *Professional'noe dvizhenie moskovskikh pishchevikov v gody pervoi revoliutsii*. Sb. 1. Moscow, 1927.

Pogozhev, A. V. *Uchet chislennosti i sostava rabochikh v Rossii: materialy po statistike truda*. St. Petersburg, 1906.

———, ed. *Adresnaia kniga fabrichno-zavodskoi i remeslennoi promyshlennosti vsei Rossii*. St. Petersburg, 1905.

Pokrovskii, M. N., ed. *1905: istoriia revoliutsionnogo dvizheniia v otdel'nykh ocherkakh*. 3 vols. Moscow-Leningrad, 1925–27.

Professional'noe dvizhenie moskovskikh pishchevikov v gody pervoi revoliutsii. Sb. 1. Moscow, 1927.

Pushkareva, I. M. *Zheleznodorozhniki Rossii v burzhuazno-demokraticheskikh revoliutsiiakh*. Moscow, 1975.

———. "Zheleznodorozhniki Rossii vo vserossiiskoi oktiabr'skoi politicheskoi stachke 1905 g.," dissertation, Akademiia nauk SSSR, Institut istorii, Moscow, 1959.

Rabochee zavoda "Serp i molot" (b. Guzhon) v 1905 godu. Sb. 2: *Russkii rabochii v revoliutsionnom dvizhenii*. Moscow, 1931.

Rashin, A. G. *Formirovanie rabochego klassa Rossii: istoriko-ekonomicheskie ocherki*. Moscow, 1958.

Romanov, V. "Dvizhenie sredi sluzhashchikh i rabochikh russkikh zheleznykh dorog v 1905 godu" (5 parts), *Obrazovanie*, nos. 10, 11, 11ᵃ, 1906; nos. 6, 7, 1907.

Rostov, N. "Zheleznodorozhniki v pervoi revoliutsii," in *Proletariat v revoliutsii 1905–1907 gg*. Moscow-Leningrad, 1930.

Rozhkova, M. K. "Rabochie Trekhgornoi manufaktury vo vtoroi polovine XIX-go veka," *Istoriia proletariata SSSR*, no. 1, 1930.

Sanburov, V. I. "Moskovskie metallisty nakanune pervoi russkoi revoliutsii (1890–1904 gg.): K voprosu o roli peredovogo otriada rabochego klassa v revoliutsionnom dvizhenii," dissertation, Moskovskii Gosudarstvennyi Pedagogicheskii Institut, 1964.

Schneiderman, Jeremiah. *Sergei Zubatov and Revolutionary Marxism: The Struggle for the Working Class in Tsarist Russia*. Ithaca, N.Y., 1976.

Schwarz, Solomon M. *The Russian Revolution of 1905*. Tr. Gertrude Vakar. Chicago, 1967.

Scott, Joan W. *The Glassworkers of Carmaux: French Craftsmen and Political Action in a Nineteenth-Century City*. Cambridge, Mass., 1974.

Sedoi [Z. Litvin], "Moskva-Presnia v piatom godu," in I. G. Batyshev, ed., *1905 na Presne: sbornik statei i vospominanii*. Moscow, 1926.

Sef, S. E. *Burzhuaziia v 1905 godu*. Moscow-Leningrad, 1926.

Semanov, S. N. *Peterburgskie rabochie nakanune pervoi russkoi revoliutsii*. Moscow-Leningrad, 1966.

Shabrov, I. Ia. "O vosstanii Rostovskogo polka v dekabre 1905 goda," *Katorga i ssylka*, no. 1(22), 1926.

Shchap, Z. *Moskovskie metallisty v professional'nom dvizhenii*. Moscow, 1927.

Sher, V. V. *Istoriia professional'nogo dvizheniia rabochikh pechatnogo dela v Moskve*. Moscow, 1911.

————. "Moskovskie pechatniki v revoliutsii 1905 goda," in A. Borshchevskii, S. Reshetov, and N. Chistov, eds., *Moskovskie pechatniki v 1905 godu*. Moscow, 1925.

Sher, V. V., and A. Svavitskii. *Ocherk polozheniia rabochikh pechatnogo dela v Moskve*. St. Petersburg, 1909.

Shestakov, P. M. "Materialy dlia kharakteristiki fabrichnykh rabochikh." *Russkaia mysl'*, no. 1, Jan. 1900.

————. *Rabochie na manufakture T-va "Emil' Tsindel'" v Moskve*. Moscow, 1900.

Shuster, U. A. *Peterburgskie rabochie v 1905–1907 gg*. Leningrad, 1976.

Sidorov, A. L., ed. *Vysshii pod'em revoliutsii 1905–1907 gg.: vooruzhennye vosstaniia, noiabr'-dekabr' 1905 goda*. Part 1. Moscow: Akademiia nauk SSSR, 1955.

Sokolov, A. V. [Stanislav Vol'skii]. "O 1905 gode," in N. Rozhkov and A. Sokolov, *O 1905 gode: vospominaniia*. Moscow, 1925.

Spektor, S. "Moskovskie tekstil'shchiki v gody pervoi revoliutsii," in *Moskovskie tekstil'shchiki v gody pervoi revoliutsii (1905–07 gg.)*. Moscow, 1929.

Spisok fabrik i zavodov evropeiskoi Rossii. St. Petersburg: Ministerstvo finansov, 1903.

Spravochnaia kniga po moskovskomu gorodskomu obshchestvennomu upravleniiu, 1904 g. Moscow, 1904.

Statisticheskii atlas goroda Moskvy. Moscow: Statisticheskii otdel gorodskoi upravy, 1911.

Statisticheskii ezhegodnik goroda Moskvy. Moscow, 1908.

Stenograficheskie otchety o sobraniiakh moskovskoi gorodskoi dumy za noiabr' i dekabr' mesiatsy 1905 goda. Moscow, 1907.

Storozhev, V. N. "F. V. Dubasov i G. A. Min na Presne v 1905 g.," *Golos minuvshego*, no. 4–6, 1918.

Surh, Gerald Dennis. "Petersburg Workers in 1905: Strikes, Workplace Democracy, and the Revolution," Ph. D. dissertation, University of California, Berkeley, 1979.

Sviatlovskii, V. *Professional'noe dvizhenie v Rossii*. St. Petersburg, 1907.

Svodnyi biulleten' po gorodu Moskve for the years 1901–5. Moscow: Statisticheskii otdel moskovskoi gorodskoi upravy, 1902–6.

Syromiatnikov, A., ed. "Moskovskii universitet v oktiabr'skie dni 1905 g.," *Krasnyi arkhiv*, 1 (74), 1936.

Tikhomirov, L. "25 let nazad," *Krasnyi arkhiv*, 3 (40), 1930.

Timofeev, P. *Chem zhivet zavodskii rabochii*. St. Petersburg: Russkoe bogatstvo, 1906.

Trotsky, Leon. *1905*. Tr. Anya Bostok. New York, 1971. Originally published in German in 1909.

Trudy Gosudarstvennogo istoricheskogo muzeia. Vyp. 41. *Materialy po istorii revoliutsii 1905–07 gg*. Moscow, 1967.

Trusova, N. S., ed. *Nachalo pervoi revoliutsii, ianvar'-mart 1905 goda*. Moscow: Akademiia nauk SSSR, 1955.

———. *Revoliutsionnoe dvizhenie v Rossii vesnoi i letom 1905 goda: aprel'-sentiabr'*. Part 1. Moscow: Akademiia nauk SSSR, 1957.

Tsentral'nyi gosudarstvennyi arkhiv Oktiabr'skoi revoliutsii. *Fond* 63 (Moscow Secret Police), *op.* 1, *d.* 773, *d.* 785; *op.* 2, *d.* 773 (vol. 4); *op.* 14, *d.* 773 (vol. 7), *d.* 784 (vol. 3), *d.* 912; *op.* 25, *d.* 773 (vols. 3, 3 *pr.*, 6 *pr.*, 8, 10, 11), *d.* 870; *op.* 26, *d.* 773 (vol. 2); *d.* 784 (part 1).

———. *Fond* 102 (Police Department, Special Division), *op.* O.O., *d.* 2100/1905.

Tsentral'nyi gosudarstvennyi istoricheskii arkhiv SSSR v Leningrade. *Fond* 1289 (Central Post and Telegraph Administration), *op.* 8, *d.* 134.

Tsukerman, G., ed. "Khronika stachechnogo dvizheniia moskovskikh tekstil'shchikov v 1905–1907 gg.," in *Moskovskie tekstil'shchiki v gody pervoi revoliutsii (1905–07 gg.)*. Moscow, 1929.

Tunnel'. *Nakanune suda: ocherk economicheskoi i politicheskoi bor'by pochtovo-telegrafnykh sluzhashchikh Rossii*. Moscow, 1908.

Tylkin, A. V. "Boevaia druzhina soiuza farmatsevtov," in Chernomordik, listed above, sb. 1.

1905 pered tsarskim sudom: sudebnye protsessy. Leningrad, 1925.

Ul'ianinskii, V. "Vosstanie Rostovskogo polka v dekabre 1905 goda," *Katorga i ssylka*, no. 6(19), 1925.

Vasil'ev-Iuzhin, M. I. "Moskovskii sovet rabochikh deputatov v 1905 godu i podgotovka im vooruzhennogo vosstaniia," *Proletarskaia revoliutsiia* (2 parts), nos. 4(39) and 5(40), 1925.

———. "Revoliutsionnoe dvizhenie v moskovskom garnizone: organizatsiia soveta soldatskikh deputatov," in *Partiia bol'shevikov v revoliutsii 1905–1907 godov*. Moscow, 1961.

Vasin, I. *Sotsial-demokraticheskoe dvizhenie v Moskve: 1883–1910 gg.* Moscow, 1955.

Verkhoven', B. P. "Promyshlennyi pod'em 90-kh godov XIX v. i krizis nachala XX v.," in *Istoriia Moskvy*, listed above, vol. 5.

Voitinskii, V. *Gody pobed i porazhenii, kniga pervaia: 1905 god*. Berlin, 1923.

Wildman, Allan K. *The Making of a Workers' Revolution: Russian Social Democracy, 1891–1903*. Chicago, 1967.

Zaiats, M. "Ekonomicheskaia bor'ba tekstil'shchikov moskovskoi oblasti v 1905 g.," in *Materialy po istorii*, listed above, sb. 5.

Index

Trade unions and other workers' organizations are indexed, by the categories and in the order given in Appendix B, pp. 231–39, only if they are referred to in the text or the notes. Some of the larger ones and the all-Russian unions have separate entries.

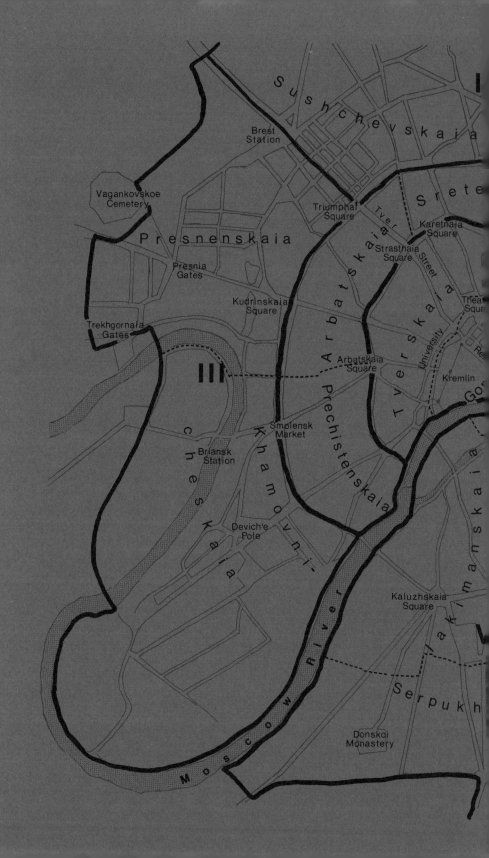